EMOTIONS IN PSYCHOLOGY AND PSYCHOTHERAPY

EMOTIONS IN

PSYCHOLOGY

—AND—

PSYCHOTHERAPY

❦

STEVEN G. BROWNLOW, PhD

SGBROWNLOW

ISBN: 978-0-9847719-0-5
Library of Congress Control Number: 2011919544

Printed in the United States of America.

First edition, 2011

Edited by Rachel Brownlow
Book design by Brion Sausser

Contents

Preface

THE REGULAR READERS of my blog (http://sgbrownlow.com) know a little about how this book came about, but it seemed appropriate that everybody else be included. Fitting my personality, this will be a story rather than a straightforward account. The progression of ideas and insights that eventually became this book started forming back in the late 1970s, when I was an undergraduate student. As I sometimes tell others, I graduated on the "Five Majors in Five Years Plan," starting off studying engineering, careening about the university studying smatterings of this and that, and finally graduating with a degree in economics. I have always been intuitive and trusted that in the end everything would work out the way it was supposed to. I have also had a tendency to combine and integrate topics that nobody else thought went together, just to see how they fit.

About my fourth year of the five, school became a burden and though I was becoming disenchanted with economics I decided I'd better go ahead and get a degree in *something*. My major problem with the way economics was taught was the assumption of rationality that went into everything. People were always assumed to make decisions that maximized their satisfaction and economic standing, and these were assumed to benefit the greatest number of people in the long term. In those years, the United States had double-digit inflation, interest rates, and unemployment. Jimmy Carter was President, OPEC was running wild and the Multilateral Commission was publishing books saying that the Western world had too much democracy and that their people should be reined in. It seemed clear that the rich and powerful were running the show (and not too well), and even the rich and powerful seemed to be miserable. Classical microeconomic assumptions clearly had little bearing on reality.

At that point, I read an early work of Daniel Kahneman's as part of a class assignment in an economics class. Now, he's a Nobel Prize laureate. Then, he was mostly unknown, but Kahneman advocated taking the novel approach of studying how people actually behaved economically instead of how others thought they ought to behave if they were rational enough. He wanted to study economics as a subset of social psychology rather than as an aspect of political philosophy. That sounded like a good starting point. Realizing how irrational people's economic behavior actually was, I wondered if maybe we shouldn't be studying truly irrational people instead of college sophomores. If the world is really run by miserable people obsessed with money and power, then to understand their thinking and behavior shouldn't we study how obsessed people actually think and behave?

I graduated with the plan that I would take some time off from school and figure out what to study next to learn something about this. If behavioral economics was in its infancy, clinical social psychology was equally so, and nobody wanted to consider granting a degree in clinical behavioral economics. I took a job in a residential treatment center for emotionally disturbed adolescent boys, thinking maybe I could learn something there about irrational behavior. Unfortunately for my hopes of becoming a brilliant economist, what I learned there instead was that I was a good therapist who felt most alive when a kid and I were in an intense, undefended, dyadic conversation in which I was helping him to acknowledge, embody, identify and regulate an intensely painful emotion he was experiencing. I gave up on economics and decided to pursue a degree in psychology. I entered graduate school in 1984.

My first semester, I took a class in clinical social psychology under Mark Leary, several of whose works are cited later in this book. Our final project for the class was to write a paper outlining some clinical problem or solution in social psychological terms. Being young and stupid, I chose a topic that was entirely too large and complex—the etiology and treatment of Borderline Personality Disorder. I had seen a lot of Borderline traits among the adolescents at the residential center and thought that people didn't understand the condition very well. I wanted to. Marsha Linehan hadn't written on BPD yet, so all of the works available were classical psychoanalytic or object-relations approaches. My brain was swimming in pathological half-selves and pathogenic introjects. The final paper translated those concepts into social psychology and speculative neuroscience (which, as it turns out, has proven to be true), but it had two major flaws that I recognized while writing it.

First, because it was my first semester and due to my basic laziness, I hadn't bothered to learn APA style yet. Knowing I would get hammered for poor style anyway, I decided to ignore it. That was the obvious problem. The less obvious problem was that the implicit model of emotion I'd gotten from the psychoanalytic texts I'd read for the paper was clearly mistaken. Their descriptions of Borderline behavior were accurate, but their descriptions of emotions weren't. People simply didn't work that way. I decided to study emotion so that I could understand psychopathology better.

It quickly became clear that all models of emotion in those years were flawed. Freud's work treated emotion as a secondary aspect of drives. Most modern analytic writers treated them as secondary aspects of internalized relationships. Cognitive psychologists treated them as secondary aspects of thinking. Systemic thinkers treated them as secondary aspects of family roles. Behaviorists pretended they didn't exist. Nobody seemed to be treating them as the primary building blocks of the self, the primary target of defensive behavior or the primary focus of treatment. Nobody seemed to be treating them as the central concern of social psychology or counseling.

I began considering emotions that way, first in the form of thought experiments. Then, I started testing my ideas in therapy. I began conceptualizing personality in terms of genuine affect and defensive efforts to avoid experiencing it. Like Freud before me, I discovered the limitations of catharsis (rather painfully) and started trying to understand what was involved in genuine "working through," which had always seemed poorly defined and explained. I was seemingly on my way to a nice career as a psychologist, but reality again intervened. Despite my goals and desires, the school wanted to train me to become a professor instead of a clinician and I started wondering whether they were truly interested in me or not. A kid at work got mad when his dad didn't show up at Thanksgiving and broke my arm with a pool cue just over a month before my research proposal was due. And, for the final coup de grace, I made the classic graduate school mistake for people intent on graduating: I met the wonderful woman who became my wife.

Before I knew it, I had a young family and a terminal Master's degree. I briefly attended a second graduate school in order to obtain my license as a professional counselor. I later became licensed as counselor supervisor. This freedom from academia allowed time to study and learn from clients, read the foundational writers and follow basic research from afar. Years passed and I believed I was finished with school, but I met a coworker who had enrolled in a distance education program to earn her Ph.D. in psychology. This was the first time I had ever considered that avenue. After discussing it with my family, I enrolled, this time with clear ideas about what to study.

This book is the result of my studies and research on how emotions actually operate in people, and it contains what was missing from the paper

Dr. Leary received back in 1984. This is the book that I would have gladly bought any time since then to help me organize my thinking about how to conceptualize emotional problems and treat people. Since others have not spent those intervening years thinking about emotions and psychotherapy in this same way, it is a book I think continues to be relevant to a larger number of people than perhaps realize it. I hope that the reader will find it enlightening and beneficial.

Emotions in Psychology and Psychotherapy could not have been written without the input and help of a number of others, who are far too numerous to note here individually. I've learned something new from nearly every client I've seen through the years, and it has been their stories that have helped me develop a framework onto which I can organize the vast amount of research evidence about emotions that has accumulated over the years. Many colleagues and professors along the way have argued against my intuitive but premature conclusions, pointed to logical flaws or suggested authors whose writing on a particular point seemed relevant. Many of them might have become sick of my constant focus on emotion through the years, but most were thankfully too kind to say so.

However, my biggest support throughout has come from my family. My wife and daughters have tolerated my late hours and occasional lack of stable employment through the intervening years of massive change and insurance upheavals in the sector. They tolerated having a "weekend dad" during the year I was away completing my doctoral internship, and my daughters have grown into responsible adults despite that. My younger daughter, Monica, who is currently a college senior, is turning out to be the academic I could never see myself becoming. She taught me one of the most pertinent questions for this project when she was about 3 years old: *How do you know that?* Speculations generally stayed out of this book unless solid research evidence supported my experience and intuitions.

My older daughter, Rachel (http://rachelbrownlow.com), has gone on to become an editor and writer. When my sister asked me once I had finally graduated what I intended to do with my degree, it was Rachel who suggested that I start posting on Twitter, blogging and writing a book. Though she has little interest in emotions as they are discussed in this book, she has provided invaluable editorial help throughout this project while continuing with her many professional responsibilities. She has preserved my writing "voice" but helped make the final product less confusing and more readable. I'm proud of her willingness to strike out on her own and grateful for her help and advice. I handed her a large manuscript and asked her to edit it carefully on a tight deadline. She should be credited with its improved readability, including removing lots of confusing commas. Any errors of scholarship are my own.

Finally and foremost, I must acknowledge my wife, Mary Lou. The first time I saw her in graduate school, I understood intuitively and immediately that she would be a great mother. I was young and thought I was on the road to becoming a professional psychologist, so at that point the idea of parenthood scared me. I understood that becoming a father would almost certainly end my graduate training at that school. As it turned out, I was correct on all counts. We both left that school with Master's degrees and she became the fantastic mother I always knew she would be. Both of our daughters have told me lately that they agree with this assessment, which has to be high praise for any mother. She has held the family together through my many years of studying and pursuing dreams. She has been my staunchest ally and the person most willing to tell me privately and compassionately when I've messed up. She has listened to the ideas contained in this book for years without rolling her eyes as they progressed and developed, asking good questions and suggesting other ways of thinking about topics. Delaying my career as a psychologist so that I could marry her and raise our daughters with her was the wisest decision I've ever made.

Introduction

HUMANS EMPLOY TWO separate computational systems, which do not always synchronize with one another (Epstein, 1994; Sloman, 1996), though each informs and influences the other (Belzung & Chevalley, 2002). One, the perceptual-cognitive system, is thoughtful, deliberate, rational and logical; the other, the emotional system, is associative, automatic, sensory and impulsive (Epstein, 1994, 1997; Greenberg, 2002a, 2004; Sloman, 1996; Smith & Kirby, 2000). Either system can be experienced consciously or remain unconscious (Greenberg, 2002a, 2002b), but the cognitive system communicates with us digitally and verbally, while the emotional system communicates via sensorimotor means, operates through pattern recognition, and expresses itself in the form of narrative stories (Epstein, 1994, 1997; Greenberg, 2002a, 2004; Panksepp, 2003a; Sloman, 1996; Smith & Kirby, 2000). Also unlike cognition, emotions rely on and process peripheral and visceral information from the body (Schulkin, Thompson, & Rosen 2003).

Nature, which has favored the increasing flexibility of organisms, designed three different aversive systems within the human brain, allowing people to reach simpler decisions more efficiently while also increasing their adaptability, flexibility and control in more complex situations (Berntson & Cacioppo, 2000). Pain, indicating a physical wound, is organized within the brain stem; emotions, which impel action to avoid future pain, is organized primarily within the limbic system; and planning, which minimizes physical and emotional pain through behavioral adaptation, is organized within the prefrontal cortex (PFC). Although each progressive level adds greater flexibility, it also requires more time, energy and information to arrive at decisions, making it more powerful but less efficient than the earlier levels, which are often sufficient at meeting task requirements (Berntson & Cacioppo, 2000).

Even rudimentary assessments about whether something is good or bad influence future goal-directed courses of action (Cacioppo & Berntson, 1999), but the brain goes further, automatically noting the existing correspondences between events and using these discoveries to predict potential threats and benefits (Greenberg, 2002a; Paivio & Greenberg, 1998). While perception and cognition describe the environment and inform us what an object is, emotions provide direct hedonic and evaluative experiences of it, tell us its meaning and predict its safeness or dangerousness (Buck, 1999; Cabanac, 2002; Cacioppo & Gardner, 1999). Emotions differentiate friendly, benign and hostile stimuli, hasten accurate decisions about whether to approach or retreat (Cacioppo & Berntson, 1999) and coordinate responses accordingly (Gross, 1999). They represent the world and account for its systematic correlations within specified contexts, especially when events predict future pain or potential danger (Cacioppo & Gardner, 1999; Crawford & Cacioppo, 2002; Zald, 2003). Such stimuli are processed more quickly than less salient stimuli and are also more capable of distracting organisms from ongoing tasks (Mackintosh & Mathews, 2003; Walz & Rapee, 2003; Zald, 2003). Using this salient information, emotions direct quick, adaptive responses (Schulkin et al., 2003).

Emotions have social, cognitive, developmental, clinical and neuropsychological facets (Cacioppo & Gardner, 1999). Unlike normal cognition, they (a) possess hedonic valences; (b) survive more types of brain damage;

(c) are easier to arouse in the young; (d) generate pan-culturally recognized expressions and behaviors; and (e) reflect motivational states (Panksepp, 2003a). They reflect the meanings an individual places on his or her transactions with the environment, real or imagined, based on that person's unique personal history, unconscious motivations and patterns of thinking and coping (Lazarus, 2006).

Though there is no action without emotion (Strasser, 1999), it is unusually difficult to define emotion, even informally (Cabanac, 2002). Operational definitions are even hazier because of the idiosyncratic manner in which individual scholars have asked their questions and pursued their research agendas (Kappas, 2002). Largely innate (Darwin, 1872/1965), emotions are processes (Sarbin & Keen, 1998) that direct homeostatic and social responses to environmental events (Hagemann, Waldstein, & Thayer, 2003). Often elicited quickly, automatically, and unconsciously (Cacioppo, Berntson, Larsen, Poehlmann, & Ito, 2000), they quickly and flexibly (Diamond & Aspinwall, 2003) respond to ongoing changes in the environment, brain and body (Greenberg, 2002a), coordinating the organism's adaptation to changing environmental demands by integrating physiological responses, subjective experience and the perceptual, cognitive and behavioral systems (Gross, 2002; Hagemann et al., 2003; Izard, 2002; Schulkin et al., 2003).

By using central, autonomic, peripheral, and visceral avenues to process information (Hagemann et al., 2003; Schulkin et al., 2003), emotions coordinate many internal systems, including those involved in sensation, perception, attention, autonomic activation, hormonal arousal, motor activity, expressive behavior, subjective feeling, goal-directed cognition and appraised valuation (Lewis & Stieben, 2004; Panksepp, 2003a), which are aspects of the individual that usually operate independently of one another (Ellgring & Smith, 1998). They coordinate neural functioning from the brain stem to the neocortex (Schulkin et al., 2003), including the frontal, temporal and parietal lobes, insula, anterior cingulate cortex (ACC), amygdala, thalamus, hypothalamus and midbrain (Hagemann et al., 2003).

Emotions integrate cognition, affect, motivation and behavior to evaluate, inform, organize, and monitor events (Greenberg, 2002a). They focus attention, organize thinking, prioritize goals, simplify decision-making, direct action and ease learning (Diamond & Aspinwall, 2003; Gross, 1999; Paivio & Greenberg, 1998). Social judgments, for example, are often made almost automatically because of their reliance on emotion (Heberlein, Adolphs, Pennebaker, & Tranel, 2001). Relying on contextual and autobiographical memory (Brosschot, 2002), emotions create flexible plans of action that can be acted upon rapidly and adjusted quickly as events warrant (Hagemann et al., 2003). Yet at times, because they bias attention, preferentially activate concepts and memories, affect cognitive capacity and are easily used as evidence for or against particular strategies, they alter processes often considered purely cognitive, such as interpretation, judgment, decision making and reasoning (Blanchette & Richards, 2010).

Emotions perform vital communicative functions (Erickson & Schulkin, 2003; Greenberg, 2002a), with emotional processes and social contexts reciprocally influencing one another (Saarni, 1997). Highly contagious, emotions produce similar states in others (Ciompi, 1998), which probably served throughout evolution to coordinate responses to salient situations (Jenkins & Oatley, 1998). By scripting complex social behavior (Gross, 1999), emotions synchronize social systems (Ellgring & Smith, 1998) and communicate individuals' intentions and desires to others (Gross, 1999). The emotions experienced and expressed within a group help regulate that group (Ellgring & Smith, 1998), while helping individual group members stabilize their attitudes, preferences and beliefs (Cacioppo & Berntson, 1999). Although no emotion is intrinsically better than another, some are better suited to particular situations. The inability to access and activate appropriate emotional responses results in poorly regulated individuals and groups (Bybee & Quiles, 1998).

Focused by nature on the present, emotions monitor the subjective wellbeing of individuals and their relationships, signal this information to others, organize future behavior and evaluate the ensuing outcomes (Greenberg, 2002a). When they are most poignant and vibrant, they are closest to genuine life experience, whether it is acknowledged or not (Greenberg & Paivio, 1997). They reflect transformations in one's relationship with the environment, with each emotion reflecting a different type of adjustment (de Rivera, 1977). They are the building blocks of more complex drive states (Kernberg, 1992). Because of memory and imagination, their influence can extend to the past and future (Greenberg, 2002a). They focus physiology (Damasio, 2001) and cognition (Lewis, 2004) for future goal-directed action and interaction (Greenberg & Pascual-Leone, 2001; Kappas, Bherer, & Theriault, 2000; Paivio & Greenberg, 1998).

Although many believe emotions are disruptive (Belzung & Chevalley, 2002), since Darwin's (1872/1965) contribution, most scientists have accepted his view that emotions are adaptive (Izard, Fine, Mostow, Trentacosta, & Campbell, 2002). Babies display many aspects of human emotion soon after birth (Sullivan & Lewis, 2003), and many discrete emotions (Izard, 2002) are individually hardwired (Darwin, 1872/1965) with differences in physiology (Herrald & Tomaka, 2002) and subsequent processing (Izard et al., 2002). However, both emotional stimuli (LeDoux, 2000; Medina, Repa, Mauk, & LeDoux, 2002; Rescorla, 1988) and attitudes (Berntson & Cacioppo, 2000) are almost completely conditioned, especially fearful ones (Sullivan and Lewis, 2003). Unconsciously conditioned responses to previously neutral stimuli can completely override normal cognition (Berntson & Cacioppo, 2000), directing behavior that either does not respond adequately to current demands or leads to harmful, impulsive actions (Gross, 1999). Because of this, maladaptive emotional patterns lead to dysfunctional interpersonal and intragroup relationships (Greenberg, 2002a, 2002b). Emotions often help solve problems elegantly, but they can also cause errors (Schulkin et al., 2003), particularly when they reflect beliefs or values that are inappropriate to the situation being faced (Gross, 1999; Lazarus, 2006).

Emotions affect the study of psychology at nearly every level, from the molecular (Buck, 1999; Graeff, 2002) to the cultural (Mesquita, 2001; Mesquita & Ellsworth, 2001). Given this vast scope of separate and dissociable levels of experience, Kappas (2002) argued that emotional impact and functioning must be studied using a coordinated approach at multiple levels. Only such integration, he reasoned, could yield a reasonably full understanding of how emotional processes function and affect human beings and relationships. This coordinated study and integration is the intent of this volume, which will examine various aspects of emotion separately and in detail before blending them to portray what is commonly seen in the counseling session. The therapeutic encounter can then be understood in a way that makes sense of the material presented, what it represents and how best to proceed.

PART ONE

EMOTIONS, AFFECT AND MOOD

Affect and Mood

By SEPARATELY CONSIDERING affect, mood and emotion, a more complete appreciation of the contribution of each can be gained. Emotion has already been briefly introduced and will be taken up more fully in succeeding chapters; in this chapter affect will be explored before attention is turned to mood. This strategy should help illuminate the important distinctions between the three constructs.

Affect

When they submitted subjective reports of emotion to factor analysis, Tellegen, Watson, and Clark (1999) found that the various discrete emotions like fear, joy and guilt resolved into the relatively independent second-order factors of positive and negative affect. At birth, children display only those two affective states rather than discernable emotions, per se (Lewis, 2003). Other researchers have found that anger does not correspond well to either factor (Debener et al., 2000), and Watson and Clark (1994, 1997) did not include either happiness or sadness as part of their affective rating scales, since each loads so poorly onto the two factors.

A long debate has since emerged over whether positive affect and negative affect are truly separable from one another or form aspects of a single bipolar dimension. Watson and Clark (1997) found that many experiences within individuals were correlated with both, and that while the various positive states correlate strongly with one another—as do the various negative states—positive affect and negative affect do not correlate with one another strongly. During calm situations, they show weak negative correlations (Zautra, Reich, Davis, Potter, & Nicolson, 2000), with various stimuli activating either, neither or both (Cacioppo & Gardner, 1999). At such times, people experience both positive and negative affective channels simultaneously, creating more fully developed, nuanced and adaptive representations of their environments (Reich & Zautra, 2002; Zautra, Berkhof, & Nicolson, 2002). In this way, people assess potential rewards and pitfalls before committing to any particular goal (Diamond & Aspinwall, 2003).

Although this carries advantages, it also requires increased time and processing capacity that cannot be afforded during stressful times (Zautra et al., 2002). Field and laboratory studies have shown that during psychologically stressful events people collapse their positive and negative affects onto one bipolar dimension, decreasing their affective complexity (Zautra et al., 2000). This process, which also takes place during states of heightened arousal, chronic pain and intense positive or negative emotion, leads to diminished differentiation, impaired discrimination, poor information processing and simplified judgment (Reich & Zautra, 2002).

Moods

Disorders of mood can emerge not only from psychiatric causes and the effects of substances, but also from neuropsychological insults, particularly lesions of the PFC caused by cardiovascular accidents or traumatic brain injuries (Liotti & Mayberg, 2001). This variety of causes makes the understanding of mood seem imperative; but to understand a topic so broad and multifaceted, perspectives must be combined from many disciplines, including psychiatry, neuropsychology and social, cognitive, developmental and clinical psychology (Cacioppo & Gardner, 1999). Yet none of these disciplines has progressed far with studying mood, as they have instead focused on emotion or affect. (Actually, it can be argued that much of the research on emotion is a study of mood, but this is another matter. The conceptual distinctions between the two have been poor.)

While emotions are intense and (usually) fleeting, most of life is experienced during less intense mood states, which current theories of emotions address poorly (Watson & Clark, 1997). Although moods sometimes cause intense affective states (Morris, 2000), when compared to emotions they last longer, have no discernable beginning or endpoint, take no fixed object, are generally less intense and are more internally influenced (Watson, 2000). Unlike emotions, moods lack clear goals or specific repertoires of behavior (Gendolla, Abele, & Krüsken, 2001) because that is not their purpose (Morris, 2000). They produce more muted physiological effects than emotions (Gendolla et al., 2001), though various combinations of mood states have been associated with differing patterns of autonomic arousal (Shapiro, Jamner, Goldstein, & Delfino, 2001).

Instead, moods measure the current balance between demands and internal resources (Morris, 2000), signaling whether an individual currently has the energy to cope with environmental demands (Martin, 2000). While emotions direct one's attention towards emergencies, moods measure the discrepancy between the internal resources needed to complete a given task and those available, with higher available energy than demand yielding positive moods and lower energy than demand turning moods negative (Martin, 2000). A highly positive mood indicates an abundant ability to solve the problems of daily life, while a highly negative mood indicates a marked insufficiency of current resources (Watson, 2000). These ongoing assessments, communicated via the endocrine and immune systems (Larsen, 2000a), help people determine how they are progressing towards their goals (Martin, 2000).

Tense tiredness yields depressed moods (Thayer, 2000), and failure, loss, and immune functioning can each negatively impact one's mood (Morris, 2000). Calm energy leads to subjective feelings of wellbeing (Thayer, 2000). Even the degree of difficulty involved in processing can affect an individual's momentary mood states (Winkielman & Cacioppo, 2001). Using naturally occurring data, Shapiro et al. (2001) found that heart rate, systolic blood pressure and diastolic blood pressure vary with the type and intensity of mood—increasing during negative moods, remaining stable during positive moods and decreasing with tiredness.

Both positive and negative moods provide motivation, with positive moods doing so through enjoyment and negative moods changing the focus to doing "good enough" (Martin, 2000). The PFC resolves any discrepancies between ongoing goals and current mood states (Davidson, Pizzagalli, Nitschke, & Putnam, 2002), and sometimes a shift in focus from one area to another can overcome a poor mood and achieve a goal (Martin, 2000). As people begin to note their likelihood of failure, their mood worsens; they focus on themselves more and they change their goals, alter their strategies or attempt to modulate their mood (Morris, 2000). However, people in highly negative moods are unlikely to do what is needed to raise their moods effectively, which involves socializing and becoming more active (Watson, 2000).

Although moods often function outside awareness, they nonetheless focus people's attention (Morris, 2000), influencing both how they act (Gendolla, 2000) and what they think (Forgas, 2000). For example, depressed moods spawn depressed cognitive and behavioral styles, which in turn reinforce the depressed mood states (Paivio & Greenberg, 1998). Wanting to retain their cognitive capacity, people generally avoid processing information more than necessary, and moods help them do this (Bower & Forgas, 2000). In general, as tasks require more thinking, an individual's mood increasingly factors into her calculations (Forgas, 2000), particularly when those moods are not consciously registered (Berkowitz, Jaffee, Jo, & Troccoli, 2000). The exception occurs when the resulting decision is likely to be highly personally salient (Forgas, 2000), a situation leading the person to overcompensate for extreme moods (Bower & Forgas, 2000). By doing so, people often falsely attribute their realistic perceptions of others and of difficult situations to their moods and discount their moods completely when they consider goals like maintaining their self-esteem (Berkowitz et al., 2000). However, as decisions become harder and require more deliberation, moods reenter the decision-making process, even in such central areas (Bower & Forgas, 2000).

People continually monitor, evaluate and regulate their moods, a process Salovey, Mayer, Goldman, Turvey, and Palfai (1995) termed the *meta-mood* experience. Though mood operates on a circadian cycle (Watson, 2000), people often try to attenuate the intensity and effects of highly positive or highly negative moods (Forgas, 2000), particularly when they are expending a lot of cognitive effort on some other task (Wenzlaff & Wegner, 2000). Much of this occurs outside awareness (Mayer & Stevens, 1994). Rather than respecting the cyclic nature of their moods, people expect to feel good all of the time and fight the lethargy that always follows periods of high energy (Watson, 2000). Effective mood regulation matches mood states to task demands (Martin, 2000; Mayer & Stevens, 1994), but most people say they regulate their moods primarily to feel better (Tice & Wallace, 2000). Once moods have been identified, it appears that people choose when to regulate them by evaluating their acceptability, typicality and influence (Mayer & Stevens, 1994). Those with higher self-esteem tend to regulate their moods more quickly, while those with lower self-esteem tend to allow their moods to linger (Forgas, 2000).

People regulate their moods by repairing, maintaining or dampening them (Mayer & Stevens, 1994). Stimulus avoidance and reappraisal, methods often used to regulate emotions, do not improve moods (Manstead & Fischer, 2000), though thoughts that oppose the mood may (Erber & Erber, 2000). Distraction, which men tend to prefer, helps modulate moods while rumination, which women tend to practice, does not (Thayer, 2000; Tice & Bratslavsky, 2000). Music and eating may alter mood (Morris, 2000), while activity generally only helps if it follows inactivity (Watson, 2000) and arousing stimuli and socializing may raise some kinds of moods but not others (Tice & Bratslavsky, 2000). After initially raising it, arousal lowers tension (Thayer, 2000), so tired people's moods can be improved by either sleeping or completely foregoing rest (Watson, 2000).

When people believe that unhealthy behavior will help them regulate their unwanted negative moods in the short term, they readily engage in such behavior (Tice, Bratslavsky, & Baumeister, 2001). They often smoke, drink caffeine and alcohol, eat sugar and unhealthy foods, procrastinate and behave in a variety of other self-destructive ways they hope will raise their moods in the short term. Ultimately, however these strategies put them at a longer-term disadvantage (Tice et al., 2001; Watson, 2000). When forced to choose between impulse control and mood regulation, people invariably chose the latter (Tice et al., 2001). If people believe that aggressive behavior will modulate their moods, they readily act aggressively even though such behavior increases their negative emotions later (Bushman, Baumeister, & Phillips, 2001). Despite their negative moods, whenever self-esteem maintenance is salient, people assess new information positively (Bower & Forgas, 2000). They also avoid seeking others' support, possibly due to the risk of potential embarrassment (Folkman, Lazarus, Dunkel-Schetter, DeLongis, and Gruen, 1986).

Since moods carry information about goal attainment, people may not regulate them if the information remains useful (Clore & Robinson,

2000). At other times, people intentionally opt for experiencing negative moods to achieve secondary gains such as attention, sympathy or a release from responsibility (Tice & Wallace, 2000). They might also adopt negative moods to demonstrate empathy (Martin, 2000) by matching others' subjective states (Greenberg, Elliot, Watson, & Bohart, 2001). Although hedonic concerns sometimes contribute to the decision (Tice & Wallace, 2000), people usually regulate their moods only when doing so is socially required (Erber & Erber, 2000), such as being somber at funerals (Hirt & McCrae, 2000). Otherwise, they tend to maintain their mood states, whether positive or negative (Erber & Erber, 2000). In general, the social appropriateness rather than the hedonic value of a mood determines whether or not it will be maintained (Martin, 2000).

As noted earlier, understanding moods is important in understanding emotions and evaluating the research on emotions. Not only do moods affect emotions (and vice versa), but much of the research on emotion probably actually induces moods. Now that moods have been addressed, the focus can turn to emotions, the primary focus of this volume.

Approaches to Studying Emotion

BECAUSE EMOTION IS such a broad topic, researchers have approached it from a variety of different perspectives and made a number of distinctions when discussing it. Emotional experiences differ from one another along at least three dimensions: arousal level, hedonic valence and the degree to which motivated behavior is either self-directed or socially directed (Buck, 1999; Cabanac, 2002; Fernández-Dols & Russell, 2003), yet although many studies have used the pleasant-unpleasant dimension as a behavioral predictor (e.g., Mackintosh & Mathews, 2003), research shows the deficiency of this approach. Emotional processes with similar hedonic valences have been shown to affect cognition (Tiedens & Linton, 2001), motivation (Lerner & Keltner, 2001) and behavior (Herrald & Tomaka, 2002) quite differently, and memories become associated by the specific emotions involved rather than based on whether it was a positive or negative emotion (Niedenthal & Halberstadt, 2000). These findings have encouraged the study of discrete emotions rather than emotional valence (Lazarus, 2001).

Evolutionary Theories

Although emotions were once thought to render people thoughtless and passive (Schulkin et al., 2003), most modern theorizing in the field can be traced to Darwin's (1872/1965) seminal work, which made current programs of studying emotion possible. In it, Darwin argued that emotions evolved to aid species in their quest for survival and that emotional expressions are attenuated behavior that helps prepare the organism for actions required for its survival. Each discrete emotion promotes survival in a unique way (Izard et al., 2002). As a secondary elaboration, Darwin believed, these expressive behaviors later became adapted as signals to others. For instance, accurately interpreting others' facial or behavioral signals of disgust may prevent someone from eating something foul, thus keeping that person alive (Erickson and Schulkin, 2003). Emotion can also be communicated by vocal tone, although this is less accurately perceived than facial expressions (Adolphs, 2002a).

Emotions appear in all animals more advanced than amphibians, suggesting that they have proven advantageous for a wide variety of animals and situations (Cabanac, 2002). Noting that evolution has added newer brain structures onto older ones, making simple explanations of emotional functioning unlikely, Kappas (2002) suggests that the study of human emotion should include analyzing the similarities and differences both with other animals and with machines. Cabanac (2002) argues that machines, having no hedonic sense, cannot experience emotions, but notes the proven value of animal studies. Believing that other mammals' cognitive abilities probably differ more from humans' than their basic emotional functioning, Panksepp (2003a) wrote that studying other animals permits researchers to use invasive techniques like surgery and drugs to formulate and confirm their hypotheses. These tactics allow for easier and cheaper testing and confirmation than human studies employing neuropsychological patients or functional brain imagery, although ultimately theories about emotional functioning should rely on convergent data from all three sources (Panksepp, 2003a).

Panksepp (2001, 2003b) believes the primordial origins of several different neural networks may have been discovered in this manner in his studies with rats, mentioning fear, joy, sadness, seeking, rage, panic, play, lust, bonding and security. While Panksepp (2003b) acknowledges that his approach may be branded both anthropomorphic and zoomorphic, he believes his research program provides scientists with the opportunity to study "basic" emotional systems. Blumberg and Sokoloff (2003), whose research employed rats, disputed some of Panksepp's interpretations of rat behavior and his assumptions about the functional equivalence of behavior across species, but acknowledged that science may progress more quickly because of the tensions between Panksepp's less cautious approach and their own.

Deficits in the animal model are readily apparent in the study of music, which taps emotional prosody reception (Panksepp & Bernatzky, 2002) and is often used to induce affective states in experimental subjects (largely for ethical or developmental reasons; see, e.g., Schmidt, Trainor, & Santesso, 2003). While music activates suspected emotional networks and raises levels of neurotransmitters associated with emotion in experimental animals, they generally respond differently to music than humans do (Panksepp & Bernatzky, 2002). To paraphrase Panksepp and Bernatzky, although music may be the language of human emotions, animals appear to speak somewhat different languages.

Many species (Cacioppo et al., 2000) experience categorical emotions like sadness and fear, suggesting that they have evolutionary roots (Fosha, 2004). Furthermore, some emotional reactions are clearly hardwired. For instance, rats raised in laboratories show fear the first time they are exposed to a fox's scent (Schulkin et al., 2003). Although humans have evolved to respond to some types of information quickly and effectively (Schulkin et al., 2003), perhaps alone among the animals they have the ability to both anticipate how their actions will affect their future emotional states and organize their goal-directed behavior accordingly (Berntson & Cacioppo, 2000).

Basic Emotion Theories

Although they have not agreed with one another on the specific emotions involved, a number of researchers (e.g., Izard, 1977, 2002; Izard et al., 2002; Plutchik, 1991, 2000; Power & Schmidt, 2004; Tomkins, 1995) have posited a small number of basic emotions, with all other emotions obtained by combining those. For example, according to these theorists, the combination of anger, disgust and contempt yields hostility (Izard, 1977), while adding fear and disgust together results in phobia (Hamm, Cuthbert, Globisch, & Vaitl, 1997). All basic emotion theorists have agreed that each basic emotion (a) has a unique function (Izard, 2002), (b) is unique both physiologically and behaviorally (Plutchik, 1991, 2000), (c) is relatively independent of the other basic emotions (Izard, 2002) and (d) is present at all levels of evolution above the one at which it appears (Plutchik, 1991, 2000). However, their lack of agreement on the number of basic emotions, let alone which emotions should be considered basic, casts doubt on whether their premise is correct.

Discrete Emotion Theories

Some emotions are fluid, while others are fixed and difficult to alter (de Rivera, 1977). Neural (Berthoz, Blair, Le Clec'h, & Martinot, 2002; Critchley, 2003) and physiological (Herrald & Tomaka, 2002; Rainville, Bechara, Naqvi, & Damasio, 2006) differences between emotions have been observed in humans. The insular cortex, among other areas, engages and disengages depending on the specific emotion evoked, its valence and intensity, and the individual's current level of satiation (Berthoz et al., 2002). Fear, anger, sadness and happiness differ in their influence on the parasympathetic nervous system (Rainville et al., 2006) while hostility leads to rising levels of low-density cholesterol and triglyceride levels (Repetti, Taylor, & Seeman, 2002).

However, using physiological indicators to differentiate among emotional reactions is extremely complex. Making fearful facial expressions increases both fear and heart rate, even when participants do not realize the expressions they adopt are fearful (Levenson, Ekman, & Friesen, 1990); meanwhile, watching frightening film clips increases fear and lowers heart rate (Fredrickson & Levenson, 1998). Exaggerating one's amusing or disgusted reactions while watching film clips raises one's heart rate compared to natural emotional expression while one is viewing the clip, but it results in a lower heart rate afterward (Demaree, Schmeichel, Robinson, & Everhart, 2004). Defensiveness increases heart rate variability and the electrical activity measured over the corrugator supercilii muscle when one is afraid, but it increases diastolic blood pressure and total peripheral resistance when one is angry (Pauls & Stemmler, 2003). Although emotions differ from one another both physiologically and behaviorally (Plutchik, 1998), it appears that they are not so much separate entities as complex mental states (Horowitz, Fridhandler, & Stinson, 1992).

Linguistic Theories

Another possibility is that emotional categories may actually be linguistic constructs rather than reflections of discrete emotions (Dailey, Cottrell, Padgett, & Adolphs, 2002), employing folk concepts rather than scientific ones (Russell, 2003). Since various cultures categorize emotions differently (Mesquita, 2001) and folk wisdom has already proven to be mistaken in a variety of other areas, we have no inherent reason to believe our folk categories of emotional experience (Kagan, 1992). Existing language categories do not accurately reflect the many possible varieties and intensities of affective processing (Fernández-Dols & Russell, 2003).

Emotional experiences with the same labels may be qualitatively different and may lead to markedly different behavior (Cacioppo et al., 2000;

Otto & Hupka, 1999). For example, fear responses can range from freezing to vigilance to flight (Cacioppo et al., 2000), while sadness can be either certain or uncertain, with certain sadness processed more heuristically, though people tend to rate the two as equally sad (Tiedens & Linton, 2001). *Disgust* may refer to noxious smells, the taste of spoiled food, or the emotional reaction to a moral transgression, each of which is associated with a different facial expression (Olatunji & Sawchuk, 2005). *Anxiety* can refer to either apprehension or arousal, each associated with its own physiological correlates (Shapiro et al., 2001). It might refer to avoidance behavior, physiology influenced by temperament, physiology influenced by specific situations (e.g., test-influenced stress responses), signals from the conscience, phobias and so forth (Kagan, 1992). Judgments of likelihood sustain the anxiety arising from physical threats, while probabilistic reasoning sustains the anxiety arising from threats to self esteem (Otto & Hupka, 1999).

Culturally conventional stories about why an action occurred are considered normal, while culturally unconventional stories are considered aberrant or crazy (Sarbin & Keen, 1998). According to Russell (2003), action depends more on an individual's ongoing goals than on his emerging emotional experience. To be effective and adaptive, he believes, action must change as situations do rather than resulting from preprogramming or preplanning. While physical changes accompany preparations for upcoming action, they do not correspond uniquely to any emotion. Instead, people organize their experience into emotional scripts based on how closely their behavior and current situation match culturally defined prototypes. By following such cultural scripts, individuals can better establish coherent and culturally appropriate narratives that help regulate their personal and interpersonal experiences. Thus, they enjoy cognitive economy and efficiency while remaining embedded in their common cultural experience (Russell, 2003).

Theorists and researchers have devised a number of ways of conceptualizing emotions, each of which has its admirers and critics. Each of the perspectives mentioned in this chapter has its applications, and each will be featured at times in the succeeding discussion.

Emotional Activation

As SIGMUND FREUD (1911/1959a) discovered, two separate types of cognitive processes exist, which appear in the literature under various names. Developing from tendencies present at birth, the first, schematic-procedural processes, quickly and tacitly encode regularities in perceptual experience by using established schemata, association and conditioning (Clyman, 1992). The second, declarative-deliberative processes, which first appear at about age 2 and only begin maturing after about age 5 (Clyman, 1992), work linguistically, follow propositional logic, organize voluntary action and may become conscious if given enough focus (Philippot & Schaefer, 2001).

Although their terminology has differed, theorists and researchers (e.g., Ben-Ze'ev, 2000; Darwin, 1872/1965; Philippot & Schaefer, 2001; Power & Schmidt, 2004; Schaefer et al., 2003) have distinguished three distinct ways by which emotions can be elicited. Here, they will be termed the schematic, associative and propositional processes. Once these are defined and explored, two types of emotional activation theories will be discussed: appraisal theories and network theories.

Types of Emotional Activation

Schematic Processes

Schematic emotional processes evaluate external environmental circumstances and prepare to deal with them effectively (Darwin, 1872/1965). Although they maintain adaptive survival (Bowlby, 1969; Darwin, 1872/1965), hardwired emotions are uncommon (Schulkin et al., 2003). Bowlby lists the fears of heights, fire, snakes, large predators, the dark, loud noises, strangeness and the enforced absence of one's caregiver—particularly in the young—as adaptive, hardwired responses that infants use to estimate their probability of survival. Far more common are conditioned emotional responses (Schulkin et al., 2003). Both the elicitors of emotional responses (LeDoux, 2000; Rescorla, 1988) and how they are expressed (Mesquita, 2001; Mesquita & Ellsworth, 2001) are largely learned, the former through Pavlovian means, the latter through operant reinforcement. Although generally adaptive, the conditions under which these emotional responses were learned may no longer apply, making them inadequate or inappropriate (Gross, 2002). Together, these two subtypes—the hardwired and the conditioned—have been grouped together as schematically activated emotions (Ben-Ze'ev, 2000; Schaefer et al., 2003).

Schematic processing takes place spontaneously (Schaefer et al., 2003) and generally occurs outside awareness (Schulkin et al., 2003). Assessing each new stimulus to determine what has occurred and how it impacts them personally, individuals compare these considerations to prior schemata (Smith & Lazarus, 1993). Formed through experience and stored in memory (Sanford, 2005), each schema corresponds to one central idea, such as "threat" for fear or "loss" for sadness (Schaefer et al., 2003). Having once learned the operative schemata, individuals with subsequent damage to their amygdalae and hippocampal areas continue to assess dynamic situations correctly, though their understanding of others' expressions is completely impaired (Adolphs, Tranel, & Damasio, 2003).

Associative Processes

Emotional processing often occurs outside awareness (Parkinson &

Manstead, 1993) via associative processing (Power & Schmidt, 2004). Previously neutral stimuli often become invested with meaning once they have been associated with emotionally salient events (Brosschot, 2002). Even subtle manipulation—whether experimental participants focus on themselves or others—changes the emotional meanings people later give to ambiguous situations (Neumann, 2000). Mood commonly acts as an associative element in emotional activation, changing both appraisals and behavioral preferences (Gendolla, 2000; Morris, 2000) through unconscious heuristic processes (Bower & Forgas, 2000). This happens because the associative processes involved in heuristic thinking (Sloman, 1996) are also those used in many emotional appraisals (Smith & Kirby, 2000).

By relying on mood and activating deep emotional processing, potent unconscious states that subtly influence behavior outside of awareness may be elicited (Berkowitz et al., 2000; Bower & Forgas, 2000; Wegner & Smart, 1997). Thus, the results of heuristic thinking tend to overrule rational and linear thought processes because of the effects of mood congruency (Bower & Forgas, 2000). Although the emotions resulting from associative processes still seem to be organized around schematic themes, they cannot be changed easily through reappraisal strategies, as people frequently do with schematically elicited emotions (Power & Schmidt, 2004).

Propositional Processes

Unlike the associative and schematic processes, propositional processes employ executive functioning to create emotional reactions that are voluntary and controlled (Schaefer et al., 2003). Using processes like those that create intellectual understanding (Walz & Rapee, 2003), propositional processes create or prolong emotional responses by consciously activating existing emotional schemata through slower, conscious and largely linear semantic processes (Ben-Ze'ev, 2000). Many emotional states contain propositional elements, especially when situational cues are used to determine how one is to react emotionally (Sanford, 2005). Schaefer et al. (2003) found that, compared to emotions elicited purely through schematic activation, propositional emotions activated the lateral PFC more and study participants rated them as less intense. However, because of their methodology, these research results were not definitive (Schaefer et al., 2003).

Emotions are sometimes elicited consciously (Gross, 2002; Philippot & Schaefer, 2001), but whether they are elicited consciously or unconsciously, emotions affect behavior (Berridge & Winkielman, 2003; Philippot & Schaefer, 2001; Schaefer et al., 2003). The emotions generated propositionally differ markedly from those elicited through schematic means in their neural underpinnings (Ochsner et al., 2009) and their effects on behavior (Izard, 2002). They also decrease people's ability to solve problems effectively (Baumann & Kuhl, 2002). Conscious propositional activation of one emotion may coincide with the unconscious activation of another emotion that will affect behavior outside awareness (Panksepp, 2001).

Propositional processing can cause pathological outcomes. Women use propositional processes more than men, not only relying more on situational cues to determine how they feel (Sanford, 2005), but also ruminating more (Nolen-Hoeksema, 1987; Nolen-Hoeksema & Jackson, 2001), which is another aspect of propositional processing (Ben-Ze'ev, 2000). Quiles and Bybee (1997; Bybee & Quiles, 1998) describe two types of guilt, which they termed *predispositional guilt* and *chronic guilt*, the former of which is schematic, the latter being propositional and pathogenic.

Appraisal Theories

Broadly, appraisal theories state that emotional processes result from cognitive evaluations of ongoing situations (Schorr, 2001), which change as situations unfold and evolve (Folkman & Lazarus, 1985; Thagard & Nerb, 2002). Both initiating and resulting from coping strategies, appraisals assess events' significance and possible future courses of action (Lazarus, 2001, 2006). Beginning as perception occurs, they include associative, schematic and propositional processes into their complex calculations (Smith & Kirby, 2001). Most theorists agree that emotional processes often begin with unconscious appraisals (e.g., Lazarus, 2001; Smith & Lazarus, 1993), but others stress that consciousness (Reisenzein & Hofmann, 1993), reflection (Strasser, 1999) or active reasoning processes (Smith & Kirby, 2000) are sometimes involved. In humans, subcortical structures make many types of appraisal quickly and automatically (Schulkin et al., 2003), but such appraisals employ associations that are easily influenced by priming and bias future appraisals (Smith & Kirby, 2001). According to Smith and Kirby, unconsciously operating schematic monitors match ongoing input with relevant emotional schemata and activate the appropriate emotion. Deliberative processes—the slowest aspect involved—enable reappraisal (Smith & Kirby, 2001) when events do not match what the prior subcortical processes had predicted (Blair, 2004).

Many appraisal theories exist, differing somewhat from one another but each holding that specific emotions are elicited through cognitive appraisals of environmental stimuli along some number of meaningful dimensions. Appraisal processes can be analyzed at either the molecular or molar level, as either a series of judgments about relevance and coping ability (Scherer, 1993; Roseman, 2001) or as a set of core relational themes (e.g., loss = sadness, being thwarted = anger; Smith & Lazarus, 1993; Lazarus, 2001). According to Scherer, emotions vary and, presumably, appraisals are made along a number of molecular dimensions such as suddenness, familiarity, predictability, intrinsic pleasantness, relevance, outcome probability, expectations, urgency, conduciveness, causal agency, causal motives, control, power, adjustment and external and internal compatibility. Scherer believes that appraisal dimensions are assessed in an invariant order, although he acknowledges that the number of necessary appraisal dimensions is in dispute.

In this scheme, various emotions are thought to employ unique patterns of appraisals along a limited number of dimensions, including certainty/uncertainty (Roseman, 2001). Some evidence has partially supported the existence of molecular appraisal processes. Although lambs apparently do not appraise predictability, suddenness startles them and increases their heart rates, and novelty leads to orientation responses and increased vagal activity, suggesting a genetic component in molecular appraisal processing (Désiré, Veissier, Després, & Boissy, 2004).

Those emotions that are "certain," such as anger, disgust, happiness and contentment, lead to heuristic and stereotypical cognitive processing in subsequent situations, while "uncertain" emotions, such as hope, surprise, worry and fear, lead instead to deeper, systematic processing (Tiedens & Linton, 2001). The bias towards cognitive efficiency and simplicity may thus help explain why, for example, people might propositionally induce defensive anger or disgust rather than experiencing schematic fear, sadness or shame, since the latter set, being uncertain, involve more intensive cognitive styles than the former set.

Core relational themes (Smith & Lazarus, 1993) account for variance beyond what molecular appraisal components do (Bennett, Lowe, & Honey, 2003). Each discrete emotion, such as fear or sadness, has a different, specific relational meaning that forms its core concept, such as danger or loss (Lazarus, 2006; Philippot, Chapelle, & Blairy, 2002; Smith & Lazarus, 1993). These molar appraisal dimensions, not emotional valence, determine how individuals predict the future, with fearful people making pessimistic assumptions and angry people making optimistic ones

(Lerner & Keltner, 2000). Appraisal models not only account for different emotions employing differing affective, cognitive, behavioral, motivational and physiological repertoires (Herrald & Tomaka, 2002) but also allow for unconsciously experienced affective processes (Berridge & Winkielman, 2003; Kihlstrom, Mulvaney, Tobias, & Tobis, 2000).

Despite the number and scope of appraisal theories, only weak evidence suggests that different emotional reactions are actually caused by differing appraisal patterns (Frijda & Zeelenberg, 2001). While Frijda (1993) agreed that different emotions are associated with different cognitive patterns, he believed that those patterns often follow rather than precede the experience of the emotion being studied. Even cognitively complex emotions like shame and humiliation, he argued, often have relatively simple cognitive antecedents, although the self-reported lists of appraisal dimensions elicited in various researchers' studies are far more elaborate.

Emotions can be elicited by temperamental influences (Izard, 2002) and through developmental and maturational processes (Izard et al., 2002). People often don't recognize the environmental causes of their emotional variability, such as subtle weather changes (Jostmann, Koole, van der Wulp, & Fockenberg, 2005). Research suggests that at least some of the time emotions can be activated more or less directly by the features of the eliciting stimulus without any formal appraisals occurring (Toates, 2002). Physiological changes often lead to changes in cognition, suggesting that appraisals do not always initiate emotional processes (Greenberg, 2002a). Pleasure, pain, physiological and motor responses, motivational states and intentional behavior may all be stimulated without prior appraisals (Frijda & Zeelenberg. 2001).

Emotional processing involves a series of changes in perceptual awareness, attention, belief and attributions, each of which might influence the cognitive elaborations that later introspection could come to regard as causal appraisals (Frijda, 1993). Frijda and Zeelenberg (2001) concluded that (a) prior affect (such as mood states) causes more emotional reactions than cognitions do; (b) inclinations determine which emotions are aroused as much as appraisals do; (c) cognitions leading to emotions are less complex than most people believe is required; and (d) appraisal cognitions and emotions influence one another without a predetermined order.

Parkinson and Manstead (1993) critiqued the process of appraisal research and found it lacking. They pointed out that most appraisal research before that time employed vignettes, which do not involve participants in the same way that real-life dramas do. Treating vignettes and experience as equivalent, they believed, is an error; vignettes only assess people's abilities to decode stylized portrayals and attach the correct label, and because stories ignore the roles of physiological, environmental and social feedback, they tell us nothing about real emotional processes (Parkinson & Manstead, 1993). Appraisal research has since incorporated this criticism (Harmon-Jones, Sigelman, Bohlig, & Harmon-Jones, 2003). Bennett et al. (2003) demonstrated that emotional appraisals of remembered situations potentially remain consistent for a week or more, but by asking for "the most stressful event of the past four weeks" they limited their research to reports of sadness, anger, anxiety and guilt. In their results, molar appraisals accounted for a significant portion of their experimental variance: almost 50% for anger, almost 40% for anxiety, but less than 20% for sadness and guilt. They believed that this might have underestimated the actual impact of molar appraisals because the design they used (questionnaires) could not measure unconscious appraisal processes. Conversely, their study failed to demonstrate that the appraisals took place prior to the emotional experience (Bennett et al., 2003).

Network Theories

Emotional processes rely not only on cognitive appraisals but also on other coordinated input from central, peripheral and visceral channels (Schulkin et al., 2003). James (1884) believed that emotions result from perceiving the changing levels and patterns of peripheral activity, motor activity and expressive activity, which differ from emotion to emotion. He further believed that voluntarily performing any action associated with a particular emotion would elicit the emotion and that halting one's emotional expression would cause listlessness (James, 1884). While appraisal theories maintain that emotions invariably begin with cognitive processes, according to network theories (a) the visceral, motor and cognitive components of various emotions are organized by and connected through innate or conditioned networks; (b) each component process triggers the automatic activation of all other component processes through associative channels; (c) physiological changes correspond to the emotion aroused and (d) automatic and implicit physical changes can activate an emotion, often completely outside of awareness (Philippot et al., 2002).

Such theories have support: amygdalar activation follows self-induced sadness (Posse et al., 2003). Moving facial muscles according to directions (e.g., tighten this muscle, loosen that one) to produce the facial expressions associated with fear, anger, sadness or disgust, even outside the awareness of the participant following the instructions, has been shown to produce thinking and behavior that match the expressions, with both the fearful and sad expressions leading to increased heart rate (Levenson et al., 1990). Further analysis of this data shows that task difficulty, the time needed to make various facial displays and the activity of other muscles did not mediate these heart rate results (Levenson & Ekman, 2002). Emotional postures, even those adopted outside awareness, lead to congruent emotional responses (Flack, Laird, & Cavallaro, 1999). Behavior consistent with various discrete emotions induces people to experience the corresponding feeling states (Clynes, 1977), as does adopting the breathing patterns associated with those emotions, even when the purpose for doing so remains unknown (Philippot et al., 2002).

The power of the emotions elicited through peripheral means increases as more elements match one another (Flack et al., 1999). People vary in how much they depend on peripheral feedback, with some individuals feeling emotions more intensely when they adopt emotional behavior and others more affected by environmental stimuli or emotional thoughts (Duclos & Laird, 2001). Duclos and Laird found that personal-cue responders induce emotional experience far better by adopting emotionally expressive behavior than do situational-cue responders, who self-induce emotional experiences better using imagery techniques. Personal-cue responders feel their emotions more intensely and later recall more memories congruent with the emotion they expressed (Schnall & Laird, 2003). Expressive inhibition lowers personal-cue responders' perceptions of their emotional state better, while situational-cue responders attenuate their emotional states more by distracting themselves (Duclos & Laird, 2001). However, when presented with false physiological feedback, at least some experimental subjects' emotional evaluations and actual physiological responses soon match the false feedback (Crucian et al., 2000).

In summary, these results suggest that (a) while peripheral activity adds to experience, emotional processing does not require it (Cacioppo et al., 2000); (b) both visceral and appraisal models have limitations (Philippot et al., 2002) and (c) cognitive and visceral processes usually reinforce one another (Cacioppo et al., 2000). Emotions can originate from visceral and subcortical activation or from more intentional, cognitive processing—though most processing is believed to combine the two (Ochsner et al., 2009).

Types of Emotional Experience

According to Greenberg (2002a, 2002b, 2004; Greenberg & Bolger, 2001; Greenberg & Paivio, 1997, 1998; Greenberg & Safran, 1989; Paivio & Greenberg, 1998), the adaptive value of an emotion rests upon whether it is a primary, secondary or instrumental emotion. Though this terminology will be changed somewhat in the following discussion, Greenberg's distinctions will form the basis for much of the discussion in later chapters.

Primary Emotions

As the initial evaluations of direct experience (Greenberg, 2002a), primary emotions (Greenberg, 2002a, 2002b, 2004; Greenberg & Bolger, 2001; Greenberg & Paivio, 1997, 1998; Greenberg & Safran, 1989; Paivio & Greenberg, 1998) respond to ongoing environmental concerns (Greenberg, 2004). Originating from schematic appraisals of environmental stimuli (Greenberg & Paivio, 1997), they prepare people to solve problems effectively (Greenberg & Safran, 1989). Primary emotions alone probably should not determine anyone's behavior, but they often provide valuable input when decisions must be made concerning future courses of action (Greenberg & Paivio, 1998). Even when they are painful and intense, they create possibilities for the individual to respond to current stimuli (Greenberg, 2002a) and help him learn to avoid similar situations in the future (Greenberg & Paivio, 1997).

Bypassed Emotions

To the above category, Greenberg (2002a, 2002b, 2004; Greenberg & Bolger, 2001; Greenberg & Paivio, 1998) add what he terms *maladaptive primary emotions*, such as longstanding emotional pain. Lewis (1971) calls a somewhat similar concept *bypassed* emotions. Bypassed emotions, which do not resolve themselves when environmental conditions change, (a) stem from past learning, (b) linger, (c) confuse and overwhelm people, (d) reduce possibilities and (e) make relationships more problematic (Greenberg, 2002a). They begin as simple but uncomfortable primary emotions that have been inadequately processed (Lewis, 1971). They often remain outside awareness, but there is no reason to assume that their effects will disappear (Greenberg, 2002a, 2002b; Panksepp, 2001). Research indicates that unconscious bypassed emotions probably continue to affect perception (Kihlstrom et al., 2000) and thinking (Berkowitz et al., 2000) and influence behavior (Lyons, 1998) much more than they would have had they been fully processed (Greenberg, 2002a, 2002b, 2004; Lewis, 1971). They often reemerge into consciousness when triggered by similar events (Urban, 2003), leading to frequent presentations for counseling and therapy because of the resulting psychological problems and lack of behavioral control (Greenberg, 2002a, 2004; Greenberg & Paivio, 1998; Lewis, 1971). When they reemerge without context, as sometimes happens, people often experience them as traumatic (Greenberg & Paivio, 1998).

Secondary Emotions

Always maladaptive (Greenberg & Paivio, 1998), secondary emotions do not correspond to ongoing environmental stimuli (Greenberg, 2004). Instead, they are either feelings about primary emotions, with much added cognition (Greenberg, 2002a) or they originate entirely from conscious thought (Greenberg, 2004). Frequently originating in the individual's interpersonal sensitivities to dependency, autonomy, control or their loss of connectedness (Greenberg & Paivio, 1997), secondary emotions usually indicate the person's defensive use of emotional processes (Greenberg, 2002a; Greenberg and Paivio, 1998) to control or avoid even more difficult or painful primary emotions that they have bypassed (Greenberg & Bolger, 2001; Greenberg & Paivio, 1997).

Depression and anxiety, two frequently experienced secondary emotions (Paivio & Greenberg, 1998), indicate the underlying presence of painful primary emotions, though they defensively obscure them (Greenberg, 2002a). Often starting with emotional predispositions and unprocessed emotions, they evolve into enduring mood states that generate cognitions. These cognitions and the secondary emotional process reciprocally reinforce one another in a circular pattern (Paivio & Greenberg, 1998). This focus and cognitive elaboration increases the duration, frequency and severity of the symptomatic episodes (Brosschot, 2002; Davis & Nolen-Hoeksema, 2000; Lyubomirsky, Kasri, & Zehm, 2003; Lyubomirsky, Tucker, Caldwell, & Berg, 1999; Nolen-Hoeksema & Jackson, 2001; Segerstrom, Stanton, Alden, & Shortridge, 2003; Treynor, Gonzalez, & Nolen-Hoeksema, 2003; Vickers & Vogeltanz-Holm, 2003).

While schematic primary emotional processes activate emotionally relevant thoughts and physiological reactions, consciously activating these same processes decreases their potency (Wegner & Smart, 1997). In Western culture, men tend to adopt anger as a defensive strategy while women adopt hurt (Satir, Banmen, Gerber, & Gomori, 1991). Even such painful (but usually adaptive) emotions as guilt may become part of these patterns (Bybee & Quiles, 1998; Quiles & Bybee, 1997). These secondary emotions help the person avoid the experience of more intense primary versions of other emotions (Greenberg, 2002a). This leads to different, more pathological outcomes (Bybee & Quiles, 1998; Quiles & Bybee, 1997), often attracts precisely those situations it is designed to defend against (Jenkins & Oatley, 1998) and frequently leads its users to seek counseling or psychotherapy (Greenberg, 2002a, 2002b).

As noted earlier, Bybee and Quiles (1998; Quiles & Bybee, 1997) distinguish predispositional from chronic guilt. A primary schematic emotion, predispositional guilt (a) responds to one's immediate transgressions; (b) is never maladaptive, despite its intensity; (c) relates positively to health, empathy, apologies, frustration tolerance, socially acceptable behavior, achievement orientation, good grades, volunteerism, religious activity and sticking to prescribed medical regimes; and (d) relates inversely to hostility and sociopathy. A secondary emotion that functions as a stable personality trait maintained through propositional processes, chronic guilt is ongoing, unattached to circumstances and leads to maladaptive outcomes such as depression and antisocial behavior (Bybee & Quiles, 1998; Quiles & Bybee, 1997).

As Beavers (1985) wrote, "I have a rule of thumb about guilt: It is useful if it doesn't last more than five minutes and produces some change in behavior" (p. 45). If it endures, it probably indicates either defensive processes (Lewis, 1971) or an attempt to evade responsibility.

Instrumental Emotions

Instrumental emotions are those emotional behaviors employed to gain momentary social advantages through manipulation (Greenberg, 2002a, 2002b, 2004; Greenberg & Paivio, 1997, 1998). An example is a child's tantrum that produces placating behavior by his parents. Employed to elicit specific behavior or emotional reactions from others by altering one's presentation, instrumental emotions are never based on genuine appraisals of actual contextual changes, so they are always maladaptive in the longer term (Greenberg & Paivio, 1998). Because instrumental emotions often elicit precisely the behavior they were intended to produce, they are frequently reinforced (Greenberg, 2002a, 2002b, 2004). Because of this, they tend to become stable parts of the personality (Greenberg, 2002b; Greenberg & Paivio, 1997) that appear automatically in similar situations (Greenberg, 2004) and are no longer experienced by the individual as inauthentic (Greenberg, 2002a, 2002b). Over time, they may become inaccessible to consciousness, making their removal difficult (Greenberg, 2002a). They are commonly seen, especially among the emotionally disordered (Greenberg, 2002b). Along with secondary emotions, instrumental emotions have led to emotion's reputation for making people behave disruptively and irrationally (Greenberg & Paivio, 1998).

In summary, we can now define what feelings are. Feelings are schematically activated primary emotions. They are first noticed through either subtle visceral feedback or by attending to the cognitions that are aroused in association with such visceral activity by the network corresponding to that particular feeling. They can generally be trusted in therapy and in life. Most insistent emotions are usually secondary or instrumental in nature, are often defensive and filled with anxiety and disrupt lives and therapy. The therapist's job is to learn to differentiate these two, encourage the one and work past the other.

Cultural Influences on Emotion

ALTHOUGH ALL HUMAN cultures recognize the existence of emotional processes, none recognize every emotion known everywhere (Mesquita, 2001). Despite this, since many emotions have evolutionary determinants (Darwin, 1872/1965), people worldwide probably have similar affective experiences (Greenberg, 2002a, 2002b). For example, in laboratory tests, European-Americans, native Chinese and Chinese-Americans all showed similar physiological reactions to reading material rapidly and loudly, as though they were angry (Drummond & Quah, 2001). Diverse samples, some with little or no formal education or contact with Western culture, endorse largely the same descriptions of visceral and peripheral emotional reactions, although various cultures emphasize somewhat different aspects and some emotions are described more similarly across cultures than others (Breugelmans et al., 2005).

Because cultures define social roles and concepts (Russell, 2003), they shape desires, which in turn shape the concerns on which emotions are based (Mesquita & Karasawa, 2002). Similar situations do not produce the same emotions in all cultures (Elster, 1999). Cultures differ in which emotions they consider basic (Mesquita, 2001) and which events or emotions they consider legitimate and worthy of notice (Elster, 1999; Fernández-Dols & Russell, 2003; Mesquita, 2001; Mesquita & Ellsworth, 2001). In China, shame is considered a basic emotion, but in many other places it is not (Mesquita, 2001). Each culture biases appraisals and some might even employ appraisal dimensions that others do not (Mesquita & Ellsworth, 2001). Some cultures, like the Chinese, define emotions based on the parties involved, since the love of one's cousin, mother and sweetheart are unlikely to be experienced the same way (Mesquita, 2001). Others, like many African cultures, view all negative emotions as unfair, externally caused and immoral (Mesquita & Ellsworth, 2001). Natives of the U.S. are more likely to appraise a situation positively than native Japanese living in either Japan or the United States (Mesquita & Karasawa, 2002), but young U.S. children experiencing pain tend to react with anger afterwards, while Japanese children tend to react with surprise and to appear less pained (Sullivan & Lewis, 2003). Cultural differences especially impact emotions with deliberative components, like shame and humiliation, because of the way that culture influences attention and cognition (Mesquita & Ellsworth, 2001).

Cultures determine which emotions are recalled and emphasized (Scollon, Diener, Oishi, & Biswas-Diener, 2004) and the permissible behaviors allowed with each emotional experience (Elster, 1999; Fernández-Dols & Russell, 2003), reinforcing some and suppressing others (Mesquita & Ellsworth, 2001). Western beliefs about bereavement (e.g., the ubiquity of depression, inappropriateness of displaying happiness following a loved one's death and need to work through grief) are culturally determined and have little or no empirical support (Lindstrom, 2002). Cultures also specify unique gender roles concerning emotional experiencing and expression, thereby biasing memories and expectations to conform to preexisting cultural mores and expectations (Hess, Philippot, & Blairy, 2000). Although each discrete emotion has a number of distinctive expressive possibilities (Clynes, 1977), seeing emotional facial expressions causes similar autonomic responses in everyone (Ekman, 1992). Natives of various rural third world countries recognize photos of American emotional expressions, and vice versa, at far greater than chance levels (Mesquita, 2001). Duchenne smiling (which involves the muscles around the eyes) signals enjoyment worldwide, and is the only kind of smiling that does so (Ekman, 1992). However, social and cultural influences mold public expressive behavior (Cacioppo et al., 2000). When unobserved, people express their emotions similarly, but when observed by others they follow their own culture's emotional display rules (Ekman, 1992).

Collectivist cultures promote relatedness while individualistic cultures promote introspection and personal goals (Basabe et al., 2003). Interdependent cultures value emotions that engage others, whether the emotion's valence is pleasant or not (Scollon et al., 2004). Their emotions rely more on context than Americans' (Oishi, Diener, Napa Scollon, & Biswas-Diener, 2004), and concordant with their cultural mores, they report more guilt and less pride than Americans (Scollon et al., 2004). Japanese display less anger than those living in individualistic cultures like the United States (Eisenberg & Zhou, 2000) and they also consistently perceive less emotional intensity in facial photos than Americans do when they view the same photos (Ekman, 1992), though when Japanese-Americans and Japanese living in the United States rate the intensity of their emotions they report scores more similar to other American residents than to Japanese living in Japan (Mesquita & Karasawa, 2002). Expressing anger causes the heart rates of white American males to increase, but causes the diastolic blood pressure of Asian Indian males to recover slowly since expressing anger is culturally incongruent in India (Suchday & Larkin, 2004). It remains unclear whether these cultural differences in the display of anger owe more to differences in behavioral control or to differences in the attention that people to pay to their internal states (Eisenberg & Zhou, 2000).

Although rich in emotional terms, language fails to capture emotional experience adequately (Cacioppo et al., 2000). Since emotion consists of cognitive, physiological, motivational, expressive and regulatory components—each of which can vary widely depending on the stimulus involved—we might predict a potentially large number of discrete emotional states, only some of which are adequately covered by any language (Kaiser & Scherer, 1998; Shapiro, 1992). Various languages label different aspects of the emotional repertoire (Russell, 2003), with some languages not containing words for emotions considered fundamental in English and some cultures considering emotions basic for which English has no words (Mesquita, 2001). In Tahiti, the reactions after losses are much like those found in Western societies, but since they have no words for sadness or guilt they attribute their dispirited crying, lethargy and depressed mood to suffering an unexpected illness (Elster, 1999; Mesquita, 2001). Although anger and sadness are thought to be among the emotions most likely to be experienced universally (Darwin, 1872/1965; Tomkins, 1965), many African languages do not differentiate them (Mesquita, 2001). However, emotional concepts can usually be explained adequately across cultures, suggesting that emotional experiences are likely to be fairly similar worldwide (Hupka, Lenton, & Hutchison, 1999). No English equivalent exists for the German word *Schadenfreude*, which means the joy people feel when their enemies encounter difficulties, but many people in English-speaking countries admit experiencing it (Mesquita, 2001).

An interesting case to consider is *amae*, a complex Japanese emotional concept without an English equivalent (Mesquita, 2001). Such difficult-to-translate emotional concepts with multiple layers also exist in other cultures, such as the Filipino (J. Guilaran, personal communication, February 15, 2011). Even defining *amae* in English is difficult and inexact (de Rivera, 1977; Gjerde, 2001), and some have suggested that it does not exist in the West (Griffiths, 1997). The Japanese define themselves with *amae*, which they believe separates them from Westerners, even though they may or may not show more of it than others do (Gjerde, 2001). As Gnepp and Klayman (1992) once argued, people (or in this case, cultures) tend to hold two sets of false beliefs about themselves and others: they believe that others think, feel and behave like them in ways they do not; and believe that they are fundamentally different from others in ways that they are not. Each of these belief systems negatively impacts the ability to understand others and gain accurate perspectives (Gnepp & Klayman, 1992). *Amae* is a complex emotional state of contentment that is connected with dependency, often signifying being cared for in a mutually dependent relationship between two people or between a person and an organization (de Rivera, 1977; Fredrickson & Branigan, 2001; Gjerde, 2001; Griffiths, 1997; Mesquita, 2001; Mesquita & Ellsworth, 2001).

Cultures differ in whether they admire or suppress various emotions and their related behaviors (Mesquita & Ellsworth, 2001). For instance, what we call "falling in love" is considered aberrant in Japan and China and is heavily sanctioned because it diminishes social conformity, but it nonetheless occurs there at times (de Rivera, 1977; Person, 1992). So it would appear to be with *amae*, which may be alive and well in the West, though the meaning assigned to it by the individual experiencing it is likely to be different. In Japan, *amae* is encouraged and treasured (Chao, 2001) but in the West it is not. In Japan, one feels good about experiencing *amae*, while in the west, with different values, people are taught to feel ashamed of enjoying their dependency and to suppress their awareness of it. That is, the reactive feelings (Satir et al., 1991) differ between the two cultures. This leads Americans in dependency-promoting situations to experience internal conflict, suppress their positive affect and ultimately experience anxiety.

Hupka et al. (1999) found that most languages add emotional categories in a fairly similar order, corresponding primarily to their social significance. Although different languages focus on various aspects of the central concepts, Hupka et al. found that most languages add words for anger and guilt first, followed by: (a) adoration, alarm, amusement and depression; (b) alienation, arousal and agony; (c) eagerness, anxiety, aggravation and pride; (d) contentment; amazement, envy and disgust; (e) pity, enthusiasm and dismay; and (f) exasperation, relief, longing, torment and enthrallment. Some languages seem to have more emotional categories than English, although the significance of this is unclear. Hope, desire and loneliness occur early in these sequences, showing that people worldwide consider social outcomes important (Hupka et al., 1999).

Hupka et al.'s findings roughly correspond to those of Widen and Russell (2010), who found that children tend to slowly differentiate unhappy emotions from anger, their first category. First, they found, children differentiate sadness, only later differentiating fear and surprise. Disgust is differentiated from anger much later, typically not before children are at least 9 years old (Widen & Russell, 2010).

There appears to be a large but finite number of different emotions possible in humans. Evidence suggests that most of them occur cross-culturally, though the secondary emotions about them do not always correspond. As children grow or cultures develop, they tend to adopt increasingly sophisticated taxonomies for differentiating their affective experiences. Yet, each culture adopts slightly different stories as the central prototypes for their emotion categories, so emotion words always have slightly different nuances, even in related languages. If all the emotion words in every language were somehow put together, they still would not adequately describe the breadth of emotional experience humans routinely experience.

PART TWO

STRESS AND PSYCHOLOGICAL THREAT

Stress and Cortisol

Two TYPES OF natural stressors exist. One type—internal threats such as hemorrhaging—causes processing that starts viscerally, while the other—external threats like predators—leads to processing that begins cognitively (Lovallo, 2006). Research has shown that responses to stress, including psychological stress, involve two separate visceral systems operating in tandem (Dickerson & Kemeny, 2004; Gaab, Rohleder, Nater, & Ehlert, 2005): the sympathetic-adreno-medullary (SAM) axis and the hypothalamus-pituitary-adrenal (HPA) axis (Brosschot, 2002; Brosschot & Thayer, 2003; Chrousos, 2000; Dienstbier, 1989; Goldstein & McEwen, 2002; Kemeny, 2003; McEwen, 2004; McEwen & Lasley, 2003; Pauls & Stemmler, 2003; Rainville et al., 2006; Repetti et al., 2002; Rohrmann, Hennig, & Netter, 1999; Schommer, Hellhammer, & Kirschbaum, 2003).

Designed to work quickly (Kemeny, 2003), the SAM matches energy output to task-dependent needs (Rohrmann et al., 1999) in order to maintain the familiar behavior patterns of fighting, fleeing or freezing (Epel, McEwen, & Ickovics, 1998). Normally, SAM activity is responsive, rising rapidly under stressful states until needs are met before falling quickly to prior levels (Epel et al., 1998). During SAM operation, signals from the hypothalamus increase blood norepinephrine (NE) levels, which triggers the medulla of the adrenal gland to secrete epinephrine (also called adrenaline) into the blood stream (Kemeny, 2003). Besides increasing sympathetic nervous system activity, such as heart rate (Kemeny, 2003), this increase in catecholamines (epinephrine, NE and dopamine) alters the operation of the immune system during acute stress, apparently promoting health (Bosch, Berntson, Cacioppo, & Marucha, 2005). Although the epinephrine released by the SAM does not cross the blood-brain barrier, some peripheral beta-adrenergic receptors project to the solitary nucleus in the brain stem, causing signals to be sent through central noradrenergic circuits that impact, among other neural areas, the amygdala (Berntson, Sarter, & Cacioppo, 2003; McGaugh, 2000).

Unlike the SAM's emphasis on task demands, the HPA appears to respond to uncertainty (Rohrmann et al., 1999), threat (Dickerson & Kemeny, 2004) and defeat (Epel et al., 1998) primarily by reacting to cognitive appraisals (Lovallo, 2006) of uncontrollability (Epel et al., 1998). Designed to maintain high energy during possibly prolonged struggling (Seery, Blascovich, Weisbuch, & Vick, 2004), the HPA axis is triggered by the release of corticotropin-releasing hormone (CRH; also called corticotropin-releasing factor, CRF) from the hypothalamus (Kemeny, 2003). Neurons from the paraventricular nuclei of the hypothalamus secrete CRH into the hypophyseal portal system, which transports it to the anterior pituitary, stimulating the pituitary to release adrenocorticotropin-releasing hormone (ACTH) into the circulatory system; this ACTH activates the cortex of the adrenal gland to release cortisol into the bloodstream (Gillespie & Nemeroff, 2005).

Once in circulation, various carrier molecules quickly bind most cortisol, with only unbound, free cortisol impacting individual cells and organs, including the brain (Kirschbaum & Hellhammer, 2000). Necessary for regulating every cell within the body (Lovallo, 2006), cortisol enters cells more easily than other hormones and produces longer-lasting effects when it does, including changing gene expressions and membrane sensitivities

(Shirtcliff et al., 2009). It elevates blood glucose levels (Dickerson & Kemeny, 2004) and regulates other systems, such as the immune, reproductive and cardiovascular systems (Gaab et al., 2005; Kemeny, 2003). Cortisol regulates its own secretion through negative feedback supplied to the pituitary gland, hippocampus and hypothalamus (Lovallo, 2006), largely by the ACC and the insula (Shirtcliff et al, 2009). Unlike the quick changes associated with SAM activity, prolonged stress can lead to cortisol elevations lasting hours (Kirschbaum & Hellhammer, 2000), and chronic stress leads to chronically dysregulated HPA output (Goldstein & McEwen, 2002; McEwen, 2004; McEwen & Lasley, 2003).

Unlike epinephrine, cortisol readily crosses the blood-brain barrier (McGaugh, 2000), where it helps regulate brain levels of catecholamines (Dickerson & Kemeny, 2004; Repetti et al., 2002). Cortisol and NE work together to activate and regulate the hippocampus, affecting memory and emotional systems (Gaab et al., 2005), and they work together in the basolateral amygdala to help retain long-term avoidance memory (Quirk & Gehlert, 2003). While suppressing the recall of negative emotional words (Wolf, Kuhlmann, Buss, Hellhammer, & Kirschbaum, 2004), cortisol enhances memory for emotional aspects of events at the expense of their neutral aspects, even when the neutral parts are integral (Payne et al., 2006). CRH, which as a neurotransmitter responds to stress and coordinates stress responses (Gillespie & Nemeroff, 2005), works together with NE to activate and regulate the amygdala, thus focusing attention, increasing arousal and scanning for danger (Chrousos, 2000). HPA products also interact with one another; together, cortisol and CRH act together to increase startle responses, although their interaction sometimes causes limbic seizures (Rosen & Schulkin, 1998).

Also unlike epinephrine, which has a half-life of about 3 minutes, the half-life of cortisol is approximately 60-90 minutes (Dienstbier, 1989). Following stressful encounters, cortisol levels reach their peaks 10-30 minutes after the stressful stimulus ends (Kirschbaum & Hellhammer, 2000), with recovery to baseline levels usually occurring 40-60 minutes after the event ends (Kemeny, 2003). In early childhood, even minor events such as feeding, changing and washing bring about these reactive increases in cortisol levels (Herbert et al., 2006). As an individual repeatedly copes successfully with similar acute stressors, the HPA habituates, cortisol elevations following each stressor become briefer and the parasympathetic nervous system releases increasing amounts of protective hormones that counteract the effects of cortisol, making the individual both physically and psychologically healthier (Epel et al., 1998).

Diurnal Cortisol Cycles

Beginning in the first 18 months of life, the amount of unbound cortisol in circulation fluctuates throughout the day, tracking predicted demands with as much as eight times more unbound cortisol present in the system at some times than at others (Herbert et al. 2006). Normally, cortisol levels track blood glucose levels (Lovallo, 2006), rising by 50-100% during the first half hour after awakening and falling steadily throughout the day, with a slight rise occurring briefly following the midday meal (Kirschbaum & Hellhammer, 2000), until they reach their lowest levels during the first half of the sleep cycle (Lovallo, 2006). Subjective distress is associated, not with high absolute cortisol levels, but with higher relative cortisol levels than the individual is accustomed to experiencing at that time of day (Vedhara et al., 2003).

Independent of body mass index, hormone replacement therapy or initial blood glucose levels (Clow, Thorn, Evans, & Hucklebridge, 2004), the awakening cortisol response occurs despite sleep duration, sleep quality, movement during sleep, morning routines or whether the awakening was spontaneous or prompted by an alarm clock (Wüst, Federenko, Hellhammer, & Kirschbaum, 2000). The effect is larger on weekdays than weekends (Clow et al., 2004; Schlotz, Hellhammer, Schulz, & Stone, 2004), a difference that increases with chronic subjective work overload and worrying. The former raises overall weekday cortisol levels while the latter magnifies the waking increase (Schlotz et al., 2004). Being awoken earlier than expected increases the awakening response (Wüst et al., 2000), though exposure to light may modulate this effect (Clow et al., 2004). Since age decreases the awakening response and most individuals tend to rise earlier as they age, the overall effect of rising time on most adults' waking cortisol levels appears to be moderate (Clow et al., 2004).

Gender, oral contraceptive use and menstrual cycle phase all affect cortisol cycles (Kirschbaum, Kudielka, Gaab, Schommer, & Hellhammer, 1999). Although postpubertal females have larger awakening cortisol responses than prepubertal females (Goodyer, Park, Netherton, & Herbert, 2001), oral contraceptives diminish such responses (Clow et al., 2004; Kirschbaum et al., 1999) because estrogen increases blood levels of corticosteroid-binding globulin, which reduces free cortisol (Herbert et al., 2006; Kirschbaum & Hellhammer, 2000). Men's awakening responses typically reach their peaks after about 30 minutes, while women's continue to rise for an additional 15 minutes or so, attaining higher levels as men's cortisol levels start to decrease (Schlotz et al., 2004). In general, cortisol levels depend more on the levels of trait affect than on the intensity of the current emotional state, positive affect lowers cortisol levels and negative affect raises initial cortisol levels and increases morning responses (Polk, Cohen, Doyle, Skoner, & Kirschbaum, 2005). Beyond that, cortisol levels and affective states correlate differently depending on gender: among women, high state positive affect lowers initial cortisol levels, while high trait positive affect flattens and lowers cortisol profiles; but among men, low trait positive affect flattens and elevates cortisol profiles, while low trait negative affect decreases awakening responses (Polk et al., 2005). The reasons for these gender differences remain unclear.

Allostasis and Allostatic Load

Cortisol activates the cardiovascular system, suppresses fluid volume during hemorrhaging, suppresses catecholamine release following stressors, inhibits glucose uptake and stimulates fat depletion (Sapolsky, Romero, & Munck, 2000). At low levels, cortisol preferentially occupies mineralocortocoid receptors (MR), found mainly in the limbic and hypothalamic areas (Goodyer et al., 2001). High in their affinity for cortisol but relatively few in number, MR help maintain fairly stable baseline cortisol levels that assist in preparing for predictable future stressors (Sapolsky et al., 2000). At low levels, cortisol: (a) is adaptive (McEwen, 2004); (b) appears to react to novelty (Buchanon, Kern, Allen, Tranel, & Kirschbaum, 2004); (c) mutually regulates human growth hormone, glucagons, catecholamines and insulin (Sapolsky et al., 2000); (d) regulates the immune system, preventing conditions such as allergic reactions, asthma, fibromyalgia, rashes, rheumatoid arthritis and multiple sclerosis (McEwen & Lasley, 2003); and (e) enhances memory and neural plasticity (Sapolsky et al., 2000). These moderate levels of basal cortisol appear to be necessary for priming the stress and emotional systems to work properly, and emotional callousness has been linked theoretically to chronically low basal cortisol levels (Shirtcliff et al., 2009).

When stressful experiences are detected or anticipated (Smyth et al., 1998), the amygdala sends signals to increase cortisol output, overriding the diurnal cycle (Lovallo, 2006). These elevations in cortisol levels remain adaptive (McEwen, 2004). Extreme stressors, such as running a marathon, might increase blood cortisol levels by 40 mg or more (Abercrombie, Kalin, & Davidson, 2005), changes that can also occur during normal awakening responses (Kirschbaum & Hellhammer, 2000). During such times, cortisol occupies a second type of neural receptor, the glucocortocoid receptors (GR; Sapolsky et al., 2000). Found in the amygdala, cerebral cortex, hippocampal region, thalamus and hypothalamus (Goodyer et al., 2001), GR have much lower affinity for cortisol than MR and initiate different processes when activated (Sapolsky et al., 2000). At these levels, cortisol makes glucose available for energy, focuses attention on arousing stimuli, improves memory and suppresses nonessential functions such as reproductive and immune responses (Abercrombie et al., 2005; Buchanon et al., 2004; Dickerson & Kemeny, 2004; Kemeny, 2003; McEwen, 2004; Quirk & Gehlert, 2003). The optimal match of initial cortisol levels with stressor severity appears to be very important to optimal functioning (Abercrombie et al., 2005).

McEwen (Goldstein & McEwen, 2002; McEwen, 2004; McEwen & Lasley, 2003) referred to what he called *allostasis*, the ability to adapt to changing conditions; brief allostatic changes might include alterations in blood pressure and/or cortisol levels. After repeated use during chronically stressful conditions these regulatory systems lose their flexibility and plasticity, creating a condition McEwen calls *allostatic load*. In this state, they no longer adequately regulate stress responses (McEwen & Lasley, 2003) because they activate inadequately, activate too fully or remain activated too long (McEwen, 2004). This accelerates physical wear, leading to harmful long-term effects (Kemeny, 2003) including neural degradation (McEwen, 2004). Although other HPA hormones such as CRH and ACTH also affect stress responses, excessive cortisol appears to be the chief factor responsible for allostatic load (Kirschbaum & Hellhammer, 2000).

The amygdala, hippocampus, and PFC usually regulate the HPA, with the amygdala maintaining vigilance for threats and activating it, the PFC monitoring and extinguishing amygdala responses and the hippocampus supplying context and deactivating it (Davidson et al., 2002; McEwen, 2004; McEwen & Lasley, 2003). Since all three areas have large numbers of GR (Goodyer et al., 2001) and prolonged exposure to cortisol can damage or kill neurons outright (Gold & Chrousos, 2002) and increase the neural dysfunction caused by damage from other sources (Herbert et al., 2006), allostatic load has devastating effects on HPA regulation (McEwen, 2004). In chronically stressful conditions, (a) all three areas decrease in size and function; (b) the amygdala becomes overly responsive to fear stimuli; (c) the PFC quits overriding amygdala responses; (d) the diurnal cortisol rhythm is distorted; (e) the stability and responsiveness of the stress system is decreased (McEwen, 2004); and (f) memory encoding and retrieval are impaired (Goldstein & McEwen, 2002; McEwen & Lasley, 2003) for verbal (Goodyer et al., 2001), association, visual-spatial (Young, Sahakian, Robbins, & Cowen, 1999) and contextual (Davidson et al., 2002) memory. Even among healthy older adults, increased baseline cortisol levels have been associated with poorer learning of verbal lists (Suhr, Demireva, & Heffner, 2008). These memory deficits appear to be caused by complex interactions between cortisol and other neural chemicals that are not yet fully understood (Kim, Song, & Kosten, 2006).

This neural loss is accompanied by multiple adverse physical changes. Cortisol normally inhibits the production of cytokines, the immune cells that regulate other immune cells, and reduces the levels of lymphocytes, the immune cells that fight infections and promote wound healing (Kemeny, 2003). Continued chronic stress leads white cells to decrease the number of immune receptors that bind glucocortocoids (Miller, Cohen, & Ritchey, 2002), often leading to excessive inflammation (Kemeny, 2003). Since the brain and body normally use the immune system and autonomic nervous system to communicate with one another, much of what we experience as stress may actually originate in the immune system (Maier & Watkins,

2000). Even minor alterations in immune functioning can, over time, accumulate and cause serious effects throughout the entire physiological system (McEwen, 2004). Among other effects, allostatic load leads to obesity (McEwen, 2004) and muscle wasting (Sapolsky et al., 2000); accelerates cardiovascular atrophy (Goldstein & McEwen, 2002) and slows cardiovascular recovery from stress (Repetti et al., 2002); suppresses immune responses (Sapolsky et al., 2000); causes bone demineralization (McEwen, 2004); reduces reproductive functioning, making male erections more difficult to maintain and both males and females less receptive sexually (Sapolsky et al., 2000); increases insulin resistance (Chrousos, 2000) and may cause steroid psychosis (McEwen, 2004).

As insulin and cortisol levels increase in tandem, body fat and atherosclerotic plaques increase (McEwen, 2004). Health effects of allostatic load thus include obesity, hypertension, osteoporosis, autoimmune disorders, atherosclerosis, type II diabetes, upper respiratory infections and cardiovascular disease (Chrousos, 2000; Goldstein & McEwen, 2002; Kemeny, 2003; McEwen & Lasley, 2003). Allostatic load also leads to increased anxiety, depression, eating disorders, premature aging, decreased self-esteem and self-confidence and quicker declines in physical and mental functioning (McEwen, 2004; McEwen & Lasley, 2003; Sapolsky et al., 2000), with the probability of these effects increasing as recovery from HPA activation slows (Dickerson & Kemeny, 2004). Among the elderly, allostatic load is also associated with Alzheimer's dementia (Starkman et al., 2001), with the degree of HPA dysfunction correlating highly with both depressive and Alzheimer's severity (McAllister-Williams et al., 1998). Clearly, given the variety and severity of the disorders listed in this section, chronic unregulated stress is a significant worldwide public health problem.

Disrupted Diurnal Cortisol Cycles

Bilateral hippocampal damage due to anoxia, surgery, stroke or encephalitis abolishes the awakening cortisol response (Buchanon et al., 2004). Besides having chronically elevated cortisol levels, such impaired individuals have attenuated awakening responses and diminished cortisol reactivity following exposure to stressors (McAllister-Williams, Ferrier, & Young, 1998), their bodies apparently attempting to compensate for sustained high cortisol levels by suppressing their awakening responses, though this cannot prevent their exposure to excessive overall cortisol levels (Chrousos, 2000). After a number of years, the cortisol levels in such individuals return to near-baseline levels (Buchanon et al., 2004).

Those with Cushing's syndrome also display this profile (McEwen, 2004; Sonino & Fava, 2001). A disorder leading to the overproduction of cortisol, Cushing's syndrome occurs in two subtypes, one resulting from too much pituitary secretion of ACTH, the other independent of ACTH and resulting from adrenal pathology (Starkman, Giordani, Berent, Schork, & Schteingart, 2001). Psychological stress may trigger Cushing's syndrome (Sonino & Fava, 2001), which like depression is associated with hyperactivity of the amygdala, atrophy of the hippocampus, bone demineralization and obesity (McEwen, 2004). Among Cushing's syndrome patients, impaired learning and memory (Young, 2004) correlate highly with cortisol levels (McAllister-Williams et al., 1998). Verbal IQ, Performance IQ, and Memory Quotient are all affected, with scores on the Block Design, Object Assembly, Digit-Symbol Learning, and Associate Learning subtests each inversely correlated with cortisol levels (Starkman et al., 2001).

Those with melancholic depression (Clow et al., 2004; Goodyer et al., 2001), Post-Traumatic Stress Disorder (Wessa, Rohleder, Kirschbaum, & Flor, 2006), binge eating disorder (Gluck, Geliebter, Hung, & Yahav, 2004) and histories of maltreatment (Goodyer et al., 2001) show this same pattern of disrupted diurnal cycles, as do those with cancer (Clow et al., 2004). Smokers (Reuter, 2002), heavy drinkers (Thayer, Hall, Sollers, &

Fischer, 2006) and drug experimenters (Lovallo, 2006) also display this pattern of flattened and elevated cortisol cycles. Genetics, worrying, social stress and the perceived lack of support play roles in this profile (Wüst et al., 2000) as does failure to disengage from unattainable goals (Wrosch, Miller, Scheier, & Brun de Pontet, 2007). The severity of negative affect and the number of recent negative events also contribute, even among non-depressed patients, particularly those with family histories of depression (Peeters, Nicholson, & Berkhof, 2003). On the other hand, in one study former depressed patients who had recovered and were no longer taking medication had double the increase in awakening cortisol as controls did (Bhagwagar, Hafizi, & Cowen, 2003).

Since alcohol and drug usage causes acute HPA activation, long-term substance abuse dysregulates both basal levels of cortisol and acute stress responses (Lovallo, 2006). Those who drink over 20 mg of alcohol per day have higher basal cortisol levels, higher blood pressure and lower heart rate variability than those who do not, suggesting impaired HPA inhibition (Thayer et al., 2006). Those who routinely take heroin or ecstasy also show disrupted cortisol cycles, with their degree of cyclical impairment directly related to the severity of their addictions (Lovallo, 2006). Lovallo, in his review, notes that (a) the degree of HPA hyporesponsiveness among chronic smokers trying to quit relates directly to their relapse potential; and (b) both alcohol intake and alcohol withdrawal can affect the diurnal cycle for up to 4 weeks, even among abstinent alcoholics. Withdrawal, like stress, triggers CRH release, leading to stress responses and triggering cravings (Lovallo, 2006), which are mediated by the basolateral amygdala (Quirk & Gehlert, 2003). Among alcoholics who drink the most, heart rate variability and cortisol levels are no longer correlated negatively, suggesting that their drinking may have deactivated their amygdalae, possibly by impacting the serotonin (5-HT, short for 5-hydroxytryptamine) system (Thayer et al., 2006).

Children from stable families that include maternal warmth and involvement, marital satisfaction and the calm discussion of differences awaken with low cortisol levels that decline rapidly (Pendry & Adam, 2007). In contrast, those children whose maternal care is disrupted in early childhood and who experience additional stressors develop dysfunctional stress responses that may last throughout their lives (Herbert et al., 2006). Children from alcoholic families show decreased heart rate variability and deficits in their inhibitory HPA regulation, conditions also seen among those with schizophrenia, depression, anxiety disorders, epilepsy and chronic stress (Thayer et al., 2006). Even among those who have not started drinking, adolescent children of such parents display attenuated HPA responses to threat (Lovallo, 2006). Since these deficits occur most frequently in those with antisocial traits, who also are at the highest risk for future drug and alcohol experimentation (Goodyer et al., 2001), this trait may be part of the genetic loading for alcoholism and drug dependency (Lovallo, 2006).

A basic understanding of the stress system is important. Much can go wrong with it, and as we shall come to appreciate in the course of this volume, the emotional system makes use of the stress system. When emotions are poorly regulated, any or all of the physiological dysfunctions noted earlier may result.

Threat, Defeat and Self-Esteem

As Dienstbier (1989) noted, challenge differs from stress, which is a threat of loss or harm characterized by minimal predictability, feedback and control. Whether events are considered challenging or threatening (including psychologically threatening) is determined through overlapping sets of appraisals (Folkman & Lazarus, 1980; Folkman, Lazarus, Gruen, & DeLongis, 1986), often made unconsciously, that vary with the person and situation (Blascovich, Mendes, Tomaka, Salomon, & Seery, 2003) and depend on how current energy capacity compares to anticipated needs (Tomaka et al., 1999; Mendes, Blascovich, Hunter, Lickel, & Jost, 2007). Mood states clearly affect this process (Martin, 2000; Morris, 2000). Not having the energy for some added demand will immediately be perceived as threatening, an appraisal often arrived at through unconscious associative processing.

While both challenge and threat appraisals activate the SAM, threat appraisals also activate the HPA (Dienstbier, 1989). In states of challenge, the increased epinephrine released by the SAM lowers peripheral resistance (Kemeny, 2003), so challenge is associated with increased arousal and cardiac output (Tomaka, Blascovich, Kelsey, & Leitten, 1993). During threatening conditions, the cortisol released by HPA activation interacts with the epinephrine (Dienstbier, 1989; Kemeny, 2003) to cause contraction rather than expansion of those same blood vessels (Blascovich et al.,

2003). This increases peripheral resistance and raises systolic blood pressure during conditions of threat or defeat (Kemeny, 2003; Tomaka et al., 1993). Subjectively, challenge is associated with positive affect and approach motivation, while threat and defeat are associated with negative affect and with avoidance or withdrawal (Mendes et al., 2007). With repeated exposure, people appraise events as less threatening and more challenging, the HPA habituates (Schommer et al., 2003) and blood pressure no longer reacts.

Self-Esteem and Psychological Threat

Although often researched, *self-esteem* confuses even those who have studied it most closely (Leary, 2003a). Optimal self-esteem can be defined as a relatively stable set of explicit and implicit positive feelings about one's self-worth that persist despite specific achievements or failures (Kernis, 2003), but only situations involving others can affect self-esteem (Leary, 2003b). Having positive qualities raises self-esteem only when others are believed to value them (Leary, 2003a). Responding to potential disapproval (Leary, 2003b) and rejection (Leary, 2003a), it provides feedback about how one stands with others (Leary, 2003b). Rejection is so stressful that people willingly act against their natural tendencies while trying to avoid it (Leary, 2003b). Merely waiting to learn if one has been rejected lowers the self-esteem of those who already have low self-esteem (Leary, 2003a).

Compared to those with stable self-esteem, people with unstable self-esteem: (a) strive for mastery less, (b) allow negative events to affect them more, (c) feel depressed by life's daily hassles more often, (d) focus more on situational threats to their self-esteem, (e) have more poorly developed self-concepts, (f) report fewer self-determined goals, and (g) overgeneralize their failures (Kernis, 2003). They engage less in assigned tasks and react more defensively while performing them, apparently because their self-doubt makes potential failure more meaningful to them (Seery et al.,

2004). Leary (2003b) believed that inconsistent feedback about whether an individual will be accepted or rejected may cause that person to develop unstable self-esteem. Compared to those with stable high self-esteem, those with unstable self-esteem appraise failure feedback as threatening and success feedback as challenging (Seery et al., 2004).

Physiological measures indicate that performing any task alone, whether rehearsed or novel, results in neither threat nor challenge appraisals (Blascovich, Mendes, Hunter, & Salomon, 1999). Mendes, Blascovich, Major, & Seery (2001) found that when individuals of differing ability levels are paired on a task, the more able of the two generally treats the task as a challenge, while the less able treats it as a threat. Yet, when differences in beliefs between task partners are also taken into account, people appraise situations as threatening when their partners either (a) perform much better, but have vastly different beliefs, or (b) perform incompetently, but have identical beliefs (Mendes et al., 2001). Compared to performing alone, people appraise performing well-learned tasks before an audience as a challenge and are more likely to perform perfectly, but they appraise performing unlearned tasks before an audience as a threat and are more likely to perform poorly (Blascovich et al., 1999). Disclosing emotionally relevant material to strangers of the same gender is challenging, while suppressing it with same-gendered strangers or revealing it to opposite-gendered strangers is threatening (Mendes, Reis, Seery, & Blascovich, 2003).

Violating expectations adds uncertainty and elicits threat responses (Mendes et al., 2007). Nonassertive women treat public speaking as threatening, while assertive women find it challenging (Tomaka et al., 1999). Interestingly, interacting with people having large facial birthmarks increases threat responses and decreases subsequent task performance (Blascovich, Mendes, Hunter, Lickel, & Kowai-Bell, 2001). Among Americans of European descent, interacting with either African-American or disadvantaged individuals leads to separate threat responses that add to one another (Mendes, Blascovich, Lickel, & Hunter, 2002) and poorer task performance, though prior exposure to members of these groups dissipates these effects (Blascovich et al., 2001). Interacting with people who violate familiar stereotypes (e.g., wealthy Hispanics, or Asian-Americans with flawless southern accents) elicits threat responses, decreases positive affect, increases avoidance behavior and lowers their interaction partners' subsequent task performance (Mendes et al., 2007).

Kemeny (2003) theorized that specific emotional responses are probably associated with different physiological stress responses. In particular, she hypothesized that appraising a situation as socially threatening leads to shame and humiliation, decreases the subjective sense of self-worth and increases HPA activity. If the appraisals of social threat were changed, cortisol levels should decrease to normal daily levels (Kemeny, 2003; Dickerson, Gruenewald, & Kemeny, 2004; Gruenewald, Kemeny, Aziz, & Fahey, 2004; Kemeny, Gruenewald, & Dickerson, 2004).

Now that the concepts of challenge and threat have been introduced, another manner of determining the differences between negative emotions and negative moods can be attempted. It seems clear that moods reflect challenges and emotions reflect threats. Nobody is threatened by having a sad mood, but the sadness caused by actual loss represents the recognition of a genuine threat to what went before. People function despite the challenge posed by timid moods but have difficulty doing so in the face of the threat that intense fear brings to awareness. There is as yet no research in this area, but it may prove a handy heuristic for keeping the distinctions between them clear as we continue through the rest of this discussion.

PART THREE

THE PHYSIOLOGY OF EMOTION

Neural Control Systems

As DISCUSSED EARLIER, the study of emotions encompasses many other areas of inquiry (Buck, 1999; Cacioppo & Gardner, 1999; Kappas, 2002). This will be the first of several chapters on the physiology of emotion. Even within the biological arena, different levels exist that do not reduce to one another but influence one another in multiple ways (Kappas, 2002). This chapter will focus briefly on three separate systems of neural control: neurotransmitter systems, electrical control through brainwaves and emotional network circuitry.

Neurotransmitters

Little will be said about the rapidly evolving research in this area, other than to note that in this case—as in many others—simple explanations are probably incorrect. Particular neurotransmitters are used in various places throughout the brain and do not always produce similar results in different areas. For instance, when found in the amygdala and septo-hippocampal system, 5-HT increases anxiety, but when found in the periaqueductal gray region of the midbrain, it diminishes anxiety (Graeff, 2002). Similar symptoms also do not always correspond to the same neurotransmitter systems. For instance, depression caused by failure responds to chemical manipulations of the 5-HT system, but depression caused by a lack of rewards responds to medication targeting NE circuitry (Buck, 1999).

Both NE and dopamine have been associated with reward (Buck,

1999), and although avoidance and escape are both conditioned by punishment and are communicated using the same neurotransmitter, they appear to be mediated in different neural structures (Graeff, 2002). Oxytocin increases attachment behavior (Buck, 1999; Schulkin et al., 2003), and both endorphins (Buck, 1999) and nicotine (Panksepp, 2003b) have been shown to reduce the separation distress of animals. Cholecystokinin injections induce anxiety attacks, vasopressin promotes male aggression and gonadotropin-releasing hormone increases sexual behavior (Buck, 1999). Opiate agonists such as naloxone and naltrexone diminish the emotional response to music (Panksepp & Bernatzky, 2002). This field is complex, confusing and continually growing.

Electrical Brainwaves

Different parts of the brain display differing brainwave patterns, as measured via electroencephalogram (EEG; Knyazev, Schutter, & van Honk, 2006). According to Knyazev et al. (2006), theta waves are associated with the hippocampus and memory. Alpha waves, associated with the thalamus (Schreckenberger et al., 2004), indicate observation, awareness and attentiveness (Knyazev et al., 2006; Orekhova, Stroganova, & Posikera, 2001). Delta waves are associated with reward and the Behavior Activating System (BAS, to be discussed in a later chapter); and beta waves signify intense cortical processing and are seen during fearful states (Knyazev et al., 2006). More recently evolved neural structures produce brainwave signals that largely, but do not completely, control and inhibit the automatic functioning of older ones (Knyazev et al., 2006; Knyazev & Slobodskaya, 2003; Orekhova et al., 2001). By doing so, the neocortex gains control of other areas (Schutter & van Honk, 2005), functioning becomes less instinctive and more voluntary (Knyazev & Slobodskaya, 2003), the information exchange between cortical and subcortical areas is enhanced (Schutter & van Honk, 2005) and emotional processing falls increasingly under higher cortical control (Izard et al., 2002). This control and exchange is enhanced by the presence of cortisol (Schutter & van Honk, 2005).

Alpha loses synchrony as excitement increases but gains it as attentiveness does (Orekhova et al., 2001). Among those with low anxiety, alpha and delta are positively correlated (Knyazev et al., 2006), meaning that attentiveness and reward go together. In those with extreme anxiety, alpha and delta rhythms become negatively correlated and beta and delta instead become synchronized (Knyazev et al., 2006). In such states, the BAS and the Behavior Inhibition System (BIS, to be discussed in a later chapter) are both active and cortisol levels increase (Knyazev et al., 2006). These people want to pursue a goal but fear doing so, and they experience heightened stress as a result.

Emotion Circuits

Sometimes survival depends on making decisions accurately, and other times it depends on making them quickly (Brosschot, 2002; Greenberg & Bolger, 2001). Because of this, emotional processing uses two pathways: a slower, more accurate one using the temporal lobes and insula, and a faster one that bypasses the cortex (Critchley, 2003; LeDoux, 1996, 2000). The subcortical path processes environmental cues (Anderson & Phelps, 2002) in as little as 150 ms (Hermans, De Houwer, & Eelen, 2001). Used during emergencies, it works completely outside awareness (Critchley, 2003; LeDoux, 2000), altering people's associations (Niedenthal & Halberstadt, 2000) and behavior, often while leaving conscious mood states untouched (Berridge & Winkielman, 2003; Winkielman & Berridge, 2004). Much emotional processing and many events remain inaccessible to consciousness (LeDoux, 2000).

By contrast, the cortical path makes use of both direct signals from the amygdala and the mixed visceral/amygdalar signal originating in the cholinergic basal nuclei (Quirk & Gehlert, 2003). This slower processing allows for reflection before acting (Critchley, 2003), something lower animals cannot do (Anderson & Phelps, 2002), and is required for the conscious experience of emotion (Berridge and Winkielman, 2003; Panksepp, 2001, 2003a). In contrast to subcortical areas, right hemispheric cortical areas process emotional input and expression (including changing skin conductance) while areas in the left hemisphere regulate its intensity and modulate its expression (Hagemann et al., 2003). After repeatedly experiencing stimuli that have proven to be benign, the right hemispheric areas responsible for emotional processing habituate, while the left hemispheric areas that recognize and categorize incoming stimuli become more sensitive (Feinstein, Goldin, Stein, Brown, & Paulus, 2002).

Regional blood flow studies have repeatedly shown that different tasks activate different parts of the brain (Drevets & Raichle, 1998). Since shifts in neural blood flow are greatest when performance anxiety is minimized and attention is most focused, extraneous factors mediating anxiety and attention can alter the observed results and make them misleading (Simpson et al, 2000). Nonetheless, it seems clear that blood flow increases to the amygdala, rostral and ventral ACC and posteromedial orbitofrontal cortex (OFC) during emotional states and decreases during intensive cognitive tasks (Drevets & Raichle, 1998). The hypothalamus, nucleus accumbens (part of the basal forebrain) and periaqueductal gray all signal other parts of the brain, both neurally and chemically, to organize them emotionally (Damasio, 2001). Emotion deactivates the dorsolateral PFC and dorsal ACC, areas that are active during working memory and discrimination tasks, respectively (Drevets & Raichle, 1998).

Although the circuitry and brain structures used for various emotions probably overlap a great deal (Schulkin et al., 2003), discrete emotions have separate processing streams that allow them to be coupled with their distinct visceral, behavioral and motor responses (Critchley, 2003; Panksepp, 2001, 2003a). The insula, second somatosensory region and ACC all vary in how their various parts activate, depending upon what emotion is aroused (Damasio, 2001). For instance, the insula is associated with negative moods (Critchley, 2003) and disgust (Adolphs et al., 2003; Taylor, Liberzon, & Koeppe, 2000), and along with the cingulate is associated with lust (Canli & Amin, 2002; Critchley, 2003). Sadness is associated with the anterior insula, happiness with the subgenual cingulate, and attention to subjective mood with the rostral anterior cingulate (Canli & Amin, 2002; Critchley, 2003). Finally, emotion circuits may be used to maintain homeostasis in other body systems, such as fluid levels (Schulkin et al., 2003) and thermal regulation (Panksepp & Bernatzky, 2002). For a review of the different activations and deactivations associated with the various discrete emotions, see Berthoz et al., (2002).

Just as there are many ways of studying emotions, there are many ways of viewing the brain's activity. Each of the control systems mentioned in this chapter will become important as we consider various aspects of the emotional system in further chapters.

The Viscera and Subcortical Neural Structures

STARTING FROM THE least evolved structures, emotions involve: (a) the viscera, (b) the brain stem, (c) the hypothalamic-pituitary system, (d) the basal ganglia, (e) the limbic system, and (f) the cerebral cortices (Buck, 1999; Schulkin et al., 2003). Lesions to any of these neural structures can cause poorer decision-making and decrease social and emotional intelligence (Bar-On, Tranel, Denburg, & Bechara, 2003). This chapter will briefly address each of these except the cortices, which will be addressed in later chapters. Particular attention will be given to the amygdala, which is a significant structure for much emotional processing.

The Viscera

James (1884) believed that emotion occurs when people become conscious of the visceral and motor responses that have already been activated by some stimulus. According to James' conception, emotional responses are essentially reflexes (Critchley, 2003) and each emotion has a distinct physiological pattern of activation (Cacioppo et al., 2000). Research data have not supported any of this (Berntson, Sarter, & Cacioppo, 2003). Evidence shows that visceral feelings are neither necessary nor sufficient for emotional processes to take place (Cacioppo et al., 2000) and suggests that emotional processing can originate in either the brain or the viscera, with each influencing and regulating the other (Berntson, Cacioppo et al., 2003; Cacioppo et al., 2000). Emotional experience clearly includes visceral and motor feedback (Berntson, Sarter et al., 2003), but different emotional states cannot be reliably distinguished by their visceral responses (Cacioppo et al., 2000).

The endocrine system provides one mechanism for visceral emotional signals to reach the brain and be incorporated (Bechara, 2004). One older model of emotional processing suggests that all emotions are built from the same undifferentiated endocrine arousal, which increases as emotional intensity does, and that emotions result from attributions made following this arousal (Philippot et al., 2002). This theory appears unlikely to be true for two reasons: (a) different emotions yield divergent patterns of activation within the autonomic nervous system (Herrald & Tomaka, 2002; Rainville et al., 2006; Schorr, 2001); and (b) studies of emotional priming and subliminal cuing have shown that people's behavior may be altered without increasing their arousal, awareness of the stimulus or consciousness of changes in their subjective affective state (Berridge & Winkielman, 2003; Hermans, De Houwer, & Eelen, 2001).

Peripheral epinephrine receptors have been found that send signals to the amygdala and alter emotional processing (Berntson, Sarter et al., 2003), so endocrine feedback may prime central systems to process emotion in various ways (Berntson, Cacioppo et al., 2003). Feedback from the viscera also takes place via the vagus nerve, which may be an important conveyor of such information (Bechara, 2004). Good vagal tone is an index of relaxation and parasympathetic activity in adults (Epel et al., 1998), predicts the future effectiveness of emotional regulation efforts and mediates the effects of marital conflict on physical health (Repetti et al., 2002).

Brain Stem

Primary emotional appraisals probably take place in the solitary and parabrachial nuclei of the brain stem (Schulkin et al., 2003); anencephalic neonates smile and react to tastes and tactile stimuli if these structures and the locus coeruleus are intact (Erickson & Schulkin, 2003). The ascending reticular system is also involved in emotion (Buck, 1999), including the dorsal raphe nucleus, which projects to both the amygdala and the dorsal periaqueductal gray via 5-HT transmission (Graeff, 2002). The periaqueductal gray, where all emotional systems converge to form a coherent self-representation, is adjacent to the inferior colliculus, which processes audition, mediates affective processing and may be where an infant's mother's voice leaves its first imprint (Panksepp & Bernatzky, 2002). Even in these evolutionarily ancient parts of the brain, emotion is being processed.

Hypothalamus

The hypothalamus directly encodes emotional experience and indirectly (largely via the brainstem and pituitary) activates the body through both neural and chemical channels (Buck, 1999). Under hypothalamic orders, the pituitary also guides the release of many of the neuropeptides found in the subcortical areas of the brain that control the visceral experience of emotion (Panksepp, 2003a).

Limbic System

At the limbic level, the brain organizes socializing emotions and behavior: vocalization; reward and depression; punishment and anxiety; fear, anger, and disgust; submission, lust, attachment, and play; and social contact (as opposed to naked self interest; Buck, 1999). All of this involves the use of three main neurotransmitters: dopamine (DA), NE, and 5-HT (Buck, 1999).

Basal Ganglia

The basal ganglia have been implicated in emotion (Erickson & Schulkin, 2003), including: (a) the corpus striatum (caudate nucleus, putamen and globus pallidus); (b) the nucleus accumbens; and (c) the olfactory tubercle (Buck, 1999). Buck believes this part of the brain to be most intimately involved in what he terms reptilian sex and aggression.

The Basal Forebrain

In the basal forebrain and all other subcortical areas, the left side of the brain processes emotional input and the right regulates emotional expression (Hagemann et al., 2003). Sitting near the amygdala and basal ganglia, the basal forebrain is involved in numerous functions, including learning, reward and punishment, and reproduction, largely as information conduits (Alheid, 2003). Signals from the viscera pass through the nucleus tractus solitarius in the brainstem and the basal forebrain cholinergic system on their way to the amygdala, basal forebrain and cortex (Berntson, Sarter et al., 2003). Acetylcholine in the basal forebrain enhances processing by boosting the relative strength of incoming sensory signals (Berntson, Cacioppo et al., 2003), and the cholinergic system combines signals from the viscera and amygdala into a single stream that regulates and modulates further cortical processing (Berntson, Sarter et al., 2003). The basal forebrain also contains beta-adrenergic receptors, which add salience to emotional memories (van Stegeren et al., 1998), enhance attention to fearful stimuli (Berntson, Cacioppo et al., 2003) and help control heart rate (van Stegeren, Everaerd, Cahill, McGaugh, & Gooren, 1998). Finally, part of this structure, little understood but considered part of the extended amygdala, appears to play a role in emotional arousal (Alheid, 2003).

The Amygdala

Many people associate emotion with one physiological structure, the amygdala, which is the most studied structure in the biopsychology of emotion (Zald, 2003). However, research evidence shows that emotion does not require its activity (Anderson & Phelps, 2002). As discussed earlier, the amygdala receives information from both the thalamus and the PFC (Critchley, 2003). A component of both the basal ganglia and limbic systems (Öhman, 2002), the activated amygdala appears to encode the emotional salience of sensory stimuli and deliver that assessment to other structures involved in the particular discrete emotional network that has been activated, such as the hippocampus, periaqueductal gray, ACC, striatum, insula and OFC (Bar-On et al., 2003; Drevets, 2003; Fanselow & Gale, 2003). Working outside conscious awareness, it increases startle responses; modulates hormonal, autonomic, motor and endocrine functioning (Zald, 2003); and directs attention (Davidson et al., 2002). Physical and emotional pain activates it, whether the pain originates in that person or in another (Decety & Jackson, 2006).

Although it is also active in top-down emotional processing beginning with cortical activity, its role is particularly vital in the activation of bottom-up emotional processing that starts in the viscera and subcortical areas (Ochsner et al., 2009). Together with the periaqueductal gray and parabrachial nucleus, it forms a conduit for information from the spinal column to the thalamus (Seeley, 2010), and its interconnections with the hypothalamus, which help it monitor peripheral states, also allow it to trigger and suppress cortisol release (Shirtcliff et al., 2009).

While the hippocampus encodes contextual memory (Davidson et al., 2002), activation of the amygdala, which occurs in laboratory studies even when experimental participants are directed to attend elsewhere, is associated with aversive conditioning, enhanced emotional memory and attention modulation (Zald, 2003). In the amygdala, emotional appraisals, peripheral signals, epinephrine and cortisol combine their influences to help consolidate lifelong memories (McGaugh, 2000; Quirk & Gehlert, 2003; Zald, 2003), especially if they involve aversive stimuli (Fanselow & Gale, 2003) or avoidance conditioning (Quirk & Gehlert, 2003). In the amygdala, norepinephrine focuses attention (Davidson et al., 2002) while epinephrine consolidates memories (McGaugh, 2000; van Stegeren et al., 1998; van Stegeren, Everaerd, & Gooren, 2002) and cortisol strengthens them (McGaugh, 2000; Quirk & Gehlert, 2003). During extreme stress, emotional memories can become much stronger than contextual ones, leading to the later dissociations that are often seen in stress-related psychiatric disorders (Shean, 2003).

During normal development, the amygdala begins at birth to weigh the motivational salience of input from the various senses, starting with smell and following a patterned sequence (Fernandez et al., 2004; Schore, 2001a; Zald, 2003). It compares ongoing, socially-relevant stimuli to what has been encountered in previous situations (Adolphs, 2002a, 2002b). The amygdala responds more to aversive stimuli than to positive ones (Schaefer et al., 2002; Zald, 2003), regardless of whether they have been consciously perceived or not (Canli & Amin, 2002). It preferentially decodes others' facial expressions, particularly those implying threat, such as scared or angry faces (Adolphs & Tranel, 2003; Öhman, 2002), probably relying largely on the configuration of eyebrows and mouths (Lundqvist, Esteves, & Öhman, 2004), especially when the presentations are overt (Phillips et al., 2004). However, any arousing stimulus with personal meaning can activate it (Taylor et al., 2000), especially if the stimulus motivates the individual or requires more perceptual processing than usual (Zald, 2003). For example, participants' amygdalae habituate to unconsciously presented pictures of members of their own racial group more quickly than they do if the pictures are of members of other groups (Canli & Amin, 2002). Such responses may remain unconscious (Zald, 2003).

Fear extinction depends on contextual learning, and when the context changes the fear reemerges (Herry et al., 2008). In mice, two sets of cells are interspersed within the basal amygdala, one set connecting to the medial PFC and the other to the hippocampus. Together, these neurons determine whether conditioned fear reactions will reappear or not after they have been extinguished (Herry et al., 2008).

The amygdala does not mediate anxious temperament (Kalin, Shelton, Davidson, & Kelley, 2001; Schulkin et al., 2003), which is instead controlled by the OFC (Davidson & Slagter, 2000). However, those predisposed to negative affect have more active amygdalae (Schaefer et al., 2002). Among others, the amygdala habituates quickly after it performs its initial evaluation (Zald, 2003). Intentionally sustaining emotional states causes longer, more intense amygdalar activity than usual (Schaefer et al., 2002), but conscious decisions to activate emotions of various types do not require amygdalar activation at all, and in such cases it rarely occurs (Zald, 2003). Suppressing emotion reduces amygdalar activity (Zald, 2003), and autistic children show significantly less amygdalar activation when presented with novel or threatening stimuli than controls do (Öhman, 2002).

Stimuli without motivational significance deactivate the amygdala (Zald, 2003). So complexly structured that it has been called a brain inside the brain (Buck, 1999), novel visual stimuli activate it, with different parts of it having different functions: the posterior parts preferentially respond to complex pictures, the anterior parts respond to specific aversive stimuli (Taylor et al., 2000), and the basolateral parts regulate drug craving (Quirk & Gehlert, 2003). Whether positive affect is also processed by the amygdala is much less clear, since the positive stimuli presented in experiments appear to be weaker than the negative stimuli, and negative stimuli are generally experienced as more salient (Zald, 2003). Zald cites Wager et al.'s unpublished manuscript, which reports 38 distinct amygdala foci responding to negative valenced stimuli and only five responding to positively valenced stimuli. Canli and Amin (2002) found in their study that greater amygdala reactivity to positive pictures was related to extraversion, while greater activation to negative pictures was related to neuroticism.

Though generally called the amygdala, as if it were singular, the topic of discussion is actually two small organs, with one located in each temporal lobe (Zald, 2003). In primates, the amygdalae do not have many connections between them (Irwin et al., 2004). The evidence for lateralization of amygdalar functioning is conflicting, partly because of methodological factors associated with functional Magnetic Resonance Imaging (fMRI). Since fMRI technology requires longer activations for more accurate measurements, most studies have asked participants to remember, amplify or sustain their targeted feelings, thus skewing their results (Zald, 2003). Although most studies have shown equal or greater activation of the left amygdala when experimental participants are presented with emotional material (Zald, 2003), some research suggests that the right amygdala—the larger of the two structures—is more involved with subliminally introduced stimuli, even those with neutral valences (Zald, 2003) and reacts more strongly when previously conditioned stimuli are presented outside awareness (Morris, Öhman, & Dolan, 1998; Öhman, 2002).

The right amygdala, which also appears to deactivate more quickly after a stimulus has been presented and habituate more rapidly to novel stimuli, is more associated with altered skin conductance (Zald, 2003). It is far less activated than the left amygdala during top-down emotional processing that originates in the cortex (Ochsner et al., 2009). According to Zald (2003), right amygdalar lesions result in greater overall impairment of memory and judgment than lesions of the left amygdala, which responds more to socially constructed meanings, linguistic material, aversive odors and cognitively mediated anticipatory anxiety—though gender, hand preference, psychopathology, and other individual difference variables may all play roles in these patterns.

The amygdalae are difficult to study using fMRI technology because of their proximity to the sphenoid sinus and because of the lack of uniform density in the surrounding tissue, which makes signal absorption and loss difficult to interpret (Zald, 2003). As Zald notes, because the surrounding structures appear to have related functions, most lesions in the area are generally treated as lesions of the amygdala itself. Animal studies also have not been very educational because the size of the amygdala in a species varies with its normal group size, implying that it evolved for social information processing (Öhman, 2002). Rat amygdalae differ from those of primates, but few studies of the primate amygdala exist (Kalin et al., 2001). In primates, bilateral amygdalar lesions lead to lowered social rank, ostracism and eventually death (Anderson & Phelps, 2000). Rhesus monkeys given amygdalar lesions retrieve food more quickly in the presence of a snake than those without lesions but more slowly than control monkeys without snakes present (Kalin et al., 2001). Kalin et al. also found that monkeys with lesions display less submissive behavior when a strange male is present, but they show similar dispositional defensive reactions as control monkeys to human presence.

Humans with damage to only one amygdala perform about as well in most emotion experiments as those without amygdalar damage (Adolphs & Tranel, 2004), but bilateral amygdalar damage can be devastating. Compared to normal controls and those with other types of brain injuries, those with unilateral or bilateral amygdalar damage have more difficulty recognizing displays of social emotion from the presentation of either entire faces or eye regions (Adolphs, Baron-Cohen, & Tranel, 2002), and those with bilateral amygdalar damage perceive situations and stimuli more positively than others do (Adolphs & Tranel, 1999). Those with bilateral amygdalar damage decode the emotion in situations as well as normal controls, but have trouble decoding the emotional cues contained in others' facial expressions (Adolphs & Tranel, 2003). These findings further suggest that the amygdala may have evolved to coordinate social emotion (Adolphs et al., 2002). Bilateral lesions also lead to attenuated startle responses and galvanic skin responses, and they end the ability of scenes associated with previous drug use to initiate drug cravings (Zald, 2003).

Anderson and Phelps (2000) studied a patient with bilateral damage, finding that he behaved emotionally, even fearfully, but he could not interpret the fearful expressions he witnessed. This patient had deficits interpreting facial expressions of fear, disgust, sadness and happiness (but not surprise or anger), but no deficits in emotional expression or in attaching labels to emotions correctly. Emotional comprehension and production, Anderson and Phelps (2000) found, are separate modular processes. Later, Anderson and Phelps (2002) compared a patient with bilateral amygdala damage to patients who had undergone either a left or right temporal lobectomy and to controls; the four groups were indistinguishable in measures of self-reported emotional experiences, both mild and intense, including fear and anxiety. The bilateral patient's daily experiences of emotion, tracked over a month, were similar to the others' but of greater magnitude, although they were remembered less intensely than the others' were (Anderson & Phelps, 2002).

A patient with similar lesions, studied by Adolphs et al. (2003), interpreted all pictures of emotions as either "happy" or "sad," interpreting surprised or scared pictures as happy and disgusted or angry pictures as sad. He organized emotional pictures according to valence, but used an idiosyncratic process to do so. Despite this, he correctly identified emotions other than disgust when they were acted out or described for him and generated correct labels for the emotions contained in stories. His problems identifying disgust were probably due to his extensively damaged insula (Adolphs et al., 2003). From this study, Adolphs et al. learned that the emotional recognition of visual stimuli is actually several separate, dissociable processes: (a) perceiving both static and dynamic emotional cues, (b) categorizing emotions, and (c) recognizing specific emotions.

When interviewed by clinical psychologists blind to her condition, another such patient with deficits in processing and expressing negative emotions (particularly fear and anger) was assessed as a heroic and resilient individual who had successfully overcome a number of potentially traumatic stumbling blocks before moving on with her life (Tranel, Gullickson, Koch, & Adolphs, 2006). However, Tranel et al. noted, the psychologists thought she seemed overly trusting of others.

In yet another study, a patient with complete bilateral amygdala lesions was nonetheless able to detect fearful faces presented to her as well as those without such damage (Tsuchiya, Moradi, Felsen, Yamazaki, & Adolphs, 2009). Though she was significantly more likely than others to rate ambiguous faces as neutral rather than fearful, she implicitly recognized fearful faces as well as they did. Also like normal controls, fearful faces broke into her consciousness far faster than neutral faces did, and as quickly as they did in the controls. However, she showed significantly more problems determining whether a face was sad or fearful than controls did. These findings suggest that rapid fear detection outside consciousness does not require the amygdala, which instead appears vital for appraising the social significance of stimuli already processed by other subcortical structures (Tsuchiya et al., 2009).

The amygdala conditions fear, among other emotions (Fanselow & Gale, 2003), and also mediates unconditioned fear responses (e.g., the sight of snakes in rodents; Kalin et al., 2001). Angry and fearful faces are discerned in a crowd much more readily than happy faces (Öhman, 2002). Fear appears to be almost totally conditioned and is largely absent at birth (Sullivan & Lewis, 2003). As opposed to other types of Pavlovian conditioning, fear conditioning may occur in a single trial, producing muscular, endocrine and autonomic changes (Medina et al., 2002). Unlike, for instance, eyelid conditioning, which is mediated by the cerebellum, Medina et al. found that fear conditioning is mediated by the lateral nucleus of the amygdala through separate inputs from the thalamus and cortex before it is relayed to the central amygdala. While lateral nucleus lesions prevent the acquisition of learned fear, lesions to the central amygdala prevent its acquisition or expression. After conditioning, the lateral nucleus activates more quickly and stays activated longer under fearful situations, consistent with learning. The dorsal regions of the lateral nucleus stay altered even after extinction, as do the thalamus and cortex, resisting further change (Medina et al., 2002).

In anxiety and many mood disorders (e.g., melancholia, familial depression, Bipolar II Disorder and Bipolar I Disorder without psychotic features), the amygdala shows abnormally strong cerebral blood flow and glucose metabolism while resting, but its responses to salient stimuli may be blunted or persist abnormally long (Drevets, 2003). According to Drevets, there appears to be less glia per neuron in those with mood disorders, occurring in parts of the amygdala that have less glia per neuron in overly stressed rodents. In depression, despite the lack of structural connections between the amygdalae, their functional connectivity increases, possibly due to the inadequacies in OFC functioning associated with mood disorders (Irwin et al., 2004).

Like those with bilateral amygdalar damage, individuals with either Asperger's Syndrome or Williams' Syndrome generally perceive basic emotions as easily as normal controls do, but have trouble recognizing social emotions and tend to rate what they perceive more positively than controls do (Adolphs, Sears, & Piven, 2001). Inhibiting the amygdala may reduce suffering in many conditions and for many individuals (Quirk & Gehlert, 2003), but it seems clear that optimal amygdalar activation—whatever that turns out to be—would be preferable. The amygdalae of those with callous traits are activated less by viewing fearful or angry faces than others' are (Dolan & Fullam, 2009; Shirtcliff et al., 2009), though this appears to be reversed in adolescents with childhood-onset Conduct Disorder (Herpertz et al., 2008).

In short, the viscera and subcortical areas are important in emotional responding, particularly when it arises through bottom-up processing. Feelings and other primary emotions (including bypassed emotions) depend on such circuitry, though propositionally activated defensive secondary emotions may not, or may do so to a far lesser extent. Even painful secondary emotions like anxiety, while they activate the amygdala (and thus the release of cortisol through its effects on the hypothalamus), may do so less intensely than bottom-up emotional processes would. However, as we've already seen, the release of cortisol, even when intense, matters less to long-term health and perceptions of wellbeing than the sustained allostatic dysregulation of cortisol output does. As we shall see later, this is precisely what occurs in major depressive and anxiety disorders.

The BAS, BIS, and Cerebral Specialization

PEOPLE VARY IN the degree to which they differentiate their emotional life into discrete categories, with some drawing fine distinctions and others treating much of their subjective experience as essentially equivalent (Feldman Barrett, Gross, Conner Christensen, & Benvenuto, 2001). Those who attend to and differentiate their emotions the least experience their emotions as ranging on a single dimension between strongly positive and strongly negative, as do those with high subjective needs for structure (Terracciano, McCrae, Hagemann, & Costa, 2003). Most others tend to experience two dimensions, with their emotions being either positive or negative and either energetic or not (Cacioppo & Gardner, 1999; Terracciano et al., 2003). Social behavior operates analogously, with the two dimensions being activity level and whether the social action is directed towards or away from others (Benjamin, 1996).

Sutton and Davidson (1997) found that those with more left frontal activity during electroencephalogram (EEG) testing had more positive affect and approach behavior, while those with more right frontal EEG activity had more negative affect and behavioral inhibition. Davidson (1998) concluded that positive affect, goal directedness and approach, on the one hand, could be differentiated from negative affect, behavioral inhibition and withdrawal, on the other. Heller and Nitschke (1998) confirmed this using both EEG and Positron Emission Tomography (PET). Desirability and danger are computed separately in the left and right prefrontal lobes, respectively, yielding positive and negative affect, respectively (Cacioppo & Gardner, 1999). Sad and scary musical selections preferentially activate the right frontal areas, while happy and joyful ones activate the left (Schmidt & Trainor, 2001).

EEG activity in the PFC is generally asymmetrical (Cacioppo, 2004), with left hemispheric activity usually greater than right (Allen, Harmon-Jones, & Cavender, 2001) even among preschool children (Pickens, Field, & Nawrocki, 2001). Those with this pattern have greater positive affect and are more likely to approach uncertain or novel stimuli (Cacioppo et al., 2000; Sutton & Davidson, 1997), qualities that co-occur (Cacioppo & Gardner, 1999; Carver & White, 1994; Davidson, 1998) and mutually reinforce one another (Urry et al., 2004). The left PFC modulates regulation of the autonomic and voluntary nervous systems (Jackson et al., 2003), and those with this pattern have greater senses of mastery, autonomy, purpose, personal growth and self-acceptance; more positive relations with others; greater life satisfaction; and both more frequent pleasant emotions and less frequent unpleasant ones than those with the opposite pattern (Urry et al., 2004).

Those with stronger right hemispheric prefrontal EEG activity experience more negative emotion, avoidance and behavioral inhibition (Cacioppo et al., 2000; Sutton & Davidson, 1997). This pattern has been observed among those with depression or panic disorder (Davidson, 1998, Davidson et al., 2002), adults recovering from depression (Allen et al., 2001) and infants with prenatal cocaine exposure (Jones, Field, Davalos, & Hart, 2004). Lesions to the amygdala do not alter these asymmetries (Kalin et al., 2001). As right prefrontal EEG dominance increases, so does the severity of depressive symptoms (Diego, Field, & Hernandez-Reif, 2001b). When startled by negative stimuli, the reactions of those with this pattern, while equally intense, tend to last much longer than they do in those with more left frontal EEG activity (Jackson et al., 2003). At least in chimpanzees, those with this pattern of right EEG dominance have higher cortisol levels than those that do not (Davidson, 1998).

By the second year of life, infants' right PFC activation is associated with distress, while left PFC activation is associated with regulating distress (Schmidt et al., 2003). Altering someone's prefrontal activation patterns through biofeedback changes her later emotional responses and self-reports of emotional experience (Allen et al., 2001). Though many researchers once thought that these asymmetries reflected dispositions toward positive or negative emotions (Cacioppo, 2004), they actually appear to reflect behavioral tendencies to approach or withdraw (Urry et al., 2004). Those high in trait anger, usually considered a negative emotional state, generally have more activity on the left (Allen et al., 2001), a pattern active when people believe their anger will help them solve a perceived problem and disappearing when they can no longer devise workable solutions and withdraw (Harmon-Jones et al., 2003). This holds despite the individual's attitudes about anger or whether or not he feels good about being angry (Harmon-Jones, 2004), though as empathy increases, the asymmetry diminishes (Harmon-Jones, 2003).

During relatively noneventful times, most people (but not the depressed) maintain a slightly positive attitude that increases exploration and risk-taking; but react more quickly and strongly to negative stimuli, promoting their safety through quick mental and behavioral adjustments (Cacioppo & Berntson, 1999; Cacioppo & Gardner, 1999). Cacioppo and Gardner (1999) refer to these well-documented phenomena as the *positivity offset* and *negativity bias*, respectively. As seen earlier, the negativity bias has its parallel in the structure and functioning of the amygdala, which negative stimuli are far more likely to activate, and to activate far more fully

(Zald, 2003). The positivity offset and negativity bias have been found in infants, who are more happy than neutral across a range of situations (Bennett, Bendersky, & Lewis, 2002), but in whom negative input elicits immediate, intense, undifferentiated negative affect (Sullivan & Lewis, 2003). As Crawford and Cacioppo (2002) conclude, recovering from missed opportunities is much easier (and better) than recovering from failed escape attempts when danger arises.

Two separate neural systems (Cacioppo & Gardner, 1999; Davidson, 1998) using different neurotransmitters (Buck, 1999) are at work. The Behavior Activating System (BAS) uses DA circuitry (Buck, 1999) to activate left prefrontal areas (Cacioppo et al., 2000) that compute the degree and likelihood of potential rewards (Carver & White, 1994), while the Behavior Inhibition System (BIS) employs a NE circuit (Buck, 1999) to activate right prefrontal areas (Cacioppo et al., 2000) that assess potential punishments (Carver & White, 1994). The BAS and BIS can operate separately or simultaneously (Cacioppo & Berntson, 1999), with various situations activating either, neither or both (Cacioppo & Gardner, 1999).

For example, though punishment frequently stops targeted approach behavior, the desire to achieve the intended goal often endures, keeping both the BAS and BIS active (Cacioppo & Berntson, 1999). When the BIS and BAS are simultaneously and intensely activated (Zautra et al., 2002) or when the individual experiences physical pain (Zautra, Hamilton, & Burke, 1999), cognitive resources become overworked, discrimination is impaired, information is processed poorly and judgment is simplified until the individual effectively regulates the emotions involved (Reich & Zautra, 2002). Internal conflict, intense anxiety and stress result (Cacioppo & Berntson, 1999; Knyazev et al., 2006).

The BIS markedly reduces reward-seeking activity and leads to fatigue (Watson & Clark, 1997) among those high in negative affect (Knyazev et al., 2006), such as those with damaged left prefrontal areas (Davidson, 1998). Since the PFC largely regulates the rest of the brain, and overall arousal levels are associated with right hemispheric parietotemporal activation, increased right prefrontal activity without accompanying right parietotemporal involvement may be responsible for producing the lethargy seen in depression (Heller & Nitschke, 1998). On the other hand, reducing the activation of the BIS results in increased energy and positive feelings, a combination experienced as serenity (Watson & Clark, 1997).

Hemispheric Specialization

The prefrontal, temporal and parietal areas are all involved in the perception of facial emotion (Erickson & Schulkin, 2003). The fusiform gyrus encodes the static properties of faces, while the superior temporal gyrus encodes their dynamic and changing aspects, like expressions and gaze direction (Adolphs, 2002a). Most people have a right hemispheric bias for visual perception (Borod, Bloom, Brickman, Nakhutina, & Curko, 2002), with the right hemisphere decoding facial displays of negative emotion more accurately than the left hemisphere and decoding positive and negative emotional faces about equally well (Jansari, Tranel, & Adolphs, 2000). The right hemispheric frontoparietal area is also better at perceiving prosody (Adolphs, 2002a; Borod et al., 2002), while the left controls emotional regulation (Berthoz et al., 2002) and is better at lexical perception (Borod et al., 2002) and decoding faces exhibiting positive emotion (Jansari et al., 2000).

The right hemisphere processes emotional input at a basic level and activates autonomic arousal (Berthoz et al., 2002). At least in chimps, its processing load correlates with blood cortisol levels (Davidson, 1998). When emotional input varies widely, as occurs in real life, a person's decoding it often depends on simulating others' perceived states to understand and predict them (Hess et al., 1998). The right hemispheric somatosensory cortices perform this task (Adolphs, 2002a), particularly the right temperoparietal juncture (TPJ; Decety & Jackson, 2006). The right anterior forebrain is involved in emotional expression in all of its forms (Erickson & Schulkin, 2003) regardless of whether the emotion is considered positive or negative (Borod et al., 2002).

Zald (2003) noted that hemispheric differences (especially in the frontal cortex) have resulted in three possible ways of interpreting the data: (a) the left is more involved in positive emotions and approach behavior, while the right is more involved with negative emotions and withdrawal; (b) the right hemisphere is more involved in emotion; and (c) the right is dominant for reception and expression, but subjective experience has a positive/negative hemispheric pattern. Buck (1999) added a fourth, that the right might be specialized for "selfish" emotions and the left for social emotions. Hagemann et al. (2003) added a fifth, that right hemispheric activation causes sympathetic arousal and left activation leads to parasympathetic arousal.

Ochsner, Bunge, Gross, and Gabrieli (2002) found that left prefrontal activity is heavily involved in attempted reappraisal of especially strong stimuli, while Feinstein et al. (2002) found that right hemispheric areas, the hypothalamus and the left cerebellum habituate to emotional input, while left hemispheric cortical areas become sensitized to it. Posse et al. (2003) showed that self-induced sadness preferentially activates the left amygdala, hippocampus and temporal lobe, although the cerebellum, fusiform gyrus, occipital cortex, brainstem and right amygdala and temporal lobes are also activated to a lesser extent. A sixth possibility might thus be advanced: the right hemisphere might be preferentially involved in the reception of emotional communication and in the activation and expression of schematically activated primary emotional states, while the left hemisphere might be preferentially involved in the activation and expression of propositionally activated emotional processes. Ochsner et al. (2009) found that emotion generated through bottom-up, schematic processing activated both amygdalae and several right-hemispheric areas, including the prefrontal and parietal areas thought to be responsible for attention and negative emotion, while emotion generated through top-down, propositional processes activated areas in the left hemispheric prefrontal, temporal and cingulate cortices implicated in working memory and information retrieval.

This points to why anger activated the left prefrontal areas in Harmon-Jones' various studies, but only as long as people thought they could do something about the situation. Anger, by and large, is an adopted strategy. It's largely an instrumental emotion rather than a primary one. The strategies employed by anger management training in its many forms rely on this but will not generalize to most other emotions. This is true because nothing else in Western culture is as likely to be adopted as a manipulative emotional strategy as anger is.

The Cerebral Cortex

As DISCUSSED EARLIER, the amygdala processes direct input from the thalamus in about 120 ms but also directs additional processing through its reciprocal feedback networks with various cortical structures (Adolphs, 2002a), particularly within the PFC. This additional processing, which takes about 170 ms (Adolphs, 2002a), includes structures such as (a) the ACC, implicated in a variety of emotional phenomena (Canli & Amin, 2002; Critchley, 2003); (b) insula, which apparently represents emotional processes as cognitive feeling states (Adolphs, 2002a); (c) medial and ventromedial prefrontal areas, which are involved in autonomic responses, social decision making and theories of mind (Canli &Amin, 2002; Schulkin et al., 2003); (d) orbitofrontal areas, which direct attention, engage associations and activate emotional states (Adolphs, 2002a); and (e) dorsolateral prefrontal areas, which are implicated in coordinating mood, attention and vigilance (Liotti & Mayberg, 2001), devising long-term goal strategies (Davidson, 1998) and regulating motivated behavior (Schmidt et al., 2003). The processing of these additional structures modulates the original, cruder responses the amygdala achieves without cortical input (Adolphs, 2002a).

Anterior Cingulate Cortex

Activation of the ACC has been related to attention processes (Berthoz et al., 2002), stress regulation (Davidson et al., 2002), emotional regulation (Drevets, 2003) and the subjective experience of emotion (Berthoz et al., 2002). It also monitors pain, both one's own and others, particularly its emotional aspects (Shirtcliff et al., 2009). The front part monitors deviations between ongoing goals and incoming sensory input (Wyland, Kelley, Macrae, Gordon, & Heatherton, 2003) and by communicating with the amygdala, nucleus accumbens, OFC, periaqueductal grey, anterior insula and autonomic brainstem nuclei (Davidson et al., 2002), the ACC helps regulate cortisol levels (Shirtcliff et al., 2009), emotional expression (Drevets, 2003) and skin conductance responses (Hagemann et al., 2003).

A neural alarm system that tracks when automatic processes should return to conscious control (Shirtcliff et al., 2009), the ACC works closely with the medial PFC (Berthoz et al., 2002) when discrepancies such as pain, moodiness or unexpected facial expressions are encountered (Davidson et al., 2002). During depressed or anxious states, the relationship between the ACC and PFC loses it efficiency (Davidson et al., 2002; Drevets, 2003). This may be at least partly because of the relative lack of gray matter many patients with Major Depressive Disorder have in the lower front portion of their ACC (Drevets, 2003).

The responsiveness of the ACC increases as cortisol levels rise (Shirtcliff et al., 2009). The right side increases expressive responses and the front left portion modulates them (Drevets, 2003). By connecting the mirror neuron system with peripheral signals it processes along with the amygdala and insula (Shirtcliff et al., 2009) and incorporating input (Davidson et al., 2002) from the back part of ACC, which processes cognition (Berthoz et al., 2002), the front part of the ACC increases the likelihood of appropriate responses to the situation at hand (Wyland et al., 2003) and helps promote empathy (Shirtcliff et al., 2009).

Insula

Located deep within the folds of the cortex, the anterior insula has a varied neuronal structure and widely disparate functions (Seeley, 2010). Playing a crucial role in monitoring body states (Decety & Jackson, 2006), it appears to integrate visceral perceptions, cognitive appraisals and autonomic responses (Guyer, McClure-Tone, Shiffrin, Pine, & Nelson, 2009) and it links emotion, cognition, and behavior (Arce, Simmons, Lovero, Stein, & Paulus, 2008).

It processes threats (Blanchette & Richards, 2010) and disgust (Olatunji, Cisler, McKay, & Phillips, 2010), along with other negative states like hunger and pain (Shirtcliff et al., 2009). It also appears to be involved in suppressing thoughts and switching tasks (Seeley, 2010). Although considered part of the gustatory cortex (Olatunji et al., 2010), it also contains key areas involved in processing autonomic and social input (Seeley, 2010) and it maintains speech and language fluency (Borg, Lieberman, & Kiehl, 2008). Part of it initiates the activity of the amygdala and ACC, sharing many connections with both (Seeley, 2010). Like those structures, it has many cortisol receptor sites (Shirtcliff et al, 2009) and monitors the activity of the viscera (Seeley, 2010). Along with the ACC, it becomes active when oneself or others are in pain (Decety & Jackson, 2006).

During adolescence, girls become more interested in dyadic relationships with desirable peers while boys become more focused on competition and group membership (Guyer et al., 2009). Guyer et al. found that among adolescent girls, as the desirability of interacting with someone increased, the activity within their anterior insula also did. Within adolescent boys, insula activity actually decreased as the peer became more desirable, suggesting that adolescent boys had less somatic responses than girls when considering whether they wanted someone to like them or not (Guyer et al., 2009).

Medial Prefrontal Cortex

More than any other area, the generation of propositional emotion is associated with the medial PFC, which is preferentially activated during that process and tracks its intensity (Ochsner et al., 2009). It also appears to be involved in controlling autonomic activity and determining the causes of naturally-occurring emotional states (Ochsner et al., 2009). Damage to the medial PFC (Berthoz et al., 2002) or its connections to the basolateral amygdala (Rosenkranz, Moore, & Grace, 2003) frequently disrupt the ability to regulate emotion. Coordinating with left hemispheric subcortical areas (Hagemann et al., 2003), the right medial PFC processes emotional input and increases autonomic arousal (Berthoz et al., 2002). Kawasaki et al. (2001) studied a single neuron in the area and discovered that it responded in between 120 and 170 ms, and only to negative stimuli. Meanwhile, left medial areas synchronize with right hemispheric subcortical areas (Hagemann et al., 2003) to dampen amygdalar activity (Davidson, 1998), regulate emotional intensity and expression (Berthoz et al., 2002) and, by activating the nucleus accumbens, match activity levels to behavioral needs (Davidson, 1998). This area may also regulate emotions by blocking amygdalar plasticity during both its learning and expressive phases (Rosenkranz et al., 2003).

Along with the precuneus and left and right TPJ, the medial PFC is involved in the theory of mind (ToM; Sabbagh, Bowman, Evraire, & Ito, 2009; Saxe, Whitfield-Gabrieli, Scholz, & Pelphrey, 2009). Taking others' perspectives activates this area (Decety & Jackson, 2006). The medial PFC is involved when there is uncertainty on these tasks or when there are response conflicts (Sabbagh et al., 2009). It seems to be involved in any thinking about people in general, while the mirror neuron system appears to be involved in assessing intentionality and the right TPJ seems to be activated specifically when one is thinking about other people's thoughts (Saxe et al., 2009). In schoolchildren, increased alpha coherence is associated with better performance on ToM tests (Sabbagh et al., 2009). The areas in the medial PFC associated with ToM show deficits in those suffering from chronic Schizophrenia, Bipolar Disorder, or their first psychotic episode (Maïza et al., 2010).

Those with Posttraumatic Stress Disorder (PTSD) have less volume in their left medial PFC than control subjects do, even those who had previously been traumatized (Eckart et al., 2011). This lack of volume is directly correlated to the extent of their prior traumatization (Eckart et al., 2011). During working memory tests, experimental participants with PTSD activate their medial PFC and posterior cingulate less than controls and also exhibit functional connectivity between their medial PFC and other neural centers that normal controls do not, resulting in additional problems with attention and performance (Daniels et al., 2010).

Ventromedial Prefrontal Cortex

The ventromedial PFC is involved when decisions are made, particularly moral ones (Shirtcliff et al., 2009). It is also used to help down-regulate emotional intensity, especially among adolescents whose brains may not yet be mature (Wang, Huettel, & De Bellis, 2008). People with lesions in their ventromedial areas cope more poorly and make less adaptive decisions than those without such damage (Bechara, 2004). They have trouble correctly identifying others' emotional expressions (Yamada et al., 2009), their capacity to experience social emotions (such as guilt, shame and compassion) is restricted and their ability to tolerate frustration without short-tempered displays is severely curtailed (Koenigs et al., 2007). Only lesions to the amygdala or insula have similar negative effects on the processing of social emotions (Bar-On et al., 2003); but unlike those with amygdalar damage, they correctly estimate the intensity of the emotional experience they see (Yamada et al., 2009). Because of these limitations, moral decisions that require the processing of social emotions are impaired, though other moral decisions are not (Koenigs et al., 2007).

The ventromedial PFC is also active in the representation of the self (Ng, Han, Mao, & Lai, 2010). Since those from collectivist cultures represent others as part of themselves, native Chinese represent both themselves and their mothers in their ventromedial PFC, while those from Western cultures represent only themselves there. In an ingenious experiment, Ng et al. found that using tacit cultural priming on a sample of bicultural natives of Hong Kong changed the area of the brain in which representations of their mothers were processed.

The area is implicated in various psychological and psychiatric disturbances. The activity of the ventromedial PFC increases with the amount of recent negative emotion (Zald, Mattson, & Pardo, 2002). The ability to coordinate the activity of the ventromedial PFC with that of the ACC predicts how fully a depressed patient will recover after 8 weeks' pharmacotherapy with citalopram (Roy et al., 2010). Schizophrenics behave as though they had both bilateral ventromedial PFC damage and bilateral amygdala damage (Yamada et al., 2009). Cocaine addicts have less gray matter in their ventromedial PFC than nonaddicts do (Quirk & Gehlert, 2003).

Orbitofrontal Cortex

Because of its location between the limbic area and the rest of the PFC, the OFC is sometimes considered part of both (Shirtcliff et al., 2009) or part of the ventromedial PFC (Bar-On et al., 2003). It continues to mature until at least early adolescence (Happaney, Zelazo, & Stuss, 2004) and plays a number of vital roles in emotional processing. However, it also has characteristics more closely resembling the PFC, including regulation and executive functioning (Shirtcliff et al., 2009). Responsible for mediating anxious temperament (Davidson & Slagter, 2000), tracking reward contingencies (Rolls, 2004) and evaluating feeling states (Adolphs, 2002a), it (a) integrates information from all senses except hearing (Rolls, 2004) to determine whether reward expectations have been violated (Blair, 2004; Rolls, 2004), (b) recognizes and responds to social cues (Blair, 2004) and (c) extinguishes conditioned responses, especially those involving fear, by forming new memories that override those retained by the lateral amygdala (Morris & Dolan, 2004; Quirk & Gehlert, 2003; Rolls, 2004).

The OFC is primarily involved in assessing the salience of an integrated stream of sensory input. Tertiary association cortices from the ventral visual "what" stream are located there, as are tertiary association cortices related to olfaction, taste and somatosensory processes (Rolls, 2004). According to Rolls, these various areas are all involved in determining what something is and what its motivational or hedonic significance might be. Smell and taste are combined to create flavor, faces are assessed for emotional significance, and internal and external feelings are assessed for pleasantness (Rolls, 2004). Emotion is important for making adequate decisions (Bechara, 2004); and the OFC, with its rich input from and reciprocal connections throughout the brain and viscera, is the area responsible for combining affective inputs from other areas (such as the insula and secondary somatosensory cortices) and combining them to decide future courses of action (Bar-On et al., 2003).

In adults and older children, when the amygdala is active, the OFC generally also is. The amount of measured resting orbitofrontal activation correlates with the self-reported experience of negative emotion within the previous month (Zald et al., 2002); and reappraisal, considered an advanced regulatory strategy (Gross, 2002), suppresses activation of both the amygdala and the medial OFC (Ochsner et al., 2002). Like the amygdala, one function of the OFC is learning reinforcement contingencies, which the OFC does more quickly (Blair, 2004). Unlike the amygdala, the OFC can also learn to reverse such conditioned emotional responses. When fear responses have been conditioned and later conditioning reverses the process, making the former "safe" stimulus threatening and the former threatening stimulus safe, the OFC activates only when the newly threatening stimulus is presented, while the amygdala persists in activating whenever the formerly threatening stimulus is presented (Morris & Dolan, 2004). The amygdala "remembers" the previous conditioning and responds accordingly (Blair, 2004), but the OFC dampens its functioning, probably by analyzing more subtle contextual cues (Toates, 2002). When the OFC is damaged, reversal learning does not take place at all and previously reinforced behavior cannot be extinguished (Happaney et al., 2004).

It is generally believed that various brain structures have different critical periods during which they mature, that insults occurring during those periods lead to the plasticity of brain functioning, that insults occurring before the critical period keep the abilities associated with that structure from developing and that those occurring after the critical period wipe out the abilities or portions of abilities already formed (Anderson, Northam, Hendy, & Wrennall, 2001; Stuss & Anderson, 2004). From what has been learned about the OFC, its initial critical period appears to span the interval between about 9 and 24 months postnatal development (Schore, 2001a), although it continues to mature until at least age 12-15 (Happaney et al., 2004), if not 21 (Bechara, 2004). We know that certain neural structures are unlikely to develop well when the brain structures from which they receive information are damaged and do not function correctly (Anderson et al., 2001), and all indications suggest that the amygdala is a structure that often shows dysfunction from birth because of any number of factors, including heredity, intrauterine environment and birth trauma.

Stuss and Anderson (2004) believe that consciousness, far from being a unitary phenomenon, has at least four developmentally and physiologically separable strata: basic arousal, sensory awareness, executive skills and self awareness. Prenatal trauma, occurring as it does before any of these functions are set, can disrupt all of them, while traumas in early childhood would only affect the latter two, since the first two abilities would be operational by then (Stuss & Anderson, 2004). It is clear that the last of these is a function of the OFC, which is linked to the development of the individual's theory of mind (Happaney et al., 2004) and thus to moral behavior (Eslinger, Flaherty-Craig, & Benton, 2004). Achieving the highest level of personal consciousness involves integrating the entire brain and viscera, as the working OFC does.

Although developmental psychology may be conceptualized as the study of how people's executive functioning changes over the lifespan (Eslinger et al., 2004), research has centered on its cognitive components, and little is known about the development of its motivational and emotional elements (Eslinger et al., 2004; Happaney et al., 2004). Schore (2001a, b) has asserted that decrements in orbitofrontal functioning should be seen in those with histories of extremely difficult attachment relationships, such as unsafe or abusive home environments that do not allow the child to learn to regulate emotions effectively. It is known that neurons in the OFC show great plasticity in their responses to abusable drugs and gonadal hormones, responding differently to each than the dorsolateral PFC does (Kolb, Pellis, & Robinson, 2004). For instance, due to hormonal influences males have more neurons in their OFC than females and learn the associated skills quicker, while females have fewer cells but thicker dendritic fields; the reverse is true in the dorsolateral PFC (Kolb et al., 2004). Such receptivity to chemical agents suggests that perhaps the children studied by Field and her associates (about whom much more will be said in later chapters) may suffer altered orbitofrontal functioning because their elevated cortisol damaged their OFC, which is rich in cortisol receptor sites.

Rats given orbitofrontal lesions behave normally except that they quit paying respect to dominant rats (Kolb et al., 2004). Human patients with orbitofrontal damage perform well on neuropsychological and intelligence tests (Bechara, 2004) but show impairments in working memory, fluid intelligence and judgment (Eslinger et al., 2004); no longer recognize others' glances or salient facial expressions accurately (Blair, 2004; Happaney et al., 2004); behave more impatiently, irritably and egocentrically (Eslinger et al., 2004); react more aggressively (Blair, 2004); and show deficits in empathy and morality (Eslinger et al., 2004). They are more likely to opt for smaller rewards gained quickly than larger rewards available in the future (Happaney et al., 2004) and they follow and negotiate rules, form friendships, learn from experience and pay attention more poorly than those without such damage (Eslinger et al., 2004). Damage localized to the right OFC causes the loss of abilities to recall one's past (Stuss & Anderson, 2004), make wise decisions using internal affective signals (Bechara, 2004) and project oneself into the future (Stuss & Anderson, 2004).

The OFC is in a particularly disadvantageous spot when considering brain damage, since the skull and orbital plate largely surround it and its neurons myelinate later in development, with both being risk factors (Anderson et al., 2001). Although orbitofrontal damage causes severe social problems whether it occurs as an adult or child (Kolb et al., 2004), with childhood damage, behavioral and emotional deficits are more severe, inadequate social behavior persists throughout life and verbal channels cannot access appropriate behavior for the situation at hand (Bechara, 2004). Early orbitofrontal damage causes deficits in social, emotional and moral development (including problems cooperating, negotiating and abiding by rules); difficulty functioning in relationships; the inability to profit from experience; and impaired executive functioning, such as attention, regulation, inhibition, planning, organization and anticipation (Eslinger et al., 2004).

Those with orbitofrontal damage behave much like 3-year-old children who need help modulating their emotional and social life (Happaney et al., 2004). Put another way, people with orbitofrontal damage acquire a personality disorder marked by having little insight and poor judgment, strong and labile emotions, and primitive moral development focused on satisfying their own immediate needs (Eslinger et al., 2004). As Blair (2004) notes, they behave much like those with Borderline Personality Disorder, displaying inappropriately intense anger, affective instability, impulsive aggression and unstable personal relationships. Those with Intermittent Explosive Disorder, who show anger completely disproportionate to the situation at hand, also show decrements in orbitofrontal functioning (Blair, 2004), which may be one reason they have difficulty recognizing other's expression of anger or disgust (Shirtcliff et al., 2009). Those with either Borderline Personality Disorder or Intermittent Explosive Disorder show difficulties on reversal tasks, making this relationship of physiology and psychology likely (Blair, 2004).

Others have referred to early damage to the OFC as *acquired sociopathy* (Fairchild et al., 2009). Children with Conduct Disorder have less overall gray matter in a number of areas, but particularly the left OFC (Vloet, Konrad, Huebner, Herpertz, & Herpertz-Dahlmann, 2008). Compared to controls, the OFCs of schizophrenics with psychopathic features do not show the same activation patterns while processing emotions (Dolan & Fullam, 2009). Sociopaths who use instrumental aggression to meet their immediate desires have impaired aversive conditioning, startle responses and avoidance learning, all associated with amygdalar but not orbitofrontal dysfunction. Children with antisocial tendencies perform tests of conditioned response reversal normally, suggesting normal orbitofrontal functioning. Because adults with Antisocial Personality Disorder no longer display normal reversal learning, it seems likely that as sociopaths age, their OFC goes "off line" (Blair, 2004).

Other developmental disorders that may also involve the OFC are Autism, Asperger's Syndrome, Attention-Deficit/Hyperactivity Disorder (ADHD) and Nonverbal Learning Disability (Stuss & Anderson, 2004). Reactive aggression, which is associated with diminished orbitofrontal modulation, decreases after lesions to the amygdala, but instrumental aggression, in which individuals attack others for personal gain, is associated with amygdalar dysfunction and a history of achieving gains through aggressive behavior (Blair, 2004). As Blair notes, orbitofrontal activity can either increase or decrease instrumental aggression, depending upon environmental factors.

This concludes our discussion of the brain. Not every neural structure involved in processing emotion has been mentioned, as some are more studied than others and some seemed to be more centrally discussed in a variety of contexts than others. Although much of it may seem technical, this discussion will provide further background for understanding much of what is to follow. These same structures will be mentioned many times within the remaining pages of this volume.

PART FOUR

PHYSIOLOGICAL MEASURES OF STRESS AND EMOTION

Electrical and Autonomic Indicators

DIRECT STUDIES OF the brain during emotional experiences have thus far not been practical. First, ethically provoking a genuine emotion in a laboratory setting has proven daunting, and such equipment cannot be transported to use *in vivo*. Second, as noted earlier, direct studies of many subcortical structures such as the amygdala have been complicated by their complexity, location and the lack of homogeneity in their surrounding tissues, which combine to make interpreting the results difficult. Even in cortical areas, studies combining EEG and PET (Oakes et al., 2004) or EEG and fMRI (Mulert et al., 2004) that would allow for the simultaneous accurate measurements of both location and duration of brain activity within a single experiment have been rare.

Studies of emotion have instead traditionally relied on self-report, though physiological measures are less easily and consciously controlled and would have provided less distorted assessments (Mendes et al., 2003). Those studies using physiological measures, which have increased in recent years, have focused on one or more of several areas: facial musculature, galvanic skin responses, autonomic activity and HPA activity. Selected findings and studies assessing muscular, skin and autonomic responses will be discussed in this chapter, with HPA activity being the focus of the next chapter.

Facial Muscles

Emotional stimulation automatically activates the facial muscles, which are the only muscles that move skin instead of bone (Öhman, 2002). The *corrugator supercilii* is the muscle over the brow that draws it down into a frown (Larsen, Norris, & Cacioppo, 2003). Electromyographic (EMG) measurements of muscle activity show that negative emotions (Cacioppo et al., 2000) and repressed anger (Pauls & Stemmler, 2003) cause corrugator activity, while positive affect inhibits it (Larsen et al., 2003). Although fear generally relaxes corrugator muscles, defending against one's fearful feelings increases corrugator tension (Pauls & Stemmler, 2003). Among those with simple phobias, seeing pictures of the feared object also increases corrugator tension (Hamm et al., 1997).

The *zygomaticus major* muscle over the cheek pulls the mouth up into a smile (Larsen et al., 2003). Positive affect (Cacioppo et al., 2000), anger and embarrassed smiles (Pauls & Stemmler, 2003) cause increased zygomaticus activity, while negative emotions have no effect on it (Larsen et al., 2003). Because zygomaticus activity is easier to control consciously than corrugator activity, it is more susceptible to social display rules (Larsen et al., 2003). This conscious control also makes anger easier to simulate. Even when instructed to suppress their responses, people watching amusing videos showed increased zygomaticus activity, as measured by EMG (Kappas, Bherer, and Theriault, 2000).

Skin Conductance

Because skin conductance apparently responds to arousal, it reacts more to both positive and negative emotional stimuli than to neutral stimuli (Hamm et al., 1997). In general, skin responses extinguish relatively easily unless they follow fearful stimuli, in which case they do not (Flykt, 2005). Those who rely on repression also show increased skin conductance following threat appraisals (Pauls & Stemmler, 2003). In their study, Hamm et al. found that those with animal phobias viewing animal pictures had increased skin conductance over controls, while those with mutilation phobias viewing mutilation pictures did not. They attribute much of this to the acknowledged disgusting nature of the mutilation pictures, which may have excited their controls. Because most of the studies measuring skin conductance focus primarily on autonomic variables, they will be addressed in the following section.

Autonomic Activity

Facially expressing emotions raises one's heart rate (Labouvie-Vief, Lumley, Jain, & Heinze, 2003), as does exaggerating the expression of what one feels (Demaree et al., 2004). Negative emotions, but not positive affect, increase heart rate 5 to 10 minutes after emotional experiences, regardless of arousal levels, physical activity levels or how long the emotions were sustained (Brosschot & Thayer, 2003). Compared to normal memories, intrusive memories cause no differences in heart rate, skin conductance or EMG (Bywaters, Andrade, & Turpin, 2004), but angry memories elevate heart rate and blood pressure (Gerin, Davidson, Christenfeld, Goyal, & Schwartz, 2006). Similar effects are found whether Americans or native Chinese are studied (Drummond & Quah, 2001).

Appraisals of challenge elicit changes in heart rate and pre-ejection period (Pauls & Stemmler, 2003) when people are motivated to try hard at difficult tasks (Eubanks, Wright, & Williams, 2002). Besides these changes, appraisals of threat also raise diastolic blood pressure and total peripheral resistance (Pauls & Stemmler, 2003). While self-reported measures of anxiety predict systolic blood pressure responses during the preparation and delivery of a speech, implicit measures of anxiety—which track how much attention is paid to a threat—also predict heart rate and diastolic blood pressure reactivity (Egloff, Wilhelm, Neubauer, Mauss, & Gross, 2002).

Heart rate and blood pressure have both sympathetic and parasympathetic determinants (Berntson, Cacioppo et al., 2003). Sympathetic activation, which relies on the quick release and slow reuptake of epinephrine, also predicts immune responses, while parasympathetic activation, mediated by the vagus nerve, also helps regulate cortisol levels (Berntson, Cacioppo et al., 2003; Rainville et al., 2006). Either can cause slow changes in heart rate, but only the parasympathetic influence can cause rapid heart rate changes (Rainville et al., 2006). Measures of vagal tone (Brosschot, 2002), respiratory sinus arrhythmia (RSA; Butler, Wilhelm, & Gross, 2006; Rottenberg, Wilhelm, Gross, and Gotlib, 2003) and heart rate variability (HRV; Pignotti & Steinberg, 2001) all reflect the balance of the sympathetic and parasympathetic systems.

During stress, the vagus withdraws and heart rate rises; following stress, the vagus reasserts control and heart rate drops below baseline levels (Mezzacappa, Kelsey, Katkin, & Sloan, 2001). The lack of either response reflects poor vagal responsiveness, which may result in later health problems (Mezzacappa et al., 2001). While low vagal tone mediates the effects of rumination and worry (Brosschot, 2002), high vagal tone is associated with increased cognitive, emotional and behavioral flexibility (Diamond & Aspinwall, 2003) and predicts how effectively emotions will be regulated as much as three years later (Repetti et al., 2002). Both exaggerated emotional expression and emotional suppression decrease vagal tone (Demaree et al., 2004).

Rapid heart rate changes are coupled with changes in respiration and the RSA (Rainville et al., 2006), a fluctuation in heart rate coinciding with respiration (Rottenberg et al., 2003). Parasympathetic influences on heart rate occur both together with and independently of RSA (Rainville et al., 2006). Higher resting RSA has been associated with increased emotional reactivity as vagal control of sympathetic activity is withdrawn (Butler, Wilhelm, & Gross, 2006), while reduced RSA has been associated with poorer attention, lower emotional regulatory functioning and greater vulnerability to stress (Rottenberg et al., 2003). After crying, naturally occurring parasympathetic activity increases RSA among those who are not depressed, but not among those who are, robbing the depressed of the allostatic regulation that crying usually initiates (Rottenberg et al., 2003). Active attempts at emotional regulation increase RSA, even when the strategies are ineffective (Butler et al., 2006).

After RSA is factored out, the parasympathetic influence remaining is the HRV (Rainville et al., 2006). Since each reflects allostatic dysregulation, both abnormally high and abnormally low HRV values increase the risk for sudden death, even among those without any prior history of heart trouble (Pignotti & Steinberg, 2001). Fearful defensiveness causes low HRV levels (Pauls & Stemmler, 2003), which are associated with higher cortisol levels and larger and more poorly modulated startle responses (Thayer et al., 2006). Low HRV levels are also found among those with depression, generalized anxiety, PTSD and specific phobias (Pignotti & Steinberg, 2001). Bornas et al. (2004) exposed a group with flight phobia to a simulated flight accompanied by the appropriate sounds, but the group's HRV values did not change significantly. Pignotti and Steinberg found that Thought Field Therapy both raises abnormally low HRV scores and lowers abnormally high ones, suggesting that it does not treat symptoms directly but instead helps reregulate the autonomic nervous system. Rainville et al. differentiated angry, sad, happy and fearful responses to stimuli solely by whether changes in HRV, RSA and respiratory variability accompanied the participants' changes in heart rate.

Because the inhibition of facial expressions increases heart rate, younger women tend to have higher heart rates during inductions of anger, which they tend to suppress (Labouvie-Vief et al., 2003). Among the elderly this effect disappears, presumably because they generally express their emotions less than young people do (Labouvie-Vief et al., 2003). Perhaps not coincidentally, increased age is also associated with decreased RSA and with increases in total peripheral resistance, systolic blood pressure and diastolic blood pressure, each of which signals increases in cardiovascular risk (Uchino, Holt-Lunstad, Bloor, & Campo, 2005).

Defensive responses are often associated with increased heart rate (Flykt, 2005). When angry, defensiveness also increases diastolic blood pressure and total peripheral resistance (Pauls & Stemmler, 2003). Alexithymia, a type of defensiveness particularly broad in its scope, consists of: (a) difficulty identifying feelings, (b) difficulty describing one's feelings, (c) a reduced capacity for fantasy and (d) a stimulus-bound, externally oriented cognitive style (Luminet, Rimé, Bagby, & Taylor, 2004). According to Luminet et al., while alexithymia is unrelated to baseline arousal levels, it is associated with increased heart rate following emotional stimulation.

Those diagnosed with PTSD display increased heart rate reactivity after subsequent stressors, whether they are male combat veterans (Goldfinger, Amdur, & Liberzon, 1998) or female sexual abuse survivors (McDonagh-Coyle et al., 2001). Combat veterans who gave Rorschach responses indicating prior trauma had higher heart rates and skin conductance measures than did veterans without such Rorschach responses or noncombat controls (Goldfinger et al., 1998); meanwhile, traumatic imagery led to more heart rate and EMG reactivity among female sexual abuse survivors than did stressful mental arithmetic tasks (McDonagh-Coyle et al., 2001). Even those traumatized by incidents unlikely to have actually occurred display such patterns. McNally et al. (2004) found that those who believed that they had been abducted by space aliens reacted to "recollections" of their abduction trauma with increased heart rate, skin conductance and EMG activation. However, nontraumatized combat veterans have even lower baseline heart rate and skin conductance levels than noncombat controls and their heart rate slows during stressful Rorschach responses, suggesting that they have developed resilience (Goldfinger et al., 1998).

vanOyen Witvliet, Ludwig, and Vander Laan (2001) studied 71 participants who each identified an individual they believed had caused them harm. Using designed scripts, they actively imagined both forgiving and unforgiving responses they might make to that individual, in random order. The researchers found that those who harbor grudges or rehearse their hurt feelings have greater heart rate, blood pressure, corrugator activity, skin conductance and negative emotion than those who imagined forgiving their transgressors.

Blascovich and his colleagues have developed a model that differentiates between threat and challenge appraisals during situations where people pressure themselves to perform well (Seery et al., 2004). Tying their model to the work of Dienstbier (1989), they believe that challenge elicits SAM activity and threat elicits both SAM and HPA activity, yet they have not measured HPA output directly. Instead, reasoning that HPA activity should decrease cardiac output and increase total peripheral resistance, they have manipulated values gained through impedance cardiography and blood pressure measurements to derive values for ventricular contractility, cardiac output and total peripheral resistance (Blascovich et al., 2003). Dienstbier never specified these variables as indicators of HPA activity, and Sherwood et al. (1990), in their guidelines for the use of impedance cardiography, specifically noted that the obtained values had yet (at that time) to be tied theoretically to anything. Wright and Kirby (2003) regarded the model in question as incoherent and self-contradictory, with poorly chosen measures, weaker than predicted results, and changes sometimes opposite those predicted. Furthermore, given the numbers of SAM and HPA chemicals involved, their various potential receptor sites, and their unknown and complex interactions with one another, inferring HPA activity on the basis of autonomic changes would be difficult and probably inaccurate, they believed (Wright & Kirby, 2003).

Blascovich et al. continue their research, which continues to achieve results that usually lie in the direction they specify (Blascovich et al., 2003). Herrald and Tomaka (2002), after using confederates to elicit emotional reactions in experimental participants, were able to distinguish anger, pride and shame not only through the participants' self-reports of the emotions elicited, state self-esteem and the core relational appraisals used, but also through cardiovascular measures such as heart rate, pre-ejection period, total peripheral resistance and cardiac output. Specifically, among those who experience them naturalistically, anger lowers peripheral resistance slightly, while shame raises it (Herrald & Tomaka, 2002). This would result if total peripheral resistance indeed measures the addition of HPA activity, given the research on shame noted in a later chapter. The major trouble with this research line is that the researchers infer HPA activity through a relatively roundabout manner rather than measuring it directly, leaving the matter of actual HPA involvement still in doubt.

Friedberg, Suchday, and Shelov (2007) measured how trait forgiveness affected a number of cardiovascular variables. They instructed participants to recall incidents within the previous 6 months in which someone had angered them. Although they measured total cardiac output, cardiovascular reactivity, total peripheral resistance, heart rate, blood pressure and stroke volume, Friedberg et al. found that trait forgiveness levels were significantly related only to diastolic reactivity (negatively) and to quicker diastolic recovery to baseline levels after recalling the incident (positively).

Although emotions clearly have physiological properties, efforts to study them and differentiate them on that basis remain in their infancy. Given what was noted in earlier chapters, self-reports are unlikely to be accurate and heart rate—since it relies on SAM activity—is unlikely to be a sensitive measure. Measuring the activation of the HPA axis is more likely to effectively reflect visceral emotional activity, but few such studies exist at this time. It is to those that we now turn.

HPA Indicators

Although the autonomic, neuroendocrine, and immune systems all interact with one another using neuropeptides (Cacioppo et al., 2000) physiological research on both stress reactions and emotional states has focused almost entirely on the autonomic nervous system (Gross, 2002), reflecting an overly narrow focus (Cacioppo et al., 2000). Although much research remains to be done in order to understand how HPA activity responds to different emotions and emotion regulation strategies (Gross, 2002), enough studies have been completed to begin to outline this picture.

The Trier Social Stress Test

Many of the discoveries about stress-related cortisol responses have resulted from use of the Trier Social Stress Test (TSST; Kirschbaum, Pirke, & Hellhammer, 1993) by various researchers. Briefly, the TSST, developed at the University of Trier, involves a 10-minute rest period, followed by the experimenter's telling the participant he or she will have 10 minutes to prepare a believable speech soliciting employment that will be videotaped, audiotaped and observed live by a three person committee, who will ask questions and evaluate the participant's speech and behavior for believability. Once the speech is completed, the participant is directed to perform serial subtractions aloud, with the committee still observing and the taping equipment still operating, starting at a large number (1687 and 2083 are each mentioned in articles) and subtracting 13 repeatedly from the difference as quickly and accurately as possible, until told to stop (Kirschbaum et al., 1993).

This task has consistently and repeatedly been found to elicit HPA and SAM responses and to elicit increased subjective ratings of stress (Kirschbaum et al., 1993). Exposure to the TSST improves the recall of emotion-colored words, no matter the valence, but decreases memory of neutral words, demonstrating that this effect does not depend on the similarity of the stress-produced emotional state (Jelicic, Geraerts, Merckelbach, & Guerrieri, 2004). Before exposing participants to the TSST, Kirschbaum, Bartussek, and Strasburger (1992) administered various scales measuring Extraversion, Neuroticism, Psychoticism, Lying, Thrill and Adventure Seeking, Experience Seeking, Disinhibition, Susceptibility to Boredom, Strength of Inhibition, Mobility, Strength of Excitation and Social Desirability. Even with the vast number of possible correlations between cortisol and personality variables, there were no significant differences on any scale variable that would predict the intensity of participants' stress reactions (Kirschbaum et al., 1992).

Specific situational variables are generally more important than personality variables in determining TSST responses, although those with low self-esteem and a negative self-concept have larger HPA responses (Gaab et al., 2005) and habituate more slowly (Gaab et al., 2003). Gaab et al. (2003) studied 48 healthy, nonsmoking male students without chronic medical or psychiatric disorders, either providing them with group cognitive-behavioral stress management (CBSM) sessions or assigning them to a control group 2 weeks before exposure to the TSST. Those given CBSM beforehand had lower stress appraisals, higher challenge appraisals, higher expectations of control, more self-confidence and attenuated cortisol responses during the TSST (Gaab et al., 2003). To determine how long the effects of CBSM last, Hammerfald et al. (2006) randomly assigned 83 healthy college students to either a CBSM or a control condition, followed 4 months later by exposure to the TSST. Again, those previously exposed to CBSM had attenuated cortisol responses compared to those who did not, though the effect size, d, was far larger among men (1.04) than among women (0.15).

In an analogous study design, Rohrmann et al. (1999) studied 60 healthy, nonsmoking males under the age of 35, preparing them to speak unprepared and be rated by people in another room. After attaching participants to devices that measured their heart rate, they then either gave each participant (a) feedback that his heart rate made him appear relaxed, (b) feedback that his heart rate made him appear nervous or (c) no feedback. Those given the relaxed feedback had the highest subsequent heart rates and cortisol levels, those given the nervous feedback had somewhat elevated levels of both and those given no feedback had somewhat elevated heart rates (as would be expected before a speech), but unchanged cortisol levels. However, those given the anxious feedback rated their own subjective anxiety and arousal highest, while those given the relaxed feedback had the lowest scores on both measures. This pattern of high measured arousal coupled with low subjective arousal is identical to what has been observed among repressors (Rohrmann et al., 1999).

Emotions

Alpers, Abelson, Wilhelm, and Roth (2003) found that exposing those with phobias to their phobic stimulus increases their cortisol levels while they anticipate the exposure. Upon exposure, their reported anxiety increases but their cortisol does not rise over its anticipatory levels; and when their anxiety level falls again, their cortisol levels remained elevated. After repeated exposures, their reported anxiety habituates but their cortisol levels do not, showing that anxiety and stress responses can be dissociated (Alpers et al., 2003). Codispoti et al. (2003) exposed 10 healthy male participants to 54 pictures: 18 pictures of household objects, 18 pictures of mutilated bodies and 18 erotic pictures. The pictures of mutilation elicited increases in cortisol, NE and ACTH, while decreasing prolactin; erotic pictures elicited increased prolactin (Codispoti et al., 2003). Hodgson, Freedman, Granger, and Erno (2004) studied 116 frail elderly residents scheduled to move from one nursing facility to another. One week before the slated move, there were no differences in the cortisol cycles of those who moved and those who did not. While the cortisol responses among those not moving did not change, baseline levels rose among movers, and their cortisol cycles flattened after the move. One week after moving, these differences reached their maximum, receding thereafter but never returning to the levels they had maintained before moving (Hodgson et al., 2004).

Lai et al. (2005) studied 80 Hong Kong Chinese subjects who provided six salivary cortisol samples on each of two consecutive workdays: upon awakening, 20 and 40 minutes after awakening, and at 11:00 AM, 4:00 PM and 7:00 PM. Following the final sampling each day, participants were also asked to chart their feelings for that day (and the previous month following the second day) using a Chinese-language mood checklist comprised of 10 positive and 10 negative descriptors, and to complete a test measuring optimism. Optimism correlated significantly with lower awakening cortisol levels, although gender and trait positive affect did not do so. On the other hand, trait positive affect correlated with lower overall cortisol readings when excluding the awakening period. Negative affect and pessimism had no effect on either score. Lai et al. concluded that positive and negative affect each influence cortisol levels independently, with the former having a more profound influence.

Quirin, Kazén, Rohrmann, and Kuhl (2009) studied an implicit measure of affect on cortisol responses. Unlike self-report measures of affect such as the PANAS scales (Watson & Clark, 1994; Watson, Clark, & Tellegen, 1988) their instrument assessed participants' current mood and emotions through the positive or negative associations they generated to nonsense words. Quirin et al. expected that, while correlated with PANAS scores that measure explicit, self-reported affect, the implicit measures they used would tap both conscious and unconscious processes and thus would more accurately predict variations in cortisol output. Demands lower positive affect but threats raise negative affect and increase cortisol reactivity (Kuhl, Kazén, & Koole, 2006). Given this, Quirin et al. predicted that their implicit measure of negative affect would relate to cortisol output more than scores on the PANAS scales did, that low levels of implicit positive affect would predict greater waking cortisol levels, and that high levels of implicit negative affect would predict more reactivity to potentially stressful encounters. Each of these predictions was realized. Those with lower levels of implicit negative affect had no cortisol reactivity, while those with higher levels reacted with increased cortisol output. Meanwhile, low implicit positive affect was associated with the elevated waking cortisol levels already associated with chronic work stress.

Social Threats

In laboratory experiments, ego involvement is a key to eliciting cortisol responses (Gruenewald et al., 2004), with demanding tasks eliciting HPA activation only when the social self is threatened (Kemeny, 2003). People experience such threats whenever (a) they try to meet central or important goals, (b) obstacles outside their control impede them and (c) others' negative evaluations of their behavior or progress in meeting these goals might cause them to lose social status (Rohleder, Beulen, Chen, Wolf, & Kirschbaum, 2007). Stimuli experienced as novel, unpredictable, uncontrollable or threatening prompt substantial cortisol secretion (Dickerson & Kemeny,

2004). Both acute and chronic social rejection elicit large cortisol responses (Gruenewald et al., 2004), part of an integrated cognitive, emotional and physiological response to social threat (Kemeny, 2003). Exclusion, having negatively valued traits or having few positive traits all serve to lower self-esteem and increase any perceived threats to the social self (Dickerson & Kemeny, 2004), as does impugning one's socially salient traits, characteristics or abilities (Gruenewald et al., 2004).

In their meta-analysis, Dickerson and Kemeny (2004) found that experiments involving an active performance that included witnesses' unpredictable, uncontrollable and potentially negative evaluations had effect sizes averaging $d = 0.92$, three times the effect size of studies involving performances with only uncontrollability or social evaluation factors. Studies with neither of these factors reported no significant effect. When uncontrollability is the only factor involved, as occurs during exposure to white noise, it produces no effects. Situations in which important goals are threatened and the desired outcome is outside one's control trigger cortisol production and delay recovery. Anonymity prevents cortisol responses, and motivated tasks without social threat yield small effect sizes if the experimenter assesses individual performance. Thus, social-evaluative stressors appear not only to be more stressful, but also to be different in kind (Dickerson & Kemeny, 2004).

Rohleder et al. (2007) found that among competitive ballroom dancers, cortisol levels began rising significantly 6 hours before the competitions began, with the magnitude of this elevation being highly correlated with how tough the participants believed their judges would be. The dancers' cortisol reactions exceeded those observed among TSST participants, and those among participants performing as couples were higher than those among the same individuals when they competed as members of 12-person teams. Cortisol reactivity showed no correspondence to activity levels or amount of previous competitive experience and did not habituate (Rohleder et al., 2007).

Pruessner, Hellhammer, and Kirschbaum (1999) subjected 52 participants to a computer-generated mental arithmetic task, to be completed under time pressure. Half of the participants received easy problems, the "success" condition, while the other half had difficult ones, the "failure" condition. Failure was associated with vastly increased cortisol ($d = 0.96$), a trend that was slightly more pronounced among those with low self-esteem ($d = 1.03$). Self-esteem levels had no effect on cortisol in the success condition. Additionally, those with higher self-esteem performed better in later trials, while those with lower self-esteem performed worse, regardless of their experimental condition (Pruessner et al., 1999).

Robles, Shaffer, Malarkey, and Kiecolt-Glaser (2006) studied the effects of marital conflict on cortisol levels. While none of their variables affected the husbands' cortisol functioning, the wives' cortisol levels depended on both the negative or positive behavior within the relationship and the negative or positive behavior each spouse exhibited individually. In couples with little overt negativity, the wives' cortisol levels fell over time as expected; but when partners exhibited negative behavior towards one another, the wife's cortisol level dropped more rapidly if her husband later took a problem-solving, supportive or humorous approach to their problems, while they flattened if she did so. Robles et al. believed these differences reflected the degree of social threat the wives assumed. At least among women, appearing to "give in" during marital conflict can apparently be risky and threatening.

Most physiological research has focused on general negative affect rather than specific emotions (Gruenewald et al., 2004). However, as noted earlier, even when "emotions" are induced, researchers often employ music or film clips rather than using naturalistic settings and stimuli likely to produce an actual emotion; thus, they are more likely to elicit somewhat challenging moods. Shame, which originates in situations involving social-evaluative threat (Dickerson & Kemeny, 2004), initiates intense cortisol responses that are not seen in the anger, guilt, anxiety, sadness or general negative affect that such experiments generate (Dickerson, Gruenewald et al., 2004; Dickerson & Kemeny, 2004). Those with lower social status tend to report more shame, but those with higher social status show more HPA reactivity to the TSST, suggesting they have more to lose from others' negative evaluations (Gruenewald, Kemeny, & Aziz, 2006). Writing about self-blaming incidents lowers cortisol levels (Dickerson, Kemeny, Aziz, Kim, & Fahey, 2004).

Gruenewald et al. (2004) altered the TSST to allow some participants to perform their speech and mental arithmetic tasks alone, while others did so before the standard committee. In this experiment, the committee members were explicitly instructed to behave in an emotionally cold and rejecting manner, since the experimenters wanted to determine if increasing participants' shame would lower their self-esteem and trigger HPA reactions. In accordance with their hypotheses, while all participants showed elevated heart rate and blood pressure, only those in the committee condition showed large increases in cortisol levels and reported higher shame and lower self-esteem (Gruenewald et al., 2004).

Dickerson and Kemeny (2004) believed that closely related emotions, such as humiliation and embarrassment, should produce similar results. Lewis and Ramsay (2002) found concordant results. They manipulated normal, healthy 4-year-old children by giving them false feedback of either success or failure while coding their facial expressions and measuring their cortisol levels. The researchers also assessed the degree of self-consciousness in the children's responses after being complimented, asked to dance, encouraged to look at their reflections and called by name. They discovered two types of embarrassment, which they termed "exposure embarrassment" and "evaluative embarrassment". Exposure embarrassment, occurring when people are intensely noticed but not negatively evaluated, is what many people feel when others sing "Happy Birthday" to them in a crowded restaurant. Evaluative embarrassment, typically seen in those children showing the most exposure embarrassment, replaced shame when children were unable to complete their tasks within the allotted time. Girls displayed more shame than boys, boys displayed more evaluative embarrassment than girls and few children displayed both. The children who exhibited either shame or evaluative embarrassment had higher cortisol levels than those who did not ($d = 0.79$).

Rumination

At least three studies have addressed the relations between HPA responses and rumination. Young and Nolen-Hoeksema (2001) found no differences in cortisol reactivity on the TSST between high and low ruminators, and found that rumination did not prolong cortisol responses. When they altered the TSST to induce rumination by providing a longer period between the introduction and the speech, all participants instead increased their problem-focused coping, and their stress responses decreased. Young and Nolen-Hoeksema believed this lack of positive results might have been due to the relative lack of rumination associated with the TSST.

Roger and Najarian (1998) studied 51 student nurses about to take an examination vital to their licensure, a context both the students and independent judges rated as highly stressful. Cortisol levels were assayed immediately after the test and again 3 weeks later, and difference scores between these two levels were computed. These difference scores correlated with the Emotion Control Questionnaire (ECQ; Roger & Najarian, 1989) Rehearsal scale, which Roger and Najarian (1998) believed measures rumination. However, this study has three major problems. First, the study is correlational, so no causality can be presumed. Second, Roger and Najarian (1998) make no mention of controlling the time of day at which the second samples were taken, which might have had a large impact on their subsequent results. Third, a perusal of the 14 items (of 56 total) on the ECQ Rehearsal scale (Roger & Najarian, 1989), especially those with highest correlations to total Rehearsal score (e.g., Question 9: I generally don't bear a grudge—when something is over, it's over, and I don't think about it again $[r = -.62]$; Question 22: I often find myself thinking over things again and again that have made me angry $[r = .59]$; Question 3: I remember things that upset me or make me angry for a long time afterwards $[r = .58]$) show that this scale addresses hostile rumination rather than rumination, per se.

McCullough, Orsulak, Brandon, and Akers (2007) studied how rumination about psychologically painful but not traumatic incidents affects cortisol levels. Of the 115 undergraduate students included in their study, 91 were female. All participants reported psychologically painful transgressions against them in the prior 7 days, such as betrayals of confidence by a romantic partner, insults by friends, romantic infidelity and rejection by romantic partners. Researchers measured participants' cortisol levels up to five times at 2-week intervals, and participants rated how frequently they had ruminated during the preceding two weeks on an 8-item, 6-point Likert scale. Scale items included, "I brooded about how he/she hurt me," "I found the offense playing over and over in my mind," and "Even when I was engaged in other tasks, I thought about how he/she had hurt me", with some items designed to address the intrusiveness of the ruminating. As predicted, the participants' reported ruminative frequency correlated strongly with their cortisol levels. McCullough, Orsulak et al. note that this study has several methodological problems: (a) its design does not lead to a clear timeline of how rumination affects cortisol levels; (b) self-reports of past rumination are unlikely to be accurate; and (c) other potential causes of cortisol activation were not controlled.

As noted in the previous chapter, the physiological study of emotion remains underdeveloped. Implicit measures of affect have provided a good addition, as they take the place of the weak laboratory manipulations that have historically been employed for ethical reasons. As they are used more frequently, the links between the intensity and frequency of negative emotion and the activation of the HPA axis may become clearer.

PART FIVE

EMOTIONAL REGULATION

Coping and Emotional Regulation

WHEN ENCOUNTERING POTENTIALLY stressful stimuli, people instinctively assess whether the events are significant and relevant to them, and if so, what they stand to lose, what behavioral options they have and which of their potential responses would best serve their needs (Folkman & Lazarus, 1985; Folkman, Lazarus, Dunkel-Schetter, DeLongis, & Gruen, 1986; Lazarus, 2001, 2006). They attempt to cope with the stressful situation through a mixture of problem-solving efforts and attempts to regulate the emotions the stressful situation has generated (Folkman & Lazarus, 1980; Lazarus, 2001; Smith & Lazarus, 1993). The primary threat-appraisal process activates the amygdala and the secondary coping appraisals activate the OFC (Ochsner et al., 2002).

Effective coping leads to the quick release of the precise amount of catecholamines needed, with slow and sparing cortisol release and a quick return to baseline cortisol levels (Dienstbier, 1989; Epel et al., 1998). It responds to environmental context, the needs of the person doing the coping and the interactions between the two (Lazarus, 2001, 2006), so people employ complex and variable mixtures of coping strategies that depend on how they appraise various situations (Folkman & Lazarus, 1985; Folkman, Lazarus, Dunkel-Schetter et al., 1986). Both problem solving and emotional regulation are probably involved in almost all coping (Folkman & Lazarus, 1980; Lazarus, 2006), with attempts to alter the situation predominating whenever it can be changed and attempts to alter emotional experiences becoming more intense and frequent whenever it cannot (Folkman & Lazarus, 1980; Folkman, Lazarus, Dunkel-Schetter et al., 1986). In general, as the stakes increase and mastery decreases, emotional coping increases but physical and psychological adjustment suffer afterwards (Folkman, Lazarus, Gruen et al., 1986).

Although distinct stressors may lead to widely contrasting emotions of various intensities, which may include contradictory impulses and feelings (Folkman & Lazarus, 1985), each individual's range of available emotional regulatory strategies tends to be far narrower than her typical range of problem solving strategies (Folkman, Lazarus, Gruen et al., 1986). Unlike defense mechanisms, emotional coping strategies are usually believed to be consciously activated (Garnefski et al., 2002), but the line between defense and coping can be blurry (Vaillant, 1998). At times, defenses may become conscious, while coping strategies sometimes become automated and are no longer accessible to consciousness (Garnefski et al., 2002).

Researchers have been unable to agree on labels for the various types of coping (Penley, Tomaka, & Wiebe, 2002). Attempts to cope by regulating emotional experience include—among other strategies—avoidance, rumination, wishful thinking, self-blaming, blaming others, catastrophizing, thought suppression, putting events into perspective, acceptance, planning, reframing, distraction and recalling positive memories (Davis & Nolen-Hoeksema, 2000; Folkman & Lazarus, 1985; Garnefski et al., 2002; Haslam & Mallon, 2003; Joormann & Siemer, 2004; Lavender & Watkins, 2004; Lyubomirsky et al., 1999; Lyubomirsky et al., 2003; Matheson & Anisman, 2003; Neumann, Waldstein, Sollers, Thayer, Sorkin, 2004; Nolen-Hoeksema & Jackson, 2001; Vickers & Vogeltanz-Holm, 2003; Wenzlaff & Luxton, 2003; Wolfradt & Engelmann, 2003). Emotion-focused avoidance coping is implicated in the subjective pain felt by those with fibromyalgia (Zautra et al., 1999), a disorder characterized by the poor regulation of positive emotions (Zautra et al., 2005). Self-blame and cata-strophizing predict clinical psychiatric and psychological symptomology, while blaming others and passive resignation are also more frequently seen within clinical populations (Garnefski et al., 2002; Wolfradt & Engel-mann, 2003). Perhaps because so many patterns of emotion-focused cop-ing are repetitive and maladaptive, researchers have largely concluded that emotion-focused coping is invariably defensive and undesirable (Diamond & Aspinwall, 2003; Stanton, Kirk, Cameron, & Danoff-Burg, 2000).

However, perspective taking, positive refocusing, and planning (all emotion-focused strategies) do not predict clinical status, and have thus far shown no negative effects (Garnefski et al., 2002). Coping strategies that lead to emotional approach can be productive and effective (Folk-man, Lazarus, Dunkel-Schetter et al., 1986; Stanton, Danoff-Burg, Cam-eron & Ellis, 1994; Stanton, Kirk et al., 2000), though rumination is also considered an emotion-focused approach strategy (Thomsen, Jørgensen, Mehlsen, & Zachariae, 2004). Stanton, Danoff-Burg et al. (2000) found that two specific types of emotional approach behavior—identifying one's emotions and expressing them—reduce emotional intensity and lead to beneficial outcomes. Although they work well independently, these two coping strategies do not effectively decrease physiological arousal or as-sist coping when performed simultaneously; one must first identify one's emotions before expressing them, and then only if an appropriate, validat-ing context can be found for doing so (Kennedy-Moore & Watson, 1999; Stanton, Danoff-Burg et al., 2000).

Emotional Regulation and Coping

Historically, the desirability of cognitively subordinating one's emo-tions has been at the heart of much philosophy (Schmidt & Schulkin, 2000). Since emotion, cognitive systems and action/motor systems each partially regulate one another (Gross, 1999; Knapp, 1992), the term *emotional regulation* can be confusing. Although the regulation of emotions is important, other functional areas such as cognition, motivation, activity, sex, aesthetics, social life and motor responses must also be regulated through executive functioning, probably using affective means (Larsen, 2000b).

As used here, emotional regulation is one form of coping, the broader construct (Gross, 1999). Since emotional activation employs a number of different neural circuits, each of which mutually and simultaneously regulate the others (Goldsmith & Davidson, 2004; Kappas, 2002), regulation is an intrinsic part of emotional arousal and experience (Lewis & Stieben, 2004) that in many ways is as important as the emotional experience itself (Greenberg, 2002a). Given the physiology involved, perhaps no emotion is ever elicited without accompanying regulation (Davidson, 1998; Diamond & Aspinwall, 2003). Because emotional regulatory mechanisms are so integral to the emotional process, separating them for experimental study can be challenging (Goldsmith & Davidson, 2004), though scientists generally resolve this problem by studying how the more consciously cognitive parts of the brain, such as the prefrontal areas, regulate those areas that are less so, such as the subcortical areas (Lewis & Stieben, 2004). However, at least some evidence suggests that the most effective regulatory strategies may involve unconscious processes operating at a holistic level (Baumann & Kuhl, 2002; Jostmann et al., 2005; Koole & Jostmann, 2004).

People continually monitor, evaluate and regulate their moods and emotions (Salovey et al., 1995) by attending to and registering their affective states (Thayer, Rossy, Ruiz-Padial, & Johnsen, 2003), trying to avoid being stuck in uncomfortable (Tice & Wallace, 2000) or inappropriate (Diamond & Aspinwall, 2003) states, and repairing negative emotional states (Thayer et al., 2003). Emotional regulation includes all of the conscious and unconscious processing used to modify the feelings, behaviors and physiological responses that make up emotional experience (Gross, 2001). Although volitional processes to regulate emotion have been studied the most (e.g., Ochsner et al., 2002), regulatory efforts tend to become automated and habitual over time (Davidson, 1998), at which time their physiological indices might change (Goldsmith & Davidson, 2004).

Emotional regulation is a means of achieving effective coping (Tugade & Fredrickson, 2006). Effective regulatory processes attempt to match the current situation, the desired goal and social expectations with the appropriate combination of responses (Diamond & Aspinwall, 2003; Martin, 2000). Regulation is required whenever conditioned physiological, motivational and behavioral responses fail to meet ongoing environmental demands (Gross, 2002) and is evident whenever someone highly motivated to complete a task believes that his negative emotional state will impede reaching this goal (Koole & Jostmann, 2004). Typically, regulation involves modifying an emotion's intensity and timing rather than its character (Sloman, Atkinson, Milligan, & Liotti, 2002), and it may decrease, increase or sustain either positive or negative emotional experiences (Gross, 2002). However, it can also be used to change which emotions are experienced or expressed when an individual is focused elsewhere or wants to replace one emotion with another (Gross, 1999, 2002). For instance, in confrontational situations where anger will be the most effective emotional response available, people preferentially choose to express anger at the expense of experiencing more hedonically satisfying emotions in the shorter term (Tamir, Mitchell, & Gross, 2008). Also, retrospective data suggest that as adults grow older, they alter their regulatory strategies to decrease their experience of negative emotions (John & Gross, 2004).

Since all aspects of emotional experience can be initiated, intensified, diminished, maintained or changed (Eisenberg and Zhou, 2000; Gross,

1999, 2002), regulation can take a variety of forms (Richards & Gross, 2000), with various strategies directed at the situational, attentional, cognitive and behavioral levels (Gross, 2001, 2002). In adults, the regulatory strategies chosen may vary widely, depending on the individual's personality, culture (Consedine, Magai, & Bonanno, 2002) and larger goals (Diamond & Aspinwall, 2003). Regulation may occur before, during or after the emotional process begins (Gross, 1999, 2002). Gross (2002) lists five common regulation strategies occurring progressively later in the emotional process: (a) situation selection (e.g., avoiding depressing acquaintances), (b) situation modification (e.g., changing the subject), (c) attentional employment (e.g., focusing on something across the room), (d) cognitive change (e.g., reappraising an ambiguous situation) and (e) expressive suppression (e.g., hiding one's embarrassment or swallowing one's anger). In general, regulatory efforts that take place earlier in this sequence have fewer and less harmful effects than those occurring later (Gross, 2001, 2002).

According to Tomkins (1995), people have four general goals regarding their moods and emotions: (a) minimize their experience of negative emotions, (b) maximize their experience of positive affect, (c) minimize their degree of emotional inhibition and (d) maximize their ability to fulfill the first three goals. However, as Fredrickson (2000) noted, people find more personal meaning in emotional states that carry more information about relevant personal or social concerns. For instance, love means more than pleasure, while shame means more than anxiety. According to Fredrickson, people strive to achieve or maintain positive states with high meaning, avoid negative states with high meaning, and ignore both positive and negative states with little meaning. Intensity plays no role in these considerations (Fredrickson, 2000), suggesting that in most situations people probably focus more on achieving their goals than on regulating their emotions (Diamond & Aspinwall, 2003).

Emotional regulation makes the person's physiology more adaptive and regulated (Fosha, 2004). Those good at regulating their physiologies have shorter startle responses and fewer enduring upsetting emotions after encountering negative stimuli (Jackson et al., 2003). This often involves managing attention and interpretation (Eisenberg & Zhou, 2000) through self-generated internal imagery (Davidson, 1998) and altered behavior (Rusting & Nolen-Hoeksema, 1998). Those who employ poor emotional regulation techniques, such as those who ruminate and worry excessively, do not adequately regulate their physiologies, instead developing decreased heart rate variability and poor vagal tone (Thayer et al., 2003).

The ability to regulate negative emotional behavior productively is considered vital for mental health (Panksepp, 2001). When negative emotions can be avoided or neutralized, people compartmentalize their emotional experiences; but when their emotions are primarily negative, they integrate their emotional experiences, a process requiring far more effort (Showers, 2000). This integration is fundamental to the formation of the self system and its components, making the regulation of mood and emotion a vital part of later personal functioning and growth (Saarni, 1997). Disrupted regulation causes dysfunctional relationship patterns (Izard, 2002) that lead to social rejection (Erickson & Schulkin, 2003), even in early childhood (Schmidt et al., 2003). Both stifled expression and venting lead to negative outcomes (Izard, 2002; Izard, et al., 2002). Conversely, proficient modulation improves cognitive and adaptive abilities (Izard, 2002; Izard et al., 2002) and increases both adults' (Erickson & Schulkin, 2003) and children's (Fabes et al., 1999) social acceptance.

Positive Affect as Emotional Regulation

THOUGH THEY ARE basic to the formation of the self (Emde, 1992), what we often call positive emotions have no defined action tendencies, no associated drives toward specific behavior and no individualized displays or arousal patterns (Fredrickson, 2003; Fredrickson & Levenson, 1998). Unlike the more numerous negative emotions, they all share a relative lack of autonomic reactivity (Fredrickson, Mancuso, Branigan, & Tugade, 2000) and the same expression, the Duchenne (natural) smile (Fredrickson, 2003; Fredrickson & Levenson, 1998). Because of this, many choose to categorize these states not as emotions, but as positive moods (Gendolla, 2000) or, more broadly, as positive affect (e.g., Isen, 2000), which is how they will be characterized here.

Encountering a negative emotional stimulus causes immediate eye blink responses (Hamm et al., 1997) and systolic blood pressure reactivity (Gendolla et al., 2001) that can last for up to two days, particularly among those with poor social connectedness (Ong & Allaire, 2005). While negative emotions organize people to solve current crises, positive affect neutralizes negative emotions' physiological and psychological effects (Fredrickson & Levenson, 1998; Fredrickson, Mancuso et al., 2000; Shapiro et al., 2001) and creates resources for solving future problems (Fredrickson, 2003). It hastens recovery from the cardiovascular effects of emotional activation and increases brain levels of DA (Fredrickson, Mancuso et al., 2000), the principal neurotransmitter used by the BAS. While experiencing positive affect does not eliminate the cardiovascular affects caused by subsequent negative emotional states (Fredrickson, Mancuso et al., 2000), it increases social connectedness (Fredrickson, 2003), which decreases cardiovascular reactivity, speeds up cardiovascular recovery from negative emotions and increases later positive affect (Ong & Allaire, 2005).

Negative emotions lead to increased reactivity (Isen, 2001) and linear thinking (Fredrickson, 2003), but positive affect increases the options people perceive (Izard et al., 2002), creates cognitive resources for future problem solving (Fredrickson, 2003), and makes good situations seem attractive (Panksepp, 2001). Those with heightened positive affect are more able to shift flexibly and adaptively between the linear, detail-focused cognitive style more often associated with negative emotion (Baumann & Kuhl, 2005b) and the global (Fredrickson, 2003) and intuitive (Bolte, Goschke, & Kuhl, 2003) processing strategies available only in positive moods states. This flexibility can be observed as people assess diverse situations and stimuli, including their social relationships and contexts (Casciaro, Carley, & Krackhardt, 1999). Positive affect fosters (a) optimism, (b) creativity, (c) social connectedness and prosocial behavior, (d) cognitive speed, complexity, elaboration and flexibility, (e) efficient problem solving, (f) perspective-taking and (g) nondefensiveness (Fredrickson, 2003; Isen, 2000, 2001). Positive affect leads to improved social skills through an increased interest in others, better awareness of others and improved cognitive quality, in turn leading to increased popularity (Casciaro et al., 1999).

Like trait negative emotionality, trait positive affect appears to be largely attributable to the environment in which one was reared (Ong & Allaire, 2005). Those high in trait positive affect are better at grasping the friendship patterns among large social networks, while those high in trait negative emotionality are better at discerning who is taking advice from whom (Casciaro et al., 1999). Because they think more clearly, rapidly, accurately, and with greater complexity and less defensiveness, those with high trait positive affect routinely make more creative, innovative, flexible and prosocial decisions (Isen, 2000, 2001).

While negative emotions narrow one's focus to fight/flight considerations (Fredrickson & Joiner, 2002), positive affect creates resiliency (Fredrickson, 2003; Isen, 2000). Negative emotions have no impact on coping (Fredrickson & Joiner, 2002), but positive affect and broadened thinking mutually enhance one another (Fredrickson, 2003). Effective broad-minded coping strategies (such as interpersonal trust and attributional optimism) and positive affect mediate one another, with the experience of positive affect leading to the increased use of broad-minded coping up to two weeks afterwards (Fredrickson & Joiner, 2002). By finding positive personal meaning in even mundane experiences, those with heightened positive affect prepare themselves to achieve better outcomes when negative events inevitably occur later in their lives (Fredrickson, 2003).

Being able to experience positive affect even in the midst of negative events is associated with resilience, which can be improved with practice (Tugade & Fredrickson, 2006). Effectively regulating grief reduces its duration (Bonanno & Kaltman, 1999). People cope with it well if their positive affect remains high (Lindstrom, 2002), and remaining primarily positive during the grieving period leads to better adjustment later (Bauer & Bonanno, 2001). Even in highly stressful conditions involving intensely negative emotions, maintaining positive affect provides protection against pathological breakdowns (Moskowitz, 2001). Since negative self-referring emotions (such as shame, embarrassment, jealousy, sadness and loneliness) negatively bias thoughts and relationships (Leary, 2000), people often try to modulate them by inducing positive affect (Shapiro et al., 2001). By inducing humor, optimism, exploration and relaxation, resilient people maintain the ability to act flexibly while limiting the intensity and duration of their negative emotional disruptions (Tugade & Fredrickson, 2006).

Across cultures, people behave in ways they predict will increase their future happiness, nearly always overestimating how happy they will become (Fredrickson, 2003). Some of these strategies do not produce affective results, and others actually decrease happiness (Tkach & Lyubomirsky, 2006). Although most of the time most people report being happier than not (Larsen, 2000b), most—even in vastly different cultures—report being only mildly so, and nobody reports being perfectly ecstatic or fulfilled (Biswas-Diener, Vitterso, & Diener, 2005). Those who are happiest, most loving and most hopeful live longer and better than those who are not (Fredrickson, 2003); and once basic needs are fulfilled within one's society one is apt to be happier than not (Biswas-Diener et al., 2005). Although many feign happiness for defensive reasons (King & Pennebaker, 1998), genuinely happy people find joy in ambiguous situations while avoiding situations likely to lower their mood, two things unhappy people rarely do (Hirt & McCrae, 2000).

Societies may socialize their members to act happy even when they are not so that social interaction can be facilitated (Biswas-Diener et al., 2005). Still, happiness, contentment, amusement and pride all contribute to a pleasurable life and take little effort to initiate or maintain (Kunzmann, Stange, & Jordan, 2005). Other positive states like joy, hope, self-worth and love are valuable for increasing optimism, resilience, and social connectedness (Fredrickson, 2000; Isen, 2001). Contentment and amusement serve as particularly good buffers against stress (Fredrickson & Levenson, 1998), while more effortful positive states—such as interest and inspiration—create active, prosocial values and an orientation towards personal growth, suggesting that pleasant feelings that promote hedonism can be separated conceptually from positive affect that fosters prosocial involvement (Kunzmann et al., 2005).

Happy people have negative emotions just like others do (Abbe, Tkach, & Lyubomirsky, 2003). They allow negative emotions to unfold naturally without disavowing them or clinging to them (Tugade & Fredrickson, 2006). According to Abbe et al., happy people have a number of distinguishing characteristics. They do not compare themselves to others. They are bolstered by their successes but are not destroyed by their failures. They take a more positive attitude towards the positive and a less negative attitude towards the negative in life than others do. They use humor to cope with their past mistakes and transgressions, and focus on the improvements they have made since committing them. They think in ways that support positive emotions and positive self-regard even when they are thinking about negative events, moods and emotions (Abbe et al., 2003).

Being or becoming happy apparently involves four qualities: one's emotional set point, attitude and expectations, circumstances and intentional behavior (Sheldon et al., 2010; Sheldon & Lyubomirsky, 2006). In general, researchers assume that everyone has an individual range of potential happiness above which they are unlikely ever to go (Sheldon et al., 2010; Sheldon & Lyubomirsky, 2006). The initial desire to become happier and the expectations that one will become happier can cause improvement separate from all other factors (Sheldon et al., 2010). Subjective interpretations of one's changes in happiness may also be more beneficial to increased happiness than any of the other factors (Sheldon & Lyubomirsky, 2006). Changing circumstances increase short-term happiness and satisfaction, but people habituate to their new circumstances quickly and these changes do not lead to long-term gains in happiness (Sheldon et al., 2010; Sheldon & Lyubomirsky, 2006).

Only goal-directed behavior (such as working to improve a relationship, become competent at a valued skill, or achieve autonomy) increases long-term happiness, and then it does so only as long as the work continues and succeeds at reaching its intended goals (Sheldon et al., 2010). By focusing energy and behavior, pursuing meaningful goals diversifies experience and increases positive affect, though negative emotion is not decreased much, if at all (Sheldon & Lyubomirsky, 2006). Continued progress towards these goals leads to feeling better, so people try harder and persist at the efforts longer (Linley, Nielsen, Wood, Gillett, & Biswas-Diener, 2010).

People generally pick strategies to improve their happiness that match their personalities: extraverts affiliate with others; conscientious people pursue goals; and agreeable people try to get along (Tkach & Lyubomirsky, 2006). Being able to choose whether to attempt to increase one's sense of wellbeing as well as which strategy to use also affects whether the attempts will be successful (Sin & Lyubomirsky, 2009). Relying on one's personal strengths to reach these goals reliably taps personal growth and autonomy, because one's strengths correspond to one's values and sense of self (Linley et al., 2010). Failure to reach one's goals to increase wellbeing leads to increased unhappiness, reflecting an inherent risk in making such attempts (Sheldon et al., 2010). Although Aristotle believed that living life to one's fullest potential in the service of others leads to the greatest happiness, and many current researchers agree (Kashdan, Biswas-Diener, & King, 2008), it remains unclear whether such activity always results in an increased sense of wellbeing (Biswas-Diener, Kashdan, & King, 2009). Ultimately, the stories one tells oneself about one's life seem to be the biggest determinant of happiness (Kashdan et al., 2008).

Positive affect provides the most effective way of managing negative emotions. While not decreasing them, positive affect nullifies many of their physiological and psychological effects. As we shall later see, it also allows for the kinds of deep, intuitive, unconscious regulation strategies that are unavailable otherwise.

The Development of Emotion Regulation

STUDIES OF EMOTION regulation in normally developing children remain sparse (Goldsmith & Davidson, 2004), with questions far outnumbering answers (Diamond & Aspinwall, 2003). In observational studies, it appears that young children experience emotions more strongly than adults, though they do so for shorter durations (Panksepp, 2001). Various emotional experiences have been hypothesized to be vital to optimal development in children, even if they first cause massive distress (Izard et al., 2002). Though young children's HPA axes are initially much more active than adults', those children whose HPA axes are initially most active when in strange situations but who later calm themselves adequately adapt better than either those whose HPA axes are initially relatively inactive or those who are unable to calm themselves (Diamond & Aspinwall, 2003). Similarly, although higher vagal tone is considered adaptive in children and adults, in whom it leads to increased emotional regulation and behavioral flexibility, higher vagal tone in young infants is associated with increased emotional reactivity (Diamond & Aspinwall, 2003).

Relatively unregulated (Izard et al., 2002), newborns respond affectively to various sensory stimuli, beginning with smell (Fernandez et al., 2004; Schore, 2001a). Eight-week-old infants born via forceps-assisted delivery exhibit the most intense stress reactions when given their scheduled immunizations, while those born through elective caesarian sections exhibit the least, suggesting that perinatal experiences can prime stress responses (Taylor, Fisk, & Glover, 2000). Learning increases the positive expressions in 4-month-old infants, while extinction increases their negative expressions and cardiovascular reactivity, but not their output of cortisol (Lewis, Hitchcock, & Sullivan, 2004). Their emotional intensity, overall daily cortisol output, timing of peak cortisol levels and efforts to regulate their emotions show no interrelationships (Ramsay & Lewis, 2003).

Frustrating 4- to 6-month-old infants by violating their expectations in either social (expecting their mother's response) or nonsocial (expecting that their movements will cause something to happen) settings results in their displaying one of two emotions (Lewis & Ramsay, 2005). When they believe their actions might resolve the situation, they behave angrily, but when they feel defeated and no longer believe their actions will benefit them, they react with sadness (Bennett et al., 2002). Their anger does not bring about cortisol reactivity, but their sadness does, with more intense sadness leading to increased cortisol reactivity (Bennett et al., 2002; Lewis & Ramsay, 2005). Once their initial expectations are again met, angry infants become more interested in the offending stimulus, while sad infants behave less joyfully (Lewis & Ramsay, 2005).

Six-month-old infants receiving inoculations respond with increased cortisol and negative emotions (Ramsay & Lewis, 2003). By 12 months of age, their expression of positive affect during feeding times predicts their weight gain (Pridham, Brown, Clark, Sondel, & Green, 2002). At that age, typical infants also begin to regulate their responses to affective stimuli like music (Schmidt et al., 2003). By 18 to 24 months, normally developing children can verbally categorize various emotional experiences (Gavazzi, 2003). From then onward, as they learn to label and regulate their emotions, their emotional lives come increasingly under cognitive control (Izard et al., 2002). By age 3, children link emotions to external causes, and between ages 3 and 4, they link their linguistic categories to others' facial expressions (Gavazzi, 2003).

By then, the children who have learned to regulate their emotions effectively stand out clearly. Those who focus their attention, enjoy low-intensity activities, inhibit their aggressive behavior and tolerate minor frustrations react less during intensely negative peer interactions (Fabes et al., 1999) and enjoy greater peer popularity (Schmidt et al., 2003). By age 4, children understand that memory makes emotions weaker; by 5, they understand that memories of a disturbing situation can reenact the emotions associated with it; and by age 6 or 7, they realize that others do not always show how they really feel (Gavazzi, 2003). During this maturation process, social and moral precepts are internalized (Izard et al., 2002).

Regulatory skills are originally learned and practiced within families, first in dyads and later individually (Diamond & Aspinwall, 2003; Fosha, 2001; Schore, 2001a, 2001b; Sloman et al., 2002). When overly aroused, infants need help maintaining their internal organization (Bowlby, 1969), and the attachment process between an infant and his or her caregiver apparently evolved primarily to help children learn to regulate their internal emotional states (Bowlby, 1973). Infants attach to their caregivers, who ideally mirror their emotional experiences but induce positive affect in them whenever they are about to become overwhelmed by intensely negative emotions (Schore, 2001a). Attachment does not reduce negative emotions directly, but instead allows reparative and prosocial positive affect to emerge through personal interactions within a caring relationship (Fosha, 2004).

These dyadic attachments allow emotional regulatory processes to reach optimal levels, with neither too little nor too much regulation of individual states, through both empathic attunement to negative states and positive affective engagement to repair those states (Diamond & Aspinwall, 2003).

Parents effectively and accurately model their infant's internal emotional environment by mirroring the child's expressions while also helping the child understand intentionality in both herself and others, beginning with the caretaker (Fonagy, 1999). Over time, the infant regulates her emotional intensity with increasing autonomy, the primary work occurring as the two partners move between individually regulating themselves and dyadically regulating one another (Diamond & Aspinwall, 2003). The child internally begins to conceptualize the external world, form a sense of herself and distinguish fantasy from reality (Fonagy, 1999).

The continual transitioning between ongoing internal regulation and adult reparative efforts, which lasts until the negative can be borne and transformed, is the essence of emotional regulation and forms the most vital aspect of the attachment process (Diamond & Aspinwall, 2003). It also assists the infant's neural growth, especially in the OFC, which is undergoing a critical growth period from about 9 to 18 months of age and which increasingly takes over regulatory functions from the caregiver as it matures (Schore, 2001a). Over time, infants' emotional behavior changes to match their parents' abilities to help them regulate it, based largely on the parents' own attachment histories (Sloman et al., 2002). Fonagy (1999) notes that (a) attachment styles persist across time between two-thirds and three-fourths of the time, (b) those with early, secure attachments are more likely to become securely attached adults and (c) those securely attached as infants are several times more likely to raise securely attached children themselves.

As long as they lead to reparative efforts by the caregiver, even small missteps in emotional mirroring by the caregiver assist the infant's growth (Schore, 2001a). Framing preschoolers' negative emotions in mildly negative terms helps them develop emotional understanding, while framing their positive emotions in mildly positive terms helps them develop both emotional understanding and emotional competence (Colwell & Hart, 2006). If a lack of attunement leads to stress, overcoming it through reparative efforts brings relief (Schore, 2001a). Like positive affect, secure attachments result in cognitive flexibility, creativity, openness, optimism and the use of positive experiences to outweigh negative ones, leading Diamond and Aspinwall (2003) to conclude that the vital element in secure attachment is the positive affect it engenders.

Secure attachments probably lead to different infant behavior in different cultures (Rothbaum, Weisz, & Pott, 2001). Conversely, a child might be very securely attached, but not necessarily the most highly adapted to the culture in which she finds herself (Gjerde, 2001). In the United States, being self-contained, autonomous and independent is acceptable and valued, while in Japan being able to get along with others harmoniously is more highly prized (de Rivera, 1977). Though it predicts future emotional and behavioral self-control, attachment security is probably related primarily to the degree of emotional acceptance and attunement between child and caretaker (Schore, 2001a) rather than the child's future behavior (Rothbaum et al., 2001). Perhaps the quality of attachment is related to the proportion of the child's emotional life he is allowed to acknowledge and feel good about experiencing fully. Children treasured while fully experiencing the complete emotional gamut should be most securely attached, but not necessarily the best adapted to their cultures (Gjerde, 2001).

The lack of adult predictability leads to insecure attachments and inadequate regulation in young children (Sloman et al., 2002). If secure attachments help the infant internalize regulatory strategies, traumatic or other less than optimal attachment patterns hinder the infant's neural growth and ability to regulate later emotional states (Schore, 2001b). Because the early and prolonged exposure to stress compromises the child's later abilities to regulate stress, emotions and relationships (Taylor, Lerner, Sage,

Lehman, & Seeman, 2004), a mother's unresponsiveness to her infant's distress at 18 months predicts that child's inability to regulate his attention effectively at age 5 (Rodriguez et al., 2005). Ineffective or nonexistent mirroring of the child's expressions can create voids in her affective regulation (Fonagy, 1999), in turn leading to later deficits in social competence (Repetti et al., 2002).

Children with hostile and traumatic backgrounds have higher baseline cortisol levels, less cortisol reactivity and more intense, frequent and prolonged stress reactions than do children from more nurturing families (Taylor et al., 2004). Dissociation and neuronal death may result (Schore, 2001a, b). Children with chaotic and traumatic backgrounds recognize their emotions poorly, lack social and emotional regulatory skills (Taylor et al., 2004) and have less successful peer relationships, with girls being more avoidant and boys being more likely to be victimized and rejected (Repetti et al., 2002). They cope poorly with their ongoing allostatic loads, reacting with hostility, depression and anxiety, which mediate the relationships between their childhood environment and their later physical and mental health (Repetti et al., 2002; Taylor et al., 2004).

Children learn to regulate their emotions in dyads through their caregivers' induction of positive affect and adequate mirroring of their negative emotional experience. When people do not get these experiences as children, they often seek them in adulthood from counselors and therapists.

Common Regulation Strategies

As NOTED EARLIER, emotional regulatory strategies can take place at any point in the sequence between choosing which situations to enter and determining how to express (or how fully to express) one's emotions (Gross, 2001, 2002). Those occurring later, Gross (2002) believes, are more likely to have adverse results. Of the various types of emotional modulation listed by Gross (2002), several have been studied extensively, but others have received little research attention. Most of the research on emotional regulation has studied a few strategies: expressive suppression, venting, reappraisal and cognitive suppression. The rest of this chapter will summarize some of this research, as well as a few other strategies. Two other often used and widely researched regulation strategies, avoidance and rumination, have been saved for separate chapters.

Reappraisal

As noted in an earlier chapter, appraisal theories of emotion posit that specific emotions are elicited by conscious or unconscious cognitive appraisals of environmental stimuli (e.g., Smith & Lazarus, 1993). Reappraisal is the intentional cognitive process of changing the emotional reaction a given situation arouses by altering its subjective meaning or reaching new conclusions regarding what a stimulus or event means, its effects and how best to respond (Butler et al., 2003; Gross, 1999, 2002; Richards & Gross, 2000). In practice, it can take at least two forms, either reinterpreting emotional contexts or taking a detached point of view towards emotional stimuli, each of which have somewhat different underlying neural mechanisms (Ochsner & Gross, 2008). Relying on propositional processing (Smith & Kirby, 2001) to change how peripheral and visceral signals have been evaluated (Ochsner et al., 2002), reappraisal aids coping (Lazarus, 2001) by decreasing negative emotions without completely eliminating them (Ochsner et al., 2002). It activates areas of the PFC and ACC normally associated with cognition while deactivating the amygdala and insula, areas more associated with emotional processing (Ochsner & Gross, 2008).

Study participants advised to reappraise their emotional experience in laboratory settings have consistently reported less intense negative emotion than those in the control groups, and unlike those who were told to suppress their emotional expression, their levels of positive affect have remained comparable to those found among the controls (Butler et al., 2003). Reappraisal has not affected verbal memory, and the nonverbal memory of those instructed to reappraise has actually exceeded that found among those in the control group (Richards & Gross, 2000). Reappraisal does not require as much attention as suppression strategies (Gross, 2001), but it sometimes requires a lot of sustained and concentrated effort to overcome continuing signals from the viscera (Ochsner et al., 2002). Using fMRI technology, Ochsner et al. (2002) found that reappraisal decreases amygdalar activity while activating the medial and lateral PFC, areas more typically involved in working memory and response selection. Neural networks required for reappraisal have been implicated in selective attention, working memory, determining emotional meaning and monitoring and regulating physiological responses (Ochsner et al., 2002; Ochsner & Gross, 2008). During reappraisal, the dorsolateral, medial and ventrolateral areas of the PFC are activated quickly (within 4.5 seconds) and they dampen the activity of the amygdala and insula in about 10.5 to 15 seconds (Goldin, McRae, Ramel, & Gross, 2008). Reappraisal also sometimes employs neural networks involved in suppressing visceral feedback, although this probably happens only during the most successful attempts to reappraise intensely negative stimuli (Ochsner et al., 2002).

Although Bennett et al. (2003) have shown that appraisals for emotionally charged events may remain stable for a week or more, several researchers have investigated the effects of reappraising such situations by altering participants' perceptions of the environmental context. In accordance with Smith's and Lazarus's (1993) ideas about secondary coping appraisals, Harmon-Jones et al. (2003) decided to deliberately anger people and measure their brain activity. They concocted a plausible story designed to anger their participants while varying the secondary appraisal conditions, which involved whether participants' actions could or could not help resolve the situation favorably. Though all participants' self-reports indicated that they experienced no emotions but anger, those who believed that their actions could have an effect showed significantly more left than right prefrontal EEG activity, while those who believed they could have no effect showed significantly more right prefrontal EEG activity (Harmon-Jones et al., 2003). As Harmon-Jones et al. noted, their evidence showed that different coping appraisals were associated with differing neural activity.

In general, individuals' choice of coping methods varies from situation to situation depending on their ongoing environmental appraisals (Folkman & Lazarus, 1985; Folkman, Lazarus, Dunkel-Schetter et al., 1986), but the degree that any one person uses reappraisal as a coping method remains fairly constant (Folkman, Lazarus, Gruen et al., 1986). Perhaps because reappraisal is related to mood repair (John & Gross, 2004), those using more reappraisal are less likely to develop clinical complaints (Garnefski et al., 2002). In particular, depression is associated with a lack of employing reappraisal (Matheson & Anisman, 2003). However, when one's new appraisals do not jibe with the clear facts of an interpersonal situation, reappraisal can result in poorer psychological health (Penley et al., 2002).

Emotional Expression

People often explicitly or implicitly believe that venting, the unrestrained release of emotions, will ease their emotional distress (Kennedy-Moore & Watson, 1999), especially when circumstances tax or exceed their personal coping resources (Mendes et al., 2003). Most modern theories of psychotherapy have posited that permitting, feeling and understanding emotional experiences are important, but expressing those emotions in a safe environment is equally important (Whelton, 2004). Available evidence suggests that expressing one's negative emotions only increases adaptation if (a) the emotions are fully processed first (Stanton, Kirk et al., 2000), (b) expressing emotions meshes with one's personal style, (c) the audience is empathic, receptive and supportive and (d) the audience validates the expresser and helps improve his self-esteem (Kennedy-Moore & Watson, 1999).

Expressing one's emotions congruently in such situations reduces stress, improves health and increases subjective life satisfaction among both males and females (Stanton, Kirk et al., 2000). Effective expression buffers the effects of stress on the immune system (Miller et al., 2002) and often precedes therapeutic change—not because the expression causes change, but because it signals that the necessary cognitive changes are taking place within an environment that accepts the client, encourages open communication and permits behavioral change (Kennedy-Moore & Watson, 1999). Even writing about previously experienced traumas reduces their impact, with the best predictor of these effects being the proportion of words in the writing that suggest insight (Pennebaker & Graybeal, 2001). Such writing leads to decreased distress; improved self-concept; increased resilience, autonomy, personal growth and self-acceptance; and an improved sense of personal mastery when measured three months later (Hemenover, 2003). Even if the writing is not shared with others, intrusive thoughts and avoidance decrease and subjective distress is reduced; but sharing one's writing decreases the effects on depression more fully and also reduces physical symptoms (Radcliffe, Lumley, Kendall, Stevenson, & Beltran, 2007).

Venting may also have negative side effects associated with its use (Izard, 2002). Bushman, Baumeister, and Phillips (2001) found that although people enjoy verbally attacking others and would continue doing so if they believed it will help them modulate their moods, this expressive behavior actually increases their subsequent negative emotion and aggression. Stroebe, Stroebe, Schut, Zech, and van den Bout (2002) found that during bereavement, greater social disclosure leads to greater distress. When emotional congruence is low and verbal, facial, postural and vocal expressions do not coincide (as often occurs among those with PTSD) the expression of emotions when discussing prior traumas can be counterproductive and lead to increased distress (Negrao, Bonanno, Noll, Putnam, & Trickett, 2005).

Distraction

People often distract themselves when they want to complete important ongoing tasks and they encounter relatively mild negative stimuli (Mackintosh & Mathews, 2003). Men generally use this strategy more than women do (Davis & Nolen-Hoeksema, 2000; Neumann et al., 2004; Nolen-Hoeksema & Jackson, 2001). Mackintosh and Mathews found that by not paying attention to previously neutral items after they have been associated with items carrying a moderately negative valence, people are able to avoid experiencing the associated negative emotions. Distraction improves the mood of dysphoric people (Joormann & Siemer, 2004; Lavender & Watkins, 2004), decreasing anger (Neumann et al., 2004) and decreasing or preventing rumination (Lavender & Watkins, 2004; Neumann et al., 2004).

Distraction allows problems to be effectively solved (Lyubomirsky et al, 1999) and moods to recover (Lavender & Watkins, 2004). It regulates mood in both the short and long terms better than rumination (Lyubomirsky et al, 1999), with those who distract themselves reporting less distress than those who ruminate (Vickers & Vogeltanz-Holm, 2003). Compared to rumination, distraction is not associated with more memories of positive events (Joormann & Siemer, 2004). Although distraction levels are unrelated to depressive severity among third graders, by seventh grade those who use more distraction have less severe depressive symptoms (Abela, Vanderbilt, & Rochon, 2004). However, long-term distraction strategies are a factor in thought suppression (Wenzlaff & Luxton, 2003), an extremely problematic strategy that will be addressed next.

Thought Suppression

The suppression of thoughts requires both (a) an unconscious monitoring mechanism that maintains vigilance for unwelcome thoughts and (b) a determined conscious effort to distract oneself from these targeted negative thoughts before they reach consciousness (Wenzlaff & Luxton, 2003). An active executive process (Anderson et al., 2004), suppressing individual thoughts increases the activation within the pregenual ACC (Wyland et al., 2003). Suppressing memories also involves, among other areas, the dorsolateral and ventrolateral PFC (Anderson et al., 2004); and suppressing all thought activates the insula (Wyland et al., 2003). Suppressing thoughts causes four unintended changes in their frequency: (a) they initially increase; (b) they intrude whenever cognitive demands change; (c) they rebound after suppression ends (Wenzlaff & Wegner, 2000); and (d) they increase during stressful times (Wenzlaff & Luxton, 2003).

Thought suppression has been shown to increase impulsivity and concrete thinking (Baumeister, 1990) and to decrease the certainty people hold regarding the accuracy of their other thoughts (Wenzlaff, Rude, & West, 2002), with the suppressed thoughts being credited to others (Wenzlaff & Wegner, 2000). Suppressing stereotypical thoughts generally leads to congruent stereotypical behavior, while suppressing personality traits often leads to their being projected onto others (Wenzlaff & Wegner, 2000). Those with invisible stigmas tend to suppress their thoughts about them; and while their social abilities are not adversely affected, their thoughts become more intrusive (Smart & Wegner, 1999). According to Wenzlaff and Wegner, since automatic thoughts occur frequently, they are generally easier to suppress than random thoughts, and thoughts connected to emotionally relevant information are generally more difficult to suppress than neutral information.

However, since targeted emotional thoughts usually recur fairly regularly, they are often relatively easy to suppress (Wenzlaff & Wegner, 2000). Though blocked from consciousness, these thoughts continue to activate emotional preparedness and behavioral readiness through associative channels, and they may continue to do so until they are brought to consciousness and released (Wegner & Smart, 1997). Such processes have been implicated in a variety of pathological outcomes, such as Obsessive-Compulsive Disorder and agoraphobia (Friman, Hayes, & Wilson, 1998; Wenzlaff & Wegner, 2000), recurrent major depressive episodes (Wenzlaff et al., 2002), PTSD (Friman et al. 1998; Wenzlaff & Wegner, 2000; Whittlesey et al., 1999), and the hypercritical behavior among families of schizophrenics that has been shown to increase the patients' psychotic symptoms (Scazufca & Kuipers, 1999). Attempting to suppress traumatic thoughts leads to PTSD and attempting to suppress intrusive thoughts leads to obsessive-compulsive disorder, with the suppression attempts in each case creating anxiety (Wenzlaff & Wegner, 2000). Attempting to suppress depressogenic thoughts and thought patterns does not change their quantity or frequency (Wenzlaff et al., 2002).

When thought suppression fails, it results in intrusive, ruminative thought patterns (Wenzlaff & Luxton, 2003; Wenzlaff et al., 2002). Ending thought suppression increases the volume of negative thoughts far beyond what would have occurred had it never been instituted (Wenzlaff & Wegner, 2000) because the unconscious monitoring processes continue to detect targeted thoughts and paradoxically bring them to conscious awareness (Wenzlaff & Luxton, 2003). Because of this, Wenzlaff and Luxton found, after controlling for initial levels of rumination and dysphoria, those who employed thought suppression under stressful conditions increased their rumination and dysphoria more than experimental controls. Firefighters, who tend to suppress thoughts associated with traumatic accidents, report frequent rumination (Haslam & Mallon, 2003).

Expressive Suppression

Although emotions help organize experience, the ability to inhibit their expression can be found in all higher primates (Consedine et al., 2002). Requiring constant self-directed attention (Gross, 2001), suppressing the expression of those negative emotions already subjectively experienced (Gross, 1999) reduces but does not eliminate the expression of a particular emotion (Gross & Levenson, 1997). Unlike reappraisal, expressive suppression is not associated with the attention, clarity or repair required to regulate moods and emotions effectively (John & Gross, 2004). Coming relatively late in the emotional process, the frontal activation involved in the expressive suppression of negative emotions increases activation of the amygdala and insula rather than decreasing it as occurs during reappraisal (Ochsner & Gross, 2008). Because of this, negative emotions actually increase; even with suppressive efforts in effect, those who employ this strategy express as much negative emotion as others do (John & Gross, 2004).

Suppressing the expression of negative emotions markedly decreases the later experience of positive affect (Butler et al., 2003; Gross, 2001; Harmon-Jones et al., 2003). However, suppressing the expression of positive affect decreases its experience directly (John & Gross, 2004). Rather than altering negative and painful emotional experiences (Gross & Levenson, 1997) or improving subjective experience (Richards & Gross, 2000), expressive suppression of negative emotions increases subjective distress (Stanton, Danoff-Burg et al., 2000) and makes emotional reactions more memorable than they otherwise would have been (Richards, Butler, & Gross, 2003). Used over time, it makes emotional experiences more intense (Whittlesey et al., 1999). By impairing verbally mediated memory (Richards & Gross, 2000) while increasing subjective anxiety (Blackledge & Hayes, 2001) and distractibility (Butler et al., 2003), it leads to forgotten conversations (Richards & Gross, 2000), diminishes people's confidence in their personal memories (Gross, 2002) and disrupts other attempts at regulation (Richards & Gross, 2000).

By reducing positive feelings about relationship partners, increasing negative feelings about others and disrupting responsiveness and communication (Butler et al., 2003), expressive suppression interferes with socializing (Gross, 2001) and interpersonal rapport (Gross, 2002). Suppressors are more likely to be socially ostracized (Butler et al., 2003) and more likely to avoid emotionally close relationships (John & Gross, 2004). Those who use it frequently report increased feelings of inauthenticity and deceitfulness (John & Gross, 2004). Lymphocyte production in the suppressor decreases (Petrie, Booth, & Pennebaker, 1998) and blood pressure increases, even before the presentation of the emotional stimuli (Gross & Levenson, 1997). During suppression, not only does the blood pressure of the suppressor remain elevated throughout the experience, but those with whom he interacts also display similar blood pressure elevations (Gross, 2001), which helps explain their lack of willingness to continue interacting with the suppressor (Butler et al., 2003). Research has not yet clarified whether thought suppression causes similar physical and interpersonal effects (Mendes et al., 2003).

Other Strategies Studied

Although many activities are associated with highly salient emotional experiences, as the activities become routine, these emotions become habituated (Wood, Quinn, & Kashy, 2002). Wood et al. (2002) found that when people engage in habitual activities, not only do they think less about their performance than people engaged in novel activities, but their emotions are also less intense and stem more from their thoughts than from the activities in which they are engaged. While novel behavior leads to more intense emotional experiences, increased feelings of helplessness and a reduced sense of control, habitual behavior is not viewed as self-relevant, so it affects self-esteem less than novel acts, for good or ill (Wood et al., 2002). Wood et al. wrote that engaging in habitual behavior is thus an understudied but widely used method of emotional regulation.

Although recalling positive memories is often used to help improve one's mood and emotional state and tends to work as well as distraction, Joormann and Siemer (2004) found that those with dysphoric moods or low self-esteem generally recall only dysphoric memories, so this strategy does not work for them.

There are a variety of emotional regulatory strategies, some of which have been mentioned in this chapter. Two of the more problematic ones, avoidance and rumination, will comprise the rest of Part 5.

Defensive Avoidance

AVOIDANCE, WHICH INCREASES when people lack self-confidence (Penley et al., 2002) and fear losing social status (Zautra et al., 1999), separates people from their innate emotional response systems (Greenberg & Paivio, 1998). Associated with elevated cortisol levels (Rosenberger, Ickovics, Epel, D'Entremont, & Jokl, 2004), avoidance is related to poorer psychological health and decreased health-promoting behavior (Penley et al., 2002). It increases knee pain and slows the functional recovery in those who receive arthroscopic knee surgery (Rosenberger et al., 2004). Though it allows emotional concealment among those who have suffered from trauma, avoidance prevents later attempts to integrate the experience (Negrao et al., 2005). After controlling for baseline levels of depression, the amount of avoidance used predicts the number and seriousness of life stressors 4 years later, which in turn predict the severity of depressive symptoms 6 years after that (Holahan, Moos, Holahan, Brennan, & Schutte, 2005).

Defenses

From the beginning, Sigmund Freud (Breuer & Freud, 1893-1895/1955) was interested in defensive behavior, which he called repression. Especially at first, his formulations of repression were fluid: either the emotional feeling or the associated cognition was blocked from consciousness, although one or the other would invariably appear (Freud, 1915/1959h). He noticed that repression was inevitably intermingled with anxiety, first believing that anxiety results from repression (Freud, 1915/1959h), later that anxiety signals danger and thus leads to repression (Freud, 1926/1959c), and finally that both are true, with anxiety and repression each able to precede the other (Freud, 1933/1965).

It fell to Anna Freud (1936/1966) to formalize thinking about defenses. In her classic treatise on the subject, she conceptually separated repression from a host of other defensive maneuvers, such as isolation. She noted that defenses were accompanied by anxiety, which might precede or follow their use. Vaillant (1993) recast defenses from Freud's conceptualizations into a framework of emotional coping. Defenses, he believed, invariably alter the sources of conflict and how the emotion is expressed by altering its valence, its attached cognition, the responsibility for eliciting the emotion or the direction of the action the emotion normally triggers. His formulation also seems to have been the first formulation of defenses to directly address emotions as the entities defended against rather than relying on hypothetical *trieben* (drives or instincts), as Freud's had done. In Vaillant's system, defenses alter emotional characteristics to protect individuals' inner experiences from the threat of overpowering negative emotional experiences.

Progress has continued on two fronts. First, researchers continue to study defenses. Mendolia (2002) discovered that, contrary to what was thought by earlier researchers, repression is a universal behavior people use when they perceive their self-concept to be under attack by highly relevant stimuli, either positive or negative. Mendolia also discovered that strong, salient negative feedback to those most inclined to repress results in increased parasympathetic activation and decreased cardiac activity. Kazén, Baumann, and Kuhl (2003) studied the conditions required for introjection, in which others' ideas and motives are accepted as personally generated. More will be said on this in a later chapter.

Second, psychoanalysts have attempted to recast theories of defense into cognitive and conditioning terms. Gillett's (1996) formulations begin with avoidance learning, while Davis's (2001) approach relies on cognitive factors. Because Gillett's and Davis's theories owe more to prior psychoanalytic writings than to current understandings of learning processes, they will not be explored deeply in this chapter, but they point toward the recognition that learning processes are involved in ego defenses.

Memory and Cognition

Although the structure and composition of one's emotional range and the expression of one's emotional states are probably largely inherited and species specific (Darwin, 1872/1965), with the possible exception of a relative handful that appear to be relatively hardwired (Schulkin et al., 2003) the stimuli activating the various emotional programs are learned through Pavlovian means (LeDoux, 2000; Rescorla, 1988). According to Stanton (2000), Pavlovian conditioning involves three types of learning, each mediated by its own neural structure: (a) sensorimotor learning, which regulates behavior, is mediated by the cerebellum; (b) emotional learning, which responds to motivational meanings and hedonic valences, is mediated by the amygdala; and (c) cognitive learning, which encodes entire episodes, including proximal and temporal representations, environmental interactions and strategies, is mediated by the hippocampus (Stanton, 2000).

According to Stanton (2000), although the amount that each contributes to learning varies with the procedure involved, every conditioning procedure involves all three types, which in normal intact individuals constantly interact. For instance, while emotional learning is processed through the amygdala, declarative learning about emotional functioning and recalling the details of specific emotional episodes are processed through the hippocampus (LeDoux, 2000). Of the three memory types, only one's cognitive memory processes are readily accessible to oneself or others, and understanding others' emotional functioning requires infer-ences based on their behavior (Stanton, 2000). These separate memory systems may explain how emotional and declarative memory can become dissociated from one another following severe trauma.

Besides memory, many other cognitive processes are involved in emo-tional activation and processing. Walz and Rapee (2003) found in a 2 x 2 test of content (neutral or angry) x expression (neutral or angry), that angry words expressed angrily are processed the quickest, while neutral words ex-pressed neutrally are processed the slowest. Walz and Rapee believe these results indicate that anger-inducing stimuli, because of their enhanced im-plications, are processed more quickly than neutral stimuli, which have only propositional meaning. Mackintosh and Mathews (2003) found that, while stimuli are processed more quickly after presenting strongly positive or negative pictures than after presenting neutral pictures, when the valence is less strong the following stimuli are processed more slowly than if neu-tral pictures had been presented. They attributed this effect to attentional avoidance, possibly to preserve the individual's ability to complete assigned cognitive tasks, but acknowledged that their pictures were organized by valence rather than discrete emotions, which may have altered their results. Combining the findings of Walz and Rapee with those of Mackintosh and Mathews, it appears likely that highly salient emotional stimuli are processed more quickly than neutral stimuli, but less salient stimuli are also less capable of distracting organisms from their ongoing tasks.

Avoidance

Extensively studied and debated by learning theorists, the precise mech-anisms underlying avoidance are still controversial. Mowrer (1960/1983) believed that avoidance required both behaviors learned through operant conditioning and emotions conditioned using Pavlovian methods. He believed that while receiving food led to hope in the rats and pigeons he studied, not receiving the expected food led to frustration and anger. He also believed that receiving shocks resulted in fear, while not receiving expected shocks led to relief. Herrnstein (1969) attacked these formulations, claiming that they relied on immeasurable constructs. Since learned avoidance behavior continued long after the administration of shocks had ended, Herrnstein doubted any accounts that relied on Pavlovian explanations, which he thought should have predicted the extinction of avoidant behavior. Instead, he advanced the theory that only operant learning was involved in avoidance.

Seligman and Johnston (1973), believing Herrnstein's (1969) theory still could not account for the lack of extinction of avoidance behavior once it had been learned, advanced a cognitive expectancy theory of avoidance. With Mowrer (1960/1983), they believed that conditioned fear provides the initial motivation to avoid, while avoidant behavior, once begun, is sustained because the animal dislikes shock and expects that it will be shocked again if it does not continue its avoidant behavior. Despite these theoretical advances, Seligman and Johnston admitted their theory could not account for many areas of interest, such as learned helplessness.

More recently, Dinsmoor (2001) equated avoidant behavior with Pavlovian safety signals. Dinsmoor believed that the act of avoiding shocks results in the animal's increased feelings of safety and security. Each time the animal acts to avoid shock, even when such shocks are no longer being presented, the resulting feelings of safety reinforce the continuation of this behavior (Dinsmoor, 2001). Dinsmoor's formulations can actually be seen in Mowrer's (1960/1983) work; if one focuses on the relief from the lack of expected shock rather than the fear due to shock, one arrives at the same result. Williams (2001) points out that if Dinsmoor's formulations are correct, then two-factor theory and safety signal theory, when taken together, account for everything now known about avoidance behavior.

Like emotional activation, learned avoidance behavior relies on Pavlovian mechanisms (Dinsmoor, 2001; Mowrer, 1960/1983). Avoidance behavior may be best conceptualized as a means of regulating internal emotional states (Mowrer, 1960/1983), providing organisms with feelings of security that in turn reinforce continued iterations of the behavior (Dinsmoor, 2001). Although cognitive evaluations may be involved in the first stages of avoidance learning (Seligman & Johnston, 1973), over time avoidance becomes habitual and routine, falling outside routine conscious awareness and becoming activated primarily by conditioned, implicit memory processes (Davis, 2001; Dinsmoor, 2001; Stanton, 2000).

The Propositional Avoidance of Emotions

Because the ability to regulate one's emotions is rewarded socially, people are motivated to present themselves as effective modulators from an early age (Erickson & Schulkin, 2003; Schmidt et al., 2003). Friman et al. (1998) pointed out that verbal abilities enable humans to label their emotional and other private inner experiences as either positive and desired, or negative and undesired. They thought that the avoidance or escape from negatively experienced emotional states is negatively reinforced behavior and that many pathological behavior manifestations result from learned avoidance of subjective experience. They believed that avoidance causes anxiety and that people avoid confronting their own anxiety, including the verbalizations that sustain it. Friman et al. believed that the control of subjective experience actually causes problems rather than solving them, as many assume. Blackledge and Hayes (2001) agree, stating that rather than negative thoughts or emotions causing problems, it is the failed attempts to avoid them that do so. Attempting to avoid thoughts and emotions both intensifies them and creates anxiety, they believe, and also carries behavioral costs. As we saw earlier, the avoidance of emotional experience is known to make traumatic experiences more severe (Whittlesey et al., 1999).

Emotionally avoidant behavior owes more to the conditioned emotional state than it does to the initial stimulus (Friman et al., 1998; Mowrer, 1960/1983). Cognitive valuations of those painful states lead first to attempts to escape them and later to avoid them completely, as the individual—with repeated trials—more accurately anticipates them and avoids awareness of their activation (Friman et al., 1998). Over time, these stimuli lose their emotional salience through habituation and are progressively treated by the individual more like initially neutral stimuli (Dijksterhuis & Smith, 2002), although the conditioned behavior remains, continually reinforced by increased feelings of wellbeing (Dinsmoor, 2001). Other learning principles discovered through experimental conditioning procedures continue to hold: (a) avoidance repertoires in particular domains are species-specific (Bolles, 1970) and related to the conditioned stimulus in fundamental ways (Seligman, 1970); (b) complex behavioral chains can be initiated through Pavlovian means and maintained by operant reinforcement, with different parts of the chain controlled by the two conditioning processes (Corbit & Balleine, 2003); and (c) emotional avoidance, while externally reinforced because of its effects on expressive modulation (Erickson & Schulkin, 2003; Schmidt et al., 2003), also receives powerful internal reinforcement because it functions as a safety signal (Dinsmoor, 2001; Williams, 2001).

Even those schematically activated emotions elicited by highly salient external stimuli can be overcome through propositional means with sufficient cognitive effort (Ochsner et al., 2002). Adopting the facial expressions, postures, vocalizations, breathing patterns, and other physiological characteristics of an alternate emotion, particularly in combination, can also instantiate different emotional experiences through physiological feedback mechanisms (Flack et al., 1999; Philippot et al., 2002). Although either type of manipulation might begin as part of a conscious plan, the activation of new emotional processes through physiological feedback mechanisms may also take place or continue outside conscious awareness (Philippot et al., 2002) and would be particularly successful among personal-cue responders (Dulclos & Laird, 2001). Some emotional expressions similar in character, such as laughing and crying, are easily substitutable for one another; Philippot et al. (2002) found that while no other manipulation made participants feel sad, those intended to produce sadness were also likely to produce joyful feelings among their participants. Indeed, in Philippot et al.'s study, the easiest emotion to arouse through feedback mechanisms was joy, precisely the emotion one might suspect to be most often aroused defensively. These results suggest the possibility of practice effects carried over from other venues.

To continue avoiding unwanted internal experiences, one must linger on a more desired one, leading to specific patterns of pathological behavior that depend upon what is avoided and what is substituted (Friman et al., 1998). As Panksepp (2001) pointed out, activating one emotion does not mean another emotion, using different circuitry within the brain, will disappear. Indeed, as Freud (1914/1959b) first noted, emotions submerged in this way will inevitably continue to compel repetitive behavior until they are acknowledged and integrated into the life of the individual. Because the potentially adaptive functions of schematic activation have been overridden, the resulting behavior will be far from optimal and may instead be extremely pathological (Blackledge & Hayes, 2001). As Friman et al. (1998) noted, the avoidance of internal states is the problem, not the solution. It leads to increased anxiety (Blackledge & Hayes, 2001; Friman, et al., 1998), which serves as an internal signal that affect is becoming undifferentiated, too much thinking is taking place, the individual is not living freely in the present moment and adaptability is suffering (Greenberg & Paivio, 1997). Meanwhile, the bypassed emotion intensifies its unconscious effects on behavior (Blackledge & Hayes, 2001).

Those best able to differentiate between various classes of negative emotional experiences are also those best able to cope with and regulate those experiences (Feldman Barrett et al., 2001), requiring experience with one's negative emotions. A full and active emotional life leads to improved modulation, problem solving and social status. While emotional modulation is important in the smooth functioning of society and within individuals' lives, emotional avoidance does not help. To be successful, it generally requires the propositional activation or sustaining of other emotions. This process, in the guise of rumination, has been much studied, and it is to those findings that we now turn.

Rumination as Coping

When performed in sequence, Attention, Clarity and Repair lead to well-regulated moods (Salovey et al., 1995) largely because Repair overcomes the urge to ruminate (Thayer et al., 2003). An ongoing, private, intensely active and intrusive cognitive style (Mor & Winquist, 2002), rumination attempts to manage emotional life through an intense inward focus (Linden et al., 2003) on one's mood and symptoms, their future implications and their possible causes (Davis & Nolen-Hoeksema, 2000; Nolen-Hoeksema & Jackson, 2001). Rumination involves perseverative negative thinking (Papageorgiou & Wells, 2003) that begins following failed attempts to reach meaningful goals (Segerstrom et al., 2003) and continues despite a lack of environmental demand for it (Mor & Winquist, 2002). This leads to intrusive brooding about one's intrusive brooding, with problems caused by both the original and subsequent brooding episodes (Verplanken, Friborg, Wang, Trafimow, & Woolf, 2007).

The ruminator repetitively reconsiders her current problems, her current poor mood, her real and imagined past failings, her feelings of disappointment and inadequacy, her lack of relatedness to others, and the futility of her existence, all without effectively addressing the underlying issues or making constructive plans to relieve her distress (Lyubomirsky et al., 1999; Wenzlaff & Luxton, 2003). Her cognitive focus narrows, she resists her emotional pain, and she magnifies the implications of her past behavior for her current sense of self-worth (Neff, 2003). By prolonging her amygdalar activation (Drevets, 2003), she maintains and strengthens her emotional states (Verona, 2005) and allostatic responses (McEwen & Lasley, 2003) long after the original eliciting events have ended. Her ruminating prolongs her search for relevant contextual and historical information, biases how she weighs that information and increases the perceived relevance she attaches to relatively neutral information (Brosschot, 2002). All of this demonstrates why rumination is often considered a failed emotional coping or regulatory strategy (Gross, 1999).

Individuals differ in the amount they ruminate (Spasojević & Alloy, 2001). Most people who ruminate begin doing so because they believe that ruminating will help them relieve their moods and solve their problems (Lyubomirsky et al., 2003) by providing insight into their emotional lives (Davis & Nolen-Hoeksema, 2000). In those who have high vagal tone, it may actually do this without causing undue ill effects by helping them access their positive memories (Brosschot, 2002; Joormann & Siemer, 2004). When depressive intensity is low and attention to one's emotional state is accompanied by emotional clarity and repair strategies, such internally focused contemplation may be helpful (Thayer et al., 2003). It causes problems only when it turns to brooding (Treynor et al., 2003), which is when it begins preventing mood repair, particularly among the dysphoric (Joormann & Siemer, 2004), even beyond what coping style, worry, and neuroticism can account for (Vickers & Vogeltanz-Holm, 2003). Dysphoric individuals may then continue ruminating despite its negative impact on their lives, feeling powerless to stop it (Papageorgiou & Wells, 2003) because only negative material is available for their cognitive review (Wenzlaff & Luxton, 2003). It may be that mere ruminating is less important than the ratio of coping attempts that consist of ruminating, since people who ruminate more than they distract themselves tend to become depressed and anxious, while those with the opposite pattern see their depression and anxiety lift (Roelofs et al., 2009)

Tests of rumination frequently correlate with one another only imperfectly, and various experimenters have discovered that different measures of rumination have predictive validity only in particular situations. For these reasons, some doubt whether the various tests of rumination measure the same construct (Siegle, Steinhauer, Carter, Ramel, & Thase, 2003). Furthermore, as Robinson and Alloy (2003) note, it is unclear whether, in their example, ruminating about one's depressive symptoms is the same process as ruminating about the negative inferences one has made following a stressful experience. They may be part of a larger construct, tendency to ruminate when distressed, or may be entirely separate constructs (Robinson & Alloy, 2003). In this book, rumination will be treated as a single construct, although the best methods of measuring it may vary by situation and likely have yet to be devised.

Who Ruminates?

Preliminary evidence suggests that rumination is not specific to Western cultures (Abdel-Khalek & Lester, 2003; Stroebe, van Vliet, Hewstone, & Willis, 2002), though race appears to influence the tendency to ruminate (McEwen & Lasley, 2003). The development of rumination mirrors the growth of cognitive functioning (Abela et al., 2004; Silk, Steinberg, & Morris, 2003), with children apparently learning to ruminate by modeling their parents' behavior (Wright et al., 2004). Female ruminators tend to internalize, growing more apprehensive and depressed, while male ruminators tend to externalize, becoming more aggressive and hostile (Verona, 2005).

A number of researchers have found that females ruminate more than males, especially when they are sad or dysphoric (Compton, Fisher, Koenig,

McKeown, & Muñoz, 2003; Davis & Nolen-Hoeksema, 2000; Neumann et al., 2004; Nolen-Hoeksema & Jackson, 2001), while men's rumination seems to be more related to general patterns of cognitive inflexibility (Davis & Nolen-Hoeksema, 2000). When rumination is statistically controlled, the differential rate of depression between men and women disappears (Nolen-Hoeksema & Jackson, 2001; Thayer et al., 2003). Societal sanctions against women's openly expressing aggression (Linden et al., 2003), their relative powerlessness compared to men (Davis & Nolen-Hoeksema, 2000) and their greater reliance on inhibitory strategies (Thayer et al., 2003) have all been suggested as reasons for women's increased likelihood of ruminating. Even after statistically controlling for expressiveness, social desirability, and reported levels of distress, all of which differentiate them from males (Nolen-Hoeksema & Jackson, 2001), women (Nolen-Hoeksema, 1987) and girls (Goodyer, Herbert, Tamplin, & Altham, 2000) still ruminate more than their male counterparts.

Men and women differ in their emotional experiences, emotional motives and basic beliefs about emotional life (Nolen-Hoeksema & Jackson, 2001). Compared to men, women (a) are more aware of their moods and feelings, (b) are more emotionally responsive, expressive and complex, (c) process emotional information more quickly and (d) are more emotionally aware and emotionally intelligent than men (Thayer et al., 2003). The expression of sadness and fear is more often encouraged among women who, being raised to be responsible for the quality of their relationships, are also extremely vigilant about their own and others' emotions (Nolen-Hoeksema & Jackson, 2001). According to Nolen-Hoeksema and Jackson, women believe that they will be unable to master their environments, that they are responsible for the success or failure of their relationships and that their emotions are uncontrollable; Nolen-Hoeksema and Jackson believe that these three beliefs account for the observed gender differences in rumination. Women realize that continued ruminating is counterproductive, but understanding this does not help them alter their behavior (Nolen-Hoeksema & Jackson, 2001).

While some people ruminate individually, others also frequently and repeatedly discuss personal problems with others, encourage others to discuss and speculate about their own personal problems and focus on others' negative emotions. Rose (2002) termed this *co-rumination* and found that in the third, fifth, seventh and ninth grades, girls co-ruminate more than boys. Co-rumination, she found, was associated both with closer relationships and with an increased likelihood of depression and anxiety.

Trait Rumination

One's style of coping can become a stable personality variable (Garnefski et al., 2002). The disposition to ruminate (Neumann et al., 2004) is a stable individual difference (Davis & Nolen-Hoeksema, 2000) that is related to worrying and neuroticism (Vickers & Vogeltanz-Holm, 2003). Trait ruminators recall more negative events when in negative emotional states than those with other personality and coping styles (Joormann & Siemer, 2004). College students with a trait ruminative style are more likely to suffer future depressive episodes, regardless of their mood when they are evaluated, than those with other coping styles (Davis & Nolen-Hoeksema, 2000).

Rumination's Relationship to Worry

Worry and rumination, constructs that originated in different research traditions that refer to similar but distinct cognitive processes, are distinguishable despite their overlap (Fresco, Frankel, Mennin, Turk, & Heimberg, 2002). Fresco et al. (p. 180) cite Borkovec et al.'s (1983) definition of worry as a chain of repetitive thoughts and images, negatively affect-laden and relatively uncontrollable; it represents an attempt to engage in mental problem-solving on an issue whose outcome is uncertain but contains the possibility of one or more negative outcomes; consequently, worry relates closely to the fear process.

A common feature in anxiety disorders and depression, worry is a superficial cognitive behavior that allows people to keep painful emotions from awareness until a sense of mastery over them can be achieved (Fresco et al., 2002). Associated with perfectionism, the intolerance of uncertainty and various health difficulties, worry's focus is the control of imagined negative outcomes in the future (Segerstrom et al., 2003). Rumination, by contrast, generally focuses on current or past behavior (Davis & Nolen-Hoeksema, 2000; Nolen-Hoeksema & Jackson, 2001; Segerstrom, Tsao, Alden, & Craske, 2000). Each is related to both depression and anxiety (Fresco et al., 2002).

Although people most frequently worry about everyday issues, such as friends, family, work and finances, some people worry about their worrying, which may be a diagnostic marker for Generalized Anxiety Disorder (Szabó & Lovibond, 2002). In a naturalistic study, Szabó and Lovibond asked their 57 participants to keep a diary listing their thoughts during worry episodes, although they did not define worrying for the participants. This intentional decision allowed a common, rather than a psychological, definition to prevail. Szabó and Lovibond found that thinking during worry episodes could be divided into nine distinct types, which included problem-solving, anticipating negative outcomes, self-blame, palliative (distracting) thoughts, devaluing threats, and fantasizing about possible solutions. Problem solving, anticipating negative outcomes, self-blame and palliative thinking did not correlate with the intensity, frequency or uncontrollability of their participants' worry episodes. Almost half of all thoughts during the episodes centered on solving problems, but only 22% of all worry episodes contained such thoughts. While approximately 20%

of all worrying was about possible future negative events, about 50% was about attempting to avoid such events. Proportionally, chronic worriers' thoughts focused on selecting workable solutions as often as others' did, but they had more difficulty reaching satisfactory solutions than others did.

Szabó & Lovibond (2002) unexpectedly discovered that rumination was also one of the nine content categories they found. Rumination comprised 11% of the total thought registered and correlated significantly with both state and trait anxiety. While those with Generalized Anxiety Disorder ruminated more and solved problems less than the rest of their sample, those two aspects were not found to vary with proneness to worry. Szabó and Lovibond believed that the unexpected presence of ruminative and self-blaming thoughts within people's worry sequences might help explain the frequently noted correlation between anxiety and depressive states.

Whether they are depressed or not, those who ruminate more also report worrying more (Vickers & Vogeltanz-Holm, 2003). Although worry and rumination overlap, the analysis of tests measuring each construct shows that their factors do not (Fresco et al., 2002). Fresco et al. gave 784 college students tests measuring anxiety, depression, worry and rumination, then factor analyzed the results. They found that worry has two factors, which they named Positive Worry Engagement and Absence of Worry; and rumination also has two factors, which they named Dwelling on the Negative and Active Cognitive Appraisal. Of these factors, Positive Worry Engagement and Dwelling on the Negative tap the most malignant aspects of depression. These two factors correlate highly with each other and with both anxiety and depression, reflecting the large diagnostic overlap between the two (Fresco et al., 2002).

In the short term, worrying and ruminating reduce the impact of stressors (Salovey et al., 1995). Though problematic themselves, they reduce visualization, which maintains stress more fully than either rumination or worry does (Stöber & Borkovec, 2002). People often talk themselves into emotional states such as hostility (Linden et al., 2003), guilt or shame, especially when their underlying schematically activated state is more painful to them (Lewis, 1971). In the longer term, not only are rumination and worry defensive maneuvers, but the depression and anxiety that result from them should be seen as defensive secondary emotions meant to replace what is underlying and believed or feared to be even more painful.

Factors in Rumination

Various researchers have found that measures of rumination actually contain two factors: one is a pondering, reflective, analytical, evaluative style while the other is a brooding self-focus on one's symptoms and experiences (Cox, Enns, & Taylor, 2001; Fresco et al., 2002; Treynor et al., 2003; Watkins & Teasdale, 2001). Pondering is associated with greater current depression but less future depression; brooding is more related than pondering to chronic strain and lack of mastery; and brooding is associated with greater depression both currently and in the future (Treynor et al., 2003). Brooding, not pondering, affects behavior only when the mood is already negative (Compton et al., 2003); brooding alone predicts depressive intensity and duration, and mediates the gender differences in depression (Treynor et al., 2003). Such brooding apparently centers on fears that depression will not end and will adversely affect one's ability to control one's cognitive functioning (Cox et al., 2001).

By brooding, people keep the amygdala and stress responses active, increasing allostatic load and causing physiological and psychological unhealthiness. Brooding on the negative is a propositional process that maintains troublesome secondary emotions like anxiety and depression and keeps people from confronting those painful but bypassed primary emotions that continue to impact their behavior. Women brood more than men, which is why they report for professional counseling more than men.

Disorders Associated with Rumination

RUMINATION HAS BEEN associated with initiating or intensifying a number of negative psychological, psychiatric and medical conditions, such as depression (Davis & Nolen-Hoeksema, 2000; Lyubomirsky, et al., 2003; Lyubomirsky, et al., 1999; Nolen-Hoeksema & Jackson, 2001; Robinson & Alloy, 2003; Spasojević & Alloy, 2001; Vickers & Vogeltanz-Holm, 2003), social phobia (Abbott and Rapee, 2004; Edwards, Rapee, & Franklin, 2003) and hostility (Neumann et al., 2004), as well as cardiovascular (Thayer et al., 2003) and other health problems. Research using clinical samples suffering from anxiety, depressive and schizophrenic disorders, which each involve negative emotion, all tend to ruminate and use other passive and avoidant coping strategies more than nonclinical samples (Wolfradt & Engelmann, 2003), while those with Major Depressive Disorder, Dysthymia and Obsessive-Compulsive Disorder use a higher proportion of distraction, rumination and containment than nonclinical samples (Matheson & Anisman, 2003).

Rumination co-occurs with negative emotional states because of stable personality characteristics rather than specific emotional stimuli or material (Salovey et al., 1995). Rumination increases hopeful thoughts about the future among even the most dysphoric ruminators, but this effect is overwhelmed by the increased pessimism it also brings about (Lavender & Watkins, 2004). While some rumination occurs even during relatively good moods, increases in rumination indicate the likelihood that dysphoria will increase, too (Matheson & Anisman, 2003). It has negative effects only in those who are already experiencing a negative affective state or who will soon experience one (Vickers & Vogeltanz-Holm, 2003). During such times, rumination, blaming of self and others, distraction and emotional containment all tend to increase, while problem solving and social support-seeking decrease (Matheson & Anisman, 2003). After statistically controlling positive reappraisal, self-blame and catastrophizing, rumination does not cause an increased incidence of psychopathology (Garnefski et al., 2002), and mood improves again when problem solving resumes (Matheson & Anisman, 2003).

Depression

Depression is characterized by a lack of problem solving and social support (Matheson & Anisman, 2003). Although activity within the left PFC dampens amygdala activity and improves moods in most people, in those with depression it is associated with increased rumination (Drevets & Raichle, 1998). This rumination predicts the onset of depression, anxiety and anxious depression (Nolen-Hoeksema, 2000) while mediating the predictive power that people's fear of cognitive dyscontrol has on the severity of their future depressive symptoms (Cox et al., 2001). Levels of rumination one month after a significant loss predict the intensity of their depressive symptoms six months after the loss (Davis & Nolen-Hoeksema, 2000). In one prospective study of previously nondepressed undergraduate students that lasted 2.5 years, Robinson and Alloy (2003) found that negative inferential styles and dysfunctional attitudes—the cognitive variables most associated with depression—predicted the onset, frequency, and duration of subsequent depressive episodes only when they interacted with a tendency to ruminate after stressful events.

Rumination has been associated repeatedly with the length and severity of depressed moods (Davis & Nolen-Hoeksema, 2000; Lyubomirsky et al., 2003; Lyubomirsky et al., 1999; Nolen-Hoeksema & Jackson, 2001; Vickers & Vogeltanz-Holm, 2003), and ruminative style predicts the severity of depressive episodes beyond the effects associated with gender, neuroticism and distractive style (Vickers & Vogeltanz-Holm, 2003). Ruminating while depressed promotes (a) lingering dysphoria, (b) negative self-evaluations, (c) less sense of personal control, (d) greater interpersonal pessimism and (e) increased gloominess about the future (Lyubomirsky et al., 2003). After accounting for the effects caused by trait ruminative and distractive response styles, worry and neuroticism, dysphoric ruminators still report more distress than dysphoric distracters (Vickers & Vogeltanz-Holm, 2003). Elevated stress levels are associated with increased insomnia, anxiety, global stress, intrusive thinking and avoidant thinking six months later, but having a ruminative style increases them still further (Morrison & O'Connor, 2005). After accounting for distress levels, ruminators attempt to get social support more often than nonruminators and benefit from good social support more than nonruminators, yet they perceive their environments as more hostile and less supportive (Nolen-Hoeksema & Davis, 1999).

Experimentally manipulating those with nondysphoric moods to ruminate does not produce dysphoria (Lyubomirsky et al., 2003), but ruminating maintains females' depression (Nolen-Hoeksema, 1987) and leads to increased risk-taking, especially when combined with low self-esteem (Goodyer et al., 2000). The resulting combination of rumination, chronic strain and lack of mastery interact with and accentuate one another to produce depression (Nolen-Hoeksema, Larson, & Grayson, 1999). The most depressed women attend to their feelings more, have more impaired interpersonal relationships and have more severe depressive symptoms (Thayer et al., 2003). A clinically depressed sample that was experimentally induced to ruminate reported worse resulting moods than those induced to distract themselves; but those from the matched, nonclinical control group did not differ in their reported moods regardless of whether they were directed to ruminate or distract themselves (Lavender & Watkins, 2004). Rumination mediates other factors that predict future depressive episodes such as social support, number of stressors, current depressive status, levels of optimism and neuroticism, negative cognitive styles, self-criticism, neediness and history of previous depressive episodes (Spasojević & Alloy, 2001).

Among children, rumination increases stress, stress reactivity and psychiatric symptoms (Wright et al., 2004). Unlike adults, young children do not differ in their gender patterns of rumination, but those children who ruminate rather than engaging in problem solving or distracting themselves report more depressive symptoms (Abela et al., 2004). In a study of 145 seventh grade girls, 45 seventh grade boys, 46 third grade girls, and 24 third grade boys, Abela et al. found that boys used distraction more and girls used it less as they got older. The younger children's ruminating was associated with both distraction and problem solving, but it tended to come at their expense among the older children. While depressed children of all ages reported receiving less social support than nondepressed children, among third graders neither social support nor rumination mediated the other's effects on depressive symptoms, but among seventh graders each partially mediated the other. As Abela et al. note, those children reporting poorer social support may ruminate more than others because nobody confronts their negative thinking, their negative cognitive patterns drive others away or their rumination leads them to mistakenly believe their social support is poorer than it is.

Among adolescents aged 12 to 17, faulty attempts at emotional regulation lead to emotional, psychiatric and behavioral problems (Silk et al., 2003). Silk et al. found that these adolescents' depressive symptoms were related to intense and labile anger and anxiety, while their behavioral problems were related to intense and labile sadness and anxiety. Emotional expression, problem solving, distraction and cognitive restructuring had little effect on their emotional intensity, but rumination, impulsive behavior, denial, avoidance, escape and wishful thinking increased their emotional intensity and lability. Those who ruminated had more depressive and problem behaviors than those who did not (Silk et al., 2003).

After statistically controlling all measured variables, Nolen-Hoeksema, Stice, Wade, and Bohon (2007), found that adolescent girls' initial levels of rumination predicted the severity of their depression one year later, and initial severity of their depressive symptoms predicted their levels of rumination one year later. Their initial levels of rumination also predicted their later symptoms of substance abuse and bulimia, while their initial levels of bulimic symptoms predicted their later levels of rumination. However, their initial levels of substance abuse did not predict their later levels of rumination. While their initial levels of rumination did not predict their later levels of externalizing symptoms, such as delinquent and aggressive behavior, their initial levels of externalizing symptoms predicted their later levels of rumination. A 3-year follow-up showed that among those who were initially symptom-free, their initial levels of rumination predicted the onset of depression, substance abuse and bulimia. At least in females, rumination thus impacts not only the onset and severity of depression but also the onset and severity of comorbid internalizing behavior hypothesized to help sufferers lower the subjective misery of their depression (Nolen-Hoeksema et al., 2007).

Anxious Depression

Chronically depressed people, even those without comorbid anxiety, have been shown to be far more sensitive to anxiety than nondepressed control group members (Cox et al., 2001). They worry about physical symptoms, cognitive dyscontrol and observable symptoms; but after statistically controlling for neuroticism, Cox et al. found that only worrying about cognitive dyscontrol predicted depressive severity. However, worrying about cognitive dyscontrol predicted rumination, which in turn predicted depressive severity. Statistically controlling for rumination removed the predictive power of worrying about cognitive dyscontrol for depressive severity. Thus, rumination perfectly mediated the effects of worrying about cognitive dyscontrol on depressive severity (Cox et al., 2001).

Posttraumatic Stress Disorder and Acute Stress Disorder

Although worry is more associated with most anxiety disorders than rumination is (Brosschot, 2002; Edwards et al., 2003), rumination plays a marked role in a few. Posttraumatic stress frequently leads to recurrent, intrusive and distressing thoughts and recollections about the traumatic events. Emergency workers who experience repeated traumatic events try to suppress their thoughts about these incidents, ruminate about their failed attempts to rescue specific individuals and worry that their loved ones might encounter similar fates, especially traffic accidents (Haslam & Mallon, 2003).

According to the Diagnostic and Statistical Manual of Mental Disorders (4th ed., text rev.; DSM-IV-TR; American Psychiatric Association, 2000), Acute Stress Disorder differs from PTSD both in its shorter duration and in its requirement that dissociation be present before a diagnosis can be made. Meiser-Stedman, Dalgleish, Smith, Yule, and Glucksman (2007) discovered that among children and adolescents with Acute Stress Disorder, demographic variables such as previous trauma history, previous mental health diagnosis and severity of the trauma did not relate to its development. However, having a greater sense of threat at the time of the incident, larger amounts of unanchored sensory memory, beliefs that worrying would aid coping and a ruminative coping style were all related to the development of the disorder (Meiser-Stedman et al., 2007).

Social Anxiety

Independently of its role in dysphoric states, rumination plays a role in social anxiety (Edwards et al., 2003), with those high in Repair having fewer anxious symptoms (Salovey et al., 1995). Social faux pas do not lead directly to social anxiety (Hiemisch, Ehlers, & Westermann, 2002), which is caused by being overly concerned with others' potentially negative evaluations (Magee, Rodebaugh, & Heimberg, 2006). When a person has high aspirations in ambiguous social situations with high perceived costs but also contends with poorly regulated emotions, low self-esteem and poorly regarded social skills, the avoidance and rumination that result will magnify his initial apprehension and increase his social anxiety (Edwards et al., 2003; Hofmann & Scepkowski, 2006). He will brood extensively on his negative self-perceptions, looking for data confirming his poor self-perceptions and perpetuating his anxiety rather than adjusting his self-perception and social expectations (Abbott & Rapee, 2004). He will get caught in cycles of deliberating when he ought to be gathering information and then failing to deliberate adequately when that would serve him better (Hiemisch et al., 2002). This is especially true when he is already socially anxious and he believes his performance was poor (Abbott & Rapee, 2004; Edwards et al., 2003).

Hostility

Anger and reactive aggression are transitive (Linden et al., 2003) and natural responses to high levels of threat or frustrating events (Blair, 2004), but hostility is a stable personality trait (Linden et al., 2003). With roots in both personal insecurity and interpersonal negativity (Repetti et al., 2002), hostility results when people with high trait anger use repetitive thought patterns to maintain their angry moods (Linden et al., 2003). Both worry (Brosschot, 2002) and rumination (Neumann, Waldstein, Sollers, Thayer,

& Sorkin, 2004) have been implicated in maintaining hostility, while distraction decreases it by allowing people to calm themselves and search for solutions later (Neumann et al., 2004). Linden et al. found that rumination is also related to delinquent acting out, possibly because such behavior is stigmatized, adding to further internal focusing or—perhaps because it maintains the focus on the wrongs suffered in the past—priming the ruminator for further aggressive behavior. Following experimental manipulations that induced anger but not depression or anxiety, only ruminators' angry moods increased as they focused on themselves and their negative moods (Rusting & Nolen-Hoeksema, 1998).

Hostility has been associated with increased LDL cholesterol levels, higher triglyceride levels, higher total cholesterol to HDL ratios and increased risk for Coronary Heart Disease (Repetti et al., 2002). It is also suspected of being a contributing factor in stress-related atherosclerosis (Fredrickson et al., 2000). Among hostility's factors, rumination is solely responsible for the ill effects it has on physical health, while also mediating the effects of the other factors (Linden et al., 2003). Hostility does not lead to increased heart rate, systolic blood pressure or diastolic blood pressure when recalling angry incidents (Neumann et al., 2004); rather, it decreases reactivity (Repetti et al., 2002) but delays cardiovascular recovery (Fredrickson, Maynard et al., 2000; Neumann et al., 2004).

Other Emotional Problems

Elite athletes are by nature very positive individuals, although like all people, their moods can vary (Scott, Stiles, Raines & Koth, 2002). Scott et al. found that athletes' preseason levels of positive and negative affect are not correlated with their athletic performance during the season; instead, their performance relates to how they respond to their ongoing affect. While knowing and labeling one's moods increases athletic performance, ruminative preoccupation with them decreases it (Scott et al., 2002).

Cancer

Cancer and depression are highly comorbid, with depression hindering treatment, decreasing survival odds and lowering the quality of life for those with cancer (Street, 2003). Rumination is a significant factor in depression among cancer patients, but its focus changes over the course of treatment. Street found that patients initially focused on personal happiness and later on social acceptance. Ruminative tendencies at diagnosis and after two months were significantly correlated with each other and with the severity of depression at the time, although the severity of depression at intake and after two months was not.

Cardiovascular Problems

Rumination worsens the blood pressure problems associated with male avoidance and also negates the healthful effects of assertiveness in women (Linden et al, 2003). Along with worry, it is associated with decreased vagal tone and vagally mediated heart rate variability (Thayer et al., 2003), signifying a lack of parasympathetic arousal (Brosschot, 2002). Continued, dispositional rumination (Neumann et al., 2004) and worry (Brosschot, 2002) have been implicated in the cardiovascular problems associated with hostility, and rumination increases systolic blood pressure among those with dysphoric moods (Vickers & Vogeltanz-Holm, 2003). Conversely, increased vagal tone and heart rate variability have been associated with increased emotional awareness (Thayer et al., 2003).

Other Physiological Problems

Ruminating about the causes of somatic symptoms increases health complaints (Lok & Bishop, 1999) and makes the symptoms worse (Lundh & Wångby, 2002). Rumination and levels of negative affect are related to attributions of physical symptoms to somatic causes (Lundh & Wångby,

2002), as decreased vagal tone leads to the decreased activation of neural opioid systems and thus to increased subjective pain and decreased emotional regulation (Brosschot, 2002). These in turn lead to misattributions of individual pain to physical rather than emotional causes (Brosschot, 2002). Following exposure to violence, asthma increases as rumination does, maintaining both unwanted thoughts about past events and physiological responses to those memories (Wright et al., 2004).

By maintaining allostatic dysregulation, rumination leads to a number of dysfunctional physical and psychological conditions. As will be seen in the next chapter, its effects of cognition are equally profound.

Cognitive Effects of Rumination

Possibly because ruminators focus solely on their negative states at the expense of attending elsewhere (Siegle, Ingram, & Matt, 2002), ruminating has been associated with a number of cognitive problems. Among these negative effects are slowed processing (Siegle et al., 2002), perseveration (Davis & Nolen-Hoeksema, 2000), impaired memory (Lyubomirsky et al., 2003; Watkins & Teasdale, 2001), diminished attention and concentration (Lyubomirsky et al., 2003; Siegle et al., 2002), disrupted problem solving (Lyubomirsky, et al., 1999) and impaired metacognitive processes (Papageorgiou & Wells, 2003). The cognitive deficits found among dysphoric ruminators are responsible for some of the biggest problems they face (Lavender & Watkins, 2004).

Processing Speed

Within the brain, the emotional and semantic aspects of environmental stimuli are processed separately, with potential processing problems attributable to poor processing of either aspect or inefficiencies combining the two (Siegle et al., 2002). Depressed people process personally significant stimuli with negative implications more slowly than nondepressed people do (Siegle et al., 2003), and they also do so more slowly than they process neutral information (Siegle et al., 2002). Siegle et al. (2003) found that other tasks requiring sustained cognition also lengthened the processing time among depressed people. The effort spent challenging individual thoughts predicted processing times, but other aspects of rumination, such as its re-petitiveness and focus on the negative, did not. Siegle et al. (2003) believed that the sustained processing of negative emotion slows processing speed by interfering with other processing.

Altered Perceptual Processing

Chimeric faces are simulated photos in which two different facial halves, often from different people, have been joined to make a complete face. Most right-handed people process chimeric faces preferentially with their right cerebral hemispheres, which correspond to their left visual fields (Compton et al., 2003). However, it is well known that depressed people display less right hemispheric parietotemporal activation than non-depressed people (Heller & Nitschke, 1998; Mineka, Watson, & Clark, 1998), even after their depression remits (Compton et al., 2003). When Compton et al. performed a chimeric faces test on depressed and nonde-pressed individuals, they found that rumination decreases left visual field bias markedly in women but not men. Dwelling on one's mood and per-sonal failings was associated with reductions in women's left visual field bias, but analytically reflecting on one's emotion and personality was not. Compton et al. concluded that either women's and men's ruminations differ in the cognitive processes they employ or common ruminative processes are localized differently in men and women.

Cognitive Inflexibility

Perseveration refers to the failure to modify thinking or behavior when environmental contingencies change. Characterized by an inflexible cogni-tive style, rumination increases the number of perseverative errors on the Wisconsin Card Sorting Test (Davis & Nolen-Hoeksema, 2000). Davis and Nolen-Hoeksema found that after controlling for gender, mood, intel-ligence, working memory and reasoning ability, ruminators still commit significantly more perseverative errors than nonruminators, yet they also abandon appropriate cognitive sets more readily. When instructed, they can switch cognitive sets, but they have difficulty doing so autonomously. They adapt poorly to environmental contingencies, become immobilized by negative feedback, abandon unproductive strategies too slowly and do not persist with strategies that work. These problems are more pronounced among male than female ruminators (Davis & Nolen-Hoeksema, 2000).

Memory Biases

Depressed people are well known to have memory biases (Edwards et al., 2003), yet while distracted dysphoric experimental participants have memories like those of nondysphoric participants, dysphoric ruminators primarily recall negative aspects of past events (Lyubomirsky et al., 2003; Lyubomirsky et al., 1999). Socially anxious people show similarly biased memories, primarily after potentially negative social evaluations (Edwards et al., 2003). Edwards et al. found that although those with social phobia ruminate heavily—continually replaying negative events and socially important information—memory biases did not increase during the week following their negative evaluations, suggesting an encoding rather than a recall bias connected with rumination. Apparently, rumination divides attention in such a way that memory is not encoded properly.

When ruminating, stimuli are processed excessively (Siegle et al., 2003) but abstractly (Williams et al., 2007). While autobiographical memories become more negative (Lyubomirsky, Caldwell, & Nolen-Hoeksema, 1998), they also become less specific (Ramponi, Barnard, & Nimmo-Smith, 2004). Many years ago, Williams and his colleagues serendipitously discovered this effect, which they called *overgeneral memory*, when they researched autobiographical memories among suicidal hospital patients (Williams et al. 2007). According to Conway and Pleydell-Pearce's (2000) model, autobiographical memories have three levels of specificity: lifetime periods (e.g., when I was in college); general events, either single or recurrent (e.g., I had a friend); and event-specific knowledge (e.g., who went bowling with me one night, and we both broke 200). Their model holds that event-specific knowledge consists of sensory and emotional knowledge, primarily visually encoded, that provides specificity to memories.

Those who ruminate never process their autobiographical memories more specifically than at the level of general events (Williams et al., 2007), producing recollections about specific situations that could apply equally well to other situations (Watkins & Teasdale, 2001). Overgeneral memory is a hallmark symptom of both PTSD and Major Depressive Disorder, which are both past-oriented, and it is believed to maintain both (Watkins & Teasdale, 2001; Williams et al., 2007). Conway and Pleydell-Pearce (2000) believe that dysphoric ruminators shut off processing at the general level to avoid emotionally painful specific memories, but Williams et al. add that (a) ruminating has compromised their executive functioning, impacting their memory; (b) they avoid even enjoyable event-specific knowledge, which might remind them of what they now lack and (c) they rely on mood-syntonic, self-conceptual heuristics, such as believing they have always made a mess of everything they have ever done.

Rumination mediates whatever specific mechanisms cause overgeneral memory (Watkins & Teasdale, 2001), and the effect disappears whenever rumination is statistically controlled (Raes et al., 2006). Dysphoric ruminators recall more distorted and dysphoric memories of past events (Lyubomirsky & Nolen-Hoeksema, 1995), believe that such events have happened more frequently (Lyubomirsky et al., 1998) and anticipate that they will happen more often in the future (Lyubomirsky & Nolen-Hoeksema, 1995). Watkins and Teasdale found that while distraction reduces overgeneral memory, rumination increases it, possibly by reducing analytic activity.

Finally, while motivated forgetting may be healthy and helpful in certain situations, sad and depressed ruminators have trouble complying after being instructed to do so (Hertel & Gerstle, 2003). Hertel and Gerstle found that rumination and intrusive thoughts related to deficient forgetting. Since memory and motivated forgetting both rely on attention, Hertel and Gerstle believe the lack of left prefrontal brain activation often associated with depression may play a role. Regardless, it is clear that rumination plays a role in reduced attention.

Impaired Concentration and Attention

Attention requires both initial perception and later associative retrieval (Siegle et al., 2002). Intrusive dysphoric rumination divides attention, leaving less capacity for other tasks (Lyubomirsky et al., 2003). Siegle et al. found that since rumination biases perception and ruminators associate affectively, dysphoric ruminators process the valence of negative environmental stimuli even more quickly than controls, but they process the meanings of those stimuli much slower than controls do. Unlike controls, they process the negative aspects of stimuli at the expense of nonemotional aspects of those stimuli, and they process the valence and meaning of positive stimuli much more slowly (Siegle et al., 2002). In a series of academic tasks, dysphoric ruminators were slower, made more errors, had more distracting thoughts and had more difficulty concentrating than nondysphoric ruminators, nondysphoric distracters or dysphoric distracters, while those three groups were similar in these outcome measures (Lyubomirsky et al., 2003). Though tasks demanding their undivided attention could disrupt their rumination, dysphoric ruminators may be unable to switch cognitive sets quickly enough to notice or avail themselves of the opportunities presented (Davis & Nolen-Hoeksema, 2000).

Impaired Future Thinking

Hopelessness leads depressed people to imagine fewer positive future events than others do, but not more negative events (Lavender & Watkins, 2004). Since ruminators expect only negative events in their futures (Lyubomirsky et al., 2003), after statistically controlling for initial hopelessness, rumination still leads to imagining significantly more negative future events among depressed people, but not among nondepressed people (Lavender & Watkins, 2004).

Problem Solving

Problem solving consists of several steps, including appraising the problem, generating possible solutions, choosing a solution and implementing it (Lyubomirsky et al., 1999). Rumination decreases problem-solving ability (Baumann & Kuhl, 2002; Wright et al., 2004), because dysphoric ruminators believe their problems are more severe and less solvable than others judge them to be, their solutions to complex problems are less likely to work effectively than others' are, and they are less likely to follow through on any constructive solutions they devise (Lyubomirsky et al., 1999). Compared to others, ruminators: (a) concentrate more poorly, (b) lack goal-directedness, (c) have more elaborate and negative inner lives, (d) engage in more introverted and antagonistic behavior, (e) dream and imagine more vividly, (f) perform cognitive tasks more slowly and poorly and (g) concern themselves less with others' impressions (Conway, Csank, Holm, & Blake, 2000; Lyubomirsky et al., 2003).

Because of these cognitive deficiencies, dysphoric ruminators solve problems more poorly than those who are not dysphoric or who do not ruminate (Lyubomirsky & Nolen-Hoeksema, 1995). They ignore evolving environmental contexts and make little effort to solve their problems (Lyubomirsky et al., 1999; Wenzlaff & Luxton, 2003). Lyubomirsky et al. (1999) found that dysphoric ruminators rated their personal problems as worse and more difficult to solve than others' are (though independent judges rated their problems as about equally severe and difficult) and considered themselves less likely to follow through with their proposed solutions to these problems (though the judges rated their solutions equal to others' and they showed as much confidence in their solutions as others did). Instead, they brood self-critically and pessimistically, focusing on their problems rather than their proposed solutions, blaming themselves, showing little confidence in their mastery and attempting to generate "perfect" solutions (Lyubomirsky et al., 1999). By contrast, those who are euthymic, no matter how much they have been ruminating, show none of the cognitive deficits listed in this section (Lyubomirsky et al., 1998; Lyubomirsky & Nolen-Hoeksema, 1995; Lyubomirsky et al., 1999). Happy people look for "good enough" solutions, enact them quickly, and move on from their problems (Abbe et al., 2003).

Self-Appraisals and Attributions

Rumination promotes pessimistic attributions about one's interpersonal problems and distorted interpretations of life events (Lyubomirsky et al., 2003). Rumination is related to increased self-deprecation, self-blame and self-criticism, along with decreased self-confidence (Lyubomirsky et al., 1999). It promotes negative self-appraisal and beliefs that one lacks control over one's life (Lyubomirsky et al., 2003).

Impaired Metacognitive Processes

The term metacognition is used to describe the monitoring, interpreting, evaluating and regulating processes that oversee the types of cognition discussed above (Papageorgiou & Wells, 2003). While rumination, as shown above, impairs those levels of cognition, it also affects higher level metacognitive processes. Papageorgiou and Wells found both positive and negative metacognitive beliefs associated with rumination. For example, as noted in a previous chapter, people believe that rumination should help them resolve their problems, yet once they start ruminating, they believe it cannot be stopped or controlled. Depression, Papageorgiou and Wells found, is correlated with both positive and negative beliefs about rumination, which were not correlated with one another. Positive beliefs are related to increased rumination, while negative beliefs increase depression by mediating the effects of rumination. These beliefs, combined with depressed mood, further reduce confidence in one's cognitive processes (Papageorgiou & Wells, 2003).

Rumination leads to a group of significant cognitive deficits that mirror those listed earlier for stress and negative emotions. However, the evidence shows that even those with intense negative affects (such as Major Depressive Disorder) who do not ruminate escape these effects. This suggests that it might be rumination itself that is causing the problems, or that rumination maintains the chronic allostatic imbalances that lead to these problems. The answers to this await further research.

Theoretical Views of Rumination

THIS CHAPTER WILL explore several of the ways in which researchers have sought to understand and characterize rumination.

Self-Focused Attention

People focus on themselves to decrease the perceived discrepancies between their ideal and real selves (Robinson & Alloy, 2003) whenever they fail to meet standards they have set for themselves (Mor & Winquist, 2002). Some people respond through self-reflective searching for actions to support their coping ability, which is related to openness; others ruminate, which is related to neuroticism (Baumann & Kuhl, 2002; Joireman, Parrott, & Hammersla, 2002). Both are considered self-focused attention, and Baumann and Kuhl have termed these two personality types action-oriented and state-oriented, respectively. Joireman et al. found that these dimensions are independent, so an individual can do either, both or neither; and while self-reflection is positively correlated with perspective taking and empathic concern, rumination is negatively related to self-esteem, empathic distress, and perspective taking.

These differences explain why self-focused attention, which may be either temporary or chronic, has been shown to reduce stereotypical thinking and increase social comparisons, internal attributions and task performance in some cases (Mor & Winquist, 2002). Though it was once believed that self-focused attention leads to psychopathological adjustment whenever it is excessive, sustained and inflexible (Ingram, 1990), if its focus is on positive aspects of the self, sustained self-focus can bring benefits, including decreasing negative emotion, suppressing stereotypical thinking, increasing internal attributions and improving task performance (Mor & Winquist, 2002).

In such cases, even rigidity and inflexibility do not increase negative emotionality, yet the sustained focus on negative self-aspects does (Mor & Winquist, 2002). In their meta-analysis of previous studies on self-focused attention, Mor and Winquist found that self-focused attention and negative emotion lead to and reinforce one another, making self-focused attention an important part of the overall process of emotional regulation. A person's self-reflective thinking about what she imagines others think or feel about her behavior increases her social anxiety and overall negative emotion, while ruminating about her own behavior increases her depression (Mor & Winquist, 2002), makes her categorical memory poorer (Watkins & Teasdale, 2001) and makes regulating her negative affect more difficult (Baumann & Kuhl, 2002).

Alone among the types of self-focus, stress-reactive rumination interacts with negative inferential styles and dysfunctional attitudes to predict future depressive episodes (Robinson & Alloy, 2003). Since both self-reflective searching and rumination correlate with depressive intensity, it is clear that they are independently responsible for maintaining depressive styles (Watkins & Teasdale, 2001). Like others, Mor and Winquist (2002) found that these effects increased among clinical samples. The difference may primarily be one indicating the differences between shame and guilt, as shame, associated with personal distress, causes ruminating about the past, while guilt, associated with perspective taking, leads to attempts to solve problems and move forward (Joireman et al., 2002).

Repetitive Thought

Segerstrom et al. (2003) differentiated repetitive thought along four dimensions: (a) either positively or negatively valenced content evaluations, (b) either a searching or solving purpose, (c) either interpersonal or achievement orientation and (d) either high or low total amount. They found the first two of these, valence and purpose, to be very robust. Searching and solving may each be contextually appropriate in their turn, since reaching optimal solutions involves understanding problems before attempting to solve them. Controlled, volitional attempts to understand one's moods and emotions are associated with positive outcomes when they are motivated by curiosity rather than by negative emotions, especially among women (Segerstrom et al., 2003). Repetitive thought may engage the deeper processing of emotionally relevant schemas, focus one's attention on goal discrepancies, or amplify one's affective states (Segerstrom et al., 2000). It may assist adaptation even following traumatic experiences if it ends quickly, leads to closure and meaning, and is shared with others, although prolonged searching without closure only increases distress (Segerstrom et al., 2003).

Affect mediates the effects of repetitive thought (Segerstrom et al., 2000) by providing valence. Introspection, rehearsal, self-analysis and emotional processing are all forms of repetitive thinking with neutral valences, while anticipation has a positive valence (Segerstrom et al., 2003). Each a pattern of negative repetitive thought (Segerstrom et al., 2000), rumination and worry differ in their purpose, as rumination is focused on searching and worry on solving problems (Segerstrom et al., 2003). Depression and anxiety are thus differentiated by their thought content rather than thinking style (Segerstrom et al., 2000). All forms of repetitive thought correlate with one another (Segerstrom et al., 2003), which almost totally accounts for the shared variance between rumination and worry (Segerstrom et al., 2000). As one's negative emotion increases, rumination increasingly has effects beyond those attributable solely to repetitive thought (Segerstrom et al., 2000). Perhaps, valence preferentially affects psychological functioning while purpose targets physiological functioning (Segerstrom et al., 2003). However, although repetitive thought factors into the genesis of both anxiety and depression, rumination has additional effects during depression, suggesting it is more powerful than mere repetitive thought (Segerstrom et al., 2000).

Conditional Goal Setting

People typically organize themselves through goals arranged in hierarchies from the distal, abstract and imprecise to the immediate, concrete and specific (Street, 2003). Street theorized that immediate concrete goals that were connected to broader future goals considered important would increase in importance themselves, and that failure to reach important goals linked to long-term happiness or wellbeing would lead to a negative self-focus, rumination and depression. In her study of 67 cancer patients, Street found that conditional goal setting contributes to rumination, which in turn contributes to depression. Once rumination was controlled statistically, conditional goal setting no longer predicted depression. At hospital admission, patients were concerned about their private wellbeing and ruminated about that. Two months later, they were concerned with social acceptance and ruminated about that. Over time, conditional goals shifted from personal happiness to social relatedness. While rumination scores at each point correlated with one another and with depression scores at that point, the two depression scores did not correlate significantly with one another (Street, 2003).

PART SIX

SOCIAL PROCESSES, INDIVIDUAL
DIFFERENCES AND PSYCHOPATHOLOGY

Social Processes

MANY CENTRAL CONCEPTS in social psychology are intimately connected with emotion. In a fairly recent survey text, Baron and Byrne (2004) identified several broad areas in social psychology relating to specific emotions or emotional processing, such as love, security, loneliness, aggression and catharsis. Second, they discussed the involvement of affective processes in areas such as: (a) nonverbal communication and the detection of deception, (b) attitude formation, (c) cognitive dissonance, (d) impression formation and management, (e) self esteem, self-concept and social identity, (f) prejudice, (g) interpersonal attraction and relationships, (h) conformity and compliance, (i) prosocial behavior, (j) cooperation and conflict and (k) advertising appeals. Finally, they noted how cognitive processes like attributions may affect mood and feeling states, such as what occurs during depressed states.

Still other social processes can be seen to have emotional components. Social desirability may be viewed as a means to avoid the rejection associated with others' negative evaluations, while group polarization can be viewed as group members' attempts to avoid ostracism because their beliefs are not "pure" enough for the group. Social facilitation, in which well-learned routines are performed better and poorly learned routines performed worse in others' presence, can be recast from neutral arousal states to states with affective valence—such as fear, humiliation, and excitement—by noting the inevitable appraisal component that accompanies such arousal. Self-efficacy, as described by Bandura (1996, 2000, 2002; Bandura & Locke, 2003), is a cognitive belief; but its properties, as listed by Bandura and Locke— including the abilities to be classically conditioned, reduce anxiety, sustain motivation and block the effects of negative emotion and feedback—reveal it to be an affective complex containing cognitive components.

Given this litany, it is clear that emotion and mood are two of the most crucial and central constructs in social psychology. Distinguishable but inseparable from cognition, affect is involved in virtually every decision made by humans, but it has historically not been well understood and has only recently been studied systematically at any level. Because few have systematically studied how the distinctions discussed earlier in this volume affect behavior, many research findings may be misleading. For instance, the distinction between schematic and propositional emotions may partly or largely explain the different effects of genuine high self-esteem and defensive self-esteem, differences in social competence, susceptibility to stereotypical thinking, individual differences in detecting deception and so forth. Clearly, much research is needed in these and related areas within social psychology.

The Self Process

The structure of the self develops from the implicit cognitive interpretation of previous emotional experiences (Epstein, 1997; Greenberg, 2002a, 2002b; Shean, 2003). Among school-age children, representations of their mothers remain stable over time while their self-representations grow ever stronger, employing parts of the brain (such as the rostral ACC) known to be preferentially involved in emotional processing (Ray et al., 2009). The self system integrates emotional life, including feelings about oneself (Saarni, 1997), though high valence stimuli that are experienced frequently are soon treated like neutral stimuli (Dijksterhuis & Smith, 2002). Because of this, not all emotional experiences are incorporated into the self structure (Greenberg & Paivio, 1997). People also experience what Satir (Satir et al., 1991) called *reactive feelings*, those feelings one has about one's primary emotions. According to Satir, these reactive feelings reflect the individual's expectations and connect strongly to his sense of self-worth and self-esteem. With both biology and culture having roles in the process, daily living produces a sense of self in three stages: the synthesis of a felt sense of self; attending to this sense; and reflecting consciously on this sense to produce a coherent self-narrative (Greenberg & Pascual-Leone, 2001). The presence of defensive and maladaptive secondary emotions like depression and anxiety signals that this development has gone awry and produced internal disorder (Greenberg, 2002a, 2002b).

Emotion Schemes

Emotions generally precede cognition and contribute independently to decision-making (Greenberg, 2004) by forming the basis of emotional-cognitive-behavioral complexes that Greenberg (2002a; 2004; Greenberg & Paivio, 1997; Greenberg & Pascual-Leone, 2001) termed *emotion schemes*. Mischel (2004) has a parallel construct he terms the *cognitive-affective unit*. Formed through prior interactions, these interactive, experience-based models of the world help the person integrate and synchronize his perceptions, memories, interpretations, expectations, motivations, physiological responses, subjective experience and behavioral tendencies (Greenberg & Paivio, 1997; Mischel, 2004). Mild emotional experience is easily integrated into these schemes; and as the schemes develop, more intense emotions (even potentially traumatic ones) become less disturbing or disintegrating (Greenberg & Paivio, 1997). Organized by emotion and intensity, these preprogrammed operations (Greenberg, 2002a) also incorporate cognitive assessments of context, increasing their subtlety and predictive accuracy (Toates, 2002) and enhancing their adaptive nature (Schulkin et al., 2003). Experiencing any particular emotion primes the knowledge structures, thinking styles and probable responses corresponding to that emotion (Blanchette & Richards, 2010).

No more potent level of integration exists among humans (Greenberg, 2002a). This uncommon synchrony improves the functioning of individuals (Greenberg, 2002a, 2004), their attachment relationships (Fosha, 2004) and their associated interpersonal groups directly, through social feedback and via expressed emotion (Ellgring & Smith, 1998). Infants form increasingly complex schemes, which regulate their behavior, help them predict how others are likely to react to them, become core components in their subjective senses of themselves and channel their further growth (Greenberg & Paivio, 1997). Maturity, learning and neural integrity all improve emotion schemes (Toates, 2002). Although emotion schemes generally lead to wiser, better-directed interactions with the world than either emotion or cognition could do when acting alone, faulty emotion schemes sometimes bias future interpretations and actions (Greenberg, 2002a; Greenberg & Paivio, 1997; Greenberg & Pascual-Leone, 2001). Activated emotion schemes can also remain unconscious but still affect behavior. Especially during loving and angry states, they may not be experienced at sufficient intensity to be consciously registered and may influence behavior outside awareness; but once they have been consciously apprehended, their character changes and their ability to control behavior decreases (Elster, 1999).

Personality and Individual Differences

Associated with decreased physical symptoms and more adaptive stress responses (Salovey et al., 1995), emotional intelligence (EI) consists of the abilities to identify and understand both one's personal emotions and the emotions of others, to regulate one's emotions, and to effectively cope with momentary stressors and meet one's needs (Mayer & Salovey, 1995; Salovey, Stroud, Woolery, & Epel, 2002). In this scheme, EI has three factors: Attention to emotions as they arise; Clarity in discriminating them; and the ability to regulate or Repair one's moods and emotions (Salovey et al., 1995). Van der Zee, Thijs, and Schakel (2002) conceptualized EI somewhat differently, as the abilities to perceive, interpret and cope with one's own and others' emotions. In their scheme, the three derived factors were Empathy, Autonomy and Emotional Control. Pellitteri (2002) found that it consisted of emotional knowledge, emotional perception and emotional regulation. In any of these schemes, a vital part of EI involves the ability to effectively relate to others in ways that engage them, keep them happy, and meet short- and long-term performance goals (Latour & Hosmer, 2002).

For EI to work most effectively, Salovey et al. (1995) found that people must follow a sequence of (1) noticing their emotional state, (2) identifying it and (3) directing their regulatory efforts; failure to follow this sequence might lead to misdirected and ineffective outcomes. Research has shown that while Attention is unrelated to Clarity and Repair, the latter two are moderately correlated with one another (Salovey et al., 1995). As Clarity increases, the Repair of negative states also increases, particularly when the states are intense (Feldman Barrett et al., 2001; Salovey et al., 1995). Attention without Clarity and Repair often leads to negative outcomes; collegiate tennis players who label their feelings accurately perform better in their matches, while those who instead merely brood on them perform more poorly (Scott et al., 2002).

According to Salovey et al. (2002), Attention, Clarity and Repair are all associated with higher self-esteem. They found that (a) attention is positively correlated with empathy, while Clarity and Repair are each associated with more satisfying relationships and decreased social anxiety and depression; (b) those higher in Attention have lower peak cortisol levels and less systolic blood pressure responsiveness following repeated stressors; (c) higher Clarity leads to increased negative affect following stressors, but to lower baseline cortisol levels and decreased cortisol responses after repeated stress; and (d) higher Repair leads to higher baseline cortisol levels when novel stressors are expected but leads to appraising repeated stressors as less threatening. Repair is associated with fewer symptoms, less social anxiety and depression, less use of passive coping strategies such as rumination, surrendering, avoiding or inhibiting responses, and more use of active coping strategies like distraction and altering noxious situations (Salovey et al., 2002).

Although the construct was originally named emotional intelligence, research has consistently shown that it has little or no relationship to intellectual intelligence but instead is highly associated with personality trait variables including Extraversion, Neuroticism, Openness and Agreeableness (Van der Zee, Thijs, & Schakel, 2002). However, unlike those enduring temperamental dimensions, EI is responsive to current environmental conditions (Faye et al., 2011) and can be developed with coaching (Latour

& Hosmer, 2002). In one study of Indian physicians, EI (particularly empathy skills) increased with family support (Faye et al., 2011).

Individual Difference Variables

Each individual's characteristic thoughts and emotional reactions tend to vary across situations but remain markedly stable in similar situations (Mischel, 2004), apparently because their characteristic emotional responses do (Oishi et al., 2004). Since emotion forms the core of personality (Izard, 2002), individual differences in emotional variables cause many of the observed differences between people. At least three of the "big five" personality dimensions have been linked to emotion. Agreeableness, a measure of how much people desire smoothness in their social relationships, is related to efforts to control the expression of negative emotions and moods (Tobin, Graziano, Vanman, & Tassinary, 2000). People high in Agreeableness also exhibit greater electromyographic activity on their brows than do those lower in it, indicating greater experience of negative affect (Tobin et al., 2000). Extraversion scores are related to greater amygdalar reactivity to positive stimuli (Canli & Amin, 2002), while Neuroticism scores are related to the disposition for having negative moods (Baumann & Kuhl, 2002) and to greater amygdalar reactivity to negative stimuli (Canli & Amin, 2002).

The following sections briefly discuss some relevant individual difference variables found in the literature. This list is by no means exhaustive.

Degree of Affective Differentiation

While some people differentiate their internal experiences finely and label them precisely using many emotional descriptors, others tend to lump their emotional experiences into two categories: the pleasant and the unpleasant (Feldman-Barrett et al., 2001). Feldman-Barrett et al. discovered that those best at differentiating their negative affect also reported using more strategies to regulate it, especially when it was intense.

Situational vs. Personal Cue Responding

Duclos and Laird (2001) discovered that the most effective methods for changing and inhibiting emotional behavior depend upon whether the individual becomes aroused more by evaluating her subjective experience or by noting environmental cues. After presenting participants a disguised facial manipulation exercise to separate their sample into these two groups, they found that personal-cue responders induced emotional experience far better by adopting emotionally expressive behavior than did situational-cue responders, who in turn self-induced emotional experiences better using imagery techniques. Although internal and external cues are usually in accord, this individual difference predicts which is most salient for a given individual. They predicted that conceptually and experimentally separating these two groups from one another in the future would yield more accurate and nuanced experimental results.

Need to Evaluate

Hermans, De Houwer, and Eelen (2001) showed that accurate emotional priming occurs in less than 300 ms. Participants with a low need to evaluate showed no emotional priming effects despite previously rating the tests' stimuli as highly valenced, either positive or negative. By contrast, those with high evaluation needs undergo significantly stronger experiences. Hermans et al. believed that individuals with high evaluation needs chronically evaluate many aspects of their environment, conditioning themselves to react emotionally even when stimuli were presented much too quickly for conscious awareness.

Belief in a Just World

Dalbert (2002) studied belief in a just world (BJW), the cognitive anticipation that good deeds are rewarded, bad ones are punished and everything works out justly in the end. Dalbert found that two types of BJW exist. Personal belief in a just world (PBJW) focuses on what James (1890/1983) termed the "me." Stretching outward from the person, through possessions, relationships, group memberships and so on, PBJW is a belief that everything in one's own life will turn out justly. General belief in a just world (GBJW) is a more universal belief that the world as a whole operates justly. When individuals believe they are unjustly impeded from reaching their goals, those without either type of BJW experience more anger than those with BJW. While GBJW and PBJW both decrease anger and increase self-esteem, PBJW provides wider protection from negative states, such as sadness, by inducing and maintaining positive moods.

Locus of Control

Lu and Chen (1996) found that individuals use four different coping styles: active interpersonal coping (e.g., seeking emotional resources); active intrapersonal coping (e.g., planning and hoping); emotional suppression; and cognitive suppression. They found that those with internal locus of control are more likely to use active coping methods, such as seeking resources and planning, while those with external locus of control are more likely to suppress their emotions and cognitions.

Coping Profiles

While the various coping strategies are generally studied singly in the laboratory, coping strategies are actually used most often in combinations or patterns (Matheson & Anisman, 2003). By changing these patterns, it is thought that the accompanying moods might be altered. Matheson and Anisman reported that (a) men generally use humor to cope more often than women do, while women seek social support, express emotions, distract and ruminate more than men do; (b) nonclinical controls use more problem solving, active distraction, humor, and social support-seeking than do clinical samples; (c) people with stable, problem-focused coping strategies are less likely to present clinically; and (d) those with profoundly dysphoric moods rely more on emotional containment, blame and rumination. Among highly dysphoric people, Matheson and Anisman found that increasing emotional containment and rumination while decreasing problem solving led to increased dysphoria a year later. However, not employing distraction, emotional expression or support-seeking led to better moods, less self-blame and more frequent support seeking a year later (Matheson & Anisman, 2003).

Action vs. State Orientation

Although effortful, deliberative top-down strategies of emotional regulation (like suppression) and efficient but rigid methods (like repression) have been studied more often, a third type known as intuitive affect regulation also exists (Baumann & Kuhl, 2002; Jostmann et al., 2005; Koole & Jostmann, 2004). Intuitive affect regulation combines executive control with implicit functioning to efficiently but flexibly regulate emotions while pursuing ongoing goals. It relies on what Kuhl termed *extension memory*, a large implicit system of associations about oneself and the environment that maintains an elaborate system of higher intuition and holistic processing (Baumann & Kuhl, 2002, 2005b; Jostmann et al., 2005; Koole & Jostmann, 2004). These associative networks, which are only accessible when one's mood is positive (Baumann & Kuhl, 2002, 2005b; Bolte et al., 2003; Kuhl et al., 2006), connect goals, motivational strategies and behavioral sequences (Baumann & Kuhl, 2002, 2005b). Guided by affect, extension memory is an essential part of the self (Kuhl et al., 2006).

Without positive affect, approach goals cannot be generated and acted upon (Baumann & Kuhl, 2005a). With high negative affect, extension memory is inaccessible (Kuhl et al., 2006). During ongoing negative emotional experiences, people adopt strategies of self-control, while in positive affective states their goals center on self-maintenance and self-regulation (Orbell, 2003). According to Orbell, this means that when one's mood is poor, one's focus is on keeping assigned tasks in mind and excluding all else. Those better able to access their extension memories are more likely to meet the personal goals they previously established (Orbell, 2003). Yet, these relationships work reciprocally, as successfully regulating negative emotions enables the access of these holistic associational networks (Gröpel & Kuhl, 2009).

Presumably because of early environmental influences, some people learn to regulate their negative emotions intuitively and maintain access to these associative networks, but those from less forgiving backgrounds featuring external control, undermining relationships and a lack of personal autonomy apparently do not (Koole & Jostmann, 2004). These two groups have been termed *action oriented* and *state oriented*, respectively. Over time, these differences become stable aspects of personality (Jostmann et al., 2005). State oriented individuals focus on their past, present or imagined future emotional states (Kazén et al., 2003). Baumann and Kuhl (2002) found that they tend to ruminate and that they have more difficulty with intuitive tasks than action oriented individuals. They also discovered that neuroticism, a measure of how quickly people enter negative mood states, is only moderately correlated with state orientation, a measure of how slowly they quit ruminating once they enter those states.

Kazén et al. (2003) found that because state oriented people have less access to their unconscious associative networks, they are more likely to mistakenly attribute external demands to their own wishes, especially when the demanded tasks are unpleasant and their moods are slightly negative. This is the source of ego-alien introjection. By contrast, both action oriented and state oriented individuals are equally likely to falsely attribute pleasant demands to their own wishes, a form of identification (Kazén et al., 2003).

Koole and Jostmann (2004) demonstrated that action oriented people focus on their goals and rely on intuitive regulation to continue pursuing them, but only when they are under potentially stressful circumstances. In their study, intuitive affect regulation operated efficiently, did not interfere with perceiving negative stimuli and strengthened access to personal memories. Its regulatory effects strengthened as time passed. By contrast, those who were state oriented remained focused on how they felt and used unexpected external rewards to help them down-regulate their reported negative emotions (Koole & Jostmann, 2004). Jostmann et al. (2005) found that the usual effects of subliminal priming were only seen among those who were state oriented. When primed with angry faces, action oriented participants' moods actually improved slightly, suggesting that they had down-regulated the primed anger. This demonstrated that intuitive affect regulation works even when negative affect is not explicitly recognized.

Baumann and Kuhl (2005a) found that when action oriented individuals resist temptation and continue on assigned tasks, it is primarily because the assigned tasks interest them. They will engage in tasks whether others assign them in an autonomy-enhancing or controlling manner, and if they like the task they will continue with it when they are no longer being monitored or expected to do so. State oriented individuals, however, avoid temptations and distraction much better when they receive externally controlling instructions. However, when they receive them, their decisions about whether to continue with the task become essentially random and no longer relate to whether they enjoy the task or not (Baumann & Kuhl, 2005a).

These distinctions between action orientation and state orientation seem to be critical, though there is no research evidence connecting these concepts to the rest of this volume. State oriented individuals are those most likely to ruminate or use equally poor regulatory strategies. They are those whose childhoods featured others' control, so they are more likely to have been subjected to undue early stress. They are thus more likely to be suffering from ongoing allostatic dysregulation and to have physical and psychological symptoms that cause them difficulty. In short, they are more likely to appear for counseling. The professional's job, among others, is to help them develop an action orientation so that this host of connected problems can be reversed, preferably in short order.

Psychopathology

BECAUSE EMOTIONAL PROCESSES are the basis of personality, their disturbance can lead to psychopathological adjustments (Izard, 2002), most of which are marked by chronically dysregulated emotions (Knapp, 1992). Over half of the Axis I disorders listed in the *DSM-IV-TR* (2000) that are not related to substance use feature some form of dysregulated emotion, as do virtually all of the AXIS II disorders (Gross & Levenson, 1997; Repetti et al., 2002). Besides such obvious candidates as schizophrenia, anxiety and mood disorders, conditions such as ADHD and the autistic spectrum disorders are also characterized by abnormalities in processing or producing emotion (Davidson & Slagter, 2000). Because of their dysregulated states, clients often believe they need to maintain their symptoms, including the substance abuse that is often their attempt to restore a subjective sense of regulation (Knapp, 1992).

Pathology relates to emotional difficulties in various ways. Some people experience emotions so overwhelming that they cannot be regulated with the personal and interpersonal resources they have available (Fosha, 2001). Others avoid or disown their primary emotional reactions (Greenberg & Paivio, 1997). Still others become fixated on particular emotions because of reinforcement, modeling or repeated exposure (Epstein, 1998). Because specific emotions are central to the routines of most families, children practice these emotional routines and as adults try to either maximize them or avoid them entirely, often not too successfully or adaptively (Magai & Hunziker, 1998). Because of faulty processing, people can produce distorted meanings (Greenberg & Paivio, 1997), become disorganized or dissociate, or have trouble balancing needs such as testing reality and protecting their self-esteem (Epstein, 1998). They may act in ways that cannot change their environment as they wish (Greenberg & Paivio, 1997) because they have developed sensitivities or compulsions that predispose them to behaving in particular ways that are currently inappropriate (Epstein, 1998).

Defenses are activated when people feel hopeless and filled with dread (Fosha & Slowiaczek, 1997). Because they alter how the intentionality and direction of primary emotions are experienced, they create uncertainty about whether, for instance, one was sent away or left voluntarily (de Rivera, 1977). Feigned happiness is a typical defensive posture (King & Pennebaker, 1998), notable for its use of the non-Duchenne (social) smile (Bonanno et al., 2002). Bypassing emotions is another (Lewis, 1971). Freud (1920/1961) postulated a death instinct responsible for the compulsion to repeat; but if Panksepp (2001) is correct, several emotion circuits may simultaneously affect behavior, with only one attaining or remaining in consciousness. If particular emotions continue to be bypassed, over time, powerful, repetitive behavior will emerge that seems foreign and context-free to both the individual and outsiders (Lewis, 1971).

Difficult emotions, as noted above, can arise in several ways. Walking alone through the woods and seeing a dangerous animal or animals (such as a big cat, a snake or a pack of wolves), will automatically arouse fear. This appears to be genetically hardwired, occurring during the first encounter (Bowlby, 1973). If one were instead walking alone through a seedy part of town at night, one might again have a fear reaction, again automatically, but this time based on prior learning and associations (LeDoux, 2000; Rescorla, 1988). Each of these is adaptive and based on schematic evaluations; and each responds quickly and surely to prior emotional schemes that are either hardwired, learned or a combination of the two (Ben-Ze'ev, 2000). Alternately, one might develop a fear reaction by worrying about a possible terrorist attack on one's community to gain control over more painful feelings (Segerstrom et al., 2003) or by an instrumental attempt at method acting (Greenberg, 2002a). The latter might be instituted because it gains payoffs such as preventing others' perceiving one as a threat to them (Greenberg & Paivio, 1997) or to bypass a more painful emotion. Finally, an anxiety reaction might be part of an emotional trauma, from which no escape exists no matter how one behaves (Freud, 1926/1959c, 1933/1965).

Another example of pathological adjustment—more culturally influenced—is aggression, which begins as neither hostile nor destructive, but as a necessary ingredient in a child's growth (Parens, 1992). Aggression that assists survival is part of our genetic makeup, can be found abundantly in the animal kingdom, and must be considered beneficial in that context (Fromm, 1973). However, Fromm notes, humans are less instinctively driven than other animals but must instead confront existential questions of meaning, power, separation from others, alienation and so forth. Some people choose to resolve the anxiety arising from these dilemmas through pursuing justice, altruism and trustworthiness, while others deviate into hatred, vindictiveness, retaliation and sadism (Fromm, 1973).

Aggression not rooted in survival can either spontaneously express unconscious urges or semi-consciously express malignant character formation (Fromm, 1973). According to Fromm, destructive cruelty helps contain these constant existential concerns, which generally remain unconscious. We thus have both murders of passion and planned genocides. Fromm believed that the latter are by far the greater distortion of human capacities. Such hatred is inherently volitional and must begin with cognition (Beck, 1999), probably in the form of rumination (Neumann et al., 2004). Rather

than being based on a schematic evaluation of one's environment, it consti-
tutes a calculated strategy for destroying one's enemies (Ben-Ze'ev, 2000).

The considerations introduced to this point lead to the following understanding of psychopathology: Actions can be divided roughly into two
main categories, those resulting from primary emotions, and those resulting from defenses erected to avoid experiencing them. Almost all people
decide somewhat consciously how their lives ought to be, including how
they should feel, and have secondary emotional reactions when their actual
lives differ from this. They imagine such deviations to be bad, worry that
perhaps they are also personally bad and brood about the decisions that
brought them to their current life situation. Finding parts of their lives
threatening, they avoid them and defend themselves against acknowledging them. Their habits maintain their avoidance and their distorted thinking, as catalogued by Ellis (1962), maintains their defenses.

Their defenses do not end their emotional experiences, however, but
merely delay their conscious recognition of them. Defensive strategies always guarantee acting in ways that force people to confront whatever they
were trying to avoid. If someone drinks to avoid facing lifelong shame, for
instance, that person's drunken behavior almost guarantees that they will
shame themselves. Whether termed addiction, repetition compulsion, or
karma (all of which are aspects of the same phenomenon), people suffer because they dread their emotional life, when integrating their emotional life
is all that can save them from endless self-imposed suffering. While most
people avoid emotional experience or force themselves to face their fate,
they could more profitably and happily embrace their lives and fulfill themselves. People do not repeat nonsensical acts because they have unconscious
death instincts but because they are compelled unconsciously to heal their
emotional lives, integrate their bypassed emotions, reform their personalities and re-configure their life narratives. Their behavior presents tangible

evidence of their bypassed emotions coupled with the defenses they use to keep them from awareness.

Humans have a very large but finite number of different emotions they can experience, many of which are not named in any language. We all experience each of them, and life's meaning, such as it is, can be found in acknowledging each experience of them, mastering and regulating each of them, putting each into perspective and integrating them all into one's conscious experience of life. Those people who regulate their behavior best while freely experiencing the biggest portion of these affective variations are those people who are considered the most mentally healthy. They are also those who tend to live the healthiest and most productive lives. Why they are motivated to do so is philosophically interesting but less important practically than determining how to induce more people to emulate that aspect of their behavior and helping them to do so. That is a more reachable ideal, although it touches upon parenting, education, social interaction and cultural mores in a profound way.

PART SEVEN

THREE PROBLEMATIC PRIMARY EMOTIONS

The Development of Shame

Most defenses use deliberative processes to keep impulses from affecting behavior (Sandler & Freud, 1985), primarily defending against unpleasant emotions, although positive affect may also be defended against (A. Freud, 1936/1966). These defensive processes always yield anxiety in their wake (Freud, 1933/1965). Repression, for instance, removes declarative thinking from consciousness, while preserving the underlying, already-unconscious procedural type (Clyman, 1992). However, before the onset of declarative processes, the child has only extremely primitive defenses and is more likely to nondefensively endorse statements indicating her belief in her own worthlessness (Balint, 1968).

Emotional processes begin at birth (Greenberg & Paivio, 1997), first arising from innately organized appraisals of situations (Ben-Ze'ev, 2000) and soon becoming biased by experiences and conditioning, but always taking place nearly automatically (Greenberg & Paivio, 1997). Each new experience may be symbolized and integrated or not, depending on the child's ability to maintain non-anxious awareness for that moment (Greenberg & Paivio, 1997). However, any affect too intense to be readily processed is experienced as disorganizing and disturbing (Freud, 1933/1965), fails to be integrated into the appropriate emotional scheme (Greenberg & Paivio, 1997), and results in the poor development of thinking, intrapsychic and behavioral regulation, emotional expression and the other relevant associated abilities (Greenspan, 1989, 1997). Traumatic reactions and emotional processing exist along a single continuum (Philippot & Rimé, 1998), with ambivalently attached individuals especially sensitive to increased distress that they cannot effectively regulate (Magai & Hunziker, 1998).

Since the irrational thinking and behavior associated with early emotional experiences comes from the faulty initial construction of the relevant emotional schemes rather than later conscious decisions, attempts to consciously confront and change them will be futile (Greenberg & Paivio, 1997). Instead, to promote health, the emphasis must be on the orderly processing of experience as it occurs. To do so, the infant must be kept reasonably calm and the experienced affect must not be too intense. Secure attachment relationships, through the effective mirroring of the child's affective experience (Fonagy, 1999), provide these parameters for neural growth and later emotional fluency (Schore, 2001a), while unhealthy ones, especially abusive ones, do not (Schore, 2001b).

According to Greenberg and Paivio (1997), as children grow, their emotional schemes form the basis for a conscious sense of self, helping the child determine how to act when feeling certain ways and predicting how others will behave in turn. The more any particular affect can be effectively integrated into its relevant emotional scheme, the less it will be experienced as disturbing or disintegrating. Throughout life, these schemes organize thinking, memory and perception while creating effective emotional and behavioral responses (Greenberg and Paivio, 1997).

Shame

Shame is one of several "social" affects, aroused by devaluation, exclusion and rejection (Leary, 2000) in a meaningful relationship (Izard, 1977). Darwin (1872/1965) believed shame was a primary emotion, as did Tomkins (1995). While guilt results from specific misbehaviors, which the individual attempts to rectify through a combination of corrective action, empathy and confession (Tangney, 1998), shame, rated a more intense emotion by most (Tangney, 1998), involves global failure attributions caused by violating standards, rules or goals (Lewis, 1992a, 1992b). Shame attributions are associated with field dependence, while guilt is associated with field independence (Lewis, 1971, 1988). Shame induces the bearer to hide, avoid or blame others (Tomkins, 1995). While guilt and shame each involve an implicit other who may be internalized, in guilt the other is horrified at what has been done, while in shame the other is contemptuous of the person doing it (de Rivera, 1977; Lewis, 1971). In children, shame is aroused by others' contempt (Lewis, 1971) and in adults, by the internalized rejecting, ridiculing and contemptuous voices of the past (Greenberg, 2002a).

Shame occurs whenever someone wants or expects something that is withheld from him; without this positive expectation, there can be no shame (Tomkins, 1995). It is a feeling of being unlovable (Lewis, 1992b), exposed (Tomkins, 1995) and lacking self-worth (Greenberg & Paivio, 1997), as well as being small, inept and vulnerable (Izard, 1977; Nathanson, 1992). Shame involves self-conscious self-contempt arising from perceptions of how others are reacting (Lewis, 2003). Unlike guilt, which involves specific appraisals of failure, shame involves global appraisals of inadequacy (Tracy & Robins, 2006). The feelings of exposure in shame also differ from those of embarrassment, since people may become embarrassed when caught doing something well, but shame always involves a sense of failure (Lewis, 1992a).

Shame varies by gender; abused children show more shame than nonabused children; and although it usually changes behavior, shame's intensity may lead to its being bypassed, causing confusion and, ultimately, narcissistic personality adjustments (Lewis, 1987). Studying those who had been victims of childhood sexual abuse, Bonanno et al. (2002) found that those controls who had not been abused showed more Duchenne smiling, those who had disclosed their abuse showed more anger and disgust, and those whose abuse had been discovered accidentally showed more intense shame and non-Duchenne smiling. Shame arose not from what had occurred to these participants previously, but from their internalized expectations of others' contempt directed towards them (Lewis, 2003).

Like all bad feelings, shame can be caused by propositional processes people use when attempting to overcome their internal dysregulation (Greenberg & Paivio, 1997). One can become ashamed of one's shame (Tomkins, 1995); and while shame in oneself or others evokes further shame (Lewis, 1988), it also leads to cycles wherein the shamed individual reacts instead with rage toward the person doing the perceived shaming, which then arouses more shame (Lewis, 1971). Shame also makes personal boundaries permeable (Lewis, 1971; Tomkins, 1995). The shame scheme thus contains a unique set of characteristics and thoughts about oneself and one's relationships that biases future interactions (Leary, 2000).

The Development of Shame Schemes

As Tangney (1998) points out, to make the attributional distinctions between guilt and shame consciously, one would first have to develop a stable concept of oneself, conscious standards of behavior, and the ability to consistently make distinctions between one's behavior and core aspects of oneself. Since this last skill is first acquired at approximately age 8, but does not develop completely until nearly adulthood (Tangney, 1998), early experiences of these emotions clearly cannot depend on conscious cognitive abilities.

Sigmund Freud (1933/1965) believed that shame and guilt, which together he classified as moral anxiety, resulted from the conflict between the ego and the superego, which grows out of the resolution of the Oedipal conflict at about age 6. Michael Lewis (1992a, 1992b) believes that shame depends on the ability to be self-referential and develops first at 24 to 36 months of age, as evidenced by children's first beginning to blush. Erik Erikson (1963) traced shame back further, to Freud's anal stage, occurring at approximately 12-36 months of age, which he believed concerned the struggle to develop personal autonomy without crippling amounts of shame and doubt. Helen Block Lewis (1988) traced shame still further back, believing it is allied with separation distress while guilt is related to fear. To her, the humiliated fury seen in attachment studies was a sign of the work of the shame-rage cycle (Lewis, 1971).

Silvan Tomkins (1995) placed shame further back still, writing that it begins in Freud's oral stage when the child is scolded for eating messily. Shame, he thought, is a violation of the intimacy contract, and occurs whenever someone receives contempt instead of an expected good reaction from an important other. Because of the other's importance, the child is unwilling to give the other up, so he instead clings to the other and attaches the bad to himself in the form of shame. To become counter-contemptuous would necessitate permanently renouncing the other, which will eventually occur should he continue to suffer from that person's continual contempt. Tomkins thus believed that children become vulnerable to shame responses when they are first able to distinguish their mother from strangers, which he put at about 7 months. Carroll Izard (1977) placed this development at around 4 to 5 months. Once this milestone is reached, Tomkins believed, after one stranger evokes a shame response, such as hiding, all strangers do so for several weeks or months. Yet, these shame responses often arouse further parental contempt, as do being too verbally outgoing with strangers or staring at them too much (Tomkins, 1995).

However, Barrett (1998) argued that emotion depends on context, not cognition, and that studies have consistently found that cognition itself precedes the theoretical estimates that experimenters had presumed for it. He further argued that emotional development consists of widening the contexts in which any particular emotion might appear, as the child's life takes on increasing breadth and depth. If we do not see a particular emotional response in a context in which we might expect it, we may only say that the response does not occur in that context, not that either the emotion or response do not exist (Barrett, 1998).

With shame, these contexts include other's contempt, emotional display taboos, failures in mirroring positive affect and increasingly, shame itself (Tomkins, 1995). Shame in oneself or others evokes further shame (Lewis, 1988). Each family's emotional life revolves around central idiosyncratic affects, which children—especially the ambivalently attached—seek to avoid (Magai & Hunziker, 1998). Failure to do so elicits shame, as does seeing one's parents struggling with shame (Tomkins, 1995). Tomkins notes that this hidden and unprocessed shame then becomes amplified and seeks expression, while the individual becomes increasingly bored.

Thus, when considering the beginning of the shame scheme's development, one must look at potential shame-inducing contexts rather than inferred cognitive abilities. Given the shame-rage cycle (Lewis, 1971), clear starting places to search for these origins are the instances when withholding expected rewards results in rage responses. These should yield at least proto-shame (Elster, 1999), which would later be incorporated into the shame scheme as it develops. Rage is present from birth (Parens, 1992), only gradually becoming attenuated to anger and irritation in normal development (Kernberg, 1992). At first, rage aids growth, although the chronic experience of unpleasant affective states may turn it into a hostile and destructive force later in development (Parens, 1992).

Another likely early component of the shame scheme involves the ongoing imprecision in parental mirroring. While close but inexact early mirroring settles the child and aids affective development (Fonagy, 1999) by providing the mild amounts of rage and shame vital to the development of these emotional schemes and the ongoing growth of autonomy (Erikson, 1963; Izard, 1977), the extreme lack of fluency in mirroring (Fonagy, 1999) creates crippling, anxiety-provoking experiences of rage and nonintegrated shame (Greenberg & Paivio, 1997). These severe, phase-inappropriate experiences would, in turn, disrupt normal affective functioning and development, causing many future difficulties since, according to the laws of respondent learning, the effects of excessive emotional stimulation can last for a lifetime (Knapp, 1992).

Shame-Related Pathology

Incompletely processed affect leads to rumination (Philippot & Rimé, 1998) and bad personal outcomes (Strasser, 1999) while complete processing deficits lead to chronic affective dispositions rather than flexible action tendencies (Lyons, 1998). In all psychopathology, the repertoire of emotional responses is stably limited and lacks flexibility (Jenkins & Oatley, 1998). While acute schematic emotions seem to be adaptive, no matter how intense, chronic ones seemingly are not (Bybee & Quiles, 1998), although such studies apparently have yet to be undertaken regarding shame.

Because very young children cannot yet defend themselves from intense shame experiences through the more advanced, propositionally produced strategies (A. Freud, 1936/1966), they either passively accept the factuality of their self-perceived badness (Balint, 1968) or resort to developmentally primitive defensive mechanisms such as splitting and disowning parts of themselves (Kaufman, 1985). Not surprisingly, unprocessed shame has been tied to narcissistic compensations (Kohut, 1966/1985; Lewis, 1987; Wurmser, 1987) along with depression (Lewis, 1971), borderline personality disorder (Lewis, 1987), obsessive-compulsive behavior (Kaufman, 1985; Lewis, 1971) and hysteria (Freud, 1893/1959f). By remaining unprocessed and bypassed, shame thus becomes the central organizing characteristic of many disordered personalities (Tomkins, 1995).

Along with anxiety, shame produces most psychiatric problems (Greenberg, 2002a). It can only be relieved if one "confesses" one's perceived transgressions to someone empowered to grant forgiveness (Lewis, 1992b), yet nonintegrated preverbal shame experiences cannot be easily accessed nor confessed. They may be best accessed through the transference process; but if therapists ignore their patients' shame, all efforts to form therapeutic bonds will fail, resulting in rage-filled attacks on therapists by their patients (Scheff, 1998). Efforts to integrate shame schemes must first begin with accepting one's shame (Greenberg, 2002a), yet the "shame phobic" nature of our culture makes this difficult (Tangney, 1998).

Conclusion

As noted earlier, appraisal theories do not explain emotional arousal as well as network theories do. Sometimes, people react emotionally and the related cognitions are attached later. When anyone, especially young children, experiences intense emotions for which they are not cognitively prepared to cope, a traumatic dissociation is likely to result. Such emotions will not be integrated into the relevant emotion schemes. With young children, this is especially likely to occur when the child's most significant attachment figures do not help regulate the emotion as it occurs.

Along with those for other affects, the emotion schemes for shame begin to form in infancy, in this case due to unexpected disruptions in the relationship between the child and her caretaker. Because these experiences occur before the advent of declarative processing, they are neither represented verbally nor accessible to memory by ordinary means. While mild and manageable amounts of shame assist development, intense shame-arousing experiences cannot be adequately processed and are thus experienced as traumatic (Freshwater & Robertson, 2002). They continue to fester and strive for behavioral expression (Freud, 1933/1965) as a means toward completing the integration of the emotional scheme.

As Greenberg (2002a) noted, emotions are adaptive when they increase possibilities and foster integration; yet, when they confuse people, overwhelm them or debilitate their relationships, they are not. Chronic, unprocessed shame prevents people from achieving their inherent potentials since it controls an inordinate amount of behavior and prevents the integration of large portions of both internal and external experience. Given the usual defensive strategies utilized against the experience of intense, unprocessed shame, our current child-rearing practices and the shame-avoidant nature of our culture make the continued prevalence of narcissistic disorders and ongoing rage-filled behavior a virtual certainty.

Humiliation

SOME TYPES OF emotions direct one's attention to one's subjective inner self, one's characteristics and how one relates to others (Leary, 2000). Examples of such self-conscious or social emotions include shame, embarrassment, humiliation, contempt, social anxiety, hurt feelings, jealousy, pride, love, respect and acceptance (Leary, 2000, 2004). These emotions, which aid survival by maintaining one's acceptance and position within important groups (Kemeny et al., 2004), always arise from the real or imagined reactions of others (Leary, 2004).

Kemeny (2003) theorized that specific emotional responses are probably associated with different physiological stress responses. In particular, she hypothesized that appraising a situation as socially threatening leads to shame and humiliation, decreases the subjective sense of self-worth and increases HPA activity. If the appraisals of social threat were changed, cortisol levels should decrease to normal daily levels (Dickerson et al., 2004; Gruenewald et al., 2004; Kemeny, 2003; Kemeny et al., 2004).

As discussed in the last chapter, shame denotes a feeling of inadequacy after an individual publicly (Kemeny et al., 2004) violates important group standards (Smith, 2001) such as group morality (Negrao et al., 2005). To result in shame, such transgressions cannot be attributed to behavior, which would result in guilt, but must be perceived as caused by stable personal characteristics outside the individual's control (Tracy & Robins, 2006).

Shame is a personal (Negrao et al., 2005) and private (Jennings & Murphy, 2000) assessment of badness or unworthiness (Gumley, White, & Power, 1999; Lewis, 1971; Nathanson, 1992; Tomkins, 1995; Tracy & Robins, 2006) that results in feelings of defeat, defectiveness and low self-worth (Negrao et al., 2005). Leading to heightened self-consciousness without feelings of injustice (Gumley et al., 1999), shame can occur without others knowing, though groups often use it to reinforce conformity (Smith, 2001). When feeling ashamed, people become increasingly depressed (Gumley et al., 1999), blush (Darwin, 1872/1965; Stoller, 1987; Tomkins, 1995) and try to maintain their social attractiveness (Gumley et al., 1999) by rededicating themselves to others in their group (Jennings & Murphy, 2000).

Like shame, embarrassment leads to feelings of self-blame and ineptitude (Negrao et al., 2005) after negative self-evaluations (Lewis & Ramsay, 2002). However, while shame stems from moral violations (Negrao et al., 2005) attributed to core personal characteristics (Kemeny et al., 2004), embarrassment occurs when the failures are relatively trivial social transgressions (Negrao et al., 2005) or stem from less central personal characteristics (Kemeny et al., 2004). Their expressions are quite different, with embarrassment causing smiling, nervousness and averted gaze (Lewis & Ramsay, 2002).

Basic emotion theorists and their followers (e.g., Izard, 1977, 2002; Lewis, 1971; Plutchik, 1991, 2000; Nathanson, 1992; Tomkins, 1995) have long believed that shame and humiliation stem from the same root emotion. Each involves self-presentational concerns (Morrison & Gilbert, 2001) and the belief that the individual has been stigmatized due to his or her core traits (Leary, 2004). This leads to social devaluation, exclusion and rejection (Leary, 2000) even if the individual does not believe he or she was not at fault (Leary, 2004). While some (e.g., Stoller, 1987; Nathanson, 1992; Tomkins, 1995) believe humiliation is merely intense shame, humiliation has no outward expression (Stoller, 1987) and each is experienced uniquely (Leary, 2000).

The word *humiliation* comes from the Latin root *humus*, meaning earth. Literally, humiliation refers to the act of thrusting others' faces into the ground by subjugating or degrading them (Lindner, 2001, 2002). Humiliation is the perception that one is being intentionally debased (Negrao et al., 2005), usually publicly (Strauchler et al., 2004), by someone in authority (Urban, 2003). It involves others' negative social evaluations (Jennings & Murphy, 2000) delivered in a manner designed to cost one his or her honor, pride, dignity (Lindner, 2002) and sense of identity (Lindner, 2001). One feels slandered and left vulnerable to attack (Negrao et al., 2005), having lost both self-respect and the respect of others (Lindner, 2002). According to Smith (2001):

> [Humiliation involves] the forced ejection and/or exclusion of individuals or groups from social roles and/or social categories with which they subjectively identify in a way that conveys the message that they are fundamentally inadequate to fill those roles or belong to those categories. Humiliation involves being violently pushed down and/or forcibly kept below the boundary line that separates the worthy from the unworthy. Humiliation may be enacted through either deliberate action or deliberate inaction. However, in all cases, its essence is to grind the face of the victim into the dirt—and leave them there, helpless. (p. 542)

More than an emotion, humiliation is a mechanism of social control (Lindner, 2001) that takes place whenever someone is made to feel less worthy than others (Smith, 2001). It produces servility (Lindner, 2001) tinged with depression (Lindner, 2002) and resentful desires to cast off the forcibly imposed negative identity (Smith, 2001). Struggling for recognition and pride, the humiliated admire, envy and want to be accepted by those who humiliate them but also feel afraid and insecure (Lindner, 2002). While wanting to save face (Jennings & Murphy, 2000) and maintain their social standing (Gumley et al., 1999), the humiliated know that showing resistance or resentment would invite additional punishment or further humiliation (Smith, 2001). This leads to strong, often impotent, desires to retaliate against those held responsible for their suffering (Morrison & Gilbert, 2001). These feelings can become as consuming as an addiction, though if the humiliated have few resources, their tactics for revenge may be reduced to passive resistance or sabotage (Lindner, 2002). Because the humiliated resent their humbled status, their oppressors often continue to humiliate them to reinforce the social order and remind them that the social chasm between them is now insurmountable (Smith, 2001; Urban, 2003).

Though the humiliated may accept their humbled status as part of the natural order (Lindner, 2002), societal beliefs in human rights make humiliation illegitimate and thus increase its painfulness (Lindner, 2001; Smith, 2001). Directed ridicule before peers increases the power of humiliation, while ridicule clearly in jest carries no humiliating power (Geiger & Fischer, 2006). Humiliations originating in rejected love are extremely hurtful (Lindner, 2002), with children often experiencing being told "no" by an adult as humiliating (Urban, 2003). Attacks on changeable aspects of oneself can be easily reappraised as constructive criticism, so they are not usually considered humiliating (Geiger & Fischer, 2006). Both daydreams (Stoller, 1987) and traditional masculine behavior (Jennings & Murphy, 2000) defend against humiliation, which is seen as a factor in domestic violence (Strauchler et al., 2004) and in the aggression of psychopaths (Morrison & Gilbert, 2001), who may kill to regain respect (Stoller, 1987). Homophobia may originate less from fears about being gay than from fears of being perceived as unacceptable, even among others attracted to members of their own gender (Jennings & Murphy, 2000).

Shame and humiliation interact with one another and often occur together, though either can occur separately (Smith, 2001). For instance, each occurs frequently among survivors of childhood sexual abuse (Negrao et al., 2005). Both shame and humiliation involve stable, uncontrollable, personal characteristics (Geiger & Fischer, 2006), and disorders of either can lead to narcissistic disorders (Lewis, 1971; Lewis, 1992b; Urban, 2003). Each is frequently bypassed to avoid experiencing emotional pain (Lewis, 1971). Children's humiliation by their parents often induces shame (Lewis, 1992b). The humiliated may not feel shame if they accept their assigned identities, though if they do not, they may feel either ashamed of their failure to reach the standards of their oppressors or ashamed of failing to assert themselves (Smith, 2001). Alternately, they may admire their oppressors and feel ashamed of admiring them (Lindner, 2002).

Humiliation differs from shame because, unlike shame, the focus in humiliation is external, on those doing the degrading (Smith, 2001). While humiliation makes one inferior to others socially, it is those who did the devaluing who receive blame (Negrao et al., 2005) for their unfairness and injustice (Gumley et al., 1999; Morrison & Gilbert, 2001). Only humiliation leads to feelings of debasement (Lindner, 2002) and the desire to retaliate (Morrison & Gilbert, 2001). While people often believe they deserve to feel shame, they rarely believe their humiliations were justified (Morrison & Gilbert, 2001; Smith, 2001). Humiliation differs from anger in its emphasis on alleged deficiencies within the self (Negrao et al., 2005), though if someone is externally blocked from rising against their oppressors, the emotion experienced is anger (Smith, 2001).

Forgiveness and Forgivingness

Since humiliation involves blame, forgiveness should logically halt its progression. Schmitt, Gollwitzer, Förster, and Montada (2004) believe that effective apologies have five components: (a) an admission of culpability, (b) an awareness of the consequences, (c) an expression of remorse, (d) a request for forgiveness and (e) a promise to compensate the victim for unjust losses. However, they found that people often infer these elements of an apology even when they go unstated; admitting fault and offering compensation have the largest impact on obtaining forgiveness, even when they are not stated explicitly; and asking for forgiveness is perceived as insincere if it is not accompanied by acknowledgement of the harm caused and an offer of restitution (Schmitt et al., 2004).

McCullough, Bono, and Root (2007) found that rumination and situational forgiveness are inversely related to one another. Those whose rumination increases in the seven days after being wronged show increased avoidance of and desire for revenge towards their wrongdoer, while decreased rumination leads (weakly) to decreases in those variables. Trait positive affect, trait negative affect and current mood states had no effects on these relationships, though anger, but not fear, towards the perpetrator mediated the effects. McCullough, Bono et al. also found that the frequency of rumination at one time predicted anger, avoidance and revenge motivation the following day, after initial levels of these variables were statistically controlled.

Berry, Worthington, O'Connor, Parrott, and Wade (2005) studied *forgivingness*, or trait forgiveness, from an emotional viewpoint. After validating a scale measuring forgivingness, they conducted three studies correlating forgivingness with a variety of constructs of interest, such as neuroticism. Of note here, they found that vengeful rumination (a disposition to hold grudges) mediated the strong relationships between forgivingness and state anger, trait anger and revenge motivation. Their studies, purely correlational, involved college students filling out forms rather than actual experiences of transgression, and it used a measure of rumination so specifically tailored to vengefulness that the results may have been a foregone conclusion.

Conclusion

Humiliated fury is a force to be reckoned with, especially among those prone to violence. Much violent crime is triggered by feelings of humiliation, as is much bullying. Compared to many other emotions, humiliation has been studied relatively little, yet its implications are huge and demand much more research. In therapeutic work with forensic populations, the understanding of humiliation and its effects is vital.

Disgust

DARWIN (1872/1965) WROTE one of the first characterizations of disgust, which he considered to have arisen originally as a precaution against contamination related to waste and tainted food. However, much as the emotional system incorporated earlier structures put in place to track physical pain (Shirtcliff et al., 2009), the disgust system evolved beyond this original purpose. Now, we find disgust directed towards that which is morally wrong or repugnant (Borg, Lieberman, & Kiehl, 2008; Calder et al., 2010). Disgust related to contamination by pathogens and by social-moral taint uses much of the same neural circuitry, adding substance to the reports that they feel similar, but each also activates unique neural structures (Borg et al., 2008).

The anterior insula, which among its other functions serves as part of the gustatory cortex, appears to have roles in processing facial expressions of disgust (Olatunji et al., 2010), which suggests that Darwin may have been correct. However, the anterior insula is not preferentially involved in processing disgust when facial recognition is not involved (Borg et al., 2008) or the presentation of the disgusting material never reaches the level of awareness (Phillips et al., 2004). Some research suggests that the anterior insula preferentially processes faces depicting moral rather than pathogen-related disgust (Calder et al., 2010), while other research suggests that it is no more activated by disgust than by any other negative emotional state (Borg et al., 2008).

By most accounts, disgust is a basic emotion along with fear, sadness, anger, happiness, surprise and, depending on the scheme, perhaps others. Darwin (1872/1965) thought that disgust was associated with a single universal facial expression, characterized by an open mouth and protruding tongue. Tomkins (1995) distinguished disgust from *dissmell*, a word he coined for the aversion to unpleasant odors, such as that of sewage, vomit, feces or rotting food. He believed that dissmell, indicated by a closed mouth and wrinkled nose (as if to block the offending smell) was also a basic emotion. Current theorists collapse the distinction between disgust and dissmell and consider both to be aspects of disgust. They have added a third expression (with curled upper lip) that is characteristic exclusively of moral disgust (Calder et al., 2010; Olatunji & Sawchuk, 2005).

Unlike Tomkins (1995), who believed that shame was a basic emotion, many researchers now believe that shame may also be an offshoot of disgust (Olatunji & Sawchuk, 2005). Nathanson (1992), agreeing with Tomkins, believes they are each basic emotions, though he believes that self-disgust complicates many instances of shame and guilt, making them more problematic and difficult to treat. Clearly, this is a complicated emotional picture and one that has still not been well-studied or well-conceptualized, especially compared to other supposedly basic emotions like anger or fear. It is not even clear how three such widely varying facial expressions could all refer to the same basic emotion (Olatunji & Sawchuk, 2005).

According to Olatunji et al. (2010), there are three main kinds of elementary disgust: concerns about rotting food and oral incorporation of human waste; reminders of our animal nature, such as death, injury, sex and feces; and contamination by disease. To these, Olatunji and Sawchuk (2005) added interpersonal and socio-moral concerns. Borg et al. (2008) argued that sexual moral disgust and nonsexual moral disgust are also separable. Freud (1905/1962) believed that this transition from food and waste to moral and sexual concerns was intended to restrict sexual fantasies to culturally acceptable topics (e.g., no incest fantasies), while Tomkins (1995) believed that disgust was a reaction to unwelcome intimacy. Evidence indicates that people find incest more disgusting than other immoral acts and that their reactions to immoral sexual acts activate more of the brain, and do so more fully, than their reactions to immoral nonsexual acts do (Borg et al., 2008).

However, though the broad categories eliciting disgust appear to be universal, what does so within these categories varies by culture and is socially disseminated and reinforced (Olatunji & Sawchuk, 2005). Each given culture has its own unique beliefs about which foods, animals and practices are considered disgusting (Teachman, 2006). According to Olatunji and Sawchuk, vomit and human waste are considered disgusting across cultures, but various cultures find different foods and animals disgusting that others do not. Sexual and hygiene practices and the rituals surrounding death are all culturally determined with an eye towards controlling what that culture considers disgusting (Olatunji & Sawchuk, 2005). Across cultures, what is considered immoral tends to be considered disgusting, though what is considered immoral varies widely from culture to culture (Borg et al., 2008). The word *disgust* even has different connotations in different cultures, essentially referring to something that tastes rotten in German but to a moral transgression in English (Calder et al., 2010).

Since what is considered disgusting is culturally determined and animals do not show disgust like humans do, disgust may be less evolutionarily prepared than other basic emotions (Olatunji & Sawchuk, 2005). Infants make the prototypical expression of disgust soon after birth, but it remains unclear what these expressions mean (McKay & Tsao, 2005). Between the ages of 2 and 9, children imitate others' expressions of disgust without understanding what they mean (Olatunji & Sawchuk, 2005). Core disgust reactions appear between about ages 4 and 6, when children begin to understand that invisible entities like germs exist (McKay & Tsao, 2005). However, when seeing universal faces of disgust that adults easily recognize, children between 4 and 9 years old do not relate stories appropriate to disgust even when the concept has been thoroughly explained to them beforehand. Instead, they tend to see the expression as conveying anger, particularly as they reach the upper end of that age range (Widen & Russell, 2010).

The appraisal criteria for eliciting disgust are simple—good/bad, like/dislike, and pleasant/unpleasant—and because they are conditioned, the appraisals occur completely outside conscious awareness, making them much harder to alter later (McKay & Tsao, 2005). People vary widely in how intensely they experience disgust (Olatunji & Sawchuk, 2005). Some people who have heightened disgust sensitivity are highly prone to experiencing it (Cisler, Olatunji, Lohr, & Williams, 2009), which appears to be a stable personality trait (Olatunji et al., 2010). Especially among such individuals, anything that has ever come into contact with something disgusting or can be associated mentally with something disgusting is itself considered disgusting (McKay & Tsao, 2005). For example, while touching a roach is generally (in American culture) considered disgusting, touching something touched by a person who recently touched a roach would also be considered disgusting. Likewise, fecal matter is considered disgusting, but edible candy shaped to resemble fecal matter is also considered disgusting. Though others do not, those highly sensitized to disgust have added difficulty maintaining their focus on other matters when extraneous stimuli they find disgusting impinge on their awareness (Cisler et al., 2009). Such sensitivity, when reinforced by the environment, sometimes leads to problems regulating disgust appropriately (Olatunji et al., 2010).

In all cases, disgust is accompanied by heightened activity of the parasympathetic nervous system, and the dominant action tendency is avoidance or withdrawal (Olatunji & Sawchuk, 2005). According to Olatunji and Sawchuk, disgust is commonly expressed by leaving, pushing offending items away, looking away, plugging one's nose and so forth. Helplessness, avoidance and submissive behavior may all be derivatives of disgust. They believe that the anti-smoking and vegetarian movements have largely been influenced by disgust. Prejudice, racial intolerance and homophobia also show the influence of disgust. Across cultures, diseased and disfigured people are commonly viewed as disgusting, as are unfamiliarity, hypocrisy, betrayal and sycophancy (Olatunji & Sawchuk, 2005).

There are no psychiatric disorders specific to disgust, but several appear to be related to inflated disgust reactions (McKay & Tsao, 2005). For instance, disgust sensitivity is heightened among those with psychotic disorders (Olatunji & Sawchuk, 2005). Theoretically, pathological aspects of disgust would lead to excessive estimations of the threats posed by the object or idea, clinically significant impairment in functioning and an inability to use logical reasoning to calm these reactions (Teachman, 2006). Theory also suggests that intense self-disgust should increase one's vulnerability to emotional disorders (Olatunji & Sawchuk, 2005). Most problems associated with pathological aspects of disgust appear to be related not to one's primary appraisals of an item or idea's disgusting nature, but instead to the secondary appraisals that one cannot cope with the offending item or idea (Teachman, 2006).

Not surprisingly, since disgust and anxiety are associated with many of the same types of cognitive biases (Blanchette & Richards, 2010), many pathological aspects of disgust are related to anxiety disorders. At least some animal phobias are mediated by exaggerated disgust reactions, which may be related to worries about contamination (Olatunji & Sawchuk, 2005). Hairy, slimy and scaly animals are frequent targets of animal phobias, as are those that live in sewage or unclean environments (Olatunji & Sawchuk, 2005). Blood injection phobias, the only phobias to cause fainting (a parasympathetic overreaction), also are mediated by disgust (Olatunji et al., 2010; Olatunji & Sawchuk, 2005). Research has shown that these phobias are associated with a universal sense of repugnance across many domains besides the one in which the specific phobia lies (Olatunji et al., 2010), and a large overlap exists between the thoughts that lead to phobic reactions and those indicative of general disgust sensitivity (Teachman, 2006). Even when phobic reactions are dampened through controlled exposure, the underlying disgust reactions remain intact (Olatunji et al., 2010).

Because people believe the intrusive thoughts symptomatic of Obsessive Compulsive Disorder indicate that something about them is disgusting, they avoid them and never learn that they are not dangerous (Teachman, 2006). Over half of those suffering from Obsessive Compulsive Disorder have excessive fears of contamination, which are also mediated by disgust (Olatunji et al., 2010; Olatunji & Sawchuk, 2005). These fears are related to chains of contagion in which people believe that once a contaminated item has been touched, everything it subsequently touches (or anything which the item or person it touches later touches) is equally tainted (Olatunji & Sawchuk, 2005). The treatment for this disorder does not remove these intrusive and irrational thoughts, but seeks to minimize their importance and alter their interpretations and the secondary appraisals suggesting that they cannot be coped with (Teachman, 2006).

Eating disorders (particularly bulimia) are associated not only with disgust related to food and eating, but also with self-disgust (McKay & Tsao, 2005). Those with bulimia have been conditioned to find overeating and fatness disgusting and show heightened disgust sensitivity only for their own bodies and for food, especially high-calorie foods (Olatunji

& Sawchuk, 2005). In remission, they are less disgusted by their bodies but remain equally disgusted by food (Olatunji & Sawchuk, 2005). Self-disgust is also implicated in the self-loathing and feelings of dirtiness that many sexual abuse and rape victims feel after being assaulted (McKay & Tsao, 2005).

Depressed patients are vigilant for others' expressions of disgust, which they may believe are directed at them (Surguladze et al., 2010). This is especially true of the disgust variety expressed with curled upper lip, which is the type most closely associated with anger and interpersonal judgment (Calder et al., 2010). Alcoholics also attribute more anger and disgust than is warranted to others' facial expressions (Pham & Philippot, 2010). Some theory suggests that depression is a coupling of sadness and self-disgust (Surguladze et al., 2010). In most people without psychiatric disorders, disgust is processed more quickly and efficiently than fear, though in one study this was reversed among patients with remitted symptoms of Bipolar Disorder (Malhi et al., 2007).

Those with Intermittent Explosive Disorder have trouble recognizing facial expressions of both disgust and anger (Fairchild et al., 2009). Psychopathy, a developmental disorder characterized by impaired social cognition and behavior that is often seen among criminals, is also notable for the inability to accurately identify facial expressions of disgust and anger, especially among those whose behavior is the most impulsive and antisocial (Hansen et al., 2008). Most psychopathic and nonpsychopathic criminals recognize the facial expressions of emotion more poorly than do control subjects, but those who are not psychopaths are poorer at recognizing fear and sadness, and psychopaths are poorer at identifying disgust, anger and happiness (Pham & Philippot, 2010). These patterns match those found among those with Conduct Disorder: those with adolescent-onset type have impaired recognition of fear, while those with childhood-onset type (who are considered more likely to develop into adult psychopaths) have marked deficits recognizing disgust, anger and happiness (Fairchild et al., 2009).

Conclusion

Disgust is an extremely complex and tangled emotional construct that, when all is finally said and done, is likely to be viewed as several related emotions rather than a single one. At this time, the vocabulary is not yet in place for this to happen. Although it is not solely associated with any single disorder, it appears clear that its recognition and the thoughts and behaviors connected with its elicitation are involved in a number of extremely problematic conditions, particularly among those who are either insensitive or hypersensitive to it. If shame (and thus, potentially, humiliation) are viewed as derivatives of disgust, it is involved in an even larger number of referrals to counseling and therapy clinics. Not yet researched extensively, it still must be understood by the clinician and treated effectively to provide the maximum benefit possible to those served.

PART EIGHT

CLINICAL CONDITIONS

Anxiety

DATING BACK TO at least 1525 (Beck & Emery, 1985), the English term "anxiety" probably comes from the Latin word *anxius*, "to choke up," through the French *angere*, apparently referring to the physical sensations commonly encountered during anxiety episodes (Beck & Emery, 1985; Vaillant, 1993). It is linguistically related to the English words "anger" and "anguish," plus words in other languages meaning grief, sorrow and longing (Bowlby, 1973). Darwin (1872/1965) connected it with grief.

Another related word is the German *angst*, popular with both existential philosophers and psychoanalysts. According to Hillman (1960), both Kierkegaard and Heidegger believed that *angst* was the primary emotion in human life, related to non-being. Kierkegaard thought sexuality, sin and alienation from natural animal life led to *angst*, while Heidegger based his entire philosophy on it. The Buddhists also believe that fear and dread are innate not just to humans but to all existence, with only the purified Buddhas existing without it (Hillman, 1960). Yet, as Solomon (1976) writes, even among the existentialists, *angst* could refer to any of the following: anxiety; dread; anguish; excruciating distress or suffering; extreme fear of the unknown, nothingness, or everything; or fear of one's own desires, emotions, or identity.

Because individual emotions do not seem to be natural categories across cultures, the lack of precise translation equivalents for *angst* is unsurprising, although its usual translation as "anxiety" creates problems. While the former is ill-defined, the latter is even more so. "Anxiety" covers a number of heterogeneous phenomena (Bowlby, 1973) and, as Tomkins (1995) noted, it now potentially refers to all negative emotions except anger. It means "stress" and is signaled by "avoidance," so anything producing negative affect is now said to cause anxiety (Tomkins, 1995). Despite this lack of clarity, this chapter will attempt to find a common meaning.

Therapeutic and Philosophical Contributions on Anxiety

Since Sigmund Freud, psychotherapists have written about many aspects of anxiety, with Freud initiating most of these lines of exploration. Although it has become commonplace to note Freud's evolving views and contrast them, he never so much gave up old thinking as added new ideas onto it (Guntrip, 1973). Therefore, Freud's thinking has largely been integrated herein, unless clear changes necessitated accounting for his developing thoughts. The context should show these areas sufficiently.

Anxiety and the Body

Freud (1894/1959d) initially believed that people develop anxiety when they are unable to deal with danger. He thought that two types of anxiety exist: normal anxiety is experienced due to external dangers, while neurotic anxiety results from perturbations of the sexual drive whenever an aroused person is unable to complete the sexual act for any reason. Anxiety thus starts as a physical phenomenon, although it has psychological ramifications.

Reich (1933/1972, 1945/1982, 1947/1973) adopted this explanation. Actual and neurotic anxieties contain and imply each other (Reich, 1945/1982, 1947/1973). Anxiety is brought about by the frustration of sexual motility (Reich 1933/1972) resulting from unresolved sexual tensions

(Reich, 1947/1973). Reich (1945/1982) measured skin conductance on the genitals and determined that, while the flow of energy is outwards in sexual excitement, anxiety reverses this flow back into the body. In anxiety, the genitals contract while the heart becomes overexcited and feels like it might explode (Reich, 1947/1973). Reich (1945/1982) also noted that blocking aggressive impulses leads to anxiety, believing this occurred because they are also directed outwards from the body.

Lowen (1958), following Reich's lead, wrote that anxiety results when the pleasurable release of tension is impossible. Mathematically put, the promise of pleasure plus the threat of pain equals anxiety (Lowen, 1975). Put still another way, anxiety is the conflict between an energetic striving in the body and a block set up to stop it (Lowen, 1975). Although not pathological unless it becomes a chronic state, anxiety is always experienced as threatening (Lowen, 1958). To defend themselves against anxiety, people avoid striving for the pleasure that originally causes anxiety to arise (Lowen, 1975).

Anxiety simultaneously activates the BAS and the BIS (Cacioppo & Berntson, 1999; Knyazev et al., 2006) and thus both the parasympathetic and the sympathetic nervous systems (Izard, 1977). It is equivalent to wanting something and not being willing to pursue it because of the punishment that will occur. Heart troubles and breathing difficulties are common correlates of anxiety (Lowen, 1975), which can feel like a choking sensation throughout the body (Vaillant, 1993) or nausea with an inability to vomit (Sullivan, 1953b), sensations associated with disgust (Nathanson, 1992).

Anxiety, Danger and Trauma

Although they seem similar, anxiety and fright are very different (Freud, 1895/1959f). Anxiety occurs when there is no possibility of mastery or emotional discharge (Freud, 1926/1959c). Freud originally believed that although fright caused trauma (Freud, 1895/1959g), neurotic anxiety required blocked sexuality. He conceded that fear and other emotions might contribute to anxiety but did not cause it (Freud, 1895/1959g). Later, he came to believe that trauma itself was the ultimate cause of anxiety (Freud, 1933/1965).

Trauma results, he believed, when one is not adequately anxious and vigilant before the devastating event occurs (Freud, 1920/1961). After suffering a trauma, individuals may develop anxiety to help maintain vigilance against future injury (Freud, 1917/1966). In this way, anxiety signals the expectation of and preparation for a future trauma but is experienced as a minor trauma itself (Freud, 1926/1959c). This anticipatory readiness to act can also be seen in the free-floating anxiety of neurosis (Freud, 1917/1966).

Traumatic dreams are attempts to restore the person to the state he was in before the trauma by retrospectively building anxiety but otherwise restoring what existed beforehand (Freud, 1920/1961). Anxiety can thus refer to a previous or current danger, or signal that one is about to occur (Freud, 1926/1959c). While anxiety is useful in establishing readiness, the disorganizing aspects of anxiety are unhelpful (Freud, 1917/1966).

Greenspan (1997) noted that as children grow, they organize their minds affectively, abstracting and differentiating their thinking and memories at ever-higher levels. He believed that during traumas or traumatic memories, the associated intense anxiety results in diminished abilities to abstract and differentiate thinking. This results in traumatic experiences being stored with memories from earlier ages, resulting in a lack of integration in the concurrent and subsequent formulations of the person's sense of self.

Anxiety, Repression, and Conflict

During repression, the act of keeping drives out of consciousness

(Freud, 1915/1959h), only the ideas connected with these drives usually become unconscious (Freud, 1915/1959h, 1915/1959j). The drive-connected affect usually remains conscious, becomes stronger and attaches to a new idea, but it sometimes changes into other affects (Freud, 1915/1959h). If the affects themselves are repressed and become unconscious, the person invariably experiences anxiety instead of the repressed affect (Freud, 1915/1959j). When an individual has conflicting impulses, both are repressed and thus become anxiety (Freud, 1926/1959c). All incompletely experienced affect becomes anxiety (Freud, 1933/1965), which then causes further repression (Freud, 1926/1959c). Thus, anxiety, which Freud took to be a fear of one's own drives, both causes and results from repression (Freud, 1933/1965).

Horney (1937) distinguished between basic and neurotic anxiety. The former is the feeling of being lost, helpless and unwanted in a cruel world, while the latter—the basis for neurosis—is a fear of one's repressed hostility (Horney, 1937). Emotional conflicts can also be involved in its generation, and anxiety is subjectively most intense when the person is caught in an acute dilemma between two or more imperative motives (Horney, 1939). For example, if one unconsciously wishes to die, one will become anxious about death (Horney, 1937). Repressed emotions create inner conflicts, which make the person unsure of what is dangerous and what is not, leading in turn to feelings of helplessness (May, 1950).

Whenever drives become too intense, defenses are engaged and anxiety results (A. Freud, 1936/1966). Even intense maturational changes, like the development of teething, can lead to anxiety (Erikson, 1963). Too much of any emotion, such as sadness, can be anxiety-provoking; but surrendering oneself to its action tendencies can bring relief, so conflict is automatically built into all intensely negative emotional experiences (Sandler & Freud 1985).

Every suppressed emotion is capable of becoming anxiety (Deutsch, 1930/1965b), but pleasant feelings tend to be less defended against than painful ones (A. Freud, 1936/1966). Repressed emotions continue to operate unconsciously, with consequent disturbing effects on both consciousness and behavior (Guntrip, 1973). A child who does not mourn experiences anxiety, which he then defends against; unaware of his continuing grief, he increasingly attracts grief-arousing situations to himself (Deutsch, 1937/1965a). This felt need to experience and master repressed emotions is stronger even than the desire to avoid emotional pain (Freud, 1920/1961).

Anxiety and Symptoms

Many theorists have noted the links between blocked symptoms and increased anxiety. Freud (1926/1959c) noted that symptoms replace repressed affect, help avoid anxiety and have to be defended against themselves. He had observed much earlier that those with obsessional neuroses show no anxiety unless their symptoms are blocked (Freud, 1917/1966); and Deutsch (1930/1965) noted the same about those with conversion hysteria. Freud (1933/1965) later stretched this understanding to all symptoms, realizing that when they are blocked, anxiety ensues. Anna Freud (1936/1966) wrote that the loss of defenses against anxiety may lead to neurosis and character warping.

Anxiety and the Ego Processes

In his structural model, Freud (1923/1960) claimed that the ego, because it must respond to demands from the id, superego and outside world, has three possible sources of danger and, thus, three separate types of anxiety. In each case, one's emotional involvement with that sphere is withdrawn and becomes anxiety. Because of this, Freud (1923/1960, 1933/1965) wrote, "The ego is the (sole) seat of anxiety." As opposed to emotional impulses and the death instinct, both thought to reside in the id (Freud, 1923/1960), anxiety has its origins in the ego, where it arises to keep the id impulses in check (Freud, 1933/1965).

Anna Freud (Sandler & Freud 1985) believed that the ego's secondary process thinking arose to interpose thoughts between impulses and action. However, this adds conflict that does not exist between impulses and results in anxiety. When ego processes are shut down (e.g., in orgies or drunkenness), there is no anxiety. Ego processes defend not only against anxiety but also against all other painful affects associated with forbidden impulses (Sandler & Freud 1985).

Anxiety as a Signal

Anxiety both causes repression and signals it (Freud, 1933/1965). Anna Freud noted that conditioned anxiety might serve as a signal to keep wishes from conscious awareness (A. Freud, 1936/1966), but psychoanalysts have identified many other emotions (such as guilt and shame) that may also serve as signals (Sandler & Freud 1985). As Reich (1945/1982) noted, signal anxiety may not be anxiety at all, but rather apprehension, which functions by transforming traumatic anxiety into thought-like communications within the psyche (Blum, 1992).

Anxiety and Birth

Freud (1917/1966) believed that anxiety repeats the act of birth, which he believed is the original source of anxiety (Freud, 1926/1959c). Rank (1929/1952) extended this thinking. Grof (1985), using LSD and specialized breathing techniques to research the mind, reached the same conclusion. According to Grof, birth features sex, pain, aggression and terror, all fused together, with a simultaneous inability to express any of these emotions. Soon after birth, babies typically receive nonempathic treatment, which compounds this trauma. Unbearable, inescapable, hopeless, mean-ingless, empty and absurd, the birth processes as re-experienced in these sessions reflect the existentialists' view of life. Later in life, people either seek situations congruent with these unresolved emotions or create those situations themselves. When the external situations they live through elicit emotions exceeding these pre-existing feelings, the feelings and drives to experience them disappear (Grof, 1985).

Anxiety, Death and Existence

Although Freud (1920/1961) posited a death instinct, he never con-nected anxiety with death. Instead, the death instinct is used to explain the compulsion to repeat earlier traumas and experience unresolved af-fect, which Freud (1920/1961), with unclear logic, equated with the urge to become lifeless and inert. Although this anxiety is experienced as a sense of annihilation, it is not an unconscious fear of death, since death is not a concept appearing in the unconscious (Freud, 1915/1959j, 1923/1960). This fear is impossible to analyze, although it occurs in the conflict between the ego processes and incorporated behavior standards. Freud instead related anxiety about death to what he said was its ultimate beginning, the anxiety about castration (Freud, 1923/1960). Very few followed his lead in this direction, although Melanie Klein (1952/1990) later claimed that all anxi-ety results from the death instinct, initially when it attacks the individual himself and later when it clashes with his loving impulses.

This lack of addressing common anxieties about death led many to con-sult existentialist philosophers and combine their insights with Freud's. For example, Tillich (1952) influenced many therapists with his claims that anxiety is the existential awareness of potential nonbeing, ultimately about death, meaninglessness and condemnation. Each, he wrote, has a distinct type of anxiety resulting from it, and each contributes to an overall sense of despair and hopelessness. Because death itself is known, we can fear it; what comes thereafter is unknowable so it must result in anxiety. While fear can be met with courage, anxiety can only be contained or defended against, so people try to turn their anxiety into concrete fears (Tillich, 1952).

Anxiety creates loneliness and alienation from the self, while the creation of meaning protects against it (Erikson, 1963). Anna Freud stated that people's primary fears were of disintegration and that people have innate drives to develop their capacities to the extent they are capable (Sandler & Freud 1985), thus somewhat disowning her father's death instinct hypothesis.

According to Irvin Yalom (1980), upcoming death is the source of most anxiety and, thus, of psychopathology, but facing death frees one from both anxiety and pathology. Death anxiety is ubiquitous but repressed, he wrote, and is rarely experienced fully. Instead, it is defended against through denial or rescue fantasies. Anxiety about death necessarily involves a projection into the future, and the potential death of the world is the biggest and deepest anxiety of all. However, he believes, unmade decisions also create anxiety. Yalom believes that one can best find one's way through life by following one's anxiety.

Rollo May (1969) agreed that imminent death creates the prototype of all anxiety. He believed anxiety is the threat of non-being or meaninglessness (May, 1950) that can occur when one's values are threatened (May, 1953). Anxieties about death and other people are normal, but a person's inability to help herself due to inner conflicts is not (May, 1950). Associated with imagination and doubt (May, 1953), anxiety destroys one's ability to decide (May, 1969), leaving one uncertain who one is, what to do next and what the outside world is really like (May, 1953). Freedom and indecision bring anxiety and apathy (May, 1981), while courage overcomes them

(May, 1972). An anxious person cannot allow herself to become aware of her feelings (May, 1953), but people develop their senses of themselves by mastering anxiety-provoking situations (May, 1950). This consciousness of one's internal self overcomes anxiety (May, 1953) and allows people to actualize their potentials (May, 1972).

Many existentially oriented writers made little place for anxiety in their works. Frankl (1962) focused on existential meaning without using the word "anxiety," although his vignettes seemingly illustrate its arising from lack of meaning. Likewise, Maslow (1968) and Rogers (1980) focused on man's existential being without mentioning anxiety. Binswanger (1949/1963) thought that existential anxiety is abnormal, indicates illness and is not about avoiding life's destruction but, rather, the "'nihilation' of existence in naked terror" (p. 323).

Erich Fromm believed that anxiety is caused by a lack of faith in life. If an individual does not acknowledge his need for relatedness, then anxiety, isolation and powerlessness result (Fromm, 1941). While aggression, drugs, sexual arousal, sleep, or others' company can be used to blunt anxiety (Fromm, 1973), living spontaneously in the present (Fromm, 1976) through love or productive work (Fromm, 1941) without trying to hold onto or control one's life (Fromm, 1976) causes anxiety to disappear. Greenberg and Paivio (1997) wrote that present-centeredness forces people to attend to their ongoing feelings and experience, helping them to symbolize these internal elements. Thus, living *in* the present and attending to one's ongoing feelings is good, while living *for* the present, in hedonistic self-indulgence, is not (Greenberg and Paivio, 1997).

Anxiety and Security

According to de Rivera (1977), a structural theorist, anxiety's object (like in depression, confidence and security) is implicit. Anxiety involves a defensive clinging to whatever makes one feel secure when security (its structural opposite) is absent. It occurs when the implicit other withdraws from the individual. Anxiety tells us we have not conformed to the rules of the group and might lose group membership. Unlike apprehension, anxiety tells one to hold on to an old identity—no matter what—to avoid losing one's relationship with others (de Rivera, 1977).

Anxiety is a subjective threat to feelings of security (Horney, 1939; Sullivan, 1953a) leading to the breakdown of the felt senses of self and other (May, 1950). When severe, it can lead to apathy (Sullivan, 1953b). Ego processes attempt to produce feelings of security rather than an absence of anxiety (Sandler & Freud 1985). Since what leads any one individual to feel secure is partly influenced by social and cultural factors, individual causes of anxiety will be both personal and shared with others (May, 1950).

Anxiety and Relationships

Anxiety causes both internal disintegration and interpersonal problems (Sullivan, 1953b). Freud (1933/1965) believed that women's neurotic anxiety was caused by their fear of losing others' love. Anxiety frequently occurs after sudden, unexpected losses, and persistent anxiety is linked to fears of further losses that are suppressed or denied (Bowlby, 1980). Neurotic anxiety leads to a fear of others (or oneself) discovering how one "really is," causing a repression of all that does not match one's façade (Horney, 1939). Anxiety preoccupies attention, causing people to avoid whatever brought it about (Sullivan, 1956). Anxiety makes people extremely defensive, and they seek to keep as great a distance from others as possible (Solomon, 1976).

Anxiety and Development

Freud (1926/1959c) noted that young infants cannot master exciting emotions or deal with the withdrawal of loving care. Diffuse anxiety patterns appear in infants before differentiated fear responses do (May, 1950). Infants as young as 1 month old become anxious whenever their mothers have intense emotional experiences, especially anxiety (Sullivan, 1953b). Sullivan thought that the baby senses the mother's anxiety through what he termed "empathy," which is an automatic, nonverbal and paralogical process. Since infants have no capacity to relieve anxiety and the mother is already unable to care for or attend to the baby adequately due to her anxiousness, the baby's subsequent crying increases the mother's anxiety, which creates a deteriorating cycle resulting in an apathetic and detached infant (Sullivan, 1953b).

Winnicott (1962/1965b) wrote that empathic mothers help their children adjust to their bodies, teaching them the abilities to bear and manage anxiety in the process. When this is not done sufficiently, he wrote, the stage is set for psychotic adjustments later in life. Greenspan (1989, 1997) noted that when parents do not mirror their children accurately because of their own anxieties, integration is not enabled and their children become more anxious. Erickson (1963) thought that children learn to fear anxiety rather than danger.

Bowlby (1973) noted that the fear of strangers differs from separation anxiety, which he equated with distress. Anxiety arises from problems attaching to and separating from attachment figures (Mahler, Pine, & Bergman, 1975). Anxiety results when attachment behavior is activated and an appropriate attachment figure is unavailable or the child becomes unsure she can find one if needed (Bowlby, 1973). If the attachment figure might return, the child grows anxious, but if the attachment figure will definitely not do so, melancholia or disordered mourning often results (Bowlby, 1980).

Anxiety often originates with the disapproval of adults, but soon any upsetting situation can lead to it (Sullivan, 1953a). While low anxiety levels help children avoid bad situations, severe anxiety contributes only confusion (Sullivan, 1953b). Although they may understand the meanings of individual emotions, children with chronic anxiety states have difficulties processing emotional intensity (Greenspan, 1989). This leads to an inability to master and integrate experiences, in turn resulting in disorganization, dedifferentiation and a loss of ego boundaries (Greenspan, 1989).

Anxiety and Related Emotions

According to Solomon (1976), dread is a fear of the unknown; anguish is the fear of oneself; and anxiety is the fear of everything. In fear, anything could be threatening, while in anxiety, everything is (Solomon, 1976). Although it differs from extreme anxiety, terror is the only emotion that approximates its intensity (Sullivan, 1953b).

Freud noted two sets of emotions connected to anxiety. The first, what he called moral anxiety (Freud, 1926/1959c), includes what we now call guilt and shame. He believed these were anxieties aroused by the conflict between the ego and superego. Sullivan (1953b) thought that anxiety is often elaborated by early experience into the following: embarrassment, shame, guilt, chagrin and humiliation. Winnicott (1958/1965a) wrote that guilt is little more than anxiety that is experienced because of a conflict between love and hate; in this case, guilt helps contain the anxiety.

The second is what Freud (1919/1959i) termed the "uncanny" emotions, which he connected with morbid anxiety. Sullivan (1953b) agreed, adding that they feel alien and make the skin crawl or the hair on the back of the neck stand up. Sullivan lists dread, awe, horror, loathing, revulsion, terror, panic and delusional jealousy in this category.

A third related category is hostility. Horney (1937) noted that once hostility is repressed the resulting anxiety is projected onto others. Once

EMOTIONS IN PSYCHOLOGY AND PSYCHOTHERAPY

this is accomplished, the projector reacts in fear and hostility toward his new "persecutor," thus justifying the hostility and resolving the anxiety into fear. Sullivan (1953b), among others, also noted the prevalence of hostility among the anxious, who feel compelled to push others away. Additionally, people often handle anxiety by envying those who have what they believe might have helped them avoid it (Sullivan, 1956).

Cognitive Perspectives

Ellis (1962) wrote that anxiety results from exaggerating the importance of possible future negative events. Beck (Beck & Emery, 1985) agreed, noting that after experiencing any provoking stimulus, automatic thoughts about an impending personal disaster will lead inexorably to physiological arousal. Like pain, Beck wrote, anxiety dramatically focuses people's attention on their contemplated or past imprudent actions. Because of this, moderate anxiety itself might be positive. For example, concerns about negative evaluations from others might stop someone from alienating others (Beck & Emery, 1985).

Contributions from Emotion Theory

Because of the kinds of imprecision contained in conceptualizing anxiety as a discrete emotion (as discussed at the beginning of this chapter) Izard (1977) decided that the term had little scientific validity. It has no single expressive pattern or single phenomenology. Instead, he believed, anxiety is composed of fear plus at least two of the following: anger, guilt, shame-shyness, distress or interest-excitement. Signal anxiety, he believed, is just another name for anticipatory fear. He hypothesized that anxiety occurs when fear persists over time and other emotions (and possibly drive states) are added to it.

Greenberg (2002; Greenberg & Paivio, 1997; Paivio & Greenberg, 1998) disagreed with that assessment, instead believing that anxiety is a secondary emotion, as discussed earlier in this book. Anxiety usually starts with incompletely processed sadness or separation distress (Paivio & Greenberg (1998), resulting in confusion rather than an action tendency (Greenberg & Paivio, 1997). Instead, it becomes a related mood, which generates corresponding catastrophic cognitions (Paivio & Greenberg (1998).

While Solomon (1976) thought that anxiety is more mood than emotion, Ben-Ze'ev (2000) believed that it fits none of these categories but is instead an example of an affective disorder. Unlike emotions, he notes, its duration tends to be long, but it tends to be much more intense than a mood. McReynolds (1998) believed that anxiety occurs naturally when there is a backlog of unassimilated perceptual material. Although this is its basis, this is not the anxiety itself, he wrote. Rather, when discrepant material cannot be assimilated, distress ensues, which leads to anxiety as the person ruminates. Anxiety may also become conditioned if a person has an experience of extreme disassimilation while doing a particular thing; afterwards, that activity will be paired classically with anxiety. Since anxiolytics reduce the painful affect but do not deal with the cognitions, the anxiety persists (McReynolds, 1998).

Contributions from Research

Anxiety can be separated into two aspects: anxious arousal is characterized by panic, while anxious anticipation is characterized by worry (Heller & Nitschke, 1998). While Heller and Nitschke associated increased right parietotemporal activation with anxious arousal, they associated increased right frontal activation with anxious anticipation. Although closely related to depression, anxiety manifests itself differently. Like depression, anxiety is characterized by a hyperactive amygdala, which is part of the disease process (Levine, Chengappa, Gershon, & Drevets, 2001). However, depressed people have biased memories and recall only the bad, but anxious ones have biased attention and perceive only the bad (Mineka et al., 1998). Anxious people are far more likely than others to rate ambiguous situations as threatening, consider future negative events more likely, and opt for the safest alternatives when choosing future courses of action (for a review of these literatures, see Blanchette & Richards, 2010). Like depression, anxiety is related to increased negative affect (Davidson, 1998), but unlike depression it is almost completely unrelated to positive affect (Mineka et al., 1998).

Perceptions of uncontrollability lead to anxiety rather than either depression (Mineka et al., 1998) or fear (Maier & Watkins, 1998). When people doubt they can cope, they become anxious, but when they know they cannot cope and they expect bad events to occur, they become depressed (Mineka et al., 1998). Maier and Watkins believe that the uncontrollability of the situation potentiates learned fear responses, making the system overly sensitive. In animal experiments, they subjected rats to either escapable or inescapable shocks and found that inescapable shocks led to increased sensitivity to even minor shocks for several days afterwards.

The central nucleus of the amygdala sends signals to other brain areas such as the ventral periaqueductal gray (freezing responses), lateral hypothalamus and dorsal motor nucleus of the vagus (autonomic responses), and the parabrachial nucleus (breathing changes), among others (Maier & Watkins, 1998). It also receives input from the dorsal raphe nucleus (DRN) of the brain stem, which seems to be the area sensitized in the rats shocked by Maier and Watkins. Part of the prelimbic region of the ventromedial PFC also has projections into the DRN that respond preferentially to controllable, but not uncontrollable, stress (Baratta et al., 2009). According to Baratta et al., it appears to be sensitive to opportunities to escape and regulates the DRN to make sure that it happens.

As the field has advanced, researchers have found ever-better ways of testing for implicit affect that do not rely on self-report. Using one such measure, Edge et al. (2009) found that explicit reports of anxiety vary directly with the amount of self-reported stress that people reported suffering as children. That is, as their childhood stress increased, their reported anxiety as adults also tended to increase. However, their implicit anxiety did not follow this linear path. Instead, those who had moderate amounts of stress in their childhoods (and who, presumably, would have learned to cope with this stress) tended to have less implicit anxiety than those who had coped with very little stress as young children.

Anxiety's Meaning

> Anxiety...in so far as it is an affective state, is the reproduction of an old event which brought a threat of danger; anxiety serves the purposes of self-preservation and is a signal of a new danger; it arises from libido that has in some way become unemployable and it also arises during the process of repression; it is replaced by the formation of a symptom, is, as it were, psychically bound—one has a feeling that something is missing here which would bring all of these pieces together into a whole. (Freud, 1933/1965, p. 75)

Emotions direct attention and motivate behavior to attain survival-related goals (Paivio & Greenberg, 1998). They also synchronize both intrapsychic subsystems and social systems (Ellgring & Smith, 1998). Yet, as we have seen, anxiety—particularly in its more intense forms—does none of these things. As Freud (1926/1959c) first noted, of all the affects only anxiety leads to neurosis and causes effects that "run counter to the movement of life" (p. 81). Also, unlike other affects, anxiety pushes for its own discharge as part of its makeup (Freud, 1926/1959c).

Yet, as Freud (1920/1961) also noted, most affects are primary process entities, while anxiety belongs to the secondary process ego (Freud, 1923/1960, 1933/1965). Anxiety is a secondary process, cognitive elaboration to guard against impulses considered dangerous (Sandler & Freud, 1985). Quoting Freud, "In...repression...the instinctual impulse still belongs to the id and the ego feels weak. The ego thereupon helps itself by a technique which is at bottom identical to thinking" (1933/1965, p. 79).

It is not, as Beck and Emery (1985) argued, the appraisal of danger, but the act of thinking itself that causes neurotic anxiety while the person seeks to defend against activating painful, traumatic or otherwise nonintegrated emotions. Clearly, thinking also causes existential anxiety by separating the individual from the immediacy of his perceptual/affective experience. Blum (1992) explicitly noted that signal anxiety transforms traumatic anxiety into thought-like communication within the psyche. Any propositional generation of emotion would also cause anxiety by the same sorts of processes. As we have already seen previously, both generating emotions propositionally and failing to acknowledge emotions that have been experienced schematically adds to one's anxiety.

Yet this idea accounts for neither Grof's (1985) findings nor Greenspan's (1989, 1997). In each case, it is not thinking, but the jumble of undifferentiated emotions that causes the anxiety. When reconsidering the neurotic and existential cases, one can see that thinking replaced ongoing emotional life with other, propositionally generated emotions (or, in the case of a complete repression, no conscious affect at all). It is this mélange of emotions—some schematic, some propositional, some suppressed by others, some unconscious—that is experienced as anxiety. This is what causes the confusion many noted, and the unsteady mixes of emotions that Izard (1977) cited. Without a steady affective foothold, life is experienced as disorienting and possibly disintegrating. As Freshwater and Robertson (2002) noted, it is not the incident itself that leads to the traumatic reaction, but the subsequent separation from the emotions connected to the incident that does so.

Anxiety is the lack of differentiated emotion occurring because of intrapsychic conflicts, the lack of emotional development or the operation of defensive propositional processes. In a similar manner, the compulsion to repeat results from ongoing tacit drives to form effective emotional schemes that would allow the individual to reintegrate their experience at higher levels of differentiation and synthesis. These formulations predict several outcomes. First, if anxiety is connected to undifferentiated emotions, then infants without stable emotional schemes should be especially prone to it. The process of emotional contagion (Ciompi, 1998) suggests that infants would need extra help regulating their emotional life and learning to distinguish one emotion from another or anxiety would ensue. We know that the first part is true and research implies that the second is, too (e.g., Fonagy, 1999; Schore 2001a, b). However, more research exploring this specific hypothesis would make the situation clearer.

Second, although all human cultures have emotions, no culture recognizes all emotions recognized anywhere (Mesquita, 2001). If Darwin (1872/1965) was correct in surmising that at least some emotions have an evolutionary substrate, then cultures not recognizing such emotions should instead experience anxiety in their places or have culturally sanctioned methods to avoid doing so. This also deserves additional directed research.

How Anxiety Assists Adaptation

Most emotion theorists have focused on either appraisal processes or putative adaptation strategies to plausibly explain the various emotions. Because the prevailing thinking about anxiety since Freud has centered on indefinite or psychological threats, little that has been written about it seems likely to be true if the formulations sketched out above are. For example, Rathus and Sanderson (1998), while correctly inferring that anxiety is about psychological rather than physical threats, groped unsuccessfully to find a survival value for anxiety, which they thought might serve as a signal to others that a floundering relationship needed attention.

Darwin (1872/1965) wrote that all emotions originally served to prepare organisms for specific actions and only secondarily (and much later) to communicate or alert others. What anxiety provides is not a signal to others but rather an internal signal to reengage in ongoing emotional experience. It signals us to get back into synchrony with our affective lives. Brief, mild anxiety may be necessary to weigh current choices against future goals, because merely considering the future detaches us from ongoing experience. Nonetheless, even this mild form of anxiety serves to remind us that we are not currently present in our bodies and experience but are instead lost in our own thinking. Freud (1920/1961) wrote that the aim of all life is death and that the compulsion to repeat serves these interests. What anxiety and the repetition compulsion actually remind us is that the aim of life is instead to live freely, in the present moment and in an affectively integrated manner.

Depression

DEPRESSION IS A stress-related response. When anticipated positive affect does not occur, the result is depression (Heller and Nitschke, 1998). Not only is depression a problem in its own right, but secondary depression after other diseases and brain injuries is also a major concern (Liotti & Mayberg, 2001), especially left hemispheric damage near the frontal pole (Davidson, 1998).

The current psychological literature contains an ongoing debate about whether depression and anxiety are actually separate processes since they co-occur over 50% of the time, anxiety symptoms tend to precede depressive ones, and people with Major Depressive Disorder have more anxiety than those with Generalized Anxiety Disorder (Mineka et al., 1998). According to Mineka et al., Generalized Anxiety Disorder, Major Depressive Disorder and neuroticism may all share a common genetic factor; but panic does not, and phobias are only weakly related. However, while both anxious and depressed people are more likely than others to believe that bad events will occur, only the depressed believe that good events will not (Mineka et al., 1998).

Those with depression have relatively inactive frontal lobes (Irwin et al., 2004). Most people have greater left than right prefrontal activity, but depressed people instead usually show the opposite pattern (Heller & Nitschke, 1998). Left prefrontal activity in depression is often associated with rumination instead of health or positive affect (Drevets & Raichle, 1998). The crying of nondepressed people activates the parasympathetic nervous system though the vagus nerve, modulating their heart rate; but depressed people lack this regulatory ability and are more likely to suffer from heart problems as a result (Rottenberg et al., 2003). Debener et al. (2000) found that activation patterns of the prefrontal areas in depressed people vary widely between individuals, but since they studied hospitalized depressed people taking antidepressant medications and did not control for secondary diagnoses such as anxiety, it is unclear what their results mean.

Compared to individuals with bipolar disorder, people with non-affective psychosis and normal controls, those with Major Depressive Disorder reported greater negative affect and less positive affect when randomly stopped at irregular intervals, while those with Bipolar Disorder reported only decreased positive affect (Myin-Germeys et al., 2003). Depressed people report more state and trait negative affect and less state and trait positive affect than controls, changing their behavior only under punishing conditions and not altering their behavior under rewarding conditions as controls do (Henriques & Davidson, 2000). Left frontal insufficiencies associated with depression make them less reactive than usual to rewards (Davidson, 1998). Working may help them regulate their moods by helping them shift their cerebral activity to neural areas more responsive to cognitive than emotional input (Drevets & Raichle, 1998).

Although researchers have generally assumed that depression makes only functional rather than any structural changes (Liotti & Mayberg, 2001), this may be untrue. The amount of gray matter in the left subgenual PFC (Brodmann's Area 24) is much reduced in those with family histories of Major Depressive Disorder compared to normal controls, the result of a lack of glia in the area and fewer and smaller neurons, which pharmacological and psychological treatments do not alter (Davidson et al., 2002;

Drevets, Ongur, & Price, 1998). Drevets et al. believed that these deficits probably impair the efficiency of the subgenual PFC's efforts to suppress amygdalar functioning. They also reported that those with Major Depressive Disorder have been shown to have a smaller caudate nucleus and larger third ventricle than normal controls, while those with Bipolar Disorder also have a larger third ventricle than controls. Depressed people have a larger left amygdala and increased amygdalar activation compared to normal controls (Davidson et al., 2002), which is part of the disease process rather than an adaptation to it (Levine et al., 2001). The hippocampus is smaller in depressed people and its functioning is impaired; since the hippocampus has many GR sites, cortisol may be destroying the hippocampus, although this has yet to be demonstrated (Davidson et al., 2002).

Because their amygdalae are overly active, depressed individuals have trouble suppressing and forgetting information that no longer has relevance (Hertel & Gerstle, 2003). They evaluate ambiguous faces and vocal intonation more negatively than others do (Luck & Dowrick, 2004). Over time, this strengthens amygdalar processing, increasing baseline cortisol levels (Goodyer et al., 2001; Young, 2004) and flattening cortisol curves (McAllister-Williams et al., 1998). The resulting allostatic load apparently results in (a) a smaller nucleus accumbens, (b) an abnormally developed hippocampus and (c) reduced glia relative to neurons within the amygdala, lateral OFC and pregenual area of the ACC (Davidson et al., 2002; Drevets, 2003). Their glucocortocoid receptors overloaded, the hippocampus quits responding readily to context, producing only overgeneral memories and prolonging depressive and anxious episodes (Davidson et al., 2002; Herbert et al., 2006). After their depressed symptoms remit, depressed individuals' baseline cortisol levels return to normal, but their cortisol levels in the first hour after wakening increase twice as much as the levels of those without histories of depression (Bhagwagar, Hafizi, & Cowen,

2003). Many depressed patients show mood improvement when administered cortisol (McAllister-Williams et al., 1998).

Since glucocortocoids like cortisol are known neurotoxins that lead to neuronal atrophy at chronically high levels (Davidson et al., 2002; Young, Gallagher, & Porter, 2002), excessive cortisol may cause the cognitive impairment in learning and memory associated with depression (Young, 2004). Healthy individuals administered corticosteroids display improvements in spatial recognition (Young et al., 1999) but deficits on neuropsychological testing, especially of memory (McAllister-Williams et al., 1998). Even relatively minor treatment employing hydrocortosone leads to reversible deficits in prefrontal cognition (Young, 2004; Young et al., 1999). Dehydroepiandrosterone (DHEA), another glucocortocoid, counteracts some of these negative cognitive effects, which remit when DHEA is injected into depressed patients (Young et al., 2002). Normally, the cortisol/DHEA ratio varies between approximately 5/1 or 7/1 in the morning and 2/1 in the evening (Goodyer et al., 2001); but the ratios among depressed patients are markedly higher, with the ratios at 8:00 AM correlating significantly with how long the depressed episode has lasted (Young et al., 2002).

Effective treatment for depression may thus involve addressing the patients' dysregulated HPA axes (Young, 2004). Antidepressant therapy suppresses overly active amygdalae (Drevets, 2003) and may also increase neural plasticity and cell survival rates (Manji, Drevets, & Charney, 2001). Many neurotransmitter systems have been implicated in depression, including the GABA, 5-HT, noradrenergic, dopaminergic, cholinergic, glutamate and CRF circuits as well as the HPA (Manji et al., 2001). Although abnormally low 5-HT levels are widely believed to maintain depression, how HPA activity and 5-HT concentrations affect one another remains unclear (Porter, Gallagher, Watson, & Young, 2004). It appears that 5-HT excites the HPA system, but HPA activity modulates 5-HT activity in a bell-shaped manner, with MR filling up faster and GR filling up later, implying that the effects of glucocortocoids on 5-HT may depend on how many glucocortocoids are currently in the system (McAllister-Williams et al., 1998). Depression also seems to involve the bidirectional interchanges between the immune system and the brain since anhedonia, anorexia, pain sensitivity, sleep disturbances, HPA activation and interference with hippocampal memory are all symptomatic of immune functioning, as are the increased leukocyte counts found among the depressed (Maier & Watkins, 2000).

Chronic adult stress apparently turns childhood risk potentials into adult patterns of depression (Repetti et al., 2002). Difficult deliveries, such as those using forceps, can increase reactivity to later stressors and make babies more difficult to soothe (Taylor, Fisk, & Glover, 2000). The quality of childhood attachment mediates the effects of stress, particularly for anxious/inhibited children (Repetti et al., 2002). As children reach separation age, securely attached children produce less reactive cortisol when facing stressors (Goodyer et al., 2001) while insecurely attached children's cortisol levels rise rapidly when they do so (Repetti et al., 2002). Those with family histories of Major Depressive Disorder and Bipolar Disorder show dysregulated HPA activity (Drevets, 2003), possibly because of adverse early environmental influences (Repetti et al., 2002). Both trait positive and trait negative affectivity may be genetic (Gendolla, 2000). However, since children born into such families receive not only biological loading, but also poorer parenting and increased household stress, not all of the family contribution to such disorders is likely to be genetic (Hammen, Davila, Brown, Ellicott, & Gitlin, 1992). Children whose family lives include chronic conflict, frequent hostility or neglectful attention tend to develop chronic patterns of poor physical and emotional health, largely because of their early allostatic load (Repetti et al., 2002).

In a series of studies, Field has shown that expectant mothers with symptoms of depression (a) have higher cortisol levels (Field, Diego, Dieter et al., 2004; Field, Diego, Hernandez-Reif, Gil, & Vera, 2005; Field, Diego, Hernandez-Reif, Schanberg, & Kuhn, 2003; Field, Diego, Hernandez-Reif et al., 2004), (b) have higher epinephrine and NE levels (Field, Diego, Hernandez-Reif, Schanberg, & Kuhn, 2003), (c) have lower DA and 5-HT levels (Field, Diego, Dieter et al., 2004), (d) have greater right than left frontal EEG (Field, Diego, Hernandez-Reif, Schanberg, & Kuhn, 2003), (e) have midterm fetuses with lower weight and activity level (Field, Diego, Hernandez-Reif et al., 2005) and (f) deliver more premature babies (Field, Diego, Dieter et al., 2004). After delivery, their cortisol and NE levels remain elevated, while these levels fall in nondepressed mothers (Field, Diego, Hernandez-Reif et al., 2004).

These signs of dysregulation translate to their children, apparently beginning before birth (Repetti et al., 2002). Although cortisol does not cross the placental barrier readily, since cortisol concentrations are much lower in fetuses than among adults, maternal cortisol may account for as much as 40% of the fetal variance (Gitau, Cameron, Fisk, & Glover, 1998). Depressed mothers bear children with higher cortisol (Field, Diego, Dieter et al., 2004; Field, Diego, Hernandez-Reif et al., 2004), higher epinephrine and NE (Field, Diego, Hernandez-Reif et al., 2004), and lower DA and 5-HT levels (Field, Diego, Dieter et al., 2004). Mothers simultaneously high in depression, anxiety and anger have babies who have (a) greater right than left frontal EEG, (b) higher cortisol levels, (c) lower DA levels, (d) less vagal tone, (e) lower Brazelton scores and (f) more disorganized sleeping patterns (Field, Diego, Hernandez-Reif, Salman et al., 2002; Field, Diego, Hernandez-Reif, Schanberg, Kuhn et al., 2003).

Those newborns whose mothers were depressed at mid-pregnancy and remain depressed shortly after delivery have higher cortisol and NE levels, lower DA levels and greater right EEG asymmetry, while those whose mothers have only midterm depression still have higher NE and right EEG dominance (Diego, Field, Hernandez-Reif et al., 2004). Those newborns with more relative right frontal EEG have mothers with higher postnatal cortisol and lower postnatal 5-HT levels (Field, Diego, Hernandez-Reif, Schanberg, & Kuhn, 2002). These elevated fetal cortisol levels could explain the low birth weight found among these children as well as neonatal brain impairment (Gitau et al., 1998). Within days, depressed mothers' infants stick objects into their mouths less often than other infants do (Hernandez-Reif, Field, Del Pino, & Diego, 2000). Those whose mothers recovered following a depressive episode during their second trimester showed raised NE levels and right asymmetries, and those whose mothers had postpartum depression did not differ from controls, but those whose mothers' chronic depression had not remitted during pregnancy showed not only raised NE levels and right asymmetry but also higher cortisol and lower DA levels compared to the other groups (Diego, Field, Hernandez-Reif et al., 2004).

Even while happy or while playing with their mothers, infants of depressed mothers show greater right frontal EEG asymmetry (Jones, Field, Fox, Davalos, & Gomez, 2001). They habituate to their mothers' faces more slowly (Hernandez-Reif, Field, Diego, & Largie, 2002) and show greater right frontal EEG during and elevated cortisol levels after being exposed to their mothers' and strangers' faces (Diego, Field, Jones et al., 2004). Compared to infants of withdrawn depressed mothers, infants of intrusive depressed mothers stare longer at strangers' emotional expressions but also have higher cortisol reactivity afterwards (Diego et al., 2002). By 12 months, infants of both intrusive and withdrawn depressed mothers show dysregulated responses after the induction of jealousy, but while the intrusive mothers' infants play and avoid contact with their mothers, the withdrawn mothers' infants approach strangers even when those strangers ignore them (Hart, Jones, & Field, 2003). Preschool children of depressed mothers have greater right EEG asymmetry, are less empathic and have fewer prosocial responses (Jones, Field, & Davalos, 2000).

Among adolescents, intense and labile emotions, together with either disengaged (e.g., denial, escape, avoidance or wishful thinking) or involuntarily engaged (e.g., rumination or acting impulsively) methods of regulation are associated with increased reports of depressive symptoms and behavioral problems (Silk et al., 2003). Among 15-year-olds, the maternal grandmother's depression affects the mother's depression and stressful context, and both—mediated by the adolescent's current stressors—affect the severity of the teen's depression and make the adolescent's experience of the mother's parenting seem more negative (Hammen, Shih, & Brennan, 2004).

Prepubescent girls and boys have similar cortisol levels, but beginning in adolescence, girls' levels are higher (Goodyer et al., 2001). Since they have more depressive symptoms, higher cortisol levels, and lower self-esteem than their male peers, regardless of risk status, adolescent girls are at higher risk of developing depression (Goodyer et al., 2000). The ratio of females to males with depression varies widely from country to country, region to region, and even group to group, with the worldwide ratio being about 2:1; women are clearly more depressed than men in a number of different cultures (Nolen-Hoeksema, 1987). Although gender bias is a factor in reporting depression (Brommelhoff, Conway, Merikangas, & Levy, 2004), female members of certain groups, such as traditional cultures and university students, have the same rates of reported depression as their male peers (Nolen-Hoeksema, 1987).

Even compared to women who are physically ill or have Bipolar Disorder, depressed women create their own stress, primarily interpersonal stress (Hammen, 1991). Their stress levels predict the severity of their later depression, mediating such factors as age of onset and family history of depression (Hammen et al., 1992). Hammen (1991) found her sample's stressors to be greater one year after initially being interviewed because of the events they had subsequently caused or contributed to. Their symptoms, dysfunctional relationships, dysfunctional families of origin, childhood maladjustment and poor skills all interacted with their poor decision-making to increase their distress (Hammen et al., 1992).

Various psychological theories of depression contain factors that fall into four main themes: faulty cognitions, negative self-feelings, poor social interactions and faulty goal setting (Street, Sheeran, & Orbell, 1999). According to Street (2003; Street et al., 2004), people develop goal hierarchies, with their more concrete, immediate goals subordinate to larger, more abstract ones. Those who believe their happiness depends upon reaching particular goals (e.g., earning a specific salary, owning a certain possession or marrying a particular individual) leave themselves prone to depression, whether those goals are reached or not (Street et al., 2004). Though renouncing unreachable goals reduces depressive symptoms (Wrosch et al., 2007), believing that happiness is an outcome-dependent state rather than a process-related one increases the likelihood of depression (Street et al., 2004), as any delay or failure in achieving one of the lesser goals puts happiness at risk and leads to depression and rumination (Street, 2003; Street et al., 2004). These links between conditional goal setting and depression have been demonstrated in both adults and children (Street et al., 2004).

Depression is a stress-related disorder. It is marked by HPA dysregulation that may or may not be maintained by rumination. Yet, depression is probably less a disorder than a symptom of one of a number of possible disorders that may have many possible causes and many possible treatments. One variety of depression, melancholia, will be considered next, which should make this point more clearly.

Melancholia

MELANCHOLIA HAS A long and involved conceptual history. Hippocrates believed melancholia (literally, black bile; Himmelhoch, Levine, & Gershon, 2001) to be related to an imbalance of this hypothesized bodily humor (Himmelhoch et al., 2001; Kagan, 1994). According to this theory, excessive black bile makes people cool and dry (Kagan, 1994), and its viscosity affects their brains (Himmelhoch et al., 2001), causing mental disorders and various serious physical ailments (Kagan, 1994). Since autumn is also cool and dry, Hippocrates reasoned that it created special risks for developing melancholia (Himmelhoch et al., 2001). Although physicians argued the purposes and organic origins of black bile, medieval Christian scholars believed its presence to be God's curse for the sins of Adam and Eve (Kagan, 1994). Under humor theory, melancholia subsumed both mood and anxiety symptoms (Kagan, 1994) including despondency, sleeplessness, aversion to food and irritability (Himmelhoch et al., 2001). According to Himmelhoch et al., the noted medieval physician Avicenna distinguished four types of melancholia: hypomanic; sluggish and listless; violent and turbulent; and one type characterized as anguished, pessimistic, withdrawn, hypochondriacal, possibly delusional and likely to commit suicide.

Freud (1917/1959e) initially described what we currently refer to as melancholic depression: responding to loss, the melancholic, like the griever, becomes dejected, listless, apathetic and forlorn; like the obsessional character, he suffers pathological grief (Bradbury, 2001) because of his inner ambivalence toward whomever or whatever was lost; and completely uniquely, he reacts with guilty self-reproach, anorexia, insomnia, shameless behavior and increased suicidal risk. Later in the 20th century, melancholia became a synonym for "endogenous" depression, those enduring, severe and somatically involved states, often seen in older people, as contrasted to "reactive" depression, the milder, transient and more neurotic states that are generally seen in younger patients (Himmelhoch et al., 2001).

The *DSM-IV-TR* (2000) contains a specifier, "With Melancholic Features," whose continued retention sparked controversy from those wanting to rid the DSM of all remaining psychoanalytic baggage (Joyce et al., 2002). This specifier is to follow any diagnosis of unipolar or bipolar depression that shows a definite loss of pleasure, plus three or more of the following: (a) a distinct depressed quality different from normal grief; (b) diurnal mood variation, with worse morning than evening mood; (c) terminal insomnia; (d) severe psychomotor retardation; (e) appetite disturbance, measured as anorexia or weight loss; and (f) excessive or inappropriate guilt.

In practice, most researchers and diagnosticians take the specifier to signify greater depressive severity (Joyce et al., 2002). Most of the other widely used modern diagnostic systems model depression dimensionally, based on severity and recurrence, rather than differentially, based upon symptom clusters (Parker & Roy, 2002). Only some researchers differentiate melancholia from other depressive types by symptom cluster (e.g., Parker, Snowdon, & Parker, 2003). Most (e.g., Bradvik, 2002; Corrigan, Denahan, Wright, Ragual, & Evans, 2000; Kienke & Rosenbaum, 2000) consider it equivalent to severe depression. Nonetheless, melancholic depression apparently possesses a unique etiology, pathophysiology, phenomenology and treatment protocol. Compared to nonmelancholic depression, it has a chronic rather than episodic course (Rothermundt et al., 2001); placebo recovery rates of approximately 5% in drug studies, compared to about 49% for other depression types (Cooper & Kelly, 2000); better one-year recovery rates (Parker, Wilhelm, Mitchell, & Gladstone, 2000); and preferential responses to different pharmacological agents (Schatzberg, Cole, & DeBattista, 2003).

Modern research provides evidence for and against considering melancholic depression a specific disorder. True melancholic depression appears to differ substantially from other forms of depression in its etiological, behavioral, phenomenological, neuropsychological, endocrine and immune manifestations, but current diagnostic strategies may also overestimate the numbers who actually have this particular disorder, since similar behavior may occur for other reasons.

Types of Depressive Disorder

Melancholic Depression

Melancholic depression, which features anxiety, dread, weight loss, morning insomnia, worse morning moods, a lack of environmental responsiveness, increased CRH levels, reduced growth hormone levels and reduced reproductive system activity, is characterized by increased HPA activity (Gold & Chrousos, 2002). Like Bipolar Disorder (Drevets, 2003), melancholic depression involves high initial cortisol levels that remit with treatment, although cortisol feedback is preserved throughout the symptomatic period (Cooney & Dinan, 2000).

Besides the distinct mood, anhedonia, diurnal mood variation, inappropriate guilt and commonly experienced anorexia and terminal insomnia that differentiate melancholia from other types of depression (Rothermundt et al., 2001), psychomotor disturbances are marked. Parker et al. (2003) accurately identified approximately 64% of all study participants' melancholic depression (or lack thereof) per *DSM-IV* criteria solely through scores on the Mental State Examination for Psychomotor Retardation and Agitation (CORE). Parker et al. thought that psychomotor retardation (PMR) is the key feature of melancholic depression and, thus, that the CORE might be more valid than DSM criteria. While noting the lack of agreement between CORE scores and *DSM-IV* diagnoses, they advocate focusing on the accuracy (or inadequacy) of *DSM-IV* criteria.

According to Freud (1917/1959e), melancholia involves a person redirecting the fury felt toward someone else onto himself or herself. The person blames himself or herself (Weiss & Lang, 2000), which is experienced as a primitive guilt with which that person then identifies (Fuchs, 2003). Compared to other depressed individuals, those with melancholic depression feel worse about themselves and their lives, and they concentrate, reach decisions and relate to others more poorly (Parker et al., 2003). They feel anxious, heavy, internally frozen and completely isolated from others (Fuchs, 2003).

Psychotic Depression

Besides the delusions and hallucinations that distinguish melancholic from psychotic depression, Parker et al. (2003) found that those with psychotic depression: (a) did not have the diurnal mood variations seen in melancholic depression, (b) thought they deserved punishment rather than feeling guilty and (c) enjoyed themselves less, avoided others more, and had more PMR, as determined by CORE scores.

Atypical Depression

Atypical depression which, like melancholic depression, has its own

DSM-IV-TR (2000) specifier and chronic course (Levitan, Vaccarino, Brown, & Kennedy, 2002), features physiological and psychological symptoms opposed to those seen in patients with melancholic depression: lethargy, fatigue, moods deteriorating over the course of the day and excessive sleeping and eating (Gold & Chrousos, 2002), especially of carbohydrates (Yamadera, Okawa, & Takahashi, 2001). Behaviorally and epidemiologically, atypical depression appears akin to somatoform disorders, chronic fatigue syndrome and fibromyalgia (Murck, 2003). Unlike the symptoms in melancholic depression, which are caused by increased HPA activity, the symptoms in atypical depression are caused by abnormal decreases in HPA functioning (Gold & Chrousos, 2002; Murck, 2003) and lower morning than evening cortisol levels (Levitan et al. 2002). The two types of depression also differ widely in how they affect the thyroid (Joyce et al., 2002) and immune system, which is dysregulated in both conditions (Rothermundt et al., 2001).

Both melancholic and atypical depression result in increased cerebral cortisol levels that may characterize depressive conditions, though they do so through different mechanisms (Murck, 2003). If diagnosed using measures of psychomotor disturbance rather than *DSM-IV-TR* (2000) criteria, those with melancholic depression have higher afternoon cortisol levels and their CRH levels correlate negatively with their number of interpersonal interactions (Joyce et al., 2002). By contrast, those with atypical depression have normal baseline cortisol levels (Young et al., 2002) but higher concentrations of cortisol in their cerebrospinal fluid than those with melancholia or nondepressed controls (Murck, 2003). Monoamine oxidase (MAO) inhibitors treat atypical depression more effectively than selective serotonin reuptake inhibitors (SSRIs) or tricyclic antidepressants (TCAs; Bruder et al., 2002; Levitan et al. 2002) and hypericum extract, which also increases HPA activity, may also be effective (Murck, 2003).

Nonmelancholic Depression

Nonmelancholic depression, a designation seen in melancholia research largely as a contrasting group in study samples, itself has several subtypes, including atypical depression. Parker and Roy (2001) distinguished two additional subtypes, anxious and irritable-hostile. Those who develop anxious depression tend to have histories of anxious temperaments, family histories of anxiety disorders, and comorbid personality disorders in Cluster C (Avoidant, Dependent, or Obsessive-Compulsive), considered the anxious personality disorders (*DSM-IV-TR*, 2000). Those who develop irritable-hostile depression tend to show interpersonal volatility, act out their rage and frustration, and display Cluster B (Antisocial, Borderline, Histrionic, Narcissistic; *DSM-IV-TR*, 2000) personality traits (Parker & Roy, 2001).

Seasonal Affective Disorder

Seasonal depression tends to have atypical features (Yamadera et al., 2001) and mood that varies by seasons, with the timing of these changes differing throughout the world (Winkler et al., 2002). When Winkler et al. compared a sample of previously treated patients with seasonal variability from Bonn with another from Vienna, they discovered that those from Bonn, treated approximately five years before those from Vienna, were also more likely to have melancholic features and to be taking TCAs, while the Viennese showed more atypical features and were more likely to be taking MAO inhibitors. While Winkler et al. believe this shows possible temporal changes in depression toward more severe symptoms, the distinction between symptom types does not appear to have been part of the original evaluations, throwing this belief into doubt.

Arias, Gutiérrez, Pintor, Gastó, & Fañanás (2001) discovered that while the 5-HT_{2A} receptor genes takes one of two patterns, 102C or 102T, those with unipolar seasonal depression, melancholic or not, differ from those without this condition. While either gene variation produces the same receptor protein, those with the 102C gene patterns were 7.57 times more likely to have patterns of seasonal depression than those with the 102T variation, suggesting that one might have either melancholic or atypical depression, with seasonal variability superimposed independently due to unrelated gene variability (Arias et al., 2001).

Differentiation of Melancholic Depression

Neuropsychological Differences

The left prefrontal area, among other tasks, responds to reward, regulates approach behavior and generates positive affect while the right prefrontal area responds to aversive stimuli, regulates withdrawal and generates negative affect (Davidson, 1998; Davidson et al., 2002). The right parietotemporal area, meanwhile, is associated with physiological arousal and is highly active during panic states (Heller & Nitschke, 1998; Mineka et al., 1998). Whenever the right prefrontal area is more active than the left, negative affect overwhelms positive affect and anxiety or depression may result (Davidson, 1998; Davidson et al., 2002; Heller & Nitschke, 1998; Jackson et al., 2003). Usually, depression is associated with a hyperaroused right prefrontal area; but in those with melancholic depression, the right prefrontal area behaves much like that of nondepressed controls and the left prefrontal and right parietotemporal areas are hypoaroused, yielding the typical melancholic symptoms of anhedonia and lack of arousal (Heller & Nitschke, 1998; Mineka et al., 1998).

The amygdala, which processes sensory stimuli, shows a preference for those with negative motivational salience (Zald, 2003). It remains hyperactive during and after depressive episodes (Drevets, 2003; Gold & Chrousos, 2002), although antidepressant medications decrease this activity (Drevets, 2003). The aroused amygdala, in turn, activates the HPA (Gold & Chrousos, 2002). Unlike atypical depression, in melancholia cortisol levels are highest in the early morning (Levitan et al., 2002). One small CRH pathway directly connecting the hypothalamus to the locus coeruleus in the brainstem, where NE is created, seems to be a key element in melancholic depression since NE levels are elevated and the CRH response to stress is excessive in melancholia (Gold & Chrousos, 2002). Elevated cortisol and NE levels, in combination, enhance perceptions of threat (Drevets, 2003); alter other hormonal levels; contribute to a variety of serious health issues (Gold & Chrousos, 2002); and are suspected of killing brain cells, especially within the hippocampus (Davidson et al., 2002).

Typically, the OFC inhibits both the amygdala and the HPA axis (Gold & Chrousos, 2002), in part by overriding previously conditioned emotional responses that no longer match current environmental demands (Morris & Dolan, 2004). In those with melancholic depression, this area is defective and malformed (Gold & Chrousos, 2002). Drevets (2003; Drevets et al., 1998) found that among those whose depressions were familial, the left subgenual area of the OFC, the left pregenual ACC and the amygdala were all smaller by volume and contained less glia per cell than the comparable parts of the brains of normal controls. The amygdalar patterns resemble those previously seen in rats that had been overstressed (Drevets, 2003). Gold and Chrousos, citing a personal communication with Drevets, confirm that these structural differences occurred mainly among those with melancholic depression.

Since subgenual metabolism increases when nondepressed experimental participants contemplate sad memories (Drevets, 2003), for some weeks following negative emotional experiences (Zald et al., 2002) and during unmedicated depression, (Drevets, 2003), this area appears vital to understanding melancholic depression. While medication alters the metabolism in the subgenual area (Davidson et al., 2002) and returns its functioning to normal (Drevets, 2003), its structural deficits remain (Davidson et al., 2002) and allow the continued hyperarousal of the amygdala and HPA axis when medication is discontinued (Gold & Chrousos, 2002). In melancholic depression, the body recovers from added excess cortisol adequately, whether the individual is taking medication or not (Cooney & Dinan, 2000); apparently the secretion of cortisol is appropriate for the amount of CRH that results from an unregulated amygdala, creating an ongoing stress response that cascades out of control (Gold & Chrousos, 2002).

Developmental Issues

Drevets (2003) reported that these structural abnormalities in the subgenual orbitofrontal area could be seen even in young children, although not among monozygotic twins discordant for depression, pointing to possible causal factors other than genetics, such as prenatal and perinatal influences. Using Centers for Epidemiological Studies-Depression (CES-D) scale data, which measures depressed mood, guilt, helplessness and hopelessness, decreased energy, and sleep and appetite disturbances (Diego et al., 2002), Tiffany Field and her research colleagues have extensively studied the offspring of depressed mothers who can classified as intrusive, withdrawn or good interaction partners. While the CES-D does not yield DSM diagnoses, it indicates the severity of depression by using constructs roughly parallel to the DSM criteria for melancholic depression.

CES-D scores correlated significantly in one study with decreased left prefrontal EEG activation (Diego, Field, & Hernandez-Reif, 2001b), which in turn related to withdrawn, rather than intrusive, depression among mothers (Diego, Field, & Hernandez-Reif, 2001a). Compared to intrusive depressed mothers, withdrawn depressed mothers have greater BIS, less BAS and display less left frontal EEG (Diego, Field, & Hernandez-Reif, 2001a). Because no formal diagnoses were made using standard criteria, however, this section of the chapter is more speculative than might be desired.

Newborns of mothers depressed during their second trimesters show more activated right than left prefrontal cortices, and compared to other newborns, also have (a) increased plasma cortisol levels, (b) lower plasma DA and 5-HT levels, (c) reduced Brazelton scores, reflecting poorer adjustment, (d) less sound sleep and (e) poorer vagal tone (Field, et al., 2003; Field et al., 2004). This diminished vagal tone reflects their compromised ability to monitor affective feedback from their viscera (Bechara, 2004), and thus to self-regulate affect and behavior (Stuss & Anderson, 2004). These infants also habituate more slowly to presentations of their mothers' faces (Hernandez-Reif et al., 2002) and process odors differently (Fernandez et al., 2004). Unlike other infants, their mothers' faces and voices elicit no particular reactions different from other faces or voices (Hernandez-Reif et al., 2002). Newborns with greater right than left prefrontal activation also have higher cortisol levels, are more maladjusted and sleep more fitfully than those with greater left prefrontal activation. Their mothers have higher postnatal cortisol levels, lower 5-HT levels, more relative right EEG asymmetry and diminished vagal tone compared to the mothers of the infants with greater left asymmetry (Field, Diego, Hernandez-Reif, Schanberg, & Kuhn, 2002).

By three months of age, infants of withdrawn depressed mothers sleep more poorly than infants of supportive depressed mothers (Field, Diego, Hernandez-Reif, Schanberg, & Kuhn, 2003) but also show less distress with strangers than infants of intrusive depressed mothers (Diego et al., 2002). Within 6 months, infants of depressed mothers show less positive affect and look at their mothers less (Diego, Field, Jones et al., 2004). By 10 months, the infants display negative emotion more intensely (Jones et al., 2001). By 1 year, withdrawn depressed mothers and their children play better together but show less overall affect than intrusive depressed mothers and their children (Hart, Jones, Field, & Lundy, 1999). By preschool, depressed mothers' children show less empathy than other children (Jones et al., 2000).

Most of the variance among children's values in the foregoing studies is accounted for by maternal variables during the second trimester of pregnancy (Field, Diego, Dieter et al., 2004). Additionally, Field et al. found that elevated maternal cortisol predicts prematurity while elevated maternal NE predicts low birth weight. Prematurity often results in defects within the amygdala, which can be particularly difficult to detect until behavior that is expected to develop does not do so (Ulfig, Setzer, & Bohl, 2003). The development of the OFC, as discussed earlier, is extremely plastic with respect to hormones such as cortisol (Kolb et al., 2004).

Personality

Those with affective disorders tend to have one of three different premorbid personality types: melancholic, manic or easy-going (von Zerssen, 2000). According to von Zerssen, the melancholic personality type is quiet, considerate, cautious, meticulous, dependent, obedient, unimaginative and emotionally restricted. They are diligent, conformist, pious and desire harmony (von Zerssen, 2000). They identify themselves with their assigned roles and strive to fulfill those roles (Weiss & Lang, 2000). They are anxious and rigid, needing direction from others but cooperating poorly (Kimura et al., 2000). They are moody, brooding even when not depressed (Ueki et al., 2001). German and Japanese tests of melancholic personality have been validated in each other's culture, indicating possible universality; but Anglo-American psychologists generally disregard this personality type, considering it a subtype of the obsessional style (Ueki et al., 2001).

Since the parents, children and siblings of those with melancholic depression also tend to have melancholic personalities, mediating variables undoubtedly exist between melancholic personality and melancholic depression (Kimura et al., 2000). When Kimura et al. analyzed their sample with melancholic personalities, they found four subgroups, one having no maladaptive personality features. They thought that the maladaptive features they identified caused melancholic depression, although evidence shows that melancholia is generally associated with less comorbidity than other types of depression (Parker & Roy, 2001), better early experiences and better personality functioning than nonmelancholic depression (Rogers et al., 2000). Unfortunately, premorbid prefrontal asymmetries, levels of various neurotransmitters and HPA axis variables like CRH and cortisol levels do not yet seem to have been researched among those with melancholic personalities to determine whether and how these individuals (particularly those who do not develop melancholic depression) compare to normal controls.

Freud Revisited

Like mourning, melancholic depression is a response to loss (Freud, 1917/1959e), but one in which the ego malfunctions (Bradbury, 2001), probably because of the orbitofrontal deficits noted previously. Individuals with melancholic depression relate to others symbiotically (Weiss & Lang, 2000). Having few internal controls and little sense of themselves or others, they organize themselves through their adherence to conformity. Following losses, which they experience as though part of themselves had died (Weiss & Lang, 2000), they identify with those lost (Bradbury, 2001), attacking the parts of themselves they do not like in order to defend against the fear that they might completely lose control (Ueki et al., 2001). They continue to seek others' help to stay organized, over-valuing everybody they meet while viciously attacking themselves (Weiss & Lang, 2000).

Differential Indicators

Recent research has shown several seemingly stable differences between those with melancholia and those with other types of depression. In the future, research might demonstrate one or more of these differences to be sufficient for developing tests to determine the presence or absence of melancholic depression, removing the guesswork and scaling currently in vogue. However, as demonstrated below, this research also demonstrates that not all "melancholic" symptoms necessarily have the same underlying physiology, making developing such differential tests all the more vital in making correct diagnoses.

Parkinsonian Symptoms

The PMR seen in melancholic depression resembles the bradykinesia (slowed motor activity) found in Parkinson's disease, whose symptoms include slowed gait, postural abnormalities and blank, fixed facial expressions (Rogers et al., 2000). Rogers et al., noting that those with Parkinson's and other basal ganglia diseases tend to become depressed before the frank onset of Parkinsonian symptoms and that those with melancholic depression also tend to score more highly on tests of Parkinsonian movement than controls, believe both Parkinson's disease and melancholic depression may share common features, including the impairment of subcortical dopaminergic networks. Using CORE scores as measures of melancholia, Rogers et al. found that for those with melancholic depression, the slowest movements occur when they are either deprived of external cues or given too many; their movement speeds match those of normal controls when they are given adequate cueing, a profile that matches Parkinsonian bradykinesia.

Rogers et al. (2002) followed the previous study with one of mental rotation. In normal controls, this process is slowed as the angle of rotation is increased, in a fairly linear manner. Rogers et al. found that in nonmelancholic patients this same linear relationship held, although rotation times were slower than those of nondepressed controls, presumably due to their motivational deficits. Among melancholic patients, the results were not only slower still but also slowed in a nonlinear pattern uncharacteristic of the other groups, with greater rotations yielding progressively larger deviations from the linear pattern shown by the other groups. Rather than diminished motivation, Rogers et al. believe this pattern reflects bradyphrenia, a major slowing of cognition, which may either be localized to the premotor cortex or reflect general cognitive slowness.

Neuropsychological Batteries

While Rogers, Bellgrove, Chiu, Mileshkin, and Bradshaw (2004) found that nonmelancholic individuals' performance did not differ from controls on four different timed neuropsychological tests of executive functioning, those with melancholic depression differed from controls on all measures and from those with nonmelancholic depression on two. Controlling for age, Naismith et al. (2003) discovered that compared to other depressed people, those with melancholic depression perform more poorly on tests of semantic fluency. They believe this reflects information processing difficulties rather than language deficits but urge the cautious use of language-based tests for premorbid cognitive functioning among this group.

Right Parietotemporal Functioning

In most right-handed people, the right parietotemporal area preferentially processes faces, but previous research has shown that those with melancholic depression exhibit processing delays in the right parietotemporal area (Bruder et al., 2002). When Bruder et al. tested an unmedicated sample of atypical and melancholic depressed patients along with normal controls by using a chimeric faces protocol, those with melancholic depression showed almost no hemispheric bias, while those with atypical depression showed a stronger right hemispheric bias than controls.

Stress Responses

Using DSM diagnostic criteria to separate their sample into nonmelancholic, melancholic and severely melancholic groups, Joyce et al. (2002) found no significant differences between groups on measures of HPA or thyroid output. However, when they used the CORE as a predictor, they found it correlated significantly with afternoon CRH levels and blunted thyroid-stimulating hormone (TSH) responses to thyrotropin-releasing hormone (TRH) challenges. Unexpectedly, on all measures (including medication response, discussed below), the largest differences Joyce et al. found were those between the nonmelancholic and melancholic groups, with the severely melancholic group tending to produce values between those of the other two groups.

Immune Responses

Because depression has been treated dimensionally in most studies, research into immune differences associated with depression has largely been mixed, contradictory and inconclusive. Testing melancholic and nonmelancholic inpatients as well as normal controls at admission, two weeks and four weeks, Rothermundt et al. (2001) found that age, gender, smoking habits, depressive severity and medication variables had no impact on immune response, but type of depression did. Specifically, those with nonmelancholic depression had raised lymphocyte, leukocyte and natural killer cell counts at all three measurements, while those with melancholic depression had reduced interleukin-2, interleukin-10 and interferon-gamma at admission only. These deficits disappeared as treatment progressed.

Melatonin

With the nighttime help of noradrenergic networks, the pineal gland synthesizes 5-HT into melatonin, which helps regulate sleep cycles but not depression (Fountoulakis et al., 2001). Measuring at both 9:00 AM and 11:00 PM, Fountoulakis et al. found that as melancholic symptoms increased in severity, melatonin levels decreased. Since sleep cycles, noradrenergic networks and serotonergic networks all show significant disturbance in this disorder, these results tie some of its symptoms together.

Additional Diagnostic Concerns

Comorbidity

Comorbid personality disorders are common among those with depression, occurring in at least 50% of all cases (Kimura et al., 2000). This trend is less true among those with melancholic depression (Rogers et al., 2000). As comorbidity rises among depressed samples, melancholic symptoms decrease (Parker & Roy, 2001). When comorbidity occurs in this population, the co-occurring condition is generally either Obsessive-Compulsive Disorder or Avoidant Personality Disorder (Joyce et al., 2002).

Body Fat

Although anorexia or weight loss is a cardinal symptom of melancholic depression, current DSM criteria allow people to be diagnosed without meeting all criteria for the disorder. In this case, that may be in error, yielding anomalous results. High plasma cortisol levels can lead to visceral obesity (Rosmond, Nilsson, & Bjorntorp, 2000), a condition reminiscent of Cushing's disease (Murck, 2003). While pituitary malfunctioning causes the heightened cortisol in Cushing's disease, the heightened cortisol in both melancholic and atypical depression serves to suppress the CRH released by an unrestrained amygdala (Gold & Chrousos, 2002). Differentiating such conditions from Cushing's disease requires advanced modern testing techniques (Chrousos, 2000).

Rosmond et al. (2000), in their Swedish study of 1464 pre-menopausal middle-aged female psychiatric patients, found that melancholic severity, as assessed through a questionnaire, correlated with both weight and waist-to-hip ratio only among Swedish natives, but not among other Nordics, Europeans or others. They believe that this indicates possible genetic variation within the disorder; but given both the diagnostic methodology and the pushes towards both dimensional and prototypical diagnostics within psychology (e.g., Westen, Heim, Morrison, Patterson, & Campbell, 2002) exemplified in this study, the results are less conclusive than the authors suggest. If, as suggested in this chapter, true melancholic depression is actually a taxonic designation (Joiner & Schmidt, 2002), their conclusions are false. Gaunt, anhedonic figures form vital parts of the "picture" of melancholic depression. If the conclusions herein are correct, patients without some aspect of the disorder will probably prove to have a different form of depression entirely, although it may resemble melancholia in certain symptomatic aspects.

Non-DSM Systems of Diagnosis

This chapter has demonstrated that melancholic depression can be distinguished from other depressive types more reliably using physiologically based measures than can be accomplished using the behavioral strategies contained in the DSM. CORE scores not only matched DSM results in approximately 64% of the sample in one study (Parker et al., 2003) but outperformed DSM criteria as physiological predictors in another (Joyce et al., 2002) and as predictors of treatment success in a third (Parker et al., 2000).

The CORE data clearly get closer to some type of meaningful differences than the DSM criteria do; but other data sources, such as overall patterns of brain arousal, neural imaging of prefrontal areas and unmedicated immune responses, each signal potential possible avenues for assessing melancholic depression more precisely. Such diagnostic precision would enable treatment options to be designed to counteract the specific conditions found in the disorder rather than guessing whether this person's depression will respond more quickly and completely to this or that medication.

Treatment of Melancholic Depression

Unfortunately, given the current trends in research that combine depression into one category and conflate different types, most of the research on treating melancholic depression as a specific type comes from the literature on medication; it is also overly sparse. Although Cognitive Behavioral Therapy is often used in treating depression, for instance, no literature was found on its relative success with different types of depression.

Nortriptyline

Many believe nortriptyline, a TCA, to be better at treating melancholic depression than fluoxetine, an SSRI. Joyce et al. (2002) found a more complex pattern of results. Among their sample of 195 patients, fluoxetine, as expected, treated nonmelancholic depression more effectively than nortriptyline, with the reverse holding for those with mild or moderate melancholic symptoms. Surprisingly, those suffering the most melancholic features, especially when determined by CORE scores, again responded better to fluoxetine. Again comparing fluoxetine and nortriptyline, Joyce, Mulder, Luty, McKenzie, and Rae (2003) found that nonmelancholic depression responded better to fluoxetine, while the results for those with melancholic depression were even more complex than those found by Joyce et al. (2002). Specifically, when assessed by CORE scores (but not DSM criteria) males over 40 with melancholic depression gained better benefit from nortriptyline, patients under 24 responded better to fluoxetine and women over 40 responded approximately equally to each. In this study, they also found that males tolerated TCAs better, while women tolerated SSRIs better.

Venlafaxine

As depression increases in severity, most antidepressant medications no longer show much effect except in combination, presumably because more neurotransmitter networks are involved and need to be treated (Kienke & Rosenbaum, 2000). In a review article, Kienke and Rosenbaum note that venlafaxine has repeatedly been shown to be effective in treating melancholic depression. Venlafaxine, a Selective Serotonin-Norepinephrine Reuptake Inhibitor (Schatzberg et al., 2003) affects two neurotransmitter systems compromised in melancholic depression.

Mirtazapine

In their review, Benkert, Muller, and Szegedi (2002) note that studies comparing success rates of venlafaxine and mirtazapine therapies among severely melancholic inpatients have failed to reach statistical significance. Like venlafaxine, mirtazapine increases neural 5-HT and norepinephrine levels (Schatzberg et al., 2003).

Olanzapine

In a review of seven cases of melancholic depression unresponsive to antidepressant treatment, Parker and Malhi (2001) report the superior results obtained when olanzapine was added to or substituted for their previous medications. Olanzapine, an atypical antipsychotic medication, affects many neurotransmitter sites and has been shown to have beneficial effects on both psychosis and depressed mood (Schatzberg et al. 2003).

Valproate

Sival, Haffmans, Jansen, Duursma, and Eikelenboom (2002) found that although valproate had no significant effect on the aggression and agitation of elderly patients, it reduced their anxious, restless and melancholic behavior significantly, as determined by global rating scales. Because the diagnoses of these patients are unclear, this result must be taken with caution.

Lithium

Melancholic features occur in both unipolar and bipolar depressive disorders, and Serretti, Lattuada, Franchini, & Smeraldi (2000) studied the efficacy of lithium with both groups, finding no significant difference in their therapeutic gains. Alongside the Sival et al. (2002) results on valproate discussed above, it seems that mood stabilizers may have a role in treating melancholic depression along with venlafaxine, mirtazapine, TCAs, SSRIs and atypical antipsychotic medications, although this remains to be researched more adequately using better methodology.

Psychotherapy

As noted earlier, little has been written concerning differences in psychotherapeutic treatment of melancholic depression. An exception was the work of Weiss and Lang (2000), who writing from the psychoanalytic tradition stated that those with melancholia present for therapy with a wooden demeanor because they have difficulty feeling strong emotions. According to Weiss and Lang, these individuals idealize others and suffer losses as if it were part of themselves that had died. Scared of further losses, they arrive in therapy behaving in an overly solicitous manner towards their therapists, afraid to argue or take a personal stand. In this relationship, they portray themselves as unworthy and, the therapist as nearly perfect;

signs of imperfection by the therapist are initially taken as signs of their own failings. Treatment progresses as the melancholic patient learns to react with disappointment and anger when the therapist does not meet the patient's perceived needs adequately. If the therapist avoids indulging in a countertransference reaction of frustration at the melancholic patient's continued self-degradation, when the patient becomes able to express such disappointment, treatment is moving toward success (Weiss & Lang, 2000).

Conclusion

Despite current diagnostic thinking, depression appears to be a symptom of several very different conditions rather than a condition itself. More than having different symptom pictures, melancholic, atypical and anxious depressions probably all correspond to differing premorbid personalities, physiological profiles, neural imaging patterns and neuropsychological deficits. Any of these should, in principle, be more amenable to distinguishing types and subtypes of depression than the current system of behavioral checklists, arbitrary time frames and proportions of relevant symptom needed to make diagnoses. Beginning in the womb as the developing progeny of withdrawn, anhedonic mothers, the HPA axis of future melancholics is overly active, and the part of their brains responsible for modulating the HPA axis does not develop properly. With little capacity for positive affect, these children develop very conventionally and without much expressed or conscious affect, a pattern that continues into adulthood. They attach and depend upon others, making few decisions themselves. When they suffer significant losses for which they defensively blame themselves, their bodies react with marked physiological changes.

Although each piece of this story has been laid out herein, it remains a story, albeit one backed by a certain amount of research. However, holes remain, specifically in the transitions and points of continuity. Future research has much to teach us about this disorder, but research progress will remain slow and uneven as long as we do not recognize that melancholia is a unitary taxonic disorder, not part of some conjectured continuum of depressive severity.

PART NINE

CONCLUSION

Putting It All Together: Empathy

It SEEMS FITTING to end this book with a discussion of empathy, which ties together many of the strands introduced throughout it. Considered by many to be a key component of emotional intelligence, if not its pinnacle (Faye et al., 2011; Latour & Hosmer, 2002; Mayer & Salovey, 1997; Saarni, 1997), empathy is considered the most important ingredient in the therapeutic relationship (Greenberg et al., 2001; Rogers, 1961, 1980). Much of psychotherapy and counseling is focused on developing empathy, particularly among those who have committed sexual offenses, though the current research indicates that its development (or lack of it) is not associated with the future risk for sexual reoffending (Rich, 2003). Finally, empathy is impaired in many clients and conditions commonly seen in counseling and psychotherapy sessions. Psychopathy, which has already been discussed briefly, is notable for the callousness and absence of empathy those having it display towards others (Shirtcliff et al., 2009).

Empathy is the recognition and sharing of others' emotional states (Shirtcliff et al., 2009). It involves an interaction between two (or more) people in which one experiences and shares the emotions of the other (Decety & Jackson, 2006). It involves the ability to understand others' perspectives and have visceral experiences like those others and, thus, has both mental and emotional aspects (Shirtcliff et al., 2009). It also requires the ability to regulate one's emotions so that self and other can be distinguished

(Decety & Jackson, 2006). It develops in families that permit the free expression of nonhostile negative emotions among their members (Eisenberg, Fabes, & Losoya, 1997), but having empathy does not imply that one will behave in a supportive or sympathetic manner at all times (Decety & Jackson, 2006).

According to Shirtcliff et al. (2009), empathy arose as the need for mother-infant attachment within species did and, on average, women remain more proficient at it than men. As attachment began using the limbic system's circuitry for emotion and pain (like friendships and pair bonding later did), it inherited a region rich in cortisol receptor sites, making it ideal for visceral feedback. Its proximity and interconnections with the mirror neuron system, which registers how others act and feel, completed the picture. The ACC and insula—both rich in cortisol sites—are active in feeling pain, and they are equally active in helping people feel others' pain. Both are highly interconnected with the amygdala, and the insula and amygdala have direct connections to the hypothalamus. Through these connections, they control the amount of free cortisol within the system (Shirtcliff et al., 2009).

Cortisol, which enters neurons more easily than other hormones and has longer-lasting effects when it does, changes neuronal membrane sensitivity and how genes are expressed (Shirtcliff et al., 2009). Its effects can permanently change how the emotional circuitry operates. According to Shirtcliff et al., basal cortisol prepares the emotional brain, and low basal cortisol levels may be implicated in callousness. Those who exhibit more cortisol reactivity to novelty are more socially competent and popular, and they interact and affiliate with others more. The insula and ACC do not react strongly among those who are callous, and the ACC's reactivity is positively related to cortisol reactivity (apparently, this has not yet been examined regarding the insula). Youth with Conduct Disorder or Oppositional

Defiant Disorder have underactive HPA systems, which become even less active over time as their PFCs regulate their cortisol levels still lower. They do not feel stress when others do and they do not feel or respond appropriately to others' pain, whether physical or emotional (Shirtcliff et al., 2009).

Even among those people who do, an additional problem remain: One's pain activates the insula and ACC, among other neural structures, but so does others'. One's own pain does so more strongly and activates additional areas within the same structures, but without adequate emotional regulation these distinctions may become lost, resulting in emotional contagion instead of empathy and leading to lost boundaries and too much arousal (Decety & Jackson, 2006). The answer can be found in the functioning of the right TPJ, which tracks personal agency. Its activity and one's consciousness of it separates empathy from emotional contagion, preventing the emotional distress caused by poor distinctions between self and other. Such consciousness requires adequate emotional regulation so the signal will not be lost in the furor of an emotional system too active to allow such distinctions (Decety & Jackson, 2006).

When I started writing this book, I wanted to help others understand how I assess and treat clientele. I initially envisioned a book that covered the essential facts about emotions and how to address them in counseling and psychotherapy, but it quickly became clear that covering only the basic research and theory about emotions would consume an entire volume. More complex phenomena like personality disorders have not been addressed and therapeutic technique has gone unmentioned, though both of these topics were in my original plans. My only response is that this project already seemed long enough to be approaching the limits of any reader's patience. Interested readers will unfortunately have to await a further volume (or possibly volumes) to learn how the unaddressed topics fit into the system that has been sketched thus far. I trust that for the interested reader the information gained will prove to be worth the wait and hope that what has been revealed thus far will prove to be beneficial in the meantime.

References

Abbe, A., Tkach, C., & Lyubomirsky, S. (2003). The art of living by dispositionally happy people. *Journal of Happiness Studies, 4*, 385-404

Abbott, M. J., & Rapee, R. M. (2004). Post-event rumination and negative self-appraisal in social phobia before and after treatment. *Journal of Abnormal Psychology, 113*, 136-144.

Abdel-Khalek, A. M., & Lester, D. (2003). Death obsession in Kuwaiti and American college students. *Death Studies, 27*, 541-553.

Abela, J. R. Z., Vanderbilt, E., & Rochon, A. (2004). A test of the integration of the response styles and social support theories of depression in third and seventh grade children. *Journal of Social and Clinical Psychology, 23*, 653-674.

Abercrombie, H. C., Kalin, N. H., & Davidson, R. J. (2005). Acute cortisol elevations cause heightened arousal ratings of objectively nonarousing stimuli. *Emotion, 5*, 354-359.

Adolphs, R. (2002a). Neural systems for recognizing emotion. *Current Opinion in Neurobiology, 12*, 169-177.

Adolphs, R. (2002b). Trust in the brain. *Nature Neuroscience, 5*, 192-193.

Adolphs, R., Baron-Cohen, S., & Tranel, D. (2002). Impaired recognition of social emotions following amygdala damage. *Cognitive Neuroscience, 14*, 1264-1274.

Adolphs, R., Sears, L., & Piven, J. (2001). Abnormal processing of social information from faces in autism. *Journal of Cognitive Neuroscience, 13*, 232-240.

Adolphs, R., & Tranel, D. (1999). Preferences for visual stimuli following amygdala damage. *Journal of Cognitive Neuroscience, 11*, 610-616.

Adolphs, R., & Tranel, D. (2003). Amygdala damage impairs emotion recognition from scenes only when they contain facial expressions. *Neuropsychologia, 41*, 1281-1289

Adolphs, R., & Tranel, D. (2004). Impaired judgments of sadness but not happiness following bilateral amygdala damage. *Journal of Cognitive Neuroscience, 16*, 453-462.

Adolphs, R., Tranel, D., & Damasio, A. R. (2003). Dissociable neural systems for recognizing emotions. *Brain and Cognition, 52*, 61-69.

Alheid, G. F. (2003). Extended amygdala and basal forebrain. *Annals of the New York Academy of Sciences, 985,* 185-205.

Allen, J. J. B., Harmon-Jones, E., & Cavender, J. H. (2001). Manipulations of frontal EEG asymmetry through biofeedback alters self-reported emotional responses and facial EMG. *Psychophysiology, 38,* 685-693.

Alpers, G. W., Abelson, J. L., Wilhelm, F. H., & Roth, W. T. (2003). Salivary cortisol response during exposure treatment in driving phobics. *Psychosomatic Medicine, 65,* 679-687.

American Psychiatric Association. (2000). *DSM-IV-TR: Diagnostic and statistical manual of mental disorders.* Washington, DC: American Psychiatric Publishing.

Anderson, A. K., & Phelps, E. A. (2000). Expression without recognition: Contributions of the human amygdala to emotional communication. *Psychological Science, 11,* 106-111.

Anderson, A. K., & Phelps, E. A. (2002). Is the human amygdala critical for the subjective experience of emotion? Evidence of intact dispositional affect in patients with amygdala lesions. *Journal of Cognitive Neuroscience, 14,* 709-720.

Anderson, M. C., Ochsner, K. N., Kuhl, B., Cooper, J., Robertson, E., Gabrieli, S. W., et al. (2004). Neural systems underlying the suppression of unwanted thoughts. *Science, 303,* 232-235.

Anderson, V., Northam, E., Hendy, J., & Wrennall, J. (2001). *Developmental neuropsychology: A clinical approach.* Hove, East Sussex: Psychology Press.

Arce, E., Simmons, A. N., Lovero, K. L., Stein, M. B., & Paulus, M. P. (2008). Escitalopram effects on insula and amygdala BOLD activation during emotional processing. *Psychopharmacology, 196,* 661-672.

Arias, B., Gutiérrez, B., Pintor, L., Gastó, C., & Fañanás, L. (2001). Variability in the 5-HT2A receptor gene is associated with seasonal pattern in major depression. *Molecular Psychiatry, 6,* 239-242.

Balint, M. (1968). *The basic fault: Theoretical aspects of regression.* Evanston, IL: Northwestern University Press.

Bandura, A. (1996). Ontological and epistemological terrains revisited. *Journal of Behavior Therapy and Experimental Psychiatry, 27,* 323-345.

Bandura, A. (2000). Social cognitive theory: An agentic perspective. *Annual Review of Psychology, 52,* 1-26.

Bandura, A. (2002). Social cognitive theory in cultural context. *Applied Psychology: An International Review, 51,* 269-290.

Bandura, A., & Locke, E. A. (2003). Negative self-efficacy and goal effects revisited. *Journal of Applied Psychology, 88,* 87-99.

Baratta, M. V., Zarza, C. M., Gomez, D. M., Campeau, S., Watkins, L. R., & Maier, S. F. (2009). Selective activation of dorsal raphe nucleus-projecting neurons in the ventral prefrontal cortex by controllable stress. *European Journal of Neuroscience, 30*, 1111-1116.

Bar-On, R., Tranel, D., Denburg, N. L., & Bechara, A. (2003). Exploring the neurological substrate of emotional and social intelligence. *Brain, 126*, 1790-1800.

Baron, R. A., & Byrne, D. (2004). *Social psychology* (10th ed.). Boston: Pearson Education.

Barrett, K. C. (1998). The origins of guilt in early childhood. In J. Bybee (Ed.), *Guilt and children* (pp. 75-90). San Diego, CA: Academic Press.

Basabe, N., Paez, D., Valencia, J., Gonzalez, J. L., Rimé, B., & Diener, E. (2002). Cultural dimensions, socioeconomic development, climate, and emotional hedonic level. *Cognition and Emotion, 16*, 103-125.

Bauer, J. J., & Bonanno, G. A. (2001). Doing and being well (for the most part): Adaptive patterns of narrative self-evaluation during bereavement. *Journal of Personality, 69*, 451-482.

Baumann, N., & Kuhl, J. (2002). Intuition, affect, and personality: Unconscious coherence judgments and self-regulation of negative affect. *Journal of Personality and Social Psychology, 83*, 1213-1223.

Baumann, N., & Kuhl, J. (2005a). How to resist temptation: The effects of external control versus autonomy support on self-regulatory dynamics. *Journal of Personality, 73*, 443-470.

Baumann, N., & Kuhl, J. (2005b). Positive affect and flexibility: Overcoming the precedence of global over local processing of visual information. *Motivation and Emotion, 29*, 123-134.

Baumeister, R. F. (1990). Suicide as escape from self. *Psychological Review, 97*, 90-113.

Beavers, W. R. (1985). *Successful Marriage: A family systems approach to couples therapy.* New York: W. W. Norton & Company.

Bechara, A. (2004). The role of emotion in decision-making: Evidence from neurological patients with orbitofrontal damage. *Brain and Cognition, 55*, 30-40.

Beck, A. T. (1999). *Prisoners of hate: The cognitive basis of anger, hostility, and violence.* New York: Harper Collins.

Beck, A. T., & Emery, G. (1985). *Anxiety disorders and phobias: A cognitive perspective.* New York: Basic Books.

Belzung, C., & Chevalley, C. (2002). Emotional behaviour as a result of stochastic interactions: A process crucial for cognition. *Behavioural Processes, 60*, 115-132.

Benjamin, L. S. (1996). A clinician-friendly version of the interpersonal circumplex: Structural analysis of social behavior. *Journal of Personality Assessment, 66*, 248-266.

Benkert, O., Muller, M., & Szegedi, A. (2002). An overview of the clinical efficacy of mirtazapine. *Human Psychopharmacology: Clinical & Experimental, 17*(Supplement 1), S23-S26.

Bennett, D. S., Bendersky, M., & Lewis, M. (2002). Facial expressivity at 4 months: A context by expression analysis. *Infancy, 3*, 97-113.

Bennett, D. S., Bendersky, M., & Lewis, M. (2004). On specifying specificity: Facial expressions at 4 months. *Infancy, 6*, 425-429.

Bennett, P., Lowe, R., & Honey, K. L. (2003). Appraisals, core relational themes, and emotions: A test of the consistency of reporting and their associations. *Cognition and Emotion, 17*, 511-520.

Ben-Ze'ev, A. (2000). *The subtlety of emotions.* Cambridge, MA: MIT Press.

Berkowitz, L., Jaffee, S., Jo, E., & Troccoli, B. T. (2000). On the correction of feeling-induced judgmental biases. In J. P. Forgas (Ed.), *Feeling and thinking: The role of affect in social cognition* (pp. 131-152). New York: Cambridge University Press.

Berntson, G. G., & Cacioppo, J. T. (2000). Psychobiology and social psychology: Past, present, and future. *Personality and Social Psychology Review, 4*, 3-15.

Berntson, G. G., Cacioppo, J. T., & Sarter, M. (2003). Bottom-up: Implications for neurobehavioral models of anxiety and autonomic regulation. In R. J. Davidson, K. R. Scherer, & H. H. Goldsmith (Eds.), *Handbook of affective sciences* (pp. 1105-1116). New York: Oxford University Press.

Berntson, G. G., Sarter, M., & Cacioppo, J. T. (2003). Ascending visceral regulation of cortical affective information processing. *European Journal of Neuroscience, 18*, 2103-2109.

Berridge, K. C., & Winkielman, P. (2003). What is an unconscious emotion? (The case for unconscious "liking"). *Cognition and Emotion, 17*, 181-211.

Berry, J. W., Worthington, E. L., Jr., O'Connor, L. E., Parrott, L., III, & Wade, N. G. (2005). Forgiveness, vengeful rumination, and affective traits. *Journal of Personality, 73*, 183-226.

Berthoz, S., Blair, R. J. R., Le Clec'h, G., & Martinot, J. L. (2002). Emotions: From neuropsychology to functional imaging. *International Journal of Psychology, 37*, 193-203.

Bhagwagar, Z., Hafizi, S., & Cowen, P. J. (2003). Increase in concentration of waking salivary cortisol in recovered patients with depression. *American Journal of Psychiatry, 160*, 1890-1891.

Binswanger, L. (1963). The case of Lola Voss (E. Angel, Trans.). In *Being-in-the-world: Selected papers of Ludwig Binswanger* (pp. 266-341). New York: Harper & Row. (Original work published 1949)

Biswas-Diener, R., Kashdan, T. B., & King, L. A. (2009). Two traditions of happiness research, not two distinct types of happiness. *Journal of Positive Psychology, 4*, 208-211.

Biswas-Diener, R., Vitterso, J., & Diener, E. (2005). Most people are pretty happy, but there is cultural variation: The Inughuit, the Amish, and the Maasai. *Journal of Happiness Studies, 6*, 205-226.

Blackledge, J. T., & Hayes, S. C. (2001). Emotion regulation in acceptance and commitment therapy. *Journal of Clinical Psychology, 57*, 243-255.

Blair, R. J. R. (2004). The roles of orbital frontal cortex in the modulation of antisocial behavior. *Brain and Cognition, 55*, 198-208.

Blanchette, I., & Richards, A. (2010). The influence of affect on higher level cognition: A review of the research on interpretation, judgement, decision making and reasoning. *Cognition and Emotion, 24*, 661-595.

Blascovich, J., Mendes, W. B., Hunter, S. B., Lickel, B., & Kowai-Bell, N. (2001). Perceiver threat in social interactions with stigmatized others. *Journal of Personality and Social Psychology, 80*, 253-267.

Blascovich, J., Mendes, W. B., Hunter, S. B., & Salomon, K. (1999). Social 'facilitation' as challenge and threat. *Journal of Personality and Social Psychology, 77*, 68-77.

Blascovich, J., Mendes, W. B., Tomaka, J., Salomon, K., & Seery, M. (2003). The robust nature of the biopsychosocial model challenge and threat: A reply to Wright and Kirby. *Personality and Social Psychology Review, 7*, 234-243.

Blum, H. P. (1992). Affect theory and the theory of technique. In T. Shapiro & R. N. Emde (Eds.), *Affect: Psychoanalytic perspectives* (pp. 265-289). Madison, CT: International Universities Press.

Blumberg, M. S., & Sokoloff, G. (2003). Hard heads and open minds: A reply to Panksepp (2003). *Psychological Review, 100*, 389-394.

Bolles, R. C. (1970). Species-specific defense reactions and avoidance learning. *Psychological Review, 77*, 32-48.

Bolte, A., Goschke, T., & Kuhl, J. (2003). Emotion and intuition: Effects of positive and negative mood on implicit judgments of semantic coherence. *Psychological Science, 14*, 416-421.

Bonanno, G. A., & Kaltman, S. (1999). Toward an integrative perspective on bereavement. *Psychological Bulletin, 125*, 760-776.

Bonanno, G. A., Keltner, D., Noll, J. G., Putnam, F. W., Trickett, P. K., LeJeune, J., et al. (2002). When the face reveals what words do not: Facial expressions of emotion, smiling, and the willingness to disclose childhood sexual abuse. *Journal of Personality and Social Psychology, 83*, 94-110.

Borg, J. S., Lieberman, D., & Kiehl, K. A. (2008). Infection, incest, and iniquity: Investigating the neural correlates of disgust and morality. *Journal of Cognitive Neuroscience, 20*, 1529-1546.

Bornas, X., Llabrés, J., Noguera, M., López, A. M., Barceló, F., Tortella-Feliu, M., et al. (2004). Self-implication and heart rate variability during simulated exposure to flight-related stimuli. *Anxiety, Stress, and Coping, 17*, 331-339.

Borod, J. C., Bloom, R. L., Brickman, A. M., Nakhutina, L., & Curko, E. A. (2002). Emotional processing deficits in individuals with unilateral brain damage. *Applied Neuropsychology, 9*, 23-36.

Bosch, J. A., Berntson, G. G., Cacioppo, J. T., & Marucha, P. T. (2005). Differential mobilization of functionally distinct natural killer subsets during acute psychologic stress. *Psychosomatic Medicine, 67*, 366-375.

Bower, G. H., & Forgas, J. P. (2000). Affect, memory, and social cognition. In E. Eich, J. F. Kihlstrom, G. H. Bower, J. P. Forgas, & P. M. Niedenthal (Eds.), *Cognition and emotion* (pp. 87-168). New York: Oxford University.

Bowlby, J. (1969). *Attachment and Loss: Vol. 1. Attachment.* New York: Basic Books.

Bowlby, J. (1973). *Attachment and loss: Vol. 2. Separation: Anxiety and anger.* New York: Basic Books.

Bowlby, J. (1980). *Attachment and loss: Vol. 3. Loss.* New York: Basic Books.

Bradbury, M. (2001). Freud's Mourning and Melancholia. *Mortality, 6*, 212-219.

Bradvik, L. (2002). The occurrence of suicide in severe depression related to the months of the year and the days of the week. *European Archives of Psychiatry and Clinical Neuroscience, 252*, 28-32.

Breuer, J., & Freud, S. (1955). J. Strachey (Ed.), *The standard edition of the complete psychological works of Sigmund Freud: Vol. 2. Studies on hysteria* (J. Strachey, Trans.). New York: Basic Books. (Original work published 1893-1895)

Breugelmans, S. M., Poortinga, Y. H., Ambadar, Z., Setiadi, B., Vaca, J. B., Widiyanto, P., et al. (2005). Body sensations associated with emotions in Raramuri Indians, rural Javanese, and three student samples. *Emotion, 5*, 166-174.

Brommelhoff, J. A., Conway, K., Merikangas, K., & Levy, B. R. (2004). Higher rates of depression in women: Role of gender bias within the family. *Journal of Women's Health, 13*, 69-76.

Brosschot, J. F. (2002). Cognitive-emotional sensitization and somatic health complaints. *Scandinavian Journal of Psychology, 43*, 113-121.

Brosschot, J. F., & Thayer, J. F. (2003). Heart rate response is longer after negative emotions than after positive emotions. *International Journal of Psychophysiology, 50*, 181-187.

Bruder, G. E., Stewart, J. W., McGrath, P. J., Ma, G. J., Wexler, B. E., & Quitkin, F. M. (2002). Atypical depression: Enhanced right hemispheric dominance for perceiving emotional chimeric faces. *Journal of Abnormal Psychology, 111*, 446-454.

Buchanon, T. W., Kern, S., Allen, J. S., Tranel, D., & Kirschbaum, C. (2004). Circadian regulation of cortisol after hippocampal damage in humans. *Biological Psychiatry, 56*, 651-656.

Buck, R. (1999). The biological affects: A typology. *Psychological Review, 106*, 301-336.

Bushman, B. J., Baumeister, R. F., & Phillips, C. M. (2001). Do people aggress to improve their mood? Catharsis beliefs, affect regulation opportunity, and aggressive responding. *Journal of Personality and Social Psychology, 81*, 17-32.

Butler, E. A., Egloff, B., Wilhelm, F. H., Smith, N. C., Erickson, E. A., & Gross, J. J. (2003). The Social Consequences of Expressive Suppression. *Emotion, 3*, 48-67.

Butler, E. A., Wilhelm, F. H., & Gross, J. J. (2006). Respiratory sinus arrhythmia, emotion, and emotion regulation during social interaction. *Psychophysiology, 43*, 612-622.

Bybee, J., & Quiles, Z. N. (1998). Guilt and mental health. In J. Bybee (Ed.), *Guilt and children* (pp. 269-291). San Diego, CA: Academic Press.

Bywaters, M., Andrade, J., & Turpin, G. (2004). Intrusive and non-intrusive memories in a non-clinical sample: The effects of mood and affect on imagery vividness. *Memory, 12*, 467-478.

Cabanac, M. (2002). What is emotion? *Behavioural Processes, 60*, 69-83.

Cacioppo, J. T. (2004). Feelings and emotions: Roles for electrophysiological markers. *Biological Psychology, 67*, 235-243.

Cacioppo, J. T., & Berntson, G. G. (1999). The affect system: Architecture and operating characteristics. *Current Directions in Psychological Science, 8*, 133-137.

Cacioppo, J. T., Berntson, G. G., Larsen, J. T., Poehlmann, K. M., & Ito, T. A. (2000). The psychophysiology of emotion. In R. Lewis & J. M. Haviland-Jones (Eds.), *The handbook of emotion* (2nd ed., pp. 173-191). New York: Guilford Press.

Cacioppo, J. T., & Gardner, W. L. (1999). Emotion. *Annual Review of Psychology, 50*, 191-214.

Calder, A. J., Keane, J., Young, A. W., Lawrence, A. D., Mason, S., & Barker, R. A. (2010). The relation between anger and different forms of disgust: Implications for emotion recognition impairments in Huntington's disease. Neuropsychologia, 48, 2719-2729.

Canli, T., & Amin, Z. (2002). Neuroimaging of emotion and personality: Scientific evidence and ethical considerations. *Brain and Cognition, 50,* 414-431.

Carver, C. S., & White, T. L. (1994). Behavioral inhibition, behavioral activation, and affective responses to impending reward and punishment: The BIS/BAS scales. *Journal of Personality and Social Psychology, 67,* 319-333.

Casciaro, T., Carley, K. M., & Krackhardt, D. (1999). Positive affectivity and accuracy in social network perception. *Motivation and Emotion, 23,* 285-306.

Chao, R. (2001). Integrating culture and attachment. *American Psychologist, 56,* 822-823.

Chrousos, G. P. (2000). The role of stress and the hypothalamic-pituitary-adrenal axis in the pathogenesis of the metabolic syndrome: Neuro-endocrine and target tissue-related causes. *International Journal of Obesity, 24*(Supplement 2), S50-S55.

Ciompi, L. (1998). Is schizophrenia an affective disease? The hypothesis of affect-logic and its implications for psychopathology. In W. F. Flack, Jr. & J. D. Laird (Eds.), *Emotions in psychopathology* (pp. 283-297). New York: Oxford University Press.

Cisler, J. M., Olatunji, B. O., Lohr, J. M., & Williams, N. L. (2009). Attentional bias differences between fear and disgust: Implications for the role of disgust in disgust-related anxiety disorders. *Cognition and Emotion, 23,* 675-687.

Clore, G. L., & Robinson, M. D. (2000). What is emotion regulation? In search of a phenomenon. *Psychological Inquiry, 11,* 163-166.

Clow, A., Thorn, L., Evans, P., & Hucklebridge, F. (2004). The awakening cortisol response: Methodological issues and significance. *Stress, 7,* 29-37.

Clyman, R. B. (1992). The procedural organization of emotions: A contribution from cognitive science to the psychoanalytic theory of therapeutic action. In T. Shapiro & R. N. Emde (Eds.), *Affect: Psychoanalytic perspectives* (pp. 349-382). Madison, CT: International Universities Press.

Clynes, M. (1977). *Sentics: The touch of emotions.* Garden City, NY: Anchor Press/ Doubleday.

Codispoti, M., Gerra, G., Montebarocci, O., Zaimovic, A., Raggi, M. A., & Baldaro, B. (2003). Emotional perception and neuroendocrine changes. *Psychophysiology, 40,* 863-868.

Colwell, M. J., & Hart, S. (2006). Emotion framing: Does it relate to children's emotion knowledge and social behavior? *Early Child Development and Care, 176*, 591-603.

Compton, R. J., Fisher, L. R., Koenig, L. M., McKeown, R., & Muñoz, K. (2003). Relationship between coping styles and perceptual asymmetry. *Journal of Personality and Social Psychology, 84*, 1069-1078.

Consedine, N. S., Magai, C., & Bonanno, G. A. (2002). Moderators of the emotion inhibition-health relationship: A review and research agenda. *Review of General Psychology, 6*, 204-228.

Conway, M., Csank, P. A. R., Holm, S. L., & Blake, C. K. (2000). On assessing individual differences in rumination on sadness. *Journal of Personality Assessment, 75*, 404-425.

Conway, M. A., & Pleydell-Pearce, C. W. (2000). The construction of autobiographical memories in the self-memory system. *Psychological Review, 107*, 261-288.

Cooney, J. M., & Dinan, T. G. (2000). Hypothalamic-pituitary-adrenal axis early-feedback responses are preserved in melancholic depression: A study of sertraline treatment. *Human Psychopharmacology: Clinical & Experimental, 15*, 351-356.

Cooper, S. J., & Kelly, C. B. (2000). Plasma noradrenaline response to a cognitive stressor in subtypes of depressive illness. *Human Psychopharmacology: Clinical & Experimental, 15*, 265-274.

Corbit, L. H., & Balleine, B. W. (2003). Instrumental and Pavlovian incentive processes have dissociable effects on components of a heterogeneous instrumental chain. *Journal of Experimental Psychology: Animal Behavior Processes, 29*, 99-106.

Corrigan, M. H., Denahan, A. Q., Wright, C. E., Ragual, R. J., & Evans, D. L. (2000). Comparison of pramipexole, fluoxetine, and placebo in patients with major depression. *Depression and Anxiety, 11*, 58-65.

Cox, B. J., Enns, M. W., & Taylor, S. (2001). The effect of rumination as a mediator of elevated anxiety sensitivity in major depression. *Cognitive Therapy and Research, 25*, 525-534.

Crawford, L. E., & Cacioppo, J. T. (2002). Learning where to look for danger: Integrating affective and spatial information. *Psychological Science, 13*, 449-453.

Critchley, H. (2003). Emotion and its disorders. *British Medical Bulletin, 65*, 35-47.

Crucian, G. P., Hughes, J. D., Barrett, A. M., Williamson, D. J. G., Bauer, R. M., Bowers, D., et al. (2000). Emotional and physiological responses to false feedback. *Cortex, 36*, 623-647.

Dailey, M. N., Cottrell, G. W., Padgett, C., & Adolphs, R. (2002). Empath: A neural network that categorizes facial expressions. *Journal of Cognitive Neuroscience, 14*, 1158-1173.

Dalbert, C. (2002). Beliefs in a just world as a buffer against anger. *Social Justice Research, 15,* 123-145.

Damasio, A. (2001). Fundamental feelings. *Nature, 413,* 781.

Daniels, J. K., McFarlane, A. C., Bluhm, R. L., Moores, K. A., Clark, C. R., Shaw, M. E., et al. (2010). Switching between executive and default mode networks in posttraumatic stress disorder: Alterations in functional connectivity. *Journal of Psychiatry & Neuroscience, 35,* 258-266.

Darwin, C. (1965). *The expression of the emotions in man and animals.* Chicago: University of Chicago. (Original work published 1872)

Davidson, R. J. (1998). Affective style and affective disorders: Perspectives from affective neuroscience. *Cognition and Emotion, 12,* 307-330.

Davidson, R. J., Pizzagalli, D., Nitschke, J. B., & Putnam, K. (2002). Depression: Perspectives from affective neuroscience. *Annual Review of Psychology, 53,* 545-574.

Davidson, R. J., & Slagter, H. A. (2000). Probing emotion in the developing brain: Functional neuroimaging in the assessment of the neural substrates of emotion in normal and disordered children and adolescents. *Mental Retardation and Developmental Disabilities Research Reviews, 6,* 166-170.

Davis, J. T. (2001). Revising psychoanalytic interpretations of the past: An examination of declarative and non-declarative memory processes. *International Journal of Psychoanalysis, 82,* 449-462.

Davis, R. N., & Nolen-Hoeksema, S. (2000). Cognitive inflexibility among ruminators and nonruminators. *Cognitive Therapy and Research, 24,* 699-711.

de Rivera, J. (1977). A structural theory of the emotions. *Psychological Issues Monograph 40.* New York: International Universities Press.

Debener, S., Beauducel, A., Nessler, D., Brocke, B., Heilemann, H., & Kayser, J. (2000). Is resting anterior EEG alpha asymmetry a trait marker for depression? *Neuropsychobiology, 41,* 31-37.

Decety, J., & Jackson, P. L. (2006). A social-neuroscience perspective on empathy. *Current Directions in Psychological Science, 15,* 54-58.

Demaree, H. A., Schmeichel, B. J., Robinson, J. L., & Everhart, D. E. (2004). Behavioral, affective, and physiological effects of negative and positive emotional exaggeration. *Cognition and Emotion, 18,* 1079-1097.

Désiré, L., Veissier, I., Després, G., & Boissy, A. (2004). On the way to assess emotions in animals: Do lambs (ovis aries) evaluate an event through its suddenness, novelty or unpredictability? *Journal of Comparative Psychology, 118,* 363-374.

Deutsch, H. (1965a). Absence of grief. In *Neuroses and character types* (pp. 226-236). Madison, CT: International Universities Press. (Original work published 1937)

Deutsch, H. (1965b). Hysterical conversion symptoms: Fits, trance states. In *Neuroses and character types* (pp. 57-73). New York: International Universities Press. (Original work published 1930)

Diamond, L. M., & Aspinwall, L. G. (2003). Emotion regulation across the life span: An integrative perspective emphasizing self-regulation, positive affect, and dyadic processes. *Motivation and Emotion, 27*, 125-156.

Dickerson, S. S., Gruenewald, T. L., & Kemeny, M. E. (2004). When the social self is threatened: Shame, physiology, and health. *Journal of Personality, 72*, 1191-1216.

Dickerson, S. S., & Kemeny, M. E. (2004). Acute stressors and cortisol responses: A theoretical integration and synthesis of laboratory research. *Psychological Bulletin, 130*, 355-391.

Dickerson, S. S., Kemeny, M. E., Aziz, N., Kim, K. H., & Fahey, J. L. (2004). Immunological effects of induced shame and guilt. *Psychosomatic Medicine, 66*, 124-131.

Diego, M. A., Field, T., Hart, S., Hernandez-Reif, M., Jones, N., Cullen, C., et al. (2002). Facial expressions and EEG in infants of intrusive and withdrawn mothers with depressive symptoms. *Depression and Anxiety, 15*, 10-17.

Diego, M. A., Field, T., & Hernandez-Reif, M. (2001a). BIS/BAS scores are correlated with frontal EEG asymmetry in intrusive and withdrawn depressed mothers. *Infant Mental Health Journal, 22*, 665-675.

Diego, M. A., Field, T., & Hernandez-Reif, M. (2001b). CES-D depression scores are correlated with frontal EEG alpha asymmetry. *Depression and Anxiety, 13*, 32-37.

Diego, M. A., Field, T., Hernandez-Reif, M., Cullen, C., Schanberg, S., & Kuhn, C. (2004). Prepartum, postpartum, and chronic depression effects on newborns. *Psychiatry, 67*, 63-80.

Diego, M. A., Field, T., Jones, N. A., Hernandez-Reif, M., Cullen, C., Schanberg, S., et al. (2004). EEG responses to mock facial expressions by infants of depressed mothers. *Infant Behavior and Development, 27*, 150-162.

Dienstbier, R. A. (1989). Arousal and physiological toughness: Implications for mental and physical health. *Psychological Review, 96*, 84-100.

Dijksterhuis, A., & Smith, P. (2002). Affective habituation: Subliminal exposure to extreme stimuli decreases their extremity. *Emotion, 2*, 203-214.

Dinsmoor, J. A. (2001). Stimuli inevitably generalized by behavior that avoids electric shock are inherently reinforcing. *Journal of the Experimental Analysis of Behavior, 75*, 311-333.

Dolan, M. C., & Fullam, R. S. (2009). Psychopathy and functional magnetic resonance imaging blood oxygenation level-dependent responses to emotional faces in violent patients with schizophrenia. *Biological Psychiatry, 66*, 570-577.

Drevets, W. C. (2003). Neuroimaging abnormalities in the amygdala in mood disorders. *Annals of the New York Academy of Sciences, 985*, 420-444.

Drevets, W. C., Ongur, D., & Price, J. L. (1998). Neuroimaging abnormalities in the subgenual prefrontal cortex: Implications for the pathophysiology of familial mood disorders. *Molecular Psychiatry, 3*, 220-226.

Drevets, W. C., & Raichle, M. E. (1998). Reciprocal suppression of regional cerebral blood flow during emotional versus higher cognitive processes: Implications for interactions between emotion and cognition. *Cognition and Emotion, 12*, 353-385.

Drummond, P. D., & Quah, S. H. (2001). The effect of expressing anger on cardiovascular reactivity and facial blood flow in Chinese and Caucasians. *Psychophysiology, 38*, 190-196.

Duclos, S. E., & Laird, J. D. (2001). The deliberate control of emotional experience through control of expressions. *Cognition and Emotion, 15*, 27-56.

Eckart, C., Stoppel, C., Kaufmann, J., Tempelmann, C., Hinrichs, H., Elbert, T., et al. (2011). Structural alterations in lateral prefrontal, parietal and posterior midline regions of men with chronic posttraumatic stress disorder. *Journal of Psychiatry & Neuroscience, 36*, 176-186.

Edge, M. D., Ramel, W., Drabant, E. M., Kuo, J. R., Parker, K. J., & Gross, J. J. (2009). For better or worse? Stress inoculation effects for implicit but not explicit anxiety. *Depression and Anxiety, 26*, 831-837.

Edwards, S. L., Rapee, R. M., & Franklin, J. (2003). Postevent rumination and recall bias for a social performance event in high and low socially anxious individuals. *Cognitive Therapy and Research, 27*, 603-617.

Egloff, B., Wilhelm, F. H., Neubauer, D. H., Mauss, I. B., & Gross, J. J. (2002). Implicit anxiety measure predicts cardiovascular reactivity to an evaluated speaking task. *Emotion, 2*, 3-11.

Eisenberg, N., Fabes, R. A., & Losoya, S. (1997). Emotional responding: Regulation, social correlates, and socialization. In P. Salovey & D. J. Sluyter (Eds.), *Emotional development and emotional intelligence* (pp. 129-163). New York: Basic Books.

Eisenberg, N., & Zhou, Q. (2000). Regulation from a developmental perspective. *Psychological Inquiry, 11*, 166-171.

Ekman, P. (1992). Facial expressions of emotion: New findings, new questions. *Psychological Science, 3*, 34-38.

Ellgring, H., & Smith, M. (1998). Affect regulation during psychosis. In W. F. Flack, Jr. & J. D. Laird (Eds.), *Emotions in psychopathology* (pp. 323-335). New York: Oxford University Press.

Ellis, A. (1962). *Reason and emotion in psychotherapy.* Secaucus, NJ: Citadel Press.

Elster, J. (1999). *Strong feelings: Emotion, addiction and human behavior* (F. Recanati, Ed.). Cambridge, MA: MIT Press.

Emde, R. N. (1992). Positive emotions for psychoanalytic theory: Surprises from infancy research and new directions. In T. Shapiro & R. N. Emde (Eds.), *Affect: Psychoanalytic perspectives* (pp. 5-44). Madison, CT: International Universities Press.

Epel, E. S., McEwen, B. S., & Ickovics, J. R. (1998). Embodying psychological thriving: Physical thriving in response to stress. *Journal of Social Issues, 54,* 301-322.

Epstein, S. (1994). Integration of the cognitive and the psychodynamic unconscious. *American Psychologist, 49,* 709-724.

Epstein, S. (1997). This I have learned from over 40 years of personality research. *Journal of Personality, 65,* 3-33.

Epstein, S. (1998). Emotions and psychopathology from the perspective of cognitive-experiential self-theory. In W. F. Flack, Jr. & J. D. Laird (Eds.), *Emotions in psychopathology* (pp. 57-69). New York: Oxford University Press.

Erber, R., & Erber, M. W. (2000). The self-regulation of moods: Second thoughts on the importance of happiness in everyday life. *Psychological Inquiry, 11,* 142-148.

Erickson, K., & Schulkin, J. (2003). Facial expressions of emotion: A cognitive neuroscience perspective. *Brain and Cognition, 52,* 52-60.

Erikson, E. H. (1963). *Childhood and society* (2nd ed.). New York: W. W. Norton & Company.

Eslinger, P. J., Flaherty-Craig, C. V., & Benton, A. L. (2004). Developmental outcomes after early prefrontal cortex damage. *Brain and Cognition, 55,* 84-103.

Eubanks, L., Wright, R. A., & Williams, B. J. (2002). Reward influence on the heart: Cardiovascular response as a function of incentive value at five levels of task demand. *Motivation and Emotion, 26,* 139-152.

Fabes, R. A., Eisenberg, N., Jones, S., Smith, M., Guthrie, I., Poulin, R., et al. (1999). Regulation, emotionality, and preschoolers' socially competent peer interactions. *Child Development, 70,* 432-442.

Fairchild, G., Van Goozen, S. H. M., Calder, A. J., Stollery, S. J., & Goodyer, I. M. (2009). Deficits in facial expression recognition in male adolescents with early-onset or adolescence-onset conduct disorder. *Journal of Child Psychology and Psychiatry, 50,* 627-636.

Fanselow, M. S., & Gale, G. D. (2003). The amygdala, fear and memory. *Annals of the New York Academy of Sciences, 985,* 125-134.

Faye, A., Kalra, G., Swamy, R., Shukla, A., Subramanyam, A., & Kamath, R. (2011). Study of emotional intelligence and empathy in medical postgraduates. *Indian Journal of Psychiatry, 53,* 140-144.

Feinstein, J. S., Goldin, P. R., Stein, M. B., Brown, G. G., & Paulus, M. P. (2002). Habituation of attentional networks during emotional processing. *NeuroReport, 13,* 1255-1258.

Feldman Barrett, L., Gross, J., Conner Christensen, T., & Benvenuto, M. (2001). Knowing what you're feeling and knowing what to do about it: Mapping the relation between emotion differentiation and emotion regulation. *Cognition and Emotion, 15,* 713-724.

Fernandez, M., Hernandez-Reif, M., Field, T., Diego, M., Sanders, C., & Roca, A. (2004). EEG during lavender and rosemary exposure in infants of depressed and non-depressed mothers. *Infant Behavior & Development, 27,* 91-100.

Fernández-Dols, J. M., & Russell, J. A. (2003). Emotion, affect, and mood in social judgments. In *Handbook of psychology: Vol. 5. Personality and social psychology* (pp. 283-298). Hoboken, NJ: John Wiley & Sons.

Field, T., Diego, M., Dieter, J., Hernandez-Reif, M., Schanberg, S., Kuhn, C., et al. (2004). Prenatal depression effects on the fetus and the newborn. *Infant Behavior & Development, 27,* 216-229.

Field, T., Diego, M., Hernandez-Reif, M., Gil, K., & Vera, Y. (2005). Prenatal maternal cortisol, fetal activity and growth. *International Journal of Neuroscience, 115,* 423-429.

Field, T., Diego, M., Hernandez-Reif, M., Salman, F., Schanberg, S., Kuhn, C., et al. (2002). Prenatal anger effects on the fetus and neonate. *Journal of Obstetrics and Gynaecology, 22,* 260-266.

Field, T., Diego, M., Hernandez-Reif, M., Schanberg, S., & Kuhn, C. (2002). Relative right versus left frontal EEG in neonates. *Developmental Psychobiology, 41,* 147-155.

Field, T., Diego, M., Hernandez-Reif, M., Schanberg, S., & Kuhn, C. (2003). Depressed mothers who are "good interaction" partners versus those who are withdrawn or intrusive. *Infant Behavior & Development, 26,* 238-252.

Field, T., Diego, M., Hernandez-Reif, M., Schanberg, S., Kuhn, C., Yando, R., & et al. (2003). Pregnancy anxiety and comorbid depression and anger: Effects on the fetus and neonate. *Depression and Anxiety, 17,* 140-151.

Field, T., Diego, M., Hernandez-Reif, M., Vera, Y., Gil, K., Schanberg, S., et al. (2004). Prenatal maternal biochemistry predicts neonatal biochemistry. *International Journal of Neuroscience, 114,* 933-945.

Flack, W. F., Jr., Laird, J. D., & Cavallaro, L. A. (1999). Separate and combined effects of facial expressions and bodily postures on emotional feelings. *European Journal of Social Psychology, 29,* 203-217.

Flykt, A. (2005). Visual search with biological threat stimuli: Accuracy, reaction times, and heart rate changes. *Emotion, 5,* 349-353.

Folkman, S., & Lazarus, R. S. (1980). An analysis of coping in a middle-aged community sample. *Journal of Health and Social Behavior, 21,* 219-239.

Folkman, S., & Lazarus, R. S. (1985). If it changes it must be a process: Study of emotion and coping during three stages of a college examination. *Journal of Personality and Social Psychology, 48,* 150-170.

Folkman, S., Lazarus, R. S., Dunkel-Schetter, C., DeLongis, A., & Gruen, R. J. (1986). Dynamics of a stressful encounter: Cognitive appraisal, coping, and encounter outcomes. *Journal of Personality and Social Psychology, 50,* 992-1003.

Folkman, S., Lazarus, R. S., Gruen, R. J., & DeLongis, A. (1986). Appraisal, coping, health status, and psychological symptoms. *Journal of Personality and Social Psychology, 50,* 571-579.

Fonagy, P. (1999, May 13). *Transgenerational consistencies of attachment: A new theory.* Paper presented to the Developmental and Psychoanalytic Discussion Group, American Psychoanalytic Association, Washington, DC. Retrieved January 18, 2003, from http://psychematters.com/papers/fonagy2.htm

Forgas, J. P. (2000). Managing moods: Toward a dual-process theory of spontaneous mood regulation. *Psychological Inquiry, 11,* 172-177.

Fosha, D. (2001). The dyadic regulation of affect. *Journal of Clinical Psychology, 57,* 227-242.

Fosha, D. (2004). 'Nothing that feels bad is ever the last step:' The role of positive emotions in experiential work with difficult emotional experiences. *Clinical Psychology and Psychotherapy, 11,* 30-43.

Fosha, D., & Slowiaczek, M. L. (1997). Techniques to accelerate dynamic psychotherapy. *American Journal of Psychotherapy, 51,* 229-251.

Fountoulakis, K. N., Karamouzis, M., Iacovides, A., Nimatoudis, J., Diakogiannis, J., Kaprinis, G., et al. (2001). Morning and evening plasma melatonin and dexamethasone suppression test in patients with nonseasonal major depressive disorder from northern Greece (latitude 40-41.5). *Neuropsychobiology, 44,* 113-117.

Frankl, V. (1962). *Man's search for meaning* (Rev. ed., I. Lasch, Trans.). Boston: Beacon Press.

Fredrickson, B. L. (2000). Extracting meaning from past affective experiences: The importance of peaks, ends, and specific emotions. *Cognition and Emotion, 14,* 577-606.

Fredrickson, B. L. (2003). The value of positive emotions. *American Scientist, 91,* 330-335.

Fredrickson, B. L., & Branigan, C. (2001). Positive emotions. In T. J. Mayne & G. A. Bonanno (Eds.), *Emotions: Current issues and future directions* (pp. 123-151). New York: Guilford.

Fredrickson, B. L., & Joiner, T. (2002). Positive emotions trigger upward spirals toward emotional well-being. *Psychological Science, 13,* 172-175.

Fredrickson, B. L., & Levenson, R. W. (1998). Positive emotions speed recovery from the cardiovascular sequelae of negative emotions. *Cognition and Emotion, 12,* 191-220.

Fredrickson, B. L., Mancuso, R. A., Branigan, C., & Tugade, M. M. (2000). The undoing effect of positive emotions. *Motivation and Emotion, 24,* 237-258.

Fredrickson, B. L., Maynard, K. E., Helms, M. J., Haney, T. L., Siegler, I. C., & Barefoot, J. C. (2000). Hostility predicts magnitude and duration of blood pressure response to anger. *Journal of Behavioral Medicine, 23,* 229-243.

Fresco, D. M., Frankel, A. N., Mennin, D. S., Turk, C. L., & Heimberg, R. G. (2002). Distinct and overlapping features of rumination and worry: The relationship of cognitive production to negative affective states. *Cognitive Therapy and Research, 26,* 179-188.

Freshwater, D., & Robertson, C. (2002). *Emotions and needs.* Philadelphia: Open University Press.

Freud, A. (1966). *The writings of Anna Freud: Vol. 2. The ego and the mechanisms of defense* (Rev. ed.) New York: International Universities Press. (Original work published 1936)

Freud, S. (1959a). Formulations regarding the two principles in mental functioning (J. Riviere, Trans.). In *Collected papers: Vol. 4. Papers on metapsychology and applied psycho-dynamics* (pp. 13-21). New York: Basic Books. (Original work published 1911)

Freud, S. (1959b). Further recommendations in the technique of psycho-analysis: Recollection, repetition and working through (J. Riviere, Trans.). In *Collected papers: Vol. 2. Clinical papers and papers on technique* (pp. 366-376). New York: Basic Books. (Original work published 1914)

Freud, S. (1959c). Inhibitions, symptoms, and anxiety (J. Strachey, Ed., A. Strachey, Trans.). New York: W. W. Norton & Company. (Original work published 1926)

Freud, S. (1959d). The justification for detaching from neurasthenia a particular syndrome: The anxiety-neurosis (J. Riviere, Trans.). In *Collected Papers: Vol. 1. Early papers* (pp. 76-106). New York: Basic Books. (Original work published 1894)

Freud, S. (1959e). Mourning and melancholia (J. Riviere, Trans.). In *Collected papers: Vol. 4. Papers on metapsychology and applied psycho-dynamics* (pp. 152-170). New York: Basic Books. (Original work published 1917)

Freud, S. (1959f). On the psychical mechanism of hysterical phenomena (J. Riviere, Trans.). In *Collected papers: Vol. 1. Early papers* (pp. 24-41). New York: Basic Books. (Original work published 1893)

Freud, S. (1959g). A reply to criticisms on the anxiety-neurosis (J. Riviere, Trans.). In *Collected papers: Vol. 1. Early papers* (pp. 107-127). New York: Basic Books. (Original work published 1895)

Freud, S. (1959h). Repression (J. Riviere, Trans.). In *Collected papers: Vol. 4. Papers on metapsychology and applied psycho-analysis* (pp. 84-97). New York: Basic Books. (Original work published 1915)

Freud, S. (1959i). The 'uncanny' (J. Riviere, Trans.). In *Collected Papers: Vol. 4. Papers on metapsychology and applied psycho-dynamics* (Vol. 4, pp. 368-407). New York: Basic Books. (Original work published 1919)

Freud, S. (1959j). The unconscious (J. Riviere, Trans.). In *Collected Papers: Vol. 4. Papers on metapsychology and applied psycho-dynamics* (pp. 98-136). New York: Basic Books. (Original work published 1915)

Freud, S. (1960). *The ego and the id* (J. Strachey, Rev. & Ed., J. Riviere, Trans.). New York: W. W. Norton & Company. (Original work published 1923)

Freud, S. (1961). *Beyond the pleasure principle* (J. Strachey, Ed. & Trans.). New York: W. W. Norton & Company. (Original work published 1920)

Freud, S. (1962). *Three essays on the theory of sexuality* (J Strachey, Ed. & Trans.). New York: W. W. Norton & Company. (Original work published 1905)

Freud, S. (1965). *New introductory lectures on psychoanalysis* (J. Strachey, Ed. & Trans.). New York: W. W. Norton & Company. (Original work published 1933)

Freud, S. (1966). *Introductory lectures on psycho-analysis* (J. Strachey, Ed. & Trans.). New York: W. W. Norton & Company. (Original work published 1917)

Friedberg, J. P., Suchday, S., & Shelov, D. V. (2007). The impact of forgiveness on cardiovascular reactivity and recovery. *International Journal of Psychophysiology, 65*, 87-94.

Frijda, N. H. (1993). The place of appraisal in emotion. *Cognition and Emotion, 7*, 357-387.

Frijda, N. H., & Zeelenberg, M. (2001). Appraisal: What is the dependent? In K. R. Scherer, A. Schorr, & T. Johnstone (Eds.), *Appraisal processes in emotion: Theory, methods, research* (pp. 141-155). New York: Oxford University Press.

Friman, P. C., Hayes, S. C., & Wilson, K. G. (1998). Why behavior analysts should study emotion: The example of anxiety. *Journal of Applied Behavior Analysis, 31*, 137-156.

Fromm, E. (1941). *Escape from freedom.* New York: Henry Holt and Company.

Fromm, E. (1973). *The anatomy of human destructiveness.* New York: Holt, Rinehart and Winston.

Fromm, E. (1976). *To have or to be.* New York: Harper & Row.

Fuchs, T. (2003). The phenomenology of shame, guilt and the body in body dysmorphic disorder and depression. *Journal of Phenomenal Psychology, 33*, 223-243.

Gaab, J., Blättler, N., Menzi, T., Pabst, B., Stoyer, S., & Ehlert, U. (2003). Randomized controlled evaluation of the effects of cognitive-behavioral stress management on cortisol responses to acute stress in healthy subjects. *Psychoneuroendocrinology, 28*, 767-779.

Gaab, J., Rohleder, N., Nater, U. M., & Ehlert, U. (2005). Psychological determinants of the cortisol stress response: The role of anticipatory cognitive appraisal. *Psychoneuroendocrinology, 30*, 599-610.

Garnefski, N., Van Den Kommer, T., Kraaij, V., Teerds, J., Legerstee, J., & Onstein, E. (2002). The relationship between cognitive emotion regulation strategies and emotional problems: Comparison between a clinical and a non-clinical sample. *European Journal of Personality, 16*, 403-420.

Gavazzi, I. G. (2003). Emotional and metaemotional competence: A developmental view. *Wirn vietri, 2859*, 367-373.

Geiger, B., & Fischer, M. (2006). Will words ever harm me? Escalation from verbal to physical abuse in sixth-grade classrooms. *Journal of Interpersonal Violence, 21*, 337-357.

Gendolla, G. H. E. (2000). On the impact of mood on behavior: An integrative theory and a review. *Review of General Psychology, 4*, 378-408.

Gendolla, G. H. E., Abele, A. E., & Krüsken, J. (2001). The informational impact of mood on effort mobilization: A study of cardiovascular and electrodermal responses. *Emotion, 1*, 12-24.

Gerin, W., Davidson, K. W., Christenfeld, N. J. S., Goyal, T., & Schwartz, J. E. (2006). The role of angry rumination and distraction in blood pressure recovery from emotional arousal. *Psychosomatic Medicine, 68*, 64-72.

Gillespie, C. F., & Nemeroff, C. B. (2005). Hypercortisolemia and depression. *Psychosomatic Medicine, 67*, S26-S28.

Gillett, E. (1996). Learning theory and intrapsychic conflict. *International Journal of Psycho-Analysis, 77*, 689-707.

Gitau, R., Cameron, A., Fisk, N. M., & Glover, V. (1998). Fetal exposure to maternal cortisol. *Lancet, 352,* 707-708.

Gjerde, P. F. (2001). Attachment, culture, and amae. *American Psychologist, 56,* 826-827.

Gluck, M. E., Geliebter, A., Hung, J., & Yahav, E. (2004). Cortisol, hunger, and desire to binge eat following a cold stress test in obese women with binge eating disorder. *Psychosomatic Medicine, 66,* 876-881.

Gnepp, J., & Klayman, J. (1992). Recognition of uncertainty in emotional inferences: Reasoning about emotionally equivocal situations. *Developmental Psychology, 28,* 145-158.

Gold, P. W., & Chrousos, G. P. (2002). Organization of the stress system and its dysregulation in melancholic and atypical depression: High vs low CRH/NE states. *Molecular Psychiatry, 7,* 254-275.

Goldfinger, D. A., Amdur, R. L., & Liberzon, I. (1998). Psychophysiologic responses to the Rorschach in PTSD patients, noncombat and combat controls. *Depression and Anxiety, 8,* 112-120.

Goldin, P. R., McRae, K., Ramel, W., & Gross, J. J. (2008). The neural bases of emotion regulation: Reappraisal and suppression of negative emotion. *Biological Psychiatry, 63,* 577-586.

Goldsmith, H. H., & Davidson, R. J. (2004). Disambiguating the components of emotion regulation. *Child Development, 75,* 361-365.

Goldstein, D. S., & McEwen, B. (2002). Allostasis, homeostats, and the nature of stress. *Stress, 5,* 55-58.

Goodyer, I. M., Herbert, J., Tamplin, A., & Altham, P. M. E. (2000). First-episode major depression in adolescents: Affective, cognitive and endocrine characteristics of risk status and predictors of onset. *British Journal of Psychiatry, 176,* 142-149.

Goodyer, I. M., Park, R. J., Netherton, C. M., & Herbert, J. (2001). Possible role of cortisol and dehydroepiandrosterone in human development and psychopathology. *British Journal of Psychiatry, 179,* 243-249.

Graeff, F. G. (2002). On serotonin and experimental anxiety. *Psychopharmacology (Berlin, Germany), 163,* 467-476.

Greenberg, L. S. (2002a). *Emotion-focused therapy: Coaching clients to work through their feelings.* Washington, DC: American Psychological Association.

Greenberg, L. S. (2002b). Integrating an emotion-focused approach to treatment into psychotherapy integration. *Journal of Psychotherapy Integration, 12,* 154-189.

Greenberg, L. S. (2004). Emotion-focused therapy. *Clinical Psychology and Psychotherapy, 11,* 3-16.

Greenberg, L. S., & Bolger, E. (2001). An emotion-focused approach to the overregulation of emotion and emotional pain. *Journal of Clinical Psychology, 57,* 197-211.

Greenberg, L. S., Elliot, R., Watson, J. C., & Bohart, A. C. (2001). Empathy. *Psychotherapy, 38,* 380-384.

Greenberg, L. S., & Paivio, S. C. (1997). *Working with emotions in psychotherapy.* New York: Guilford.

Greenberg, L. S., & Paivio, S. C. (1998). Allowing and accepting painful emotional experiences. *International Journal of Action Methods, 51,* 47-61.

Greenberg, L. S., & Pascual-Leone, J. (2001). A dialectical constructivist view of the creation of personal meaning. *Journal of Constructivist Psychology, 14,* 165-186.

Greenberg, L. S., & Safran, J. D. (1989). Emotion in psychotherapy. *American Psychologist, 44,* 19-29.

Greenspan, S. I. (1989). *The development of the ego.* Madison, CT: International Universities Press.

Greenspan, S. I. (1997). *The growth of the mind.* Reading, MA: Addison-Wesley Publishing Company.

Griffiths, P. E. (1997). *What emotions really are.* Chicago: University of Chicago Press.

Grof, S. (1985). *Beyond the brain.* Albany, NY: State University of New York Press.

Gröpel, P., & Kuhl, J. (2009). Work-life balance and subjective well-being: The mediating role of need fulfillment. *British Journal of Psychology, 100,* 365-375.

Gross, J. J. (1999). Emotion regulation: Past, present, future. *Cognition and Emotion, 13,* 551-573.

Gross, J. J. (2001). Emotion regulation in adulthood: Timing is everything. *Current Directions in Psychological Science, 10,* 214-219.

Gross, J. J. (2002). Emotion regulation: Affective, cognitive, and social consequences. *Psychophysiology, 39,* 281-291.

Gross, J. J., & Levenson, R. W. (1997). Hiding feelings: The acute effects of inhibiting negative and positive emotion. *Journal of Abnormal Psychology, 106,* 95-103.

Gruenewald, T. L., Kemeny, M. E., & Aziz, N. (2006). Subjective social status moderates cortisol responses to social threat. *Brain, Behavior, and Immunity, 20,* 410-419.

Gruenewald, T. L., Kemeny, M. E., Aziz, N., & Fahey, J. L. (2004). Acute threat to social self: Shame, social self-esteem, and cortisol activity. *Psychosomatic Medicine, 66,* 915-924.

Gumley, A., White, C. A., & Power, K. (1999). An interacting cognitive subsystems model of relapse and the course of psychosis. *Clinical Psychology and Psychotherapy, 6*, 261-278.

Guntrip, H. (1973). *Psychoanalytic theory, therapy, and the self.* New York: Basic Books.

Guyer, A. E., McClure-Tone, E. B., Shiffrin, N. D., Pine, D. S., & Nelson, E. E. (2009). Probing the neural correlates of anticipated peer evaluation in adolescence. *Child Development, 80*, 1000-1015.

Hagemann, D., Waldstein, S. R., & Thayer, J. F. (2003). Central and autonomic nervous system integration in emotion. *Brain and Cognition, 52*, 79-87.

Hamm, A. O., Cuthbert, B. N., Globisch, J., & Vaitl, D. (1997). Fear and the startle reflex: Blink modulation and autonomic response patterns in animal and mutilation fearful subjects. *Psychophysiology, 34*, 97-107.

Hammen, C. (1991). Generation of stress in the course of unipolar depression. *Journal of Abnormal Psychology, 100*, 555-561.

Hammen, C., Davila, J., Brown, G., Ellicott, A., & Gitlin, M. (1992). Psychiatric history and stress: Predictors of severity of unipolar depression. *Journal of Abnormal Psychology, 101*, 45-52.

Hammen, C., Shih, J. H., & Brennan, P. A. (2004). Intergenerational transmission of depression: Test of an interpersonal stress model in a community sample. *Journal of Consulting and Clinical Psychology, 72*, 511-522.

Hammerfald, K., Eberle, C., Grau, M., Kinsperger, A., Zimmerman, A., Ehlert, U., et al. (2006). Persistent effects of cognitive-behavioral stress management on cortisol responses to acute stress in healthy subjects—A randomized control trial. *Psychoneuroendocrinology, 31*, 333-339.

Hansen, A. L., Johnsen, B. H., Hart, S., Waage, L., & Thayer, J. F. (2008). Psychopathy and recognition of facial expressions of emotion. *Journal of Personality Disorders, 22*, 639-645.

Happaney, K., Zelazo, P. D., & Stuss, D. T. (2004). Development of orbitofrontal function: Current themes and future directions. *Brain and Cognition, 55*, 1-10.

Harmon-Jones, E. (2003). Clarifying the emotive functions of asymmetrical frontal cortical activity. *Psychophysiology, 40*, 838-848.

Harmon-Jones, E. (2004). On the relationship of frontal brain activity and anger: Examining the role of attitude toward anger. *Cognition and Emotion, 18*, 337-361.

Harmon-Jones, E., Sigelman, J. D., Bohlig, A., & Harmon-Jones, C. (2003). Anger, coping, and frontal cortical activity: The effect of coping potential on anger-induced left frontal activity. *Cognition and Emotion, 17*, 1-24.

Hart, S., Jones, N. A., & Field, T. (2003). Atypical expressions of jealousy in infants of intrusive- and withdrawn-depressed mothers. *Child Psychiatry and Human Development, 33*, 193-207.

Hart, S., Jones, N. A., Field, T., & Lundy, B. (1999). One-year-old infants of intrusive and withdrawn depressed mothers. *Child Psychiatry and Human Development, 30*, 111-120.

Haslam, C., & Mallon, K. (2003). A preliminary investigation of post-traumatic stress symptoms among firefighters. *Work & Stress, 17*, 277-285.

Heberlein, A. S., Adolphs, R., Pennebaker, J. W., & Tranel, D. (2001). Effects of damage to right-hemispheric brain structures on spontaneous emotional and social judgments. *Political Psychology, 24*, 705-726.

Heller, W., & Nitschke, J. B. (1998). The puzzle of regional brain activity in depression and anxiety: The importance of subtypes and comorbidity. *Cognition and Emotion, 12*, 421-447.

Herbert, J., Goodyer, I. M., Grossman, A. B., Hastings, M. H., de Kloet, E. R., Lightman, S. L., et al. (2006). Do corticosteroids damage the brain? *Journal of Neuroendocrinology, 18*, 393-411.

Hermans, D., De Houwer, J., & Eelen, P. (2001). A time course analysis of the emotional priming effect. *Cognition and Emotion, 15*, 143-165.

Herpertz, S. C., Huebner, T., Marx, I., Vloet, T. D., Fink, G. R., Stoecker, T., et al. (2008). Emotional processing in male adolescents with childhood-onset conduct disorder. *Journal of Child Psychology and Psychiatry, 49*, 781-791.

Hemenover, S. H. (2003). The good, the bad, and the healthy: Impacts of emotional disclosure of trauma on resilient self-concept and psychological distress. *Personality and Social Psychology Bulletin, 29*, 1236-1244.

Henriques, J. B., & Davidson, R. J. (2000). Decreased responsiveness to reward in depression. *Cognition and Emotion, 14*(5), 711-724.

Hermans, D., De Houwer, J., & Eelen, P. (2001). A time course analysis of the emotional priming effect. *Cognition and Emotion, 15*, 143-165.

Hernandez-Reif, M., Field, T., Del Pino, N., & Diego, M. (2000). Less exploring by mouth occurs in newborns of depressed mothers. *Infant Mental Health Journal, 21*, 204-210.

Hernandez-Reif, M., Field, T., Diego, M., & Largie, S. (2002). Depressed mother's newborns show longer habituation and fail to show face/voice preference. *Infant Mental Health Journal, 23*, 643-653.

Herrald, M. M., & Tomaka, J. (2002). Patterns of emotion-specific appraisal, coping, and cardiovascular reactivity during an ongoing emotional episode. *Journal of Personality and Social Psychology, 83*, 434-450.

Herrnstein, R. J. (1969). Method and theory in the study of avoidance. *Psychological Review, 76,* 49-69.

Herry, C., Ciocchi, S., Senn, V., Demmou, L., Müller, C., & Lüthi, A. (2008). Switching on and off fear by distinct neuronal circuits. *Nature, 454,* 600-608.

Hertel, P. T., & Gerstle, M. (2003). Depressive deficits in forgetting. *Psychological Science, 14,* 573-578.

Hess, U., Philippot, P., & Blairy, S. (1998). Facial reactions to emotional facial expressions: Affect or cognition? *Cognition and Emotion, 12,* 509-531.

Hess, U., Senécal, S., Kirouac, G., Herrera, P., Philippot, P., & Kleck, R. E. (2000). Emotional expressivity in men and women: Stereotypes and self-perceptions. *Cognition and Emotion, 14,* 609-642.

Hiemisch, A., Ehlers, A., & Westermann, R. (2002). Mindsets in social anxiety: A new look at selective information processing. *Journal of Behavior Therapy, 33,* 103-114.

Hillman, J. (1960). *Emotion.* Evanston, IL: Northwestern University Press.

Himmelhoch, J., Levine, J., & Gershon, S. (2001). Historical overview of the relationship between anxiety disorders and affective disorders. *Depression and Anxiety, 14,* 53-66.

Hirt, E. R., & McCrea, S. M. (2000). Beyond hedonism: Broadening the scope of affect regulation. *Psychological Inquiry, 11,* 180-183.

Hodgson, N., Freedman, V. A., Granger, D. A., & Erno, A. (2004). Biobehavioral correlates of relocation in the frail elderly: Salivary cortisol, affect, and cognitive function. *Journal of the American Geriatric Society, 52,* 1856-1862.

Hofmann, S. G., & Scepkowski, L. A. (2006). Social self-reappraisal therapy for social phobia: Preliminary findings. *Journal of Cognitive Psychotherapy, 20,* 45-57.

Holahan, C. J., Moos, R. H., Holahan, C. K., Brennan, P. L., & Schutte, K. K. (2005). Stress generation, avoidance coping, and depressive symptoms: A 10-year model. *Journal of Consulting and Clinical Psychology, 4,* 658-666.

Horney, K. (1937). *The neurotic personality of our time.* New York: W. W. Norton & Company.

Horney, K. (1939). *New ways in psychoanalysis.* New York: W. W. Norton & Company.

Horowitz, M., Fridhandler, B., & Stinson, C. (1992). Person schemas and emotions. In T. Shapiro & R. N. Emde (Eds.), *Affect: Psychoanalytic perspectives* (pp. 173-208). Madison, CT: International Universities Press.

Hupka, R. B., Lenton, A. P., & Hutchison, K. A. (1999). Universal development of emotion categories in natural language. *Journal of Personality and Social Psychology, 77,* 247-278.

Ingram, R. E. (1990). Self-focused attention in clinical disorders: Review and a conceptual model. *Psychological Bulletin, 107*, 156-176.

Irwin, W., Anderle, M. J., Abercrombie, H. C., Schaefer, S. M., Kalin, N. H., & Davidson, R. J. (2004). Amygdalar interhemispheric functional connectivity differs between the non-depressed and depressed human brain. *NeuroImage, 21*, 674-686.

Isen, A. M. (2000). Some perspectives on positive affect and self-regulation. *Psychological Inquiry, 11*, 184-187.

Isen, A. M. (2001). An influence of positive affect on decision making in complex situations: Theoretical issues with practical implications. *Journal of Consumer Psychology, 11*, 75-85.

Izard, C. E. (1977). *Human emotions.* New York: Plenum Press.

Izard, C. E. (2002). Translating emotion theory and research into preventive interventions. *Psychological Bulletin, 128*, 796-824.

Izard, C. E., Fine, S., Mostow, A., Trentacosta, C., & Campbell, J. (2002). Emotion processes in normal and abnormal development and preventive intervention. *Development and Psychopathology, 14*, 761-787.

Jackson, D. C., Mueller, C. J., Dolski, I., Dalton, K. M., Nitschke, J. B., Urry, H. L., et al. (2003). Now you feel it, now you don't: Frontal brain electrical asymmetry and individual differences in emotion regulation. *Psychological Science, 14*, 612-617.

James, W. (1983). *The principles of psychology.* Cambridge, MA: Harvard University Press. (Original work published 1890)

James, W. (1884). What is an emotion? *Mind, 9*, 188-205.

Jansari, A., Tranel, D., & Adolphs, R. (2000). A valence-specific lateral bias for discriminating emotional facial expressions in free field. *Cognition and Emotion, 14*, 341-353.

Jelicic, M., Geraerts, E., Merckelbach, H., & Guerrieri, R. (2004). Acute stress enhances memory for emotional words, but impairs memory for neutral words. *International Journal of Neuroscience, 114*, 1343-1351.

Jenkins, J. M., & Oatley, K. (1998). The development of emotion schemas in children: Processes that underlies psychopathology. In W. F. Flack, Jr. & J. D. Laird (Eds.), *Emotions in psychopathology* (pp. 45-56). New York: Oxford University Press.

Jennings, J. R. (1987). Editorial policy on analyses of variance with repeated measures. *Psychophysiology, 24*, 474-475.

Jennings, J. L., & Murphy, C. M. (2000). Male-male dimensions of male-female battering: A new look at domestic violence. *Psychology of Men and Masculinity, 1,* 21-29.

John, O. P., & Gross, J. J. (2004). Healthy and unhealthy emotion regulation: Personality processes, individual differences, and life span development. *Journal of Personality, 72,* 1301-1334.

Joiner, T. E., & Schmidt, N. B. (2002). Taxometrics can "do diagnostics right" (and isn't quite as hard as you think). In L. E. Beutler & M. L. Malik (Eds.), *Rethinking the DSM: A psychological perspective* (pp. 107-120). Washington, DC: American Psychological Association.

Joireman, J. A., Parrott, L., III, & Hammersla, J. (2002). Empathy and the self-absorption paradox: Support for the distinction between self-rumination and self-reflection. *Self and Identity, 1,* 53-65.

Jones, N. A., Field, T., & Davalos, M. (2000). Right frontal EEG asymmetry and lack of empathy in preschool children of depressed mothers. *Child Psychiatry and Human Development, 30,* 189-204.

Jones, N. A., Field, T., Davalos, M., & Hart, S. (2004). Greater right frontal EEG asymmetry and nonempathic behavior are observed in children prenatally exposed to cocaine. *International Journal of Neuroscience, 114,* 459-480.

Jones, N. A., Field, T., Fox, N. A., Davalos, M., & Gomez, C. (2001). EEG during different emotions in 10-month-old infants of depressed mothers. *Journal of Reproductive and Infant Psychology, 19,* 295-312.

Joormann, J., & Siemer, M. (2004). Memory accessibility, mood regulation, and dysphoria: Difficulties in repairing sad mood with happy memories? *Journal of Abnormal Psychology, 113,* 179-188.

Jostmann, N. B., Koole, S. L., van der Wulp, N. Y., & Fockenberg, D. A. (2005). Subliminal affect regulation: The moderating role of action vs. state orientation. *European Psychologist, 10,* 209-217.

Joyce, P. R., Mulder, R. T., Luty, S. E., McKenzie, J. M., & Rae, A. M. (2003). A differential response to nortriptyline and fluoxetine in melancholic depression: The importance of age and gender. *Acta Psychiatrica Scandinavica, 108,* 20-23.

Joyce, P. R., Mulder, R. T., Luty, S. E., McKenzie, J. M., Sullivan, P. E., Abbott, R. M., et al. (2002). Melancholia: Definitions, risk factors, personality, neuroendocrine markers and differential antidepressant response. *Australian and New Zealand Journal of Psychiatry, 36,* 376-383.

Kagan, J. (1992). A conceptual analysis of the affects. In T. Shapiro & R. N. Emde (Eds.), *Affect: Psychoanalytic perspectives* (pp. 109-129). Madison, CT: International Universities Press.

Kagan, J. (1994). *Galen's prophecy: Temperament in human nature.* New York: Basic Books.

Kaiser, S., & Scherer, K. R. (1998). Models of "normal" emotions applied to facial and verbal expression in clinical disorders. In W. F. Flack, Jr. & J. D. Laird (Eds.), *Emotions in psychopathology* (pp. 81-98). New York: Oxford University Press.

Kalin, N. H., Shelton, S. E., Davidson, R. J., & Kelley, A. E. (2001). The primate amygdala mediates acute fear but not the behavioral and physiological components of anxious temperament. *Journal of Neuroscience, 21,* 2067-2074.

Kappas, A. (2002). The science of emotion as a multidisciplinary research paradigm. *Behavioural Processes, 60,* 85-98.

Kappas, A., Bherer, F., & Theriault, M. (2000). Inhibiting facial expressions: Limitations to the voluntary control of facial expressions of emotion. *Motivation and Emotion, 24,* 259-270.

Kashdan, T. B., Biswas-Diener, R., & King, L. A. (2008). Reconsidering happiness: The costs of distinguishing between hedonics and eudaimonia. *Journal of Positive Psychology, 3,* 219-233.

Kaufman, G. (1985). *Shame: The power of caring* (2nd ed.). Cambridge, MA: Schenkman Publishing Company.

Kawasaki, H., Adolphs, R., Kaufman, O., Damasio, H., Damasio, A. R., Granner, M., et al. (2001). Single-neuron responses to emotional visual stimuli recorded in human ventral prefrontal cortex. *Nature Neuroscience, 4,* 15-16.

Kazén, M., Baumann, N., & Kuhl, J. (2003). Self-infiltration and self-compatibility checking in dealing with unattractive tasks: The moderating influence of state vs. action orientation. *Motivation and Emotion, 27,* 157-197.

Kemeny, M. E. (2003). The psychobiology of stress. *Current Directions in Psychological Science, 12,* 124-129.

Kemeny, M. E., Gruenewald, T. L., & Dickerson, S. S. (2004). Shame as the emotional response to threat to the social self: Implications for behavior, physiology, and health. *Psychological Inquiry, 15,* 153-160.

Kennedy-Moore, E., & Watson, J. C. (1999). *Expressing emotion: Myths, realities, and therapeutic strategies.* New York: Guilford Press.

Kernberg, O. (1992). The psychopathology of hatred. In T. Shapiro & R. N. Emde (Eds.), *Affect: Psychoanalytic perspectives* (pp. 209-238). Madison, CT: International Universities Press.

Kernis, M. H. (2003). Toward a conceptualization of optimal self-esteem. *Psychological Inquiry, 14,* 1-26.

Keselman, H. J. (1998). Testing treatment effects in repeated measures designs: An update for psychophysiological researchers. *Psychophysiology, 35*, 470-478.

Kienke, A. S., & Rosenbaum, J. F. (2000). Efficacy of venlafaxine in the treatment of severe depression. *Depression and Anxiety, 12*(Supplement 1), 50-54.

Kihlstrom, J. F., Mulvaney, S., Tobias, B. A., & Tobis, I. P. (2000). The emotional unconscious. In E. Eich, J. F. Kihlstrom, G. H. Bower, J. P. Forgas, & P. M. Niedenthal (Eds.), *Cognition and emotion* (pp. 30-86). New York: Oxford University Press.

Kim, J. J., Song, E. Y., & Kosten, T. A. (2006). Stress effects in the hippocampus: Synaptic plasticity and memory. *Stress, 9*, 1-11.

Kimura, S., Sato, T., Takahashi, T., Narita, T., Hirano, S., & Goto, M. (2000). Typus melancholicus and the Temperament and Character Inventory personality dimensions in patients with major depression. *Psychiatry and Clinical Neurosciences, 54*, 181-189.

King, L. A., & Pennebaker, J. W. (1998). What's so great about feeling good? *Psychological Inquiry, 9*, 53-56.

Kirschbaum, C., Bartussek, D., & Strasburger, C. J. (1992). Cortisol responses to psychological stress and correlations with personality traits. *Personality and Individual Differences, 13*, 1353-1357.

Kirschbaum, C., & Hellhammer, D. H. (2000). Salivary cortisol. In G. Fink (Ed.), *Encyclopedia of stress* (Vol. 3, pp. 379-383). San Diego, CA: Academic Press.

Kirschbaum, C., Kudielka, B. M., Gaab, J., Schommer, N. C., & Hellhammer, D. H. (1999). Impact of gender, menstrual cycle phase, and oral contraceptives on the activity of the hypothalamus-pituitary-adrenal axis. *Psychosomatic Medicine, 61*, 154-162.

Kirschbaum, C., Pirke, K.-M., & Hellhammer, D. H. (1993). The 'Trier Social Stress Test'—A tool for investigating psychobiological stress responses in a laboratory setting. *Neuropsychobiology, 28*, 76-81.

Klein, M. (1990). The origins of transference. In A. H. Esman (Ed.), *Essential papers on transference* (pp. 236-245). New York: New York University Press. (Original work published 1952)

Knapp, P. H. (1992). Emotion and the psychoanalytic encounter. In T. Shapiro & R. N. Emde (Eds.), *Affect: Psychoanalytic perspectives* (pp. 239-264). Madison, CT: International Universities Press.

Knyazev, G. G., Schutter, D. J. L. G., & van Honk, J. (2006). Anxious apprehension increases coupling of delta and beta oscillations. *International Journal of Psychophysiology, 61*, 283-287.

Knyazev, G. G., & Slobodskaya, H. R. (2003). Personality trait of behavioral inhibition is associated with oscillatory systems reciprocal relationships. *International Journal of Psychophysiology, 48*, 247-261.

Koenigs, M., Young, L., Adolphs, R., Tranel, D., Cushman, F., Hauser, M., et al. (2007). Damage to the prefrontal cortex increases utilitarian moral judgements. *Nature, 446*, 908-911.

Kohut, H. (1985). Forms and transformations of narcissism. In C. B. Strozier (Ed.), *Self psychology and the humanities* (pp. 97-123). New York: Norton. (Original work published 1966)

Kolb, B., Pellis, S., & Robinson, T. E. (2004). Plasticity and functions of the orbital frontal cortex. *Brain and Cognition, 55*, 104-115.

Koole, S. L., & Jostmann, N. B. (2004). Getting a grip on your feelings: Effects of action orientation and external demands on intuitive affect regulation. *Journal of Personality and Social Psychology, 87*, 974-990.

Kuhl, J., Kazén, M., & Koole, S. L. (2006). Putting self-regulatory theory into practice: A user's manual. *Applied Psychology: An International Review, 55*, 408-418.

Kunzmann, U., Stange, A., & Jordan, J. (2005). Positive affectivity and lifestyle in adulthood: Do you do what you feel? *Personality and Social Psychology Bulletin, 31*, 574-588.

Labouvie-Vief, G., Lumley, M. A., Jain, E., & Heinze, H. (2003). Age and gender differences in cardiac reactivity and subjective emotion responses to emotional autobiographical memories. *Emotion, 3*, 115-126.

Lai, J. C., Evans, P. D., Ng, S. H., Chong, A. M. L., Siu, O. T., Chan, C. L. W., et al. (2005). Optimism, positive affectivity, and salivary cortisol. *British Journal of Health Psychology, 10*, 467-484.

Larsen, J. T., Norris, C. J., & Cacioppo, J. T. (2003). Effects of positive and negative affect on electromyographic activity over zygomaticus major and corrugator supercilii. *Psychophysiology, 40*, 776-785.

Larsen, R. J. (2000a). Toward a science of mood regulation. *Psychological Inquiry, 11*, 129-141.

Larsen, R. J. (2000b). Maintaining hedonic balance: Reply to commentaries. *Psychological Inquiry, 11*, 218-225.

Latour, S. M., & Hosmer, B. C. (2002). Emotional intelligence: Implications for United States Air Force leaders. *Air & Space Power Journal, 16*(4), 27-35.

Lavender, A., & Watkins, E. (2004). Rumination and future thinking in depression. *British Journal of Clinical Psychology, 43*, 129-142.

Lazarus, R. S. (2001). Relational meaning and discrete emotions. In K. R. Scherer, A. Schorr, & T. Johnstone (Eds.), *Appraisal processes in emotions: Theory, methods, research* (pp. 37-67). New York: Oxford University Press.

Lazarus, R. S. (2006). Emotions and interpersonal relationships: Toward a person-centered conceptualization of emotions and coping. *Journal of Personality, 74,* 9-46.

Leary, M. R. (2000). Affect, cognition, and social emotions. In J. P. Forgas (Ed.), *Feeling and thinking: The role of affect in social cognition* (pp. 331-356). New York: Cambridge University.

Leary, M. R. (2003a). Commentary on self-esteem as an interpersonal monitor: The sociometer hypothesis (1995). *Psychological Inquiry, 14,* 270-274.

Leary, M. R. (2003b). Interpersonal aspects of optimal self-esteem and the authentic self. *Psychological Inquiry, 14,* 52-54.

Leary, M. R. (2004). Digging deeper: The fundamental nature of "self-conscious" emotions. *Psychological Inquiry, 15,* 129-131.

LeDoux, J.E. (1996). *The emotional brain.* New York: Touchstone.

LeDoux, J. E. (2000). Emotion circuits in the brain. *Annual Review of Neuroscience, 23,* 155-184.

Lerner, J. S., & Keltner, D. (2000). Beyond valence: Toward a model of emotion-specific influences on judgement and choice. *Cognition and Emotion, 14,* 473-493.

Levenson, R. W., & Ekman, P. (2002). Difficulty does not account for emotion-specific heart rate changes in the directed facial action task. *Psychophysiology, 39,* 397-405.

Levenson, R. W., Ekman, P., & Friesen, W. V. (1990). Voluntary facial action generates emotion-specific autonomic nervous system activity. *Psychophysiology, 27,* 363-384.

Levine, J., Chengappa, K. N. R., Gershon, S., & Drevets, W. (2001). Differentiating primary pathophysiologic from secondary adaptational processes. *Depression and Anxiety, 14,* 105-111.

Levitan, R. D., Vaccarino, F. J., Brown, G. M., & Kennedy, S. H. (2002). Low-dose dexamethasone challenge in women with atypical major depression: Pilot study. *Journal of Psychiatry & Neuroscience, 27,* 47-51.

Lewis, H. B. (1971). *Shame and guilt in neurosis.* New York: International Universities Press.

Lewis, H. B. (1987). Shame and the narcissistic personality. In D. L. Nathanson (Ed.), *The many faces of shame* (pp. 93-132). New York: The Guilford Press.

Lewis, H. B. (1988). The role of shame in symptom formation. In M. Clynes & J. Panksepp (Eds.), *Emotions and psychopathology* (pp. 95-106). New York: Plenum Publishing Corporation.

Lewis, M.D. (2003). The role of the self in shame. *Social Research, 70*(4), 1181-1204.

Lewis, M.D. (2004). Emotional development: Past, present and future. *Human Development, 47,* 66-70.

Lewis, M. D., & Stieben, J. (2004). Emotion regulation in the brain: Conceptual issues and directions for developmental research. *Child Development, 75,* 371-376.

Lewis, M., Hitchcock, D. F. A., & Sullivan, M. W. (2004). Physiological and emotional reactivity to learning and frustration. *Infancy, 6,* 121-143.

Lewis, M., & Ramsay, D. (2002). Cortisol response to embarrassment and shame. *Child Development, 73,* 1034-1045.

Lewis, M., & Ramsay, D. (2005). Infant emotional and cortisol responses to goal blockage. *Child Development, 76,* 518-530.

Lewis, M. L. (1992a). Self-conscious emotions and the development of self. In T. Shapiro & R. N. Emde (Eds.), *Affect: Psychoanalytic perspectives* (pp. 45-73). Madison, CT: International Universities Press.

Lewis, M. L. (1992b). *Shame: The exposed self.* New York: Free Press.

Linden, W., Hogan, B. E., Rutledge, T., Chawla, A., Lenz, J. W., & Leung, D. (2003). There is more to anger coping than "in" or "out". *Emotion, 3,* 12-29.

Lindner, E. G. (2001). Humiliation and human rights: Mapping a minefield. *Human Rights Review, 2*(2), 46-63.

Lindner, E. G. (2002). Healing the cycles of humiliation: How to attend to the emotional aspects of "unsolvable" conflicts and the use of "humiliation entrepreneurship". *Peace and Conflict: Journal of Peace Psychology, 8,* 125-138.

Lindstrom, T. C. (2002). "It ain't necessarily so" . . . Challenging mainstream thinking about bereavement [Special issue: Bereavement in families and the community]. *Family & Community Health, 25,* 11-21.

Linley, P. A., Nielsen, K. M., Wood, A. M., Gillett, R., & Biswas-Diener, R. (2010). Using signature strengths in pursuit of goals: Effects on goal progress, need satisfaction, and well-being, and implications for coaching psychologists. *International Coaching Psychology Review, 5,* 6-15.

Liotti, M., & Mayberg, H. S. (2001). The role of functional neuroimaging in the neuropsychology of depression. *Journal of Clinical and Experimental Neuropsychology, 23,* 121-136.

Lok, C., & Bishop, G. D. (1999). Emotion control, stress, and health. *Psychology & Health, 14,* 813-827.

Lovallo, W. R. (2006). Cortisol secretion patterns in addiction and addiction risk. *International Journal of Psychophysiology, 59,* 195-202.

Lowen, A. (1958). *The language of the body.* New York: Collier Books.

Lowen, A. (1975). *Bioenergetics.* New York: Penguin Books.

Lu, L., & Chen, C. S. (1996). Correlates of coping behaviours: Internal and external resources. *Counseling Psychology Quarterly, 9,* 297-307.

Luck, P., & Dowrick, C. F. (2004). 'Don't look at me in that tone of voice!' Disturbances in the perception of emotion in facial expression and vocal intonation by depressed patients. *Primary Care Mental Health, 2,* 99-106.

Luminet, O., Rimé, B., Bagby, R. M., & Taylor, G. J. (2004). A multimodal investigation of emotional responding in alexithymia. *Cognition and Emotion, 18,* 741-766.

Lundh, L.-G., & Wångby, M. (2002). Causal thinking about somatic symptoms—How is it related to the experience of symptoms and negative affect? *Cognitive Therapy and Research, 26,* 701-717.

Lundqvist, D., Esteves, F., & Öhman, A. (2004). The face of wrath: The roles of features and configurations in conveying social threat. *Cognition and Emotion, 18,* 161-182.

Lyons, W. (1998). Philosophy, the emotions, and psychopathology. In W. F. Flack, Jr. & J. D. Laird (Eds.), *Emotions in psychopathology* (pp. 1-19). New York: Oxford University Press.

Lyubomirsky, S., Caldwell, N. D., & Nolen-Hoeksema, S. (1998). Effects of ruminative and distracting responses to depressed mood on retrieval of autobiographical memories. *Journal of Personality and Social Psychology, 75,* 166-177.

Lyubomirsky, S., Kasri, F., & Zehm, K. (2003). Dysphoric rumination impairs concentration on academic tasks. *Cognitive Therapy and Research, 27,* 309-330.

Lyubomirsky, S., & Nolen-Hoeksema, S. (1995). Effects of self-focused rumination on negative thinking and interpersonal problem solving. *Journal of Personality and Social Psychology, 69,* 176-190.

Lyubomirsky, S., Tucker, K. L., Caldwell, N. D., & Berg, K. (1999). Why ruminators are poor problem solvers: Clues from the phenomenology of dysphoric rumination. *Journal of Personality and Social Psychology, 77,* 1041-1060.

Mackintosh, B., & Mathews, A. (2003). Don't look now: Attentional avoidance of emotionally valenced cues. *Cognition and Emotion, 17,* 623-646.

Magai, C., & Hunziker, J. (1998). "To bedlam and part way back": Discrete emotions theory and borderline symptoms. In W. F. Flack, Jr. & J. D. Laird (Eds.), *Emotions in psychopathology* (pp. 380-393). New York: Oxford University Press.

Magee, L., Rodebaugh, T. L., & Heimberg, R. G. (2006). Negative evaluation is the feared consequence of making others uncomfortable: A response to Rector, Kocovski, and Ryder. *Journal of Social and Clinical Psychology, 25,* 929-936.

Mahler, M. S., Pine, F., & Bergman, A. (1975). *The psychological birth of the infant.* New York: Basic Books.

Maier, S. F., & Watkins, L. R. (1998). Stressor controllability, anxiety, and serotonin. *Cognitive Therapy and Research, 22,* 595-613.

Maier, S. F., & Watkins, L. R. (2000). The immune system as a sensory system: Implications for psychology. *Current Directions in Psychological Science, 9,* 98-102.

Maïza, O., Razafimandimby, A., Brazo, P., Lecardeur, L., Delamillieure, P., Mazoyer, B., et al. (2010). Functional deficit in the medial prefrontal cortex in patients with chronic schizophrenia, first psychotic episode, and bipolar disorders. *Bipolar Disorders, 12,* 450-452.

Malhi, G. S., Lagopoulos, J., Sachdev, P. S., Ivanoski, B., Shnier, R., & Ketter, T. (2007). Is a lack of disgust something to fear? A functional magnetic resonance imaging facial emotion recognition study in euthymic bipolar disorder patients. *Bipolar Disorders, 9,* 345-357.

Malhi, G. S., Lagopoulos, J., Ward, P. B., Kumari, V., Parker, G. B., Ivanovski, B., et al. (2004). Cognitive generation of affect in bipolar depression: an fMRI study. *European Journal of Neuroscience, 19,* 741-754.

Manji, H. K., Drevets, W. C., & Charney, D. S. (2001). The cellular neurobiology of depression. *Nature Medicine, 7,* 541-547.

Manstead, A. S. R., & Fischer, A. H. (2000). Emotion regulation in full. *Psychological Inquiry, 11,* 188-191.

Martin, L. L. (2000). Wag the dog: Do individuals regulate moods or do moods regulate individuals? *Psychological Inquiry, 11,* 191-196.

Maslow, A. H. (1968). *Toward a psychology of being* (2nd ed.). New York: D. Van Nostrand Company.

Matheson, K., & Anisman, H. (2003). Systems of coping associated with dysphoria, anxiety and depressive illness: A multivariate profile perspective. *Stress, 6,* 223-234.

May, R. (1950). *The meaning of anxiety.* New York: Ronald Press Company.

May, R. (1953). *Man's search for himself.* New York: W. W. Norton & Company.

May, R. (1969). *Love and will.* New York: W. W. Norton & Company.

May, R. (1972). *Power and innocence.* New York: W. W. Norton & Company.

May, R. (1981). *Freedom and destiny.* New York: W. W. Norton & Company.

Mayer, J. D., & Salovey, P. (1997). What is emotional intelligence? In P. Salovey & D. J. Sluyter (Eds.), *Emotional development and emotional intelligence* (pp. 3-31). New York: Basic Books.

Mayer, J. D., & Stevens, A. A. (1994). An emerging understanding of the reflective (meta-) experience of mood. *Journal of Research in Personality, 28,* 351-373.

McAllister-Williams, R. H., Ferrier, I. N., & Young, A. H. (1998). Mood and neuropsychological function in depression: The role of corticosteroids and serotonin. *Psychological Medicine, 28,* 573-584.

McCullough, M. E., Bono, G., & Root, L. M. (2007). Rumination, emotion, and forgiveness: Three longitudinal studies. *Journal of Personality and Social Psychology, 92,* 490-505.

McCullough, M. E., Orsulak, P., Brandon, A., & Akers, L. (2007). Rumination, fear, and cortisol: An in vivo study of interpersonal transgressions. *Health Psychology, 26,* 126-132.

McDonagh-Coyle, A., McHugo, G. J., Friedman, M. J., Schnurr, P. P., Zayfert, C., & Descamps, M. (2001). Psychophysiological reactivity in female sexual abuse survivors. *Journal of Traumatic Stress, 14,* 667-683.

McEwen, B. S. (2004). Protection and damage from acute and chronic stress: Allostasis and allostatic load and relevance to the pathophysiology of psychiatric disorders. *Annals of the New York Academy of Sciences, 1032,* 1-7.

McEwen, B. S., & Lasley, E. N. (2003). Allostatic load: When protection gives way to damage. *Advances in Mind-Body Medicine, 19,* 28-33.

McGaugh, J. L. (2000). Memory—A century of consolidation. *Science, 287,* 248-251.

McKay, D., & Tsao, S. D. (2005). A treatment most foul: Handling disgust in cognitive-behavioral therapy. *Journal of Cognitive Psychotherapy: An International Quarterly, 19,* 355-367.

McNally, R. J., Lasko, N. B., Clancy, S. A., Macklin, M. L., Pitman, R. K., & Orr, S. P. (2004). Psychophysiological responding during script-driven imagery in people reporting abduction by space aliens. *Psychological Science, 15,* 493-497.

McReynolds, P. (1998). The role of anxiety in psychopathology. In W. F. Flack, Jr. & J. D. Laird (Eds.), *Emotions in psychopathology* (pp. 243-253). New York: Oxford University Press.

Medina, J. F., Repa, J. C., Mauk, M. D., & LeDoux, J. E. (2002). Parallels between cerebellum- and amygdala-dependent conditioning. *Nature Reviews Neuroscience, 3,* 122-131.

Meiser-Stedman, R., Dalgleish, T., Smith, P., Yule, W., & Glucksman, E. (2007). Diagnostic, demographic, memory quality, and cognitive variables associated with acute stress disorder in children and adolescents. *Journal of Abnormal Psychology, 116,* 65-79.

Mendes, W. B., Blascovich, J., Hunter, S. B., Lickel, B., & Jost, J. T. (2007). Threatened by the unexpected: Physiological responses during social interactions with expectancy-violating partners. *Journal of Personality and Social Psychology, 92*, 698-716.

Mendes, W. B., Blascovich, J., Lickel, B., & Hunter, S. (2002). Challenge and threat during social interaction with white and black men. *Personality and Social Psychology Bulletin, 28*, 939-952.

Mendes, W. B., Blascovich, J., Major, B., & Seery, M. (2001). Challenge and threat responses during downward and upward social comparisons. *European Journal of Social Psychology, 31*, 477-497.

Mendes, W. B., Reis, H. T., Seery, M. D., & Blascovich, J. (2003). Cardiovascular correlates of emotional expression and suppression: Do content and gender context matter? *Journal of Personality and Social Psychology, 84*, 771-792.

Mendolia, M. (2002). An index of self-regulation and the study of repression in social contexts that threaten or do not threaten self-concept. *Emotion, 2*, 215-232.

Mesquita, B. (2001). Culture and emotion: Different approaches to the question. In T. J. Mayne & G. A. Bonanno (Eds.), *Emotions: Current issues and future directions* (pp. 214-250). New York: Guilford.

Mesquita, B., & Ellsworth, P. C. (2001). The role of culture in appraisal. In K. R. Scherer, A. Schorr, & T. Johnstone (Eds.), *Appraisal processes in emotion* (pp. 233-248). New York: Oxford University.

Mesquita, B., & Karasawa, M. (2002). Different emotional lives. *Cognition and Emotion, 16*, 127-141.

Mezzacappa, E. S., Kelsey, R. M., Katkin, E. S., & Sloan, R. P. (2001). Vagal rebound and recovery from psychological stress. *Psychosomatic Medicine, 63*, 650-657.

Miller, G. E., Cohen, S., & Ritchey, A. K. (2002). Chronic psychological stress and the regulation of pro-inflammatory cytokines: A glucocortocoid-resistance model. *Health Psychology, 21*, 531-541.

Mineka, S., Watson, D., & Clark, L. A. (1998). Comorbidity of anxiety and unipolar mood disorders. *Annual Review of Psychology, 49*, 377-412.

Mischel, W. (2004). Toward in integrated science of the person. *Annual Review of Psychology, 55*, 1-22.

Mor, N., & Winquist, J. (2002). Self-focused attention and negative affect: A meta-analysis. *Psychological Bulletin, 128*, 638-662.

Morris, J. S., & Dolan, R. J. (2004). Dissociable amygdala and orbitofrontal responses during reversal fear conditioning. *NeuroImage, 22*, 372-380.

Morris, J. S., Öhman, A., & Dolan, R. (1998). Conscious and unconscious emotional learning in the human amygdala. *Nature, 393*(6684), 467-470.

Morris, W. N. (2000). Some thoughts about mood and its regulation. *Psychological Inquiry, 11,* 200-202.

Morrison, D., & Gilbert, P. (2001). Social rank, shame and anger in primary and secondary psychopaths. *Journal of Forensic Psychiatry, 12,* 330-356.

Morrison, R., & O'Connor, R. C. (2005). Predicting psychological distress in college students: The role of rumination and stress. *Journal of Clinical Psychology, 61,* 447-460.

Moskowitz, J. T. (2001). Emotion and coping. In T. J. Mayne & G. A. Bonanno (Eds.), *Emotions: Current issues and future directions* (pp. 311-336). New York: Guilford Press.

Mowrer, O. H. (1983). Learning theory and behavior. In *Leaves from many seasons: Selected papers* (pp. 117-145). New York: Praeger Publishing. (Original work published 1960)

Mulert, C., Jäger, L., Schmitt, R., Bussfeld, P., Pogarell, O., Möller, H.-J., et al. (2004). Integration of fMRI and simultaneous EEG: Towards a comprehensive understanding of localization and time-course of brain activity in target detection. *NeuroImage, 22,* 83-94.

Murck, H. (2003). Atypical depression spectrum disorder - neurobiology and treatment. *Acta Neuropsychiatrica, 15,* 227-241.

Myin-Germeys, I., Peeters, F., Havermans, R., Nicolson, N. A., deVries, M. W., Delespaul, P., et al. (2003). Emotional reactivity to daily life stress in psychosis and affective disorder: An experience sampling study. *Acta Psychiatrica Scandinavica, 107,* 124-131.

Naismith, S. L., Hickie, I. B., Turner, K., Little, C. L., Winter, V., Ward, P. B., et al. (2003). Neuropsychological performance in patients with depression is associated with clinical, etiological and genetic risk factors. *Journal of Clinical and Experimental Neuropsychology, 25,* 866-877.

Nathanson, D. L. (1992). *Shame and pride: Affect, sex, and the birth of the self.* New York: W.W. Norton.

Neff, K. (2003). Self-compassion: An alternative conceptualization of a healthy attitude toward oneself. *Self and Identity, 2,* 85-101.

Negrao, C., II, Bonanno, G. A., Noll, J. G., Putnam, F. W., & Trickett, P. K. (2005). Shame, humiliation, and childhood sexual abuse: Distinct contributions and emotional coherence. *Child Maltreatment, 10,* 350-363.

Neumann, R. (2000). The causal influences of attributions on emotions: A procedural priming approach. *Psychological Science, 11,* 179-182.

Neumann, S. A., Waldstein, S. R., Sollers, J. J., III, Thayer, J. F., & Sorkin, J. D. (2004). Hostility and distraction have differential influences on cardiovascular recovery from anger recall in women. *Health Psychology, 23,* 631-640.

Ng, S. H., Han, S., Mao, L., & Lai, J. C. L. (2010). Dynamic bicultural brains: fMRI study of their flexible neural representation of self and significant others in response to culture primes. *Asian Journal of Social Psychology, 13,* 83-91.

Niedenthal, P. M., & Halberstadt, J. B. (2000). Emotional response as conceptual coherence. In E. Eich, J. F. Kihlstrom, G. H. Bower, J. P. Forgas, & P. M. Niedenthal (Eds.), *Cognition and emotion* (pp. 169-203). New York: Oxford University Press.

Nolen-Hoeksema, S. (1987). Sex differences in unipolar depression: Evidence and theory. *Psychological Bulletin, 101,* 259-282.

Nolen-Hoeksema, S. (2000). The role of rumination in depressive disorders and mixed anxiety/depressive symptoms. *Journal of Abnormal Psychology, 109,* 504-511.

Nolen-Hoeksema, S., & Davis, C. G. (1999). "Thanks for sharing that": Ruminators and their social support networks. *Journal of Personality and Social Psychology, 77,* 801-814

Nolen-Hoeksema, S., & Jackson, B. (2001). Mediators of the gender difference in rumination. *Psychology of Women Quarterly, 25,* 37-47.

Nolen-Hoeksema, S., Larson, J., & Grayson, C. (1999). Explaining the gender difference in depressive symptoms. *Journal of Personality and Social Psychology, 77,* 1061-1072.

Nolen-Hoeksema, S., Stice, E., Wade, E., & Bohon, C. (2007). Reciprocal relations between rumination and bulimic, substance abuse, and depressive symptoms in female adolescents. *Journal of Abnormal Psychology, 116,* 198-207.

Oakes, T. R., Pizzagalli, D. A., Hendrick, A. M., Horras, K. A., Larson, C. L., Abercrombie, H. C., et al. (2004). Functional coupling of simultaneous electrical and metabolic activity in the human brain. *Human Brain Mapping, 21,* 257-270.

Ochsner, K. N., Bunge, S. A., Gross, J. J., & Gabrieli, J. D. E. (2002). Rethinking feelings: an fMRI study of the cognitive regulation of emotion. *Journal of Cognitive Neuroscience, 14,* 1215-1229.

Ochsner, K. N., & Gross, J. J. (2008). Cognitive emotional regulation. *Current Directions in Psychological Science, 17,* 153-158.

Ochsner, K. N., Ray, R. R., Hughes, B., McRae, K., Cooper, J. C., Weber, J., et al. (2009). Bottom-up and top-down processes in emotion generation. *Psychological Science, 20,* 1322-1331.

Öhman, A. (2002). Automaticity and the amygdala: Nonconscious responses to emotional faces. *Current Directions in Psychological Science, 11,* 62-66.

Oishi, S., Diener, E., Scollon, C. N., & Biswas-Diener, R. (2004). Cross-situational consistency of affective experiences across cultures. *Journal of Personality and Social Psychology, 86*, 460-472.

Olatunji, B. O., Cisler, J., McKay, D., & Phillips, M. L. (2010). Is disgust associated with psychopathology? Emerging research in the anxiety disorders. *Psychiatry Research, 175*, 1-10.

Olatunji, B. O., & Sawchuk, C. N. (2005). Disgust: Characteristic features, social manifestations, and clinical implications. *Journal of Social and Clinical Psychology, 24*, 932-962.

Ong, A. D., & Allaire, J. C. (2005). Cardiovascular intraindividual variability in later life: The influence of social connectedness and positive emotions. *Psychology and Aging, 20*, 476-485.

Orekhova, E. V., Stroganova, T. A., & Posikera, I. N. (2001). Alpha activity as an index of cortical inhibition during sustained internally controlled attention in infants. *Clinical Neurophysiology, 112*, 740-749.

Orbell, S. (2003). Personality systems interactions theory and the theory of planned behaviour: Evidence that self-regulatory volitional components enhance enactments of studying behaviour. *British Journal of Social Psychology, 42*, 95-112.

Otto, J. H., & Hupka, R. B. (1999). Change of anxiety states by probabilistic processing. *Anxiety, Stress, and Coping, 12*, 265-283.

Paivio, S. C., & Greenberg, L. S. (1998). Experiential theory of emotion applied to anxiety and depression. In W. F. Flack, Jr. & J. D. Laird (Eds.), *Emotions in psychopathology* (pp. 229-242). New York: Oxford University Press.

Panksepp, J. (2001). The long-term psychobiological consequences of infant emotions: Prescriptions for the twenty-first century. *Infant Mental Health Journal, 22*, 132-173.

Panksepp, J. (2003a). At the interface of the affective, behavioral, and cognitive neurosciences: Decoding the emotional feelings of the brain. *Brain and Cognition, 52*, 4-14.

Panksepp, J. (2003b). Can anthropomorphic analyses of separation cries in other animals inform us about the emotional nature of social loss in humans? Comment on Blumberg and Sokoloff (2001). *Psychological Review, 110*, 376-388.

Panksepp, J., & Bernatzky, G. (2002). Emotional sounds and the brain: The neuro-affective foundations of musical appreciation. *Behavioural Processes, 60*, 133-155.

Papageorgiou, C., & Wells, A. (2003). An empirical test of a clinical metacognitive model of rumination and depression. *Cognitive Therapy and Research, 27*, 261-273.

Parens, H. (1992). A view of the development of hostility in early life. In T. Shapiro & R. N. Emde (Eds.), *Affect: Psychoanalytic perspectives* (pp. 75-108). Madison, CT: International Universities Press.

Parker, G., & Malhi, G. (2001). Are atypical antipsychotic drugs also atypical antidepressants? *Australian and New Zealand Journal of Psychiatry, 35,* 631-638.

Parker, G., & Roy, K. (2001). Adolescent depression: A review. *Australian and New Zealand Journal of Psychiatry, 35,* 572-580.

Parker, G., & Roy, K. (2002). Examining the utility of a temperament model for modelling non-melancholic depression. *Acta Psychiatrica Scandinavica, 106,* 54-61.

Parker, G., Snowdon, J., & Parker, K. (2003). Modelling late-life depression. *International Journal of Geriatric Psychiatry, 18,* 1102-1109.

Parker, G., Wilhelm, K., Mitchell, P., & Gladstone, G. (2000). Predictors of 1-year outcome in depression. *Australian and New Zealand Journal of Psychiatry, 34,* 56-64.

Parkinson, B., & Manstead, A. S. R. (1993). Making sense of emotion in stories and social life. *Cognition and Emotion, 7,* 295-323.

Pauls, C. A., & Stemmler, G. (2003). Repressive and defensive coping during fear and anger. *Emotion, 3,* 284-302.

Payne, J. D., Jackson, E. D., Ryan, L., Hoscheidt, S., Jacobs, W. J., & Nadel, L. (2006). The impact of stress on neutral and emotional aspects of episodic memory. *Memory, 14,* 1-16.

Peeters, F., Nicholson, N. A., & Berkhof, J. (2003). Cortisol responses to daily events in major depressive disorder. *Psychosomatic Medicine, 65,* 836-841.

Pellitteri, J. (2002). The relationship between emotional intelligence and ego defense mechanisms. *Journal of Psychology, 136,* 182-194.

Pendry, P., & Adam, E. K. (2007). Associations between parents' marital functioning, maternal parenting quality, maternal emotion and child cortisol levels. *International Journal of Behavioral Development, 31,* 218-231.

Penley, J. A., Tomaka, J., & Wiebe, J. S. (2002). The association of coping to physical and psychological health outcomes: A meta-analytic review. *Journal of Behavioral Medicine, 25,* 551-603.

Pennebaker, J. W., & Graybeal, A. (2001). Patterns of natural language use: Disclosure, personality, and social integration. *Current Directions in Psychological Science, 10,* 90-93.

Person, E. S. (1992). Romantic Love: At the intersection of the psyche and the cultural unconscious. In T. Shapiro & R. N. Emde (Eds.), *Affect: Psychoanalytic perspectives* (pp. 383-411). Madison, CT: International Universities Press.

Petrie, K. J., Booth, R. J., & Pennebaker, J. W. (1998). The immunological effects of thought suppression. *Journal of Personality and Social Psychology, 75*, 1264-1272.

Pham, T. H., & Philippot, P. (2010). Decoding of facial expressions of emotion in criminal psychopaths. *Journal of Personality Disorders, 24*, 445-459.

Philippot, P., Chapelle, G., & Blairy, S. (2002). Respiratory feedback in the generation of emotion. *Cognition and Emotion, 16*, 605-627.

Philippot, P., & Rimé, B. (1998). Social and cognitive processing in emotion: A heuristic for psychopathology. In W. F. Flack, Jr. & J. D. Laird (Eds.), *Emotions in psychopathology* (pp. 114-129). New York: Oxford University Press.

Philippot, P., & Schaefer, A. (2001). Emotion and memory. In T. J. Mayne & G. A. Bonanno (Eds.), *Emotions: Current issues and future directions* (pp. 82-122). New York: Guilford Press.

Phillips, M. L., Williams, L. M., Heining, M., Herba, C. M., Russell, T., Andrew, C., et al. (2004). Differential neural responses to overt and covert presentations of facial expression of fear and disgust. *NeuroImage, 21*, 1484-1496.

Pickens, J., Field, T., & Nawrocki, T. (2001). Frontal EEG asymmetry in response to emotional vignettes in preschool age children. *International Journal of Behavioral Development, 25*, 105-112.

Pignotti, M., & Steinberg, M. (2001). Heart rate variability as an outcome measure for thought field therapy in clinical practice. *Journal of Clinical Psychology, 57*, 1193-1206.

Plutchik, R. (1991). *The emotions* (Rev. ed.). Lanham, MD: University Press of America.

Plutchik, R. (1998). Emotions, diagnoses, and ego defense: A psychoevolutionary perspective. In W. F. Flack, Jr. & J. D. Laird (Eds.), *Emotions in psychotherapy* (pp. 367-379). New York: Oxford University Press.

Plutchik, R. (2000). *Emotions in the practice of psychotherapy: Clinical implications of affect theories.* Washington, DC: American Psychological Association.

Polk, D. E., Cohen, S., Doyle, W. J., Skoner, D. P., & Kirschbaum, C. (2005). State and trait affect as predictors of salivary cortisol in healthy adults. *Psychoneuroendocrinology, 30*, 261-272.

Porter, R. J., Gallagher, P., Watson, S., & Young, A. H. (2004). Corticosteroid-serotonin interactions in depression: A review of the human evidence. *Psychopharmacology, 17*, 1-17.

Posse, S., Fitzgerald, D., Gao, K., Habel, U., Rosenberg, D., Moore, G. J., et al. (2003). Real-time fMRI of temporolimbic regions detects amygdala activation during single-trial self-induced sadness. *NeuroImage, 18*, 760-768.

Power, M. J., & Schmidt, S. (2004). Emotion-focused treatment of unipolar and bipolar mood disorders. *Clinical Psychology and Psychotherapy, 11*, 44-57.

Pridham, K. F., Brown, R., Clark, R., Sondel, S., & Green, C. (2002). Infant and caregiving factors affecting weight-for-age and motor development of full-term and premature infants at 1 year post-term. *Research in Nursing & Health, 25*, 394-410.

Pruessner, J. C., Hellhammer, D. H., & Kirschbaum, C. (1999). Low self-esteem, induced failure and the adrenocortical stress response. *Personality and Individual Differences, 27*, 477-489.

Quiles, Z. N., & Bybee, J. (1997). Chronic and predispositional guilt: Relations to mental health, prosocial behavior, and religiosity. *Journal of Personality Assessment, 69*, 104-126.

Quirin, M., Kazén, M., Rohrmann, S., & Kuhl, J. (2009). Implicit but not explicit affectivity predicts circadian and reactive cortisol: Using the implicit positive and negative affect test. *Journal of Personality, 77*, 401-426.

Quirk, G. J., & Gehlert, D. R. (2003). Inhibition of the amygdala: Key to pathological states? *Annals of the New York Academy of Sciences, 985*, 263-272.

Radcliffe, A. M., Lumley, M. A., Kendall, J., Stevenson, J. K., & Beltran, J. (2007). Written emotional disclosure: Testing whether social disclosure matters. *Journal of Social and Clinical Psychology, 26*, 362-384.

Raes, F., Hermans, D., Williams, J. M. G., Beyers, W., Brunfaut, E., & Eelen, P. (2006). Reduced autobiographical memory specificity and rumination in predicting the course of depression. *Journal of Abnormal Psychology, 115*, 699-704.

Rainville, P., Bechara, A., Naqvi, N., & Damasio, A. R. (2006). Basic emotions are associated with distinct patterns of cardiorespiratory activity. *International Journal of Psychophysiology, 61*, 5-18.

Ramponi, C., Barnard, P. J., & Nimmo-Smith, I. (2004). Recollection deficits in dysphoric mood: An affect of schematic models and executive mode? *Memory, 12*, 655-670.

Ramsay, D., & Lewis, M. (2003). Reactivity and regulation in cortisol and behavioral responses to stress. *Child Development, 74*, 456-464.

Rank, O. (1952) *The trauma of birth.* New York: Robert Brunner. (Original work published 1929)

Rathus, J. H., & Sanderson, W. C. (1998). The role of emotion in the psychopathology and treatment of anxiety disorders. In W. F. Flack, Jr. & J. D. Laird (Eds.), *Emotions in psychopathology* (pp. 254-264). New York: Oxford University Press.

Ray, R. D., Shelton, A. L., Garber Hollon, N., Michel, B. D., Frankel, C. B., Gross, J. J., et al. (2009). Cognitive and neural development of individuated self-representation in children. *Child Development, 80*, 1232-1242.

Reich, J. W., & Zautra, A. J. (2002). Arousal and the relationship between positive and negative affect: An analysis of the data of Ito, Cacioppo, and Lang (1998). *Motivation and Emotion, 26*, 209-222.

Reich, W. (1972). *Character analysis* (3rd ed., M. Higgins & C. M. Raphael, Eds., V. R. Carfagno, Trans.). New York: Farrar, Straus and Giroux. (Original work published 1933)

Reich, W. (1973). *The discovery of the orgone: Vol. 1. The function of the orgasm* (V. R. Carfagno, Trans.). New York: Farrar, Straus and Giroux. (Original work published 1947)

Reich, W. (1982). *The bioelectric investigation of sexuality and anxiety* (M. Faber, D. Jordan, & I. Jordan, Trans.). New York: Farrar, Straus, and Giroux. (Original work published 1945)

Reisenzein, R., & Hofmann, T. (1993). Discriminating emotions from appraisal-relevant situational information: Baseline data for structural models of cognitive appraisals. *Cognition and Emotion, 7*, 271-293.

Repetti, R. L., Taylor, S. E., & Seeman, T. E. (2002). Risky families: Family social environments and the mental and physical health of offspring. *Psychological Bulletin, 128*, 330-366.

Rescorla, R. A. (1988). Pavlovian conditioning: It's not what you think it is. *American Psychologist, 43*, 151-160.

Reuter, M. (2002). Impact of cortisol on emotions under stress and nonstress conditions: A pharmacopsychological approach. *Neuropsychobiology, 46*, 41-48.

Rich, P. (2003). *Understanding juvenile sexual offenders: Assessment, treatment, and rehabilitation.* New York: John Wiley & Sons.

Richards, J. M., Butler, E. A., & Gross, J. J. (2003). Emotion regulation in romantic relationships: The cognitive consequences of concealing feelings. *Journal of Social and Personal Relationships, 20*, 599-620.

Richards, J. M., & Gross, J. J. (2000). Emotion regulation and memory: The cognitive costs of keeping one's cool. *Journal of Personality and Social Psychology, 79*, 410-424.

Robinson, M. S., & Alloy, L. B. (2003). Negative cognitive styles and stress-reactive rumination interact to predict depression: A prospective study. *Cognitive Therapy and Research, 27*, 275-292.

Robles, T. F., Shaffer, V. A., Malarkey, W. B., & Kiecolt-Glaser, J. K. (2006). Positive behaviors during marital conflict: Influences on stress hormones. *Journal of Social and Personal Relationships, 23*, 305-325.

Rodriguez, M. L., Ayduk, O., Aber, J. L., Mischel, W., Sethi, A., & Shoda, Y. (2005). A contextual approach to the development of self-regulatory competencies: The role of maternal unresponsivity and toddlers' negative affect in stressful situations. *Social Development, 14,* 136-157.

Roelofs, J., Rood, L., Meesters, C., te Dorsthorst, V., Bögels, S., Alloy, L., et al. (2009). The influence of rumination and distraction on depressed and anxious mood: A prospective examination of the response styles theory in children and adolescents. *European Child & Adolescent Psychiatry, 18,* 635-642.

Roger, D., & Najarian, B. (1989). The construction of a new scale for measuring emotion control. *Personality and Individual Differences, 8,* 845-853.

Roger, D., & Najarian, B. (1998). The relationship between emotional rumination and cortisol secretion under stress. *Personality and Individual Differences, 24,* 531-538.

Rogers, C. R. (1961). *On becoming a person.* Boston: Houghton Mifflin Company.

Rogers, C. R. (1980). *A way of being.* Boston: Houghton Mifflin Company.

Rogers, M. A., Bellgrove, M. A., Chiu, E., Mileshkin, C., & Bradshaw, J. L. (2004). Response selection deficits in melancholic but not nonmelancholic unipolar major depression. *Journal of Clinical and Experimental Neuropsychology, 26,* 169-179.

Rogers, M. A., Bradshaw, J. L., Phillips, J. G., Chiu, G., Mileshkin, C., & Vaddadi, K. (2002). Mental rotation in unipolar major depression. *Journal of Clinical and Experimental Neuropsychology, 24,* 101-106.

Rogers, M. A., Bradshaw, J. L., Phillips, J. G., Chiu, E., Vaddadi, K., Presnel, I., et al. (2000). Parkinsonian motor characteristics in unipolar major depression. *Journal of Clinical and Experimental Neuropsychology, 22,* 232-244.

Rohleder, N., Beulen, S. E., Chen, E., Wolf, J. M., & Kirschbaum, C. (2007). Stress on the dance floor: The cortisol stress response to social-evaluative threat in competitive ballroom dancers. *Personality and Social Psychology Bulletin, 33,* 69-84.

Rohrmann, S., Hennig, J., & Netter, P. (1999). Changing psychobiological stress reactions by manipulating cognitive processes. *International Journal of Psychophysiology, 33,* 149-161.

Rolls, E. T. (2004). The functions of the orbitofrontal cortex. *Brain and Cognition, 55,* 11-29.

Rose, A. J. (2002). Co-rumination in the friendships of girls and boys. *Child Development, 73,* 1830-1843.

Roseman, I. J. (2001). A model of appraisal in the emotion system: Integrating theory, research, and applications. In K. R. Scherer, A. Schorr, & T. Johnstone (Eds.), *Appraisal processes in emotion: Theory, methods, research* (pp. 68-91). New York: Oxford University Press.

Rosen, J. B., & Schulkin, J. (1998). From normal fear to pathological anxiety. *Psychological Review, 105,* 325-350.

Rosenberger, P. H., Ickovics, J. R., Epel, E. S., D'Entremont, D., & Jokl, P. (2004). Physical recovery in arthroscopic knee surgery: Unique contributions of coping behaviors to clinical outcomes and stress reactivity. *Psychology and Health, 19,* 307-320.

Rosenkranz, J. A., Moore, H., & Grace, A. A. (2003). The prefrontal cortex regulates lateral amygdala neuronal plasticity and responses to previously conditioned stimuli. *Journal of Neuroscience, 23,* 11054-11064.

Rosmond, R., Nilsson, A., & Björntorp, P. (2000). Psychiatric ill health and distribution of body fat mass among female immigrants in Sweden. *Public Health, 114,* 45-51.

Rothbaum, F, Weisz, J., & Pott, M. (2001). Deeper into attachment and culture. *American Psychologist, 56,* 827-829.

Rothermundt, M., Arolt, V., Fenker, J., Gutbrodt, H., Peters, M., & Kirchner, H. (2001). Different immune patterns in melancholic and non-melancholic major depression. *European Archives of Psychiatry & Clinical Neuroscience, 251,* 90-97.

Rottenberg, J., Wilhelm, F. H., Gross, J. J., & Gotlib, I. H. (2003). Vagal rebound during resolution of tearful crying among depressed and nondepressed individuals. *Psychophysiology, 40,* 1-6.

Roy, M., Harvey, P.-O., Berlim, M. T., Mamdani, F., Beaulieu, M.-M., Turecki, G., et al. (2010). Medial prefrontal cortex activity during memory encoding of pictures and its relation to symptomatic improvement after citalopram treatment in patients with major depression. *Journal of Psychiatry & Neuroscience, 35,* 152-162.

Russell, J. A. (2003). Core affect and the psychological construction of emotion. *Psychological Reviews, 110,* 145-172.

Rusting, C. L., & Nolen-Hoeksema, S. (1998). Regulating responses to anger: Effects of rumination and distraction on angry mood. *Journal of Personality and Social Psychology, 74,* 790-803.

Saarni, C. (1997). Emotional competence and self-regulation in childhood. In P. Salovey & D. J. Sluyter (Eds.), *Emotional development and emotional intelligence* (pp. 35-66). New York: Basic Books.

Sabbagh, M. A., Bowman, L. C., Evraire, L. E., & Ito, J. M. B. (2009). Neurodevelopmental correlates of theory of mind in preschool children. *Child Development, 80*, 1147-1162.

Salovey, P., Mayer, J. D., Goldman, S. L., Turvey, C., & Palfai, T. P. (1995). Emotional attention, clarity, and repair: Exploring emotional intelligence using the Trait Meta-Mood Scale. In J. W. Pennebaker (Ed.), *Emotion, disclosure, and health* (pp. 125-154). Washington, DC: American Psychological Association.

Salovey, P., Stroud, L. R., Woolery, A., & Epel, E. S. (2002). Perceived emotional intelligence, stress reactivity, and symptom reports: Further explorations using the Trait Meta-Mood Scale. *Psychology and Health, 17*, 611-627.

Sandler, J., & Freud, A. (1985). *The analysis of defense: The ego and the mechanisms of defense revisited.* New York: International Universities Press.

Sanford, K. (2005). Attributions and anger in early marriage: Wives are event-dependent and husbands are schematic. *Journal of Family Psychology, 19*, 180-188.

Sapolsky, R. M., Romero, L. M., & Munck, A. U. (2000). How do glucocortocoids influence stress responses? Integrating permissive, suppressive, stimulatory, and preparative actions. *Endocrine Reviews, 21*, 55-89.

Sarbin, T. R., & Keen, E. (1998). Sanity and madness: Conventional and unconventional narratives of emotional life. In W. F. Flack, Jr. & J. D. Laird (Eds.), *Emotions in psychopathology* (pp. 130-142). New York: Oxford University Press.

Satir, V., Banmen, J., Gerber, J., & Gomori, M. (1991). *The Satir model: Family therapy and beyond.* Palo Alto, CA: Science and Behavior Books.

Saxe, R. R., Whitfield-Gabrieli, S., Scholz, J., & Pelphrey, K. A. (2009). Brain regions for perceiving and reasoning about other people in school-aged children. *Child Development, 80*, 1197-1209.

Scazufca, M., & Kuipers, E. (1999). Coping strategies in relatives of people with schizophrenia before and after psychiatric admission. *British Journal of Psychiatry, 174*, 154-158.

Schaefer, A., Collette, F., Philippot, P., Van der Linden, M., Laureys, S., Delfiore, G., et al. (2003). Neural correlates of "hot" and "cold" emotional processing: A multilevel approach to the functional anatomy of emotion. *NeuroImage, 18*, 938-949.

Schaefer, S. M., Jackson, D. C., Davidson, R. J., Aguirre, G. K., Kimberg, D. Y., & Thompson-Schill, S. L. (2002). Modulation of amygdalar activity by the conscious regulation of negative emotion. *Journal of Cognitive Neuroscience, 14*, 913-921.

Schatzberg, A. F., Cole, J. O., & DeBattista, C. (2003). *Manual of clinical psychopharmacology* (4th ed.). Washington, DC: American Psychiatric Publishing.

Scheff, T. J. (1998). Therapeutic alliance: Microanalysis of shame and the social bond. In W. F. Flack, Jr. & J. D. Laird (Eds.), *Emotions in psychopathology* (pp. 99-113). New York: Oxford University Press.

Scherer, K. R. (1993). Studying the emotion-antecedent appraisal process: An expert system approach. *Cognition and Emotion, 7,* 325-355.

Schlotz, W., Hellhammer, J., Schulz, P., & Stone, A. A. (2004). Perceived work overload and chronic worrying predict weekend-weekday differences in the cortisol awakening response. *Psychosomatic Medicine, 66,* 207-214.

Schmidt, L. A., & Schulkin, J. (2000). Toward a computational affective neuroscience. *Brain and Cognition, 42,* 95-98.

Schmidt, L. A., & Trainor, L. J. (2001). Frontal brain electrical activity (EEG) distinguishes valence and intensity of musical emotions. *Cognition and Emotion, 15,* 487-500.

Schmidt, L. A., Trainor, L. J., & Santesso, D. L. (2003). Development of frontal electroencephalogram (EEG) and heart rate (ECG) responses to affective musical stimuli during the first 12 months of post-natal life. *Brain and Cognition, 52,* 27-32.

Schmitt, M., Gollwitzer, M., Förster, N., & Montada, L. (2004). Effects of objective and subjective account components on forgiving. *Journal of Social Psychology, 144,* 465-485.

Schnall, S., & Laird, J. D. (2003). Keep smiling: Enduring effects of facial expressions and postures on emotional experience and memory. *Cognition and Emotion, 17,* 787-797.

Schommer, N. C., Hellhammer, D. H., & Kirschbaum, C. (2003). Dissociation between reactivity of the hypothalamus-pituitary-adrenal axis and the sympathetic-adrenal-medullary system to repeated psychosocial stress. *Psychosomatic Medicine, 65,* 450-460.

Schore, A. N. (2001a). The effects of a secure attachment relationship on right brain development, affect regulation, and infant mental health. *Infant Mental Health Journal, 22,* 7-66.

Schore, A. N. (2001b). The effects of early relational trauma on right brain development, affect regulation, and infant mental health. *Infant Mental Health Journal, 22,* 201-269.

Schorr, A. (2001). Appraisal: The evolution of an idea. In K. R. Scherer, A. Schorr, & T. Johnstone (Eds.), *Appraisal processes in emotion: Theory, methods, research* (pp. 20-34). New York: Oxford University Press.

Schreckenberger, M., Lange-Asschenfeld, C., Lochmann, M., Mann, K., Siessmeier, T., Buchholz, H.-G., et al. (2004). The thalamus as the generator and modulator of EEG alpha rhythm: A combined PET/EEG study with lorazepam challenge in humans. *NeuroImage, 22,* 637-644.

Schulkin, J., Thompson, B. L., & Rosen, J. B. (2003). Demythologizing the emotions: Adaptation, cognition, and visceral representations of emotion in the nervous system. *Brain and Cognition, 52,* 15-23.

Schutter, D. J. L. G., & van Honk, J. (2005). Salivary cortisol and the coupling of midfrontal delta-beta oscillations. *International Journal of Psychophysiology, 55,* 127-129.

Scollon, C. N., Diener, E., Oishi, S., & Biswas-Diener, R. (2004). Emotions across cultures and methods. *Journal of Cross-Cultural Psychology, 35,* 304-326.

Scott, V. B., Jr., Stiles, K. B., Raines, D. B., & Koth, A. W. (2002). Mood, rumination, and mood awareness in the athletic performance of collegiate tennis players. *North American Journal of Psychology, 4,* 457-468.

Seeley, W. W. (2010). Anterior insula degeneration in frontotemporal dementia. *Brain Structure & Function, 214,* 465-475.

Seery, M. D., Blascovich, J., Weisbuch, M., & Vick, S. B. (2004). The relationship between self-esteem level, self-esteem stability, and cardiovascular reactions to performance feedback. *Journal of Personality and Social Psychology, 87,* 133-145.

Segerstrom, S. C., Stanton, A. L., Alden, L. E., & Shortridge, B. E. (2003). A multidimensional structure for repetitive thought: What's on your mind, and how, and how much? *Journal of Personality and Social Psychology, 85,* 909-921.

Segerstrom, S. C., Tsao, J. C. I., Alden, L. E., & Craske, M. G. (2000). Worry and rumination: Repetitive thought as a concomitant and predictor of negative mood. *Cognitive Therapy and Research, 24,* 671-688.

Seligman, M. E. P. (1970). On the generality of the laws of learning. *Psychological Review, 77,* 406-418.

Seligman, M. E. P., & Johnston, J. C. (1973). A cognitive theory of avoidance learning. In F. J. McGuigan & D. B. Lumsden (Eds.), *Contemporary approaches to conditioning and learning* (pp. 69-110). Washington, DC: V. H. Winston & Sons.

Serretti, A., Lattuada, E., Franchini, L., & Smeraldi, E. (2000). Melancholic features and response to lithium prophylaxis in mood disorders. *Depression and Anxiety, 11,* 73-79.

Shapiro, D., Jamner, L. D., Goldstein, I. B., & Delfino, R. J. (2001). Striking a chord: Moods, blood pressure, and heart rate in everyday life. *Psychophysiology, 38,* 197-204.

Shapiro, T. (1992). Words and feelings in the psychoanalytic dialogue. In T. Shapiro & R. N. Emde (Eds.), *Affect: Psychoanalytic perspectives* (pp. 321-348). Madison, CT: International Universities Press.

Shean, G. D. (2003). Is cognitive therapy consistent with what we know about emotions? *Journal of Psychology, 137,* 195-208.

Sheldon, K. M., Abad, N., Ferguson, Y., Gunz, A., Houser-Marko, L., Nichols, C. P., et al. (2010). Persistent pursuit of need-satisfying goals leads to increased happiness: A 6-month experimental longitudinal study. *Motivation and Emotion, 34,* 39-48.

Sheldon, K. M. & Lyubomirsky, S. (2006). Achieving sustainable gains in happiness: Change your actions, not your circumstances. *Journal of Happiness Studies, 7,* 55-86.

Sherwood, A., Allen, M. T., Fahrenberg, J., Kelsey, R. M., Lovallo, W. R., & van Doornen, L. J. P. (1990). Methodological guidelines for impedance cardiography. *Psychophysiology, 27,* 1-23.

Shirtcliff, E. A., Vitacco, M. J., Graf, A. R., Gostisha, A. J., Merz, J. L., & Zahn-Waxler, C. (2009). Neurobiology of empathy and callousness: Implications for the development of antisocial behavior. *Behavioral Sciences and the Law, 27,* 137-171.

Showers, C. J. (2000). Self-organization in emotional contexts. In J. P. Forgas (Ed.), *Feeling and thinking: The role of affect in social cognition* (pp. 283-307). New York: Cambridge University.

Siegle, G. J., Ingram, R. E., & Matt, G. E. (2002). Affective interference: An explanation for negative attention biases in dysphoria? *Cognitive Therapy and Research, 26,* 73-87.

Siegle, G. J., Steinhauer, S. R., Carter, C. S., Ramel, W., & Thase, M. E. (2003). Do the seconds turn into hours? Relationships between sustained pupil dilation in response to emotional information and self-reported rumination. *Cognitive Therapy and Research, 27,* 365-382.

Silk, J. S., Steinberg, L., & Sheffield Morris, A. (2003). Adolescents' emotion regulation in daily life: Links to depressive symptoms and problem behavior. *Child Development, 74,* 1869-1880.

Simpson, J. R., Ongur, D., Akbudak, E., Conturo, T. E., Ollinger, J. M., Snyder, A. Z., et al. (2000). The emotional modulation of cognitive processing: An fMRI study. *Journal of Cognitive Neuroscience, 12,* 157-170.

Sin, N. L. & Lyubomirsky, S. (2009). Enhancing well-being and alleviating depressive symptoms with positive psychology interventions: A practice-friendly meta-analysis. *Journal of Clinical Psychology: In Session, 65,* 467-487.

Sival, R. C., Haffmans, P. M. J., Jansen, P. A. F., Duursma, S. A., & Eikelenboom, P. (2002). Sodium valproate in the treatment of aggressive behavior in patients with dementia--A randomized placebo controlled clinical trial. *International Journal of Geriatric Psychiatry, 17,* 579-585.

Sloman, L., Atkinson, L., Milligan, K., & Liotti, G. (2002). Attachment, social rank, and affect regulation: Speculations on an ethological approach to family interaction. *Family Process, 41,* 313-328.

Sloman, S. A. (1996). The empirical case for two systems of reasoning. *Psychological Bulletin, 119,* 3-22.

Smart, L., & Wegner, D. M. (1999). Covering up what can't be seen: Concealable stigma and mental control. *Journal of Personality and Social Psychology, 77,* 474-486.

Smith, C. A., & Kirby, L. D. (2000). Consequences require antecedents: Toward a process model of emotion elicitation. In J. P. Forgas (Ed.), *Feeling and thinking: The role of affect in social cognition* (pp. 83-106). New York: Cambridge University Press.

Smith, C. A., & Kirby, L. D. (2001). Toward delivering on the promise of appraisal theory. In K. R. Scherer, A. Schorr, & T. Johnstone (Eds.), *Appraisal processes in emotion: Theory, methods, research* (pp. 121-138). New York: Oxford University Press.

Smith, C. A., & Lazarus, R. S. (1993). Appraisal components, core relational themes, and the emotions. *Cognition and Emotion, 7,* 233-269.

Smith, D. (2001). Organizations and humiliation: Looking beyond Elias. *Organization, 8,* 537-560.

Smyth, J., Ockenfels, M. C., Porter, L., Kirschbaum, C., Hellhammer, D. H., & Stone, A. A. (1998). Stressors and mood measured on a momentary basis are associated with salivary cortisol secretion. *Psychoneuroendocrinology, 23,* 353-370.

Solomon, R. C. (1976). *The passions.* Garden City, NY: Anchor Press/Doubleday.

Sonino, N., & Fava, G. A. (2001). Psychiatric disorders associated with Cushing's syndrome: Epidemiology, pathophysiology and treatment. *CNS Drugs, 15,* 361-373.

Spasojević, J., & Alloy, L. B. (2001). Rumination as a common mechanism relating depressive risk factors to depression. *Emotion, 1,* 25-37.

Stanton, A. L., Danoff-Burg, S., Cameron, C. L., Bishop, M., Collins, C. A., Kirk, S. B., et al. (2000). Emotionally expressive coping predicts psychological and physical adjustment to breast cancer. *Journal of Consulting and Clinical Psychology, 68,* 875-882.

Stanton, A. L., Danoff-Burg, S., Cameron, C. L., & Ellis, A. P. (1994). Coping through emotional approach: Problems of conceptualization and confounding. *Journal of Personality and Social Psychology, 66,* 350-362.

Stanton, A. L., Kirk, S. B., Cameron, C. L., & Danoff-Burg, S. (2000). Coping through emotional approach: Scale construction and validation. *Journal of Personality and Social Psychology, 78,* 1150-1169.

Stanton, M. E. (2000). Multiple memory systems, development, and conditioning. *Behavioural Brain Research, 110,* 25-37.

Starkman, M. N., Giordani, B., Berent, S., Schork, M. A., & Schteingart, D. E. (2001). Elevated cortisol levels in Cushing's disease are associated with cognitive decrements. *Psychosomatic Medicine, 63,* 985-993.

Stöber, J., & Borkovec, T. D. (2002). Reduced concreteness of worry in generalized anxiety disorder: Findings from a therapy study. *Cognitive Therapy and Research, 26,* 89-96.

Stoller, R. J. (1987). Pornography: Daydreams to cure humiliation. In D. L. Nathanson (Ed.), *The many faces of shame* (pp. 292-307). New York: Guilford Press.

Strasser, F. (1999). *Emotions: Experiences in existential psychotherapy and life.* London: Duckworth.

Strauchler, O., McCloskey, K., Malloy, K., Sitaker, M., Grigsby, N., & Gillig, P. (2004). Humiliation, manipulation, and control: Evidence of centrality in domestic violence against an adult partner. *Journal of Family Violence, 19,* 339-354.

Street, H. (2003). The psychosocial impact of cancer: Exploring relationships between conditional goal setting and depression. *Psycho-Oncology, 12,* 580-589.

Street, H., Nathan, P., Durkin, K., Morling, J., Dzahari, M. A., Carson, J., & et al. (2004). Understanding the relationships between wellbeing, goal-setting and depression in children. *Australian and New Zealand Journal of Psychiatry, 38,* 155-161.

Street, H., Sheeran, P., & Orbell, S. (1999). Conceptualizing depression: An integration of 27 theories. *Clinical Psychology and Psychotherapy, 6,* 175-193.

Stroebe, M., Stroebe, W., Schut, H., Zech, E., & van den Bout, J. (2002). Does disclosure of emotions facilitate recovery from bereavement? Evidence from two prospective studies. *Journal of Consulting and Clinical Psychology, 70,* 169-178.

Stroebe, M., van Vliet, T., Hewstone, M., & Willis, H. (2002). Homesickness among students in two cultures: Antecedents and consequences. *British Journal of Psychology, 93,* 147-168.

Stuss, D. T., & Anderson, V. (2004). The frontal lobes and theory of mind: Developmental concepts from adult focal lesion research. *Brain and Cognition, 55*, 69-83.

Suchday, S., & Larkin, K. T. (2004). Psychophysiological responses to anger provocation among Asian Indian and white men. *International Journal of Behavioral Medicine, 11*, 71-80.

Suhr, J., Demireva, P., & Heffner, K. (2008). The relation of salivary cortisol to patterns of performance on a word list learning task in healthy older adults. *Psychoneuroendocrinology, 33*, 1293-1296.

Sullivan, H. S. (1953a). *Conceptions of modern psychiatry.* New York: W. W. Norton & Company.

Sullivan, H. S. (1953b). *The interpersonal theory of psychiatry.* New York: W. W. Norton & Company.

Sullivan, H. S. (1956). *Clinical studies in psychiatry.* New York: W. W. Norton & Company.

Sullivan, M. W., & Lewis, M. (2003). Emotional expressions of young infants and children. *Infants & Young Children: An Interdisciplinary Journal of Special Care Practices, 16*, 120-142.

Surguladze, S. A., El-Hage, W., Dalgleish, T., Radua, J., Gohier, B., & Phillips, M. L. (2010). Depression is associated with increased sensitivity to signals of disgust: A functional magnetic resonance imaging study. *Journal of Psychiatric Research, 44*, 894-902.

Sutton, S. K., & Davidson, R. J. (1997). Prefrontal brain asymmetry: A biological substrate of the behavioral approach and inhibition systems. *Psychological Science, 8*, 204-210.

Szabó, M., & Lovibond, P. F. (2002). The cognitive content of naturally occurring worry episodes. *Cognitive Therapy and Research, 26*, 167-177.

Tamir, M., Mitchell, C., & Gross, J. J. (2008). Hedonic and instrumental motives in anger regulation. *Psychological Science, 19*, 324-328.

Tangney, J. P. (1998). How does guilt differ from shame? In J. Bybee (Ed.), *Guilt and children* (pp. 1-17). San Diego, CA: Academic Press.

Taylor, A., Fisk, N. M., & Glover, V. (2000). Mode of delivery and subsequent stress response. *Lancet, 355*, 120.

Taylor, S. E., Lerner, J. S., Sage, R. M., Lehman, B. J., & Seeman, T. E. (2004). Early environment, emotions, responses to stress, and health. *Journal of Personality, 72*, 1365-1394.

Taylor, S. F., Liberzon, I., & Koeppe, R. A. (2000). The effect of graded aversive stimuli on limbic and visual activation. *Neuropsychologia, 38*, 1415-1425.

Teachman, B. A. (2006). Pathological disgust: In the thoughts, not the eye, of the beholder. *Anxiety, Stress, and Coping, 19,* 335-351.

Tellegen, A., Watson, D., & Clark, L. A. (1999). On the dimensional and hierarchical structure of affect. *Psychological Science, 10,* 297-303.

Terracciano, A., McCrae, R. R., Hagemann, D., & Costa, P. T., Jr. (2003). Individual difference variables, affective differentiation, and the structures of affect. *Journal of Personality, 71,* 669-703.

Thagard, P., & Nerb, J. (2002). Emotional gestalts: Appraisal, change, and the dynamics of affect. *Personality and Social Psychology Review, 6,* 274-282.

Thayer, J. F., Hall, M., Sollers, J. J., III, & Fischer, J. E. (2006). Alcohol use, urinary cortisol, and heart rate variability in apparently healthy men: Evidence for impaired inhibitory control of the HPA axis in heavy drinkers. *International Journal of Psychophysiology, 56,* 244-250.

Thayer, J. F., Rossy, L. A., Ruiz-Padial, E., & Johnsen, B. H. (2003). Gender differences in the relationship between emotional regulation and depressive symptoms. *Cognitive Therapy and Research, 27,* 349-364.

Thayer, R. E. (2000). Mood regulation and general arousal systems. *Psychological Inquiry, 11,* 202-204.

Thomsen, D. K., Jørgensen, M. M., Mehlsen, M. Y., & Zachariae, R. (2004). The influence of rumination and defensiveness on negative affect in response to experimental stress. *Scandinavian Journal of Psychology, 45,* 253-258.

Tice, D. M., & Bratslavsky, E. (2000). Giving in to feel good: The place of emotion regulation in the context of general self-control. *Psychological Inquiry, 11,* 149-159.

Tice, D. M., Bratslavsky, E., & Baumeister, R. F. (2001). Emotional distress regulation takes precedence over impulse control: If you feel bad, do it! *Journal of Personality and Social Psychology, 80,* 53-67.

Tice, D. M., & Wallace, H. (2000). Mood and emotion control: Some thoughts on the state of the field. *Psychological Inquiry, 11,* 214-217.

Tiedens, L. Z., & Linton, S. (2001). Judgment under emotional certainty and uncertainty: The effects of specific emotions on information processing. *Journal of Personality and Social Psychology, 81,* 973-988.

Tillich, P. (1952). *The courage to be.* New Haven, CT: Yale University Press.

Tkach, C., & Lyubomirsky, S. (2006). How do people pursue happiness?: Relating personality, happiness-increasing strategies, and well-being. *Journal of Happiness Studies, 7,* 183-225.

Toates, F. (2002). Application of a multilevel model of behavioural control to understanding emotions. *Behavioural Processes, 60,* 99-114.

Tobin, R. M., Graziano, W. G., Vanman, E. J., & Tassinary, L. G. (2000). Personality, emotional experience, and efforts to control emotions. *Journal of Personality and Social Psychology, 79,* 656-669.

Tomaka, J., Blascovich, J., Kelsey, R. M., & Leitten, C. L. (1993). Subjective, physiological, and behavioral effects of threat and challenge appraisal. *Journal of Personality and Social Psychology, 65,* 248-260.

Tomaka, J., Palacios, R., Schneider, K. T., Colotla, M., Concha, J. B., & Herrald, M. M. (1999). Assertiveness predicts threat and challenge reactions to potential stress among women. *Journal of Personality and Social Psychology, 76,* 1008-1021.

Tomkins, S. (1995). *Shame and its sisters: A Silvan Tomkins reader* (E. K. Sedgwick & A. Frank, Eds.). Durham, NC: Duke University Press.

Tranel, D., Gullickson, G., Koch, M., & Adolphs, R. (2006). Altered experience of emotion following bilateral amygdala damage. *Cognitive Neuropsychiatry, 11,* 219-232.

Tracy, J. L., & Robins, R. W. (2006). Appraisal antecedents of shame and guilt: Support for a theoretical model. *Personality and Social Psychology Bulletin, 32,* 1339-1351.

Trapnell, P. D., & Campbell, J. D. (1999). Private self-consciousness and the five-factor model of personality: Distinguishing rumination from reflection. *Journal of Personality and Social Psychology, 76,* 284-304.

Treynor, W., Gonzalez, R., & Nolen-Hoeksema, S. (2003). Rumination reconsidered: A psychometric analysis. *Cognitive Therapy and Research, 27,* 247-259.

Tsuchiya, N., Moradi, F., Felsen, C., Yamazaki, M., & Adolphs, R. (2009). Intact rapid detection of fearful faces in the absence of the amygdala. *Nature Neuroscience, 12,* 1224-1225.

Tugade, M. M., & Fredrickson, B. L. (2006). Regulation of positive emotions: Emotion regulation strategies that promote resilience. *Journal of Happiness Studies, 8,* 311-333.

Uchino, B. N., Holt-Lunstad, J., Bloor, L. E., & Campo, R. A. (2005). Aging and cardiovascular reactivity to stress: Longitudinal evidence for changes in stress reactivity. *Psychology and Aging, 20,* 134-143.

Ueki, H., Holzapfel, C., Washino, K., Inoue, M., Ogawa, N., & Takai, A. (2001). Reliability and validity of Kasahara's scale of melancholic type of personality (typus melancholicus) in a German sample population. *Psychiatry and Clinical Neurosciences, 55,* 31-35.

Ulfig, N., Setzer, M., & Bohl, J. (2003). Ontogeny of the human amygdala. *Annals of the New York Academy of Sciences, 9985,* 22-33.

Urban, E. (2003). Developmental aspects of trauma and traumatic aspects of development. *Journal of Analytical Psychology, 48,* 171-190.

Urry, H. L., Nitschke, J. B., Dolski, I., Jackson, D. C., Dalton, K. M., Mueller, C. J., et al. (2004). Making a life worth living: Neural correlates of well-being. *Psychological Science, 15,* 367-372.

Vaillant, G. E. (1993). *The wisdom of the ego.* Cambridge, MA: Harvard University Press.

Vaillant, G. E. (1998). Where do we go from here? *Journal of Personality, 98,* 1147-1157.

Van der Zee, K., Thijs, M., & Schakel, L. (2002). The relationship of emotional intelligence with academic intelligence and the big five. *European Journal of Personality, 16,* 103-125.

van Stegeren, A. H., Everaerd, W., Cahill, L., McGaugh, J. L., & Gooren, L. J. G. (1998). Memory for emotional events: Differential effects of centrally versus peripherally acting beta-blocking agents. *Psychopharmacology, 138,* 305-310.

van Stegeren, A. H., Everaerd, W., & Gooren, L. J. G. (2002). The effect of beta-adrenergic blockade after encoding on memory of an emotional event. *Psychopharmacology, 163,* 202-212.

vanOyen Witvliet, C., Ludwig, T. E., & Vander Laan, K. L. (2001). Granting forgiveness or harboring grudges: Implications for emotion, physiology, and health. *Psychological Science, 12,* 117-123.

Vedhara, K., Miles, J., Bennett, P., Plummer, S., Tallon, D., Brooks, E., et al. (2003). An investigation into the relationship between salivary cortisol, stress, anxiety and depression. *Biological Psychology, 62,* 89-96.

Verona, E. (2005). Moderating effects of rumination and gender on context-specific aggression. *Aggressive Behavior, 31,* 420-436.

Verplanken, B., Friborg, O., Wang, C. E., Trafimow, D., & Woolf, K. (2007). Mental habits: Metacognitive reflection on negative self-thinking. *Journal of Personality and Social Psychology, 92,* 526-541.

Vickers, K. S., & Vogeltanz-Holm, N. D. (2003). The effects of rumination and distraction tasks on psychophysiological responses and mood in dysphoric and nondysphoric individuals. *Cognitive Therapy and Research, 27,* 331-348.

Vloet, T. D., Konrad, K., Huebner, T., Herpertz, S., & Herpertz-Dahlmann, B. (2008). Structural and functional MRI-findings in children and adolescents with antisocial behavior. *Behavioral Sciences and the Law, 26,* 99-111.

von Zerssen, D. (2000). Variants of premorbid personality and personality disorder: A taxonomic model of their relationships. *European Archives of Psychiatry & Clinical Neuroscience, 250,* 234-248.

Walz, P. G., & Rapee, R. M. (2003). Disentangling schematic and conceptual processing: A test of the Interacting Cognitive Subsystems framework. *Cognition and Emotion, 17,* 65-81.

Wang, L., Huettel, S., & De Bellis, M. D. (2008). Neural substrates for processing task-irrelevant sad images in adolescents. *Developmental Science, 11,* 23-32.

Watkins, E., & Teasdale, J. D. (2001). Rumination and overgeneral memory in depression: Effects of self-focus and analytic thinking. *Journal of Abnormal Psychology, 110,* 353-357.

Watson, D. (2000). Basic problems in positive mood regulation. *Psychological Inquiry, 11,* 205-209.

Watson, D., & Clark, L. A. (1994). *Manual for the Positive and Negative Affect Schedule - Expanded Form.* Retrieved November 28, 2006, from http://www.psychology.uiowa.edu/Faculty/Watson/PANAS-X.pdf

Watson, D., & Clark, L. A. (1997). Measurement and mismeasurement of mood: Recurrent and emergent issues. *Journal of Personality Assessment, 68,* 267-296.

Watson, D., Clark, L. A., & Tellegen, A. (1988). Development and validation of brief measures of positive and negative affect: The PANAS scales. *Journal of Personality and Social Psychology, 54,* 1063-1070.

Wegner, D. M., & Smart, L. (1997). Deep cognitive activation: A new approach to the unconscious. *Journal of Consulting and Clinical Psychology, 65,* 984-995.

Weiss, H., & Lang, H. (2000). Object relations and intersubjectivity in depression. *American Journal of Psychotherapy, 54,* 317-328.

Wenzlaff, R. M., & Luxton, D. D. (2003). The role of thought suppression in depressive rumination. *Cognitive Therapy and Research, 27,* 293-308.

Wenzlaff, R. M., Rude, S. S., & West, L. M. (2002). Cognitive vulnerability to depression: The role of thought suppression and attitude certainty. *Cognition and Emotion, 16,* 533-548.

Wenzlaff, R. M., & Wegner, D. M. (2000). Thought suppression. *Annual Review of Psychology, 51,* 59-91.

Wessa, M., Rohleder, N., Kirschbaum, C., & Flor, H. (2006). Altered cortisol awakening response in posttraumatic stress disorder. *Psychoneuroendocrinology, 31,* 209-215.

Westen, D., Heim, A. K., Morrison, K., Patterson, M., & Campbell, L. (2002). Simplifying diagnosis using a prototype-matching approach: Implications for the next edition of the DSM. In L. E. Beutler & M. L. Malik (Eds.), *Rethinking the DSM: A psychological perspective* (pp. 221-250). Washington, DC: American Psychological Association.

Whelton, W. J. (2004). Emotional processes in psychotherapy: Evidence across therapeutic modalities. *Clinical Psychology and Psychotherapy, 11,* 58-71.

Whittlesey, S. W., Allen, J. R., Bell, B. D., Lindsey, E. D., Speed, L. F., Lucas, A. F., et al. (1999). Avoidance in trauma: Conscious and unconscious defense, pathology, and health. *Psychiatry, 62,* 303-312.

Widen, S. C., & Russell, J. A. (2010). The "disgust face" conveys anger to children. *Emotion, 10,* 455-466.

Williams, B. A. (2001). Two-factor theory has strong empirical evidence of validity. *Journal of the Experimental Analysis of Behavior, 75,* 362-365.

Williams, J. M. G., Barnhofer, T., Crane, C., Hermans, D., Raes, F., Watkins, E., et al. (2007). Autobiographical memory specificity and emotional disorder. *Psychological Bulletin, 133,* 122-148.

Winkielman, P., & Berridge, K. C. (2004). Unconscious emotion. *Current Directions in Psychological Science, 13,* 120-123.

Winkielman, P., & Cacioppo, J. T. (2001). Mind at ease puts a smile on the face: Psychophysiological evidence that processing facilitation elicits positive affect. *Journal of Personality and Social Psychology, 81,* 989-1000.

Winkler, D., Willeit, M., Praschak-Rieder, N., Lucht, M. J., Hilger, E., Konstantinidis, A., et al. (2002). Changes of clinical pattern in seasonal affective disorder (SAD) over time in a German-speaking sample. *European Archives of Psychiatry & Clinical Neuroscience, 252,* 54-62.

Winnicott, D. W. (1965a). Psycho-analysis and the sense of guilt. In *The maturational processes and the facilitating environment* (pp. 15-28). Madison, CT: International Universities Press. (Original work published 1958)

Winnicott, D. W. (1965b). Ego integration in child development. In *The maturational processes and the facilitating environment* (pp. 56-63). Madison, CT: International Universities Press. (Original work published 1962)

Wolf, O. T., Kuhlmann, S., Buss, C., Hellhammer, D. H., & Kirschbaum, C. (2004). Cortisol and memory retrieval in humans: Influence of emotional valence. *Annals of the New York Academy of Sciences, 1032,* 195-197.

Wolfradt, U., & Engelmann, S. (2003). Depersonalization, fantasies, and coping behavior in clinical context. *Journal of Clinical Psychology, 59,* 1117-1124.

Wood, W., Quinn, J. M., & Kashy, D. A. (2002). Habits in everyday life: Thought, emotion, and action. *Journal of Personality and Social Psychology, 83,* 1281-1297.

Wright, R. A., & Kirby, L. D. (2003). Cardiovascular correlates of challenge and threat appraisals: A critical examination of the biopsychosocial analysis. *Personality and Social Psychology Review, 7,* 216-233.

Wright, R. J., Mitchell, H., Visness, C. M., Cohen, S., Stout, J., Evans, R., et al. (2004). Community violence and asthma morbidity: The inner-city asthma study. *American Journal of Public Health, 94,* 625-632.

Wrosch, C., Miller, G. E., Scheier, M. F., & Brun de Pontet, S. (2007). Giving up on unattainable goals: Benefits for health? *Personality and Social Psychology Bulletin, 33,* 251-265.

Wurmser, L. (1987). Shame: The veiled companion of narcissism. In D. L. Nathanson (Ed.), *The many faces of shame* (pp. 64-92). New York: Guilford.

Wüst, S., Federenko, I., Hellhammer, D. H., & Kirschbaum, C. (2000). Genetic factors, perceived chronic stress, and the free cortisol response to awakening. *Psychoneuroendocrinology, 25,* 707-720.

Wyland, C. L., Kelley, W. M., Macrae, C. N., Gordon, H. L., & Heatherton, T. F. (2003). Neural correlates of thought suppression. *Neuropsychologia, 41,* 1863-1867.

Yalom, I. D. (1980). *Existential psychotherapy.* New York: Basic Books.

Yamada, M., Ueda, K., Namiki, C., Hirao, K., Hayashi, T., Ohigashi, Y., et al. (2009). Social cognition in schizophrenia: Similarities and differences of emotional perception from patients with focal frontal lesions. *European Archives of Psychiatry & Clinical Neuroscience, 259,* 227-233.

Yamadera, H., Okawa, M., & Takahashi, K. (2001). Open study of effects of alprazolam on seasonal affective disorder. *Psychiatry and Clinical Neurosciences, 55,* 27-30.

Young, A. H. (2004). Cortisol in mood disorders. *Stress, 7,* 205-208.

Young, E. A., & Nolen-Hoeksema, S. (2001). Effect of ruminations on the salivary cortisol response to a social stressor. *Psychoneuroendocrinology, 26,* 319-329.

Young, A. H., Gallagher, P., & Porter, R. J. (2002). Elevation of the cortisol-dehydroepiandrosterone ratio in drug-free depressed patients. *American Journal of Psychiatry, 159,* 1237-1239.

Young, A. H., Sahakian, B. J., Robbins, T. W., & Cowen, P. J. (1999). The effects of chronic administration of hydrocortosone on cognitive function in normal male volunteers. *Psychopharmacology, 145,* 260-266.

Zald, D. H. (2003). The human amygdala and the emotional evaluation of sensory stimuli. *Brain Research Reviews, 41,* 88-123.

Zald, D. H., Mattson, D. L., & Pardo, J. V. (2002). Brain activity in ventromedial prefrontal cortex correlates with individual differences in negative affect. *PNAS: Proceeding of the National Academy of Sciences of the United States of America, 99,* 2450-2454.

Zautra, A. J., Berkhof, J., & Nicolson, N. A. (2002). Changes in affect interrelations as a function of stressful events. *Cognition and Emotion, 16*, 309-318.

Zautra, A. J., Fasman, R., Reich, J. W., Harakas, P., Johnson, L. M., Olmstead, M. E., et al. (2005). Fibromyalgia: Evidence for deficits in positive affect regulation. *Psychosomatic Medicine, 67*, 147-155.

Zautra, A. J., Hamilton, N. A., & Burke, H. M. (1999). Comparison of stress responses in women with two types of chronic pain: Fibromyalgia and osteoarthritis. *Cognitive Therapy and Research, 23*, 209-230.

Zautra, A. J., Reich, J. W., Davis, M. C., Potter, P. T., & Nicolson, N. A. (2000). The role of stressful events in the relationship between positive and negative affects: Evidence from field and experimental studies. *Journal of Personality, 68*, 927-951.

Index

www.ingramcontent.com/pod-product-compliance
Lightning Source LLC
Chambersburg PA
CBHW071619270326
41928CB00010B/1689